D1606419

Before the Shining Path

Before the Shining Path

Politics in Rural Ayacucho, 1895–1980

Jaymie Patricia Heilman

STANFORD UNIVERSITY PRESS

STANFORD, CALIFORNIA

Stanford University Press
Stanford, California

This book has been published with the assistance of the
Faculty of Arts of the University of Alberta.

A portion of Chapter 3 appeared previously in
"We Will No Longer Be Servile: Aprismo in 1930s Ayacucho,"
Journal of Latin American Studies 38:3, 491–518, 2006
© Cambridge Journals, published by Cambridge University Press,
reproduced with permission.

Printed in the United States of America on acid-free,
archival-quality paper

Library of Congress Cataloging-in-Publication Data
Heilman, Jaymie Patricia.
Before the Shining Path : politics in rural Ayacucho, 1895–1980 /
Jaymie Patricia Heilman.
p. cm.
Includes bibliographical references and index.
ISBN 978-0-8047-7094-1 (cloth : alk. paper)
1. Ayacucho (Peru : Dept.)—Politics and government—20th century.
I. Title. F3451.A9H456 2010
985'.29063—dc22
2010008178

Typeset by Thompson Type in 10/12 Sabon

For my parents

Contents

Acknowledgments

My first thanks go to the archivists at the Archivo Regional de Ayacucho. Juan Gutiérrez, Teófilo Cuba, and Virgilio Gutiérrez showed me enormous kindness and generosity, and I could not have written this book without them. These archivists' dedication to their work was clearest to me on the day they climbed up into the archive's rafters and pulled down fifty-two dusty and heavy boxes of untouched documents from the Cangallo subprefecture. It was an enormous privilege to be the first scholar to work with these documents, and I thank Don Juan, Don Virgilio, and Don Teófilo for their efforts in acquiring, preserving, and sharing these documents. Thanks to Hermelinda Barreto and Fermina Villar for helping me catalogue the ARA's Supreme Court records. I also owe thanks to the staff of the Proyecto Especial de Titulación de Tierras (PETT) and the keepers of the periodicals collection of the San Francisco Convent. The Huanta subprefecture kindly allowed me to access and organize their archive, granting me a desk and laughingly enduring Huantinos' questions about their new gringa secretary. In Lima, I benefited from the assistance of archivists at the Archivo General de la Nación, the Archivo Público de la Biblioteca Nacional, and the Archivo Histórico Militar.

Ayacucho quickly worked its way into my heart and head, not least because of the many amazing Ayacuchanos who welcomed me into their lives. My compadres Faustino Flores and Mercedes Yauri made me part of their family, and their friendship has meant the world to me. Their children, Diosdado and Natividad, continue to delight and impress me with their many achievements and escapades. During my longest stretch of fieldwork in Ayacucho, I shared a home with Caroline Yezer and Arthur Scarritt. Caroline facilitated just about every part of my life and work in Ayacucho, and I am enormously grateful to her. Arthur Scarritt and I had many long conversations about rural Ayacucho, the Peruvian state, and the challenges of fieldwork. Arthur's moral support and friendship got me through many a rough moment. I also shared many laughs with Wendy Coxshall, Kairos Marquardt, and the members of the Carrasco Gutiérrez family.

Ayacucho has long drawn the attention of bright scholars and terrific human beings, and I benefited from their insights, ideas, and suggestions. Isabel Coral made an early intervention in this project, leading me to change my geographic focus to include Carhuanca. Caroline Yezer generously shared her knowledge about 1960s Huanta with me and introduced me to a number of Huantinos who assisted my research. Kimberly Theidon gave exactly the right words of encouragement at exactly the right time, and I learned much from Nelson Pereyra's insights on the 1920s. I also enjoyed many spirited discussions and friendly debates with Iván Caro. José (Pepe) Coronel helped me see the importance of my own project, and his commitment to rural Ayacuchanos is exemplary. Special thanks go to Ponciano del Pino, who has been a source of much insight and assistance.

A number of individuals helped me with the oral history component of my research. Alejandro Coronado accompanied me on my first visit to Huayllay, Reina Vargas accompanied me to Pampay, and Jorge Álvarez traveled with me on my first visit to Carhuanca. My great thanks go to Alicia Carrasco Gutiérrez. After several difficult solo visits to Carhuanca, I hired Alicia to accompany me as a research assistant. Her support made a world of difference. Alicia's kindness, warmth, and compassion make her a cherished friend, while her insights helped me better understand what we saw and heard in Carhuanca.

The bulk of my oral historical research took place in the district of Carhuanca. I want to say yet another round of heartfelt thanks to the young and elderly Carhuanquinos who welcomed Alicia and me into their homes for meals, chicha, stories, and laughter. I will never forget the way these women and men and trusted us with their historical memories, their sorrows, and their hopes. I thank these individuals for their kindness and generosity. This study also owes a major intellectual debt to Jorge Cárdenas, a Carhuanquino educated at San Marcos. Not only did Jorge provide Alicia and me with a home inside Carhuanca, he also proved an unending source of historical information about his beloved district. Through his lengthy answers to my endless questions, Jorge provided an astonishing amount of detailed information about Carhuanca's past. Although Don Jorge will staunchly disagree with many of the conclusions I draw about Carhuanca, I hope he will nonetheless accept my gratitude for the keen historical analysis he so regularly shared with me.

I did my graduate training at the University of Wisconsin-Madison, where I had the great fortune to work closely with several fine scholars. Frank Salomon's methodological rigor and passionate commitment to Andean peoples provided a model for humanistic scholarship, while Francisco Scarano (gently) pushed me to consider questions of economics that I would otherwise have left unasked. Steve J. Stern's teaching, his feedback on my work, and his scholarship opened and reopened my mind. On the very first day I met Steve, he asked me if I had considered studying Ayacucho; I haven't looked back since. My greatest debts are owed to Florencia Mallon. From the outset, Florencia pushed me to think harder and better about indigenous peoples, nation-states, and politics. Her research and her writing continue to inspire me. It was Florencia who first introduced me to the idea of collaborative oral history research, and I learned much from her methods and counsel. At a moment when the difficulties of ethnographic research in a postwar context threatened to overwhelm me, Florencia gave me the support, encouragement, and friendship that allowed me to persevere. And, in her continuing generosity, she also helped me find a home for this book. Mil gracias, Florencia.

For their friendship, criticisms, and support, I thank Marc Hertzman, Andrés Matías Ortíz, Cynthia Milton, Ana Schaposchnik, Julie Gibbings, Tamara Feinstein, and Gabi Kuenzli. Ileana Rodríguez-Silva won my heart as she wins the hearts of all who meet her, and her fine scholarship has transformed the way I think about race and racism. Ili has also provided more advice, guidance, and reassurance than I can ever properly acknowledge. Solsi del Moral consistently took me to task when my analysis went too far or not far enough and always helped me to laugh at myself. My dear friend Gladys McCormick deserves an entire page of acknowledgments just to herself. Gladys has been my toughest critic and staunchest supporter throughout the research and writing of this book. I cannot thank her enough.

I had the tremendous fortune to begin my academic career at Dalhousie University. Dalhousie's history department has been absolutely terrific to me—supportive, collegial, and intellectually engaging. I will always be incredibly grateful for my years at Dalhousie. Special thanks go to my colleagues Claire Campbell, Amal Ghazal, and Paddy Riley, who made me laugh as often as they made me think. I joined the University of Alberta History and Classics department in the summer of 2010, excited to return to the institution where I took my very first course in Latin American history. Hearty thanks go to David C. Johnson for introducing me to Latin America all those years ago and for his continuing friendship, advice, and encouragement.

I thank Norris Pope, Sarah Crane Newman, and Margaret Pinette for their terrific editorial support. Marc Becker showed much academic generosity with his comments and critiques, while the second (anonymous) reader helped me immeasurably with her keen insights and recommendations. This book is better because of these two scholars, and I thank them warmly. Funding for this project included grants from the Social Science Research Council, the University of Wisconsin-Madison, Dalhousie University, and a Sir James Lougheed Award. I also thank the University of Alberta for a timely publication grant.

I have saved the most important thanks for last. Sheri Michelson has been my best ally and friend since the 1980s. Thanks, Sheri, for always standing by me. Ken Mah came into my life just as I began revising the first draft of this book. He makes me happy each and every day. Loving thanks go to my mother and father. Throughout the research, writing, and rewriting of this book, they heard me worry, complain, lament, and worry some more, and they always responded with boundless encouragement, love, and teasing. Thanks, Mom and Dad, for everything.

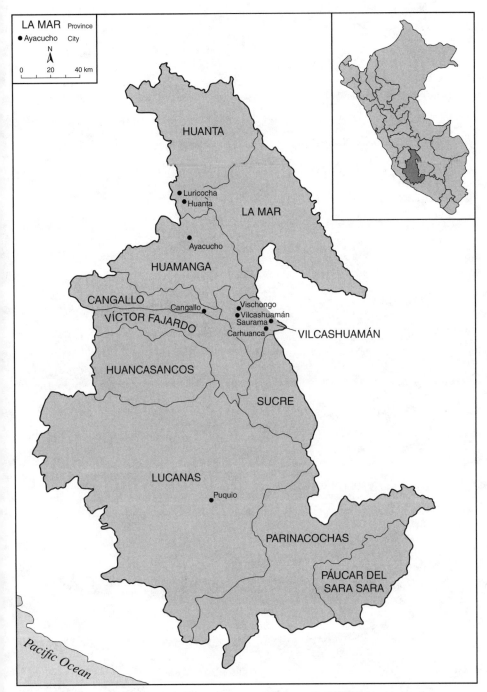

LA MAR Province
● Ayacucho City
N
0   20   40 km

HUANTA

● Luricocha
● Huanta

LA MAR

● Ayacucho

HUAMANGA

CANGALLO
Cangallo ●
VÍCTOR FAJARDO
● Vischongo
● Vilcashuamán
Saurama ●
Carhuanca ●
VILCASHUAMÁN

HUANCASANCOS

SUCRE

LUCANAS
● Puquio

PARINACOCHAS

PÁUCAR DEL
SARA SARA

Pacific Ocean

Ayacucho, circa 2000. Source: Jaymie Patricia Heilman, "We Will No Longer Be
Servile: Aprismo in 1930s Ayacucho," *Journal of Latin American Studies* 38:3,
p. 498, 2006 © Cambridge Journals, published by Cambridge University Press,
reproduced with permission.

Before the Shining Path

Introduction

꒰

Resting two newly polished rifles against his shoulders as he spoke, Don Isaac Escobar looked at the ground and then at me. "Those were years of crying, miss," he told me, "a life of crying."[1] An indigenous man from rural Ayacucho, Don Isaac was speaking of Peru's 1980 to 1992 civil war, a war fought by Maoist Shining Path (PCP-SL) rebels, Peruvian state forces, and Andean peasants. According to the final report of Peru's Truth and Reconciliation Commission, this conflict left over 69,000 people dead, the overwhelming majority of whom were indigenous men and women from rural Andean communities. One of the most troubling of the Truth Commission's findings was its allocation of blame: PCP-SL militants were responsible for the majority (54 percent) of these deaths, having enacted violent punishments, public executions, and massacres against the very same oppressed peoples they claimed to be liberating through their revolutionary struggle. Still more troubling is the fact that most of the individuals filling the PCP-SL's ranks were themselves of rural Andean origins: They were the recently urbanized sons and daughters of indigenous peasants.[2]

Much has been written about the Shining Path—the *Partido Comunista del Perú–Por el Sendero Luminoso de Mariátegui* or the Peruvian Communist Party–For the Shining Path of Mariátegui—so much so that studies of the party and its war have become popularly known as "Senderology."[3] Attempting to make sense of the Maoist party and its incredibly violent insurrection, early studies of the PCP-SL placed emphasis on late-twentieth-century economic crises, failed state reform efforts, and radical Maoist party leaders. The very best of these early studies extended a detailed analysis of the PCP-SL's origins and founders.[4] The very worst of these studies wrongly cast the PCP-SL's armed struggle as a millenarian uprising of the Inkaic masses. Many of these works—and particularly those by North American scholars—received sharp criticism for misconstruing popular support for the PCP-SL in the countryside, overstating Sendero's popularity and understating the party's horrifying punitive violence against indigenous campesinos.[5] Such shortcomings were perhaps inevitable: The civil war violence consuming the Andean countryside rendered impossible the kind of direct investigation and observation, as well as the slow and careful reflection, that became possible once the war ended. I am one of several scholars who has had the luck and the privilege to take advantage of this changed historical and political moment.[6]

This book attempts to make sense of Shining Path by looking backward in time, tracing eighty-five years of historical processes that prefaced the party and its war. I use a combination of archival research and oral history interviews to turn attention away from the standard emphases on the economic and political crises of the 1970s. I instead interpret the PCP-SL as the last and most extreme of a series of radical political movements that garnered strength in Peru's countryside during the twentieth century. Focusing on the Andean department of Ayacucho, this book examines the political history of a rural indigenous district from 1895 until the 1980 launch of the Shining Path's insurrection. This study thus represents an active response to historian Steve J. Stern's call for scholars to move "beyond enigma," to get past their dismay at the Shining Path's frequently bizarre and incredibly cruel uses of violence by thoroughly contextualizing the PCP-SL and its war.[7]

The work of historicizing the PCP-SL began well before I put pen to paper. Breaking the path for a historical consideration of the party, Carlos Iván Degregori brilliantly situated the PCP-SL inside a long history of local provincial elites. Like the nonindigenous rural elites who preceded them, PCP-SL militants (or *Senderistas*) melded genuine concern for the plight of indigenous peasants with violence and authoritarianism.[8] Although the pages that follow depart from Degregori's arguments in significant and sometimes forceful ways, this study's intellectual debt to Degregori is unmistakable. Iván Hinojosa also helped anchor the PCP-SL in historical time, tracing the long and complicated political genealogy of the Peruvian left.[9] Marisol de la Cadena similarly placed PCP-SL militants inside a lengthy historical trajectory of provincial "insurgent intellectuals," who advocated Peru's sociopolitical transformation while they remained mired in their own racial prejudices.[10] Florencia Mallon drew subtle connections between the making of an exclusionary political order in nineteenth-century Peru and the Shining Path's emergence a century later.[11] Lewis Taylor, in turn, ably connected the rise and development of the APRA (Alianza Popular Revolucionaria Americana) party in Cajamarca with the PCP-SL's emergence in that department.[12] My work echoes many of these scholars' findings and builds on them by casting the PCP-SL as one of numerous political efforts undertaken in rural Ayacucho from the 1920s forward.

Across the twentieth century, rural Andean men and women denounced the grave abuses perpetrated by their neighbors and rued chronic government inattention to their concerns. These men and women also advanced a series of creative political projects designed to overhaul local and national systems of power. Those projects included the Tawantinsuyo indigenous rights movement of the 1920s, promotion of the populist APRA party in the 1930s and 1940s, support for Trotskyism and the reformist Acción Popular party in the 1960s, and cooperation with Peru's progressive military government in the 1970s. Although these political projects took different shapes and attracted varying levels of popular support, all of them proposed to transform Peru's grossly unequal distribution of political, economic, and social power. And all of them proved unable to realize that transformation. Those failures came not for lack of effort but instead because of the Peruvian state's policies of repression and malign neglect and because of the unremitting force of racial and class denigration at the national, regional, and local levels.

This context of prolonged political frustration and failure helps explain the initial attraction of the PCP-SL in the countryside. Historically unable to transform their country's systems of power, many young Ayacucho men and women eagerly joined the PCP-SL because that party promised to raze those systems entirely. Yet for all their determination to create a new order inside Peru, Shining Path militants remained trapped in the tight grasp of racism and class prejudice that had long shaped politics inside Peru. Members of the Shining Path thus reproduced the very same race and class hatreds that their People's War aimed to defeat, perpetrating violent acts of cruelty against the humblest sectors of Peruvian society.

The PCP-SL's violence was so terrible, and the Peruvian military's punishment of Senderista supporters (both real and assumed) so extreme, that many rural Ayacuchanos have understandably minimized their early sympathy for the PCP-SL. Both during and after the war, Ayacucho campesinos regularly cast themselves as straightforward victims who were caught between Shining Path militants and the Peruvian military. Scholars like Kimberly Theidon, Ponciano del Pino, and Caroline Yezer have provided thoughtful analyses of Ayacuchanos' traumatic postwar memories, showing how and why those memories obscure campesinos' early involvement with the PCP-SL.[13] This study comes at the issue of campesino participation in the PCP-SL's ranks from a different angle, showing that the Shining

Path was part of a long historical course of political thought, action, and reaction inside rural Ayacucho communities.

The 1895 start of the Aristocratic Republic represents an ideal entry point into this study, as this period of reconstruction following the disastrous War of the Pacific set the stage of political exclusion, repression, and neglect that shaped rural Ayacucho's history across the twentieth century. From the end of the Aristocratic Republic, I trace the next sixty years of Ayacucho's history, exploring the changing dimensions of campesinos' interactions with state, regional, and local authorities and with each other. This study's chronologically organized chapters reflect the book's political focus. The first chapter examines the late-nineteenth-century and early-twentieth-century circumstances that conditioned the political projects that emerged after 1919. Chapter Two considers the Tawantinsuyo movement of the 1920s, while the next chapter treats the emergence and growth of the populist APRA party in the 1930s. Chapter Four considers the struggles I deem "literacy politics"—conflicts over the uses and abuses of education during the 1940s and 1950s. Chapter Five explores the promise and problems of Trotskyism and the reformist Acción Popular party in the 1960s, while Chapter Six examines the military reformism of the early 1970s. The final chapter focuses on the rise of the PCP-SL during the late 1970s. I close this book in 1980, the year that Shining Path militants declared the start of their People's War.

Ayacucho is the best theater for a study of the political preludes to the Shining Path War; it was the department where PCP-SL militants initiated their People's War, and it was the region that suffered the most war deaths. The department is also one of the most impoverished and indigenous areas of Peru. Together with Apurímac and Huancavelica, Ayacucho ranks as the poorest of Peru's two dozen departments, and it forms part of the country's so-called *mancha india* (Indian stain).[14] A focus on Ayacucho department therefore brings issues of racism and structural neglect into sharp relief.

Negotiating the difficult balance between analytical depth and breadth, I focus my analysis on the eastern Ayacucho district of Carhuanca in the province of Cangallo.[15] Shining Path militants prioritized work in eastern Ayacucho in the years immediately before the 1980 launch of their armed struggle, and their party realized considerable success in Carhuanca. Several Carhuanca residents (*Carhuanquinos*) formally joined the PCP-SL, assuming leadership positions within the movement and promoting the party inside the district. More Carhuanquinos offered tacit support, aiding the rebels or joining as fighters. Most Carhuanquinos simply fled the district, leaving Carhuanca for Lima to live as refugees in the capital. The PCP-SL was then able to gain total control of Carhuanca for two entire years.

Carhuanca was (and remains) geographically remote. Located in the easternmost corner of central Ayacucho, Carhuanca was approximately fifty kilometers from the city of Cangallo and over one hundred kilometers away from the Ayacucho capital. Without a highway connecting Carhuanca to either of these cities until the end of the 1960s, Carhuanca had few connections to urban Ayacucho. Indeed, Carhuanca's articulation to urban Ayacucho was so weak that most of the Carhuanquinos who migrated out of the district traveled all the way to the nation's capital of Lima. Because of its small size, its lack of a highway until the late 1960s, and its geographic location at the province's easternmost edge, Carhuanca was relatively unimportant to Cangallo province's political and economic life.

Carhuanca's economic marginality was a consequence of both geography and local land tenure patterns. Until 1940, Carhuanca was home to three haciendas, but those estates were all confined to the district's lower valleys on the Río Pampas. These haciendas were distant from the district capital of Carhuanca town, and they covered only a small portion of district land. While these haciendas grew produce like sugar, *tuna* (prickly pear), and oranges, they were also prisoner to the opposing problems of drought and flooding. These haciendas were not especially lucrative; their owners usually marketed their produce only inside Carhuanca itself. Nor were these haciendas particularly enduring. Carhuanca's church-owned Champacancha estate was the district's lone well-established hacienda, and Carhuanca residents purchased the hacienda in 1940. Carhuanca's Encuentro and Virán haciendas, in contrast, took shape only in the late nineteenth century, and the owners of these unprofitable haciendas abandoned them in the mid-1940s. Carhuanca's peripheral hacienda presence along the Río Pampas was far overshadowed by campesino smallholdings at higher elevations. The 2,301 individuals who lived in Carhuanca in 1940 typically owned several tiny private plots of familial land, usually well under one hectare in size, and eked out their livings from these holdings.[16]

Close attention to a district like Carhuanca allows a degree of analytic depth and complexity impossible to achieve with a broader regional or national analysis. Looking at one district allows us to trace the political triumphs, failures, hatreds, and allegiances of specific individuals and families across time. Although the specific details of its past are unique to Carhuanca, the district's history resonates with other districts in the easternmost zones of Cangallo, districts that today form the province of Vilcashuamán (created in 1984).[17] The Truth Commission notes that these areas were "marked by an extremely weak articulation as much to the state as to the market."[18] Like Carhuanca, these districts had twentieth-century histories rife with conflict. The Truth Commission reported that these easternmost districts were home to fights between neighboring communities and heated litigation over community borders. The Truth Commission also established that in these districts wealthy community members, mayors, governors, justices of the peace, and community presidents assumed the role of abusive local strongmen in the absence of a significant hacendado class. And, as in Carhuanca, it was in these eastern districts that the PCP-SL realized many of its greatest successes.[19]

To temper my discussion of Carhuanca and to show a different face of rural Ayacucho's twentieth-century history, I offer comparative considerations of Luricocha district in Huanta, the district that Don Isaac Escobar called home.[20] Unlike Carhuanca, Luricocha was a district defined by haciendas. Several large haciendas, including Huayllay, Atalambra, Atoccpuquio, Pampay I, Pampay II, Iribamba, Huanchacc, Vado, Cedro Huerta, and Meccayra, dominated Luricocha's land tenure system, leaving only a few scattered campesino smallholdings free from hacienda control. Most of these haciendas were held in usufruct; hacendados divided their estates among campesino tenants who worked the land in exchange for a yearly rent paid in cash and/or in kind. Luricocha district included warm, well-irrigated valley haciendas like Pampay and Iribamba and higher, cooler haciendas like Huayllay. On valley haciendas, fruits like oranges, lemons, and avocados grew, while higher-elevation estates grew crops like potatoes, barley, and tubers. The 6,337 men and women who resided in Luricocha at the time of the 1940 census lived in a district characterized by the presence of haciendas.[21]

A second difference between Luricocha and Carhuanca involves geography. Whereas Carhuanca was extremely isolated geographically, Luricocha was relatively close to two major urban centers. Located only seven kilometers from Huanta city and thirty kilometers from the departmental capital, Luricocha was tightly articulated with these urban centers. Luricocha hacendados usually lived and even worked in these cities, visiting their haciendas only occasionally, and Luricocha's campesinos were able to sell some of their agricultural produce in these cities. The district of Luricocha was also relatively close to Huanta's jungle (*selva*) regions, and, like most Huanta campesinos, Luricocha's peasants regularly migrated to the jungle for seasonal agricultural labor.

These differences of land tenure and geography situated Luricocha and Carhuanca in somewhat opposing positions in relation to provincial and departmental power structures. So closely connected to the city of Huanta, Luricocha was tied into that city's vibrant political and economic life. One observer noted in 1924 that Huanta was home to a "first-rate commercial plaza," visited by merchants from urban Ayacucho and especially from the city of Huancayo, to buy coca, coffee, *chancaca* (solidified sugar), and other goods.[22] The city's commercial importance and geographical proximity to the city of Ayacucho, combined with the fact that most of the province's landlords chose to reside in urban Huanta, meant that the city of Huanta became a bastion of regional power, second only to urban Ayacucho within the larger department.[23]

Luricocha's connections to the Shining Path were also different from—but no less complex than—those of Carhuanca. The PCP-SL's second-in-command, Augusta La Torre Carrasco or Comrade Norah, was the daughter of a Luricocha hacendado and the wife of Abimael Guzmán Reynoso, the founder of the Shining Path. Augusta La Torre, Guzmán, and other PCP-SL leaders transformed the La Torre family's Iribamba hacienda into one of their first military training schools. But while the La Torre example is striking, it was also unusual inside Luricocha. The indigenous peasants who formed the vast majority of Luricocha's population proved largely disinterested in the Shining Path. Only a few Luricocha peasants sympathized with the PCP-SL, and fewer still actively joined the party. In addition, Shining Path militants met staunch resistance from Luricocha residents (*Luricochanos*) who actively fought the rebels through civil defense patrols, or *rondas campesinas*. Don Isaac Escobar had those two rifles with him precisely because he was a member of one such patrol; he was taking the just-repaired rifles back to his home community in Luricocha.[24]

One of this book's central assertions is that the PCP-SL's emergence and actions inside rural Ayacucho had historical precedents and historical explanations. The PCP-SL's first killings in the district of Carhuanca reflected animosities that stretched back decades. The past suggests other patterns, too. Throughout the twentieth century, men and women in Carhuanca joined diverse political movements and parties, hoping to transform local and national power relationships. There was an established tradition of party politics and affiliation inside Carhuanca, meaning that it was not historically unusual for Carhuanquinos to embrace a political party like the PCP-SL. That assertion holds true even though the Shining Path was far more extreme than any of the numerous political parties that preceded it inside Ayacucho's countryside.

History also helps explain the course of the Shining Path war in
Luricocha, where a hacienda-owning family produced a leading PCP-SL
militant and where indigenous peasants chose partnership with the
Peruvian military over affiliation with the Shining Path. For most of the
twentieth century, party politics were hacendados' domain. Luricocha's
landlords joined a broad variety of political parties and movements,
advancing political agendas that ranged from radical to conservative.
The district's campesinos, in contrast, shied away from membership in
political parties and repeatedly stressed their allegiance to the Peruvian
state. That was true in the 1920s, 1930s, and 1960s, and it was true
in the 1980s. It was also true across the entire province of Huanta:
Anthropologist Kimberly Theidon and historian Ponciano del Pino have
each established that Huanta campesinos defined themselves as patriotic
defenders of the Peruvian homeland and government.[25] My argument
is not that the past predetermined the course of the Shining Path War
or that the insurgency was inevitable or predictable. Instead, this book
asserts that, by looking at the long historical course of political engagement inside communities, we can contextualize a devastating war that
might otherwise seem utterly incomprehensible.

THE POLITICS OF POLITICS

Across its seven chapters, this book demonstrates that politics—
understood here as efforts to maintain, reform, or overhaul systems of
power—suffused rural Ayacucho life. Historians like Florencia Mallon,
Cecilia Méndez, Mark Thurner, and Charles Walker have shown the
manifold ways that rural, indigenous men and women shaped the course
of nineteenth-century nation building in Peru.[26] This book serves as a
coda to those fine studies, for the twentieth century was characterized by
popular efforts to overhaul the resultant economic, political, and social
structures. Just as the nineteenth century was a time of nation-state formation, the twentieth was a time of nation-state *transformation*. Much
as Laura Gotkowitz has shown for Bolivia and Marc Becker has shown
for Ecuador, this study demonstrates that women and men living in Ayacucho's countryside embraced a variety of political parties, movements,
and opportunities, by turns eager and desperate for political change.[27]

The assertion that political parties and projects were central to rural Ayacuchanos' lives from the 1920s onward is surprisingly novel
for the Peruvian case. While scholars have recognized that the 1920s
Tawantinsuyo Committee had both urban and rural branches, no one
has yet studied how the organization affected political life in rural in-

digenous communities or examined the local consequences of the national government's concerted repression of the Tawantinsuyo movement. Similarly, while the academic literature on the populist APRA party is considerable, scholars have focused almost exclusively on APRA sympathy in urban settings and on industrialized sugar plantations, leaving APRA's place in the indigenous countryside largely unstudied. I make similar considerations of the Acción Popular party, demonstrating how the party generated considerable local enthusiasm and hope. Read together, these projects show that politics sat at the very core of rural Ayacucho society.

Inside areas like Carhuanca, rural Ayacuchanos carried out their political projects in a context of malign state neglect, a condition of (mis) governance I deem "rule by abandon." *Abandon* is in some ways an imperfect term, as it necessarily implies an earlier historical moment when the state acknowledged, remembered, and tended to now-orphaned regions. Yet *abandon* is the term Ayacuchanos themselves mobilized to describe their twentieth-century political condition, and so I take up their label.[28] Rule by abandon implies governance that operates on a principle of intentional and detrimental neglect instead of dominance or hegemony and that reinforces state rule through sporadic bursts of punitive violence. Rather than creating situations of political autonomy and sovereignty, rule by abandon fostered a culture of impunity within much of rural Ayacucho. Given that culture of impunity, grave crimes like homicide, arson, and robbery frequently went unpunished by the courts, and regional authorities rarely heeded popular complaints about abusive local authorities. Due to the fundamental lack of recourse against these local authorities, there was a consistent perpetuation of abuses at the district level. Often the only remaining tool against such authorities or local strongmen was physical violence. The absent state did not perpetrate this violence, but its policies of neglect fostered it.

Wanting to change this condition of state abandon, rural Ayacuchanos took up a tremendous number of distinct political projects. Politics appealed across rural lines of class and race. Inside the district of Carhuanca, richer and poorer peasants alike embraced parties, movements, and political alliances. But if the pull of politics was general, the specific paths were not. The appeal of a given political party or current usually depended on a campesino's social and economic standing. The Tawantinsuyo movement of the 1920s attracted Carhuanca's humblest, most "Indian" peasants, whereas the Acción Popular party of the 1960s won support from the district's wealthiest residents.

Politics were equally significant, and equally diverse, in Luricocha. District hacendados were a surprisingly complex set of political actors, straying far from the stereotype of reactionary feudal lords. Luricocha's landlords joined conservative, populist, and even Marxist parties and movements, looking to participate in national political life. As Aaron Bobrow-Strain has argued for Chiapas, landlords did not always act in the ways we might expect of rural "bad guys."[29] Luricocha peasants were also politically engaged; they lobbied for better social, economic, and political conditions. But these campesinos did so largely outside the realm of formal parties and organizations, purposefully abstaining from a political course that government officials might deem radical.

The Luricocha case also establishes the conceptual limits of "rule by abandon." Because of Luricocha's geographical proximity to the major economic, social, and political center of Huanta city and because of Huanta's own proximity to urban Ayacucho, provincial, departmental, and even national authorities kept nervous watch over the district. State attention to Luricocha—and to the province of Huanta in general—was all the sharper because of a powerful, racialized stereotype of Huanta's indigenous peasantry as inherently prone to resistance and rebellion. Cecilia Méndez's invaluable work on Huanta's early republican history traces the rise and evolution of this stereotype—a stereotype that hardened with the events of the late nineteenth century.[30] What emerged by the last years of the nineteenth century, then, was a system of "rule by reaction." Even the slightest hint of political protest or mobilization by Luricocha's indigenous peasants brought either the threat or the display of military force, often accompanied by inflammatory denunciations of looming "race war." The combination of bloody military repression and threats to resume that repression led most Luricocha campesinos to pursue an extremely staid course of political moderation, shying away from engagement with political parties and movements and seeking only modest reforms for their communities. All the while, these campesinos stressed their loyalty to the Peruvian state. One biting irony of "rule by reaction" in Luricocha was that government repression and invective targeted at indigenous peasants actually left unchecked the much more radical and aggressive political activities of nonindigenous Luricocha landlords.

Local differences of class and race were easy to spot in areas like Luricocha, where a set of nonindigenous hacendados owned the lands on which indigenous peasants labored. But racial and class differences proved equally relevant in places like Carhuanca, where haciendas were only a peripheral presence. Inside Carhuanca, class disparities emerged between a wealthier, literate set of peasants and their poorer, less educated neighbors. Richer campesinos were easily identifiable inside the district. They self-defined as "local notables" and dominated appointed positions of political power in the district. These local notables had the most plots of land, the best-quality land, and the largest extensions of land. Although affluent campesinos' wealth was reflected in the quality and quantity of their holdings, their lands' yields were rarely the primary source of their wealth. Almost none of Carhuanca's production was sold outside the district, and richer campesinos derived their wealth instead from salaries paid them as local schoolteachers, wealth inherited from relatives, money sent from relatives in Lima, and/or income from the sale of land itself. Affluent campesinos' wealth showed, too, in the number and size of their homes, the presence of tile instead of straw roofs, and whitewash over their homes' adobe bricks. It need be remembered, though, that most of these local notables were still dreadfully poor. They regularly lost their babies in infancy; they lacked potable water, sewage removal, and electricity; and while they had enough food to fill their stomachs, their food was not sufficiently varied to provide good nutrition. These local notables were "rich" only in comparison to their poorer neighbors, who suffered a more extreme poverty. Those poorer campesinos sometimes lacked food and almost always lacked the money needed to travel out of their district, adequately educate their children, or pay for lawsuits and notaries.

Many of Carhuanca's local notables gained their initial economic leverage inside the district through migration: Their families came into Carhuanca in the late nineteenth century as priests or as would-be farmers, settling in the district because they were able to purchase plots of land. These migrants soon initiated a process of land commoditization inside Carhuanca. Carhuanca's weak articulation to regional and national economic markets meant that the primary commodity sold from and to Carhuanquinos was land itself. Valuable much less for its market production capacities than for its centrality to peasants' subsistence and its connection to local prestige and power hierarchies, land was the most precious commodity inside Carhuanca. Buying and reselling district land, and sometimes stealing land for resale or private use, Carhuanca's more affluent peasants amassed significant profit and numerous tracts of land. Without goods to sell and without ready opportunity to sell their labor, campesinos needing cash often had little choice but to sell their holdings to their neighbors. Because land was such a treasured commodity, neighbors fought neighbors over boundaries with astonishing frequency, while crop theft, fraudulent sales, and land invasions were commonplace. Deep and enduring enmities came as a result.

Those enmities had many political repercussions. Local notables wrestled continuously for power and control of the district, fighting bitterly with one another. Their fights were often materially motivated, but Carhuanca's local notables also sought power for power's sake.

Geographically distant from any urban center, the district's wealthier peasants made Carhuanca the focus of their political aspirations and intrigues. Political fights between wealthy campesinos existed alongside poorer campesinos' protests against these more affluent and frequently abusive local notables. But poorer campesinos also sought out allies among wealthier Carhuanquinos, using those partnerships to fight against their equally impoverished neighbors. Within this district context of heated political and economic conflict, political parties and movements flourished. Richer and poorer Carhuanquinos alike looked to a broad range of political movements, parties, and alliances to transform their local and national political worlds and to gain ground against their district rivals.

Crucially, these local divides of class mapped onto local differences of race. Carhuanca's peasant notables typically described themselves as "not indigenous," defining themselves in opposition to the district's poorer, more Indian masses. That self-definition came even though the phenotypical differences between these two groups were often slight and even though many of these local notables spoke Quechua before they learned Spanish. During our weeks together in Carhuanca, my research assistant Alicia Carrasco and I heard many commentaries about race from elderly local notables. One Carhuanquino told me that "the Indian" was "lazy, miserable, and gluttonous," and he defined an Indian as a man who stole a widow's bread from the mouths of her fatherless children.[31] A Carhuanca woman, in turn, explained to me that she was "not of the same race" as indigenous Carhuanquinos, as her parents had been born in the city of Ayacucho. She informed me that her husband was "not of the Carhuanquino race," either, as he had been born elsewhere and had very straight, angular nose.[32] One Carhuanquino man went beyond these comparisons when he learned of my German heritage. He leaned in toward Alicia and me and confided his opinion that Hitler had been right to kill the Jews, opining that "we Spaniards should have killed the Indians."[33] Had the Spaniards done so, he explained, Peru would not be suffering the poverty and violence experienced today. The documentary record offers equally inflammatory statements about race. Carhuanquina Manuela Quijana requested the subprefect's guarantees on her properties against encroaching indigenous peasants, explaining the problem through implicit reference to her own whiteness and explicit reference to her enemies' Indianness. Worried that these campesinos would not only steal her land but also kill her and her husband, she reminded the authorities that "because Indian people are like savages, they could increase their demands, as they are so accustomed to doing."[34] Humbler Carhuanquinos also invoked the concept of race, casting themselves as stereotypically weak and defenseless Indians who were ruthlessly exploited by whiter community elites.[35]

Although Carhuanquinos participated in a court system that based race on phenotype, with court documents listing litigants' physical traits like skin and hair color, along with more bluntly racialized traits like lip size, hair texture, and nose shape, Carhuanquinos did not make a priority of phenotype in their local racial classifications. Instead, Carhuanquinos employed a highly specific and also highly racialized trait to clarify who was Indian and who was not. That trait was literacy. Certainly, literacy and education were signposts of class. For most of the twentieth century, education was a luxury that only Carhuanca's wealthiest campesinos could afford, as only those families with an above-average quantity of livestock, productive lands, and access to cash were able to send their children to school. As such, literacy was as important to a campesino's class standing as were the number of animals and number of hectares he owned. But it must be understood that literacy was also central to a Carhuanquino's racial identity. As Marisol de la Cadena showed so well in her study *Indigenous Mestizos*, ideas of culture are central to ideas of race inside Peru, with education being the primary tool of "de-Indianization."[36] Baldly put, to be poor and illiterate within Carhuanca was to be Indian; to be rich and well educated was to be non-Indian. This construct of race existed as much in the legal realm of the state as it did in everyday popular consciousness. Florencia Mallon's book *Peasant and Nation* demonstrates that Peruvian lawmakers' late-nineteenth-century decision to disenfranchise illiterates was a decision that aimed to exclude Peru's indigenous population from the nation.[37]

Literacy's centrality in local experiences of race underscores another of this book's central arguments: A painful ambivalence toward education overshadowed and informed political life in rural Ayacucho. Without question, indigenous peasants prized education. They sacrificed to send their children (especially their sons) to school, and they flooded government offices with requests for dedicated, competent teachers.[38] Yet just as campesinos longed for education, they also denounced the abuses perpetrated inside their communities by the educated. Wealthier and poorer peasants alike criticized their educated neighbors for using their literacy to cheat, steal, and manipulate for their own private advantage. During the 1920s, ambivalence over education helped fuel the local Tawantinsuyo movement. In that movement, humble campesinos called for more and better schools while they simultaneously protested against the crimes of "those who could read and write." In the 1940s and 1950s, contradictory attitudes toward literacy propelled *tinterillos*—literally "users of little ink pots"—into the center of district political life. Often translated as "shyster lawyer," but better translated as "shyster scribe," a tinterillo was someone who manipulated the written word to his private benefit, composing (and sometimes forging) letters of protest, petitions, and official documents, usually to his own economic or political gain. Tinterillos very rarely had formal legal training or clout; they were simply men who took full advantage of their literacy, resources, and ambition to the detriment of others. Rural Ayacucho men and women lambasted tinterillos for their abuses, but they continued to depend on these scribes to pen the letters and documents they needed. Contradictions about education again came into the foreground in the 1970s, when a young generation of teachers inspired by Maoism began work in Carhuanca schools. Those young educators taught alongside an older generation of decidedly nonrevolutionary teachers firmly ensconced inside the ranks of the district's local notables. Fights were not long in coming. Those fights reflected local differences of class and race, but they also reflected the vibrancy of district political ideas, passions, and agendas. Much was at stake. Tragically, even more was lost.

A NOTE ON METHODOLOGY

Although based primarily on archival documents, this study also draws substantially on oral history interviews I conducted in communities throughout the districts of Luricocha and Carhuanca. Together, my research assistant Alicia Carrasco and I conducted approximately two dozen formal and informal interviews in Carhuanca, complementing the dozen interviews I conducted alone or with friends in Luricocha communities. Alicia and I also conducted several additional interviews in the cities of Huanta, Ayacucho, and Lima. These interviews gave details and insights absent from the archival record, and the process of sharing documents with Luricochanos and Carhuanquinos allowed me to give considerable nuance to my archival findings. With their permission, I have included the names of a few of my interviewees. Usually, these were men with prominent reputations at the departmental and national level, and pseudonyms would do little to disguise their identities. In the majority of cases, however, I have changed my interviewees' names to provide anonymity. Names that appear in archival documents are left unchanged as they are a matter of public record, but in a few cases I have changed these names and withheld the specific documentary references to help protect the individuals involved.

CHAPTER ONE

Small Towns and Giant Hells

The Politics of Abandon in Rural Ayacucho, 1895–1919

Handing me the flower held tucked beneath his faded lapel, ninety-three-year-old Hernán Carrillo invited me to sit down beside him in Carhuanca's central plaza. That afternoon, Don Hernán spoke to me of his district's history, recounting tales of abusive authorities, priests, and the local gentry. Shrugging his shoulders and sighing, Don Hernán remarked, "small town, giant hell."[1] That same summation of political life inside Peru's rural indigenous communities—"our minor towns, rightly called major hells"—appeared in Peruvian novelist Clorinda Matto de Turner's acclaimed 1889 work *Aves sin nido.*[2] Matto de Turner's portrayal of malicious governors, lustful priests, and corrupt tax collectors very much resembled the stories Don Hernán told me about Carhuanca's politics and echo Peruvian thinker Manuel González Prada's argument that nineteenth-century indigenous communities suffered "the tyranny of the justice of the peace, the governor, and the priest, that unholy trinity responsible for brutalizing the Indian."[3] These comments all push for a closer consideration of the mechanics of local authority and the processes of rule inside Ayacucho's rural, indigenous communities during the late nineteenth and early twentieth centuries, a period that cemented the local power relationships and abuses, as well as the practice of state neglect, that propelled and delimited Ayacucho campesinos' political struggles from 1919 forward.

Known as the "Aristocratic Republic," the period between 1895 and 1919 consolidated a national political order premised on the exclusion of indigenous campesinos.[4] Broadly defined by political stability and economic development, these twenty-four years amounted to a period of reconstruction following the disastrous 1879–1883 War of the Pacific, a conflict fought among Chile, Peru, and Bolivia over the nitrate-rich

Atacama Desert. The story of indigenous campesinos' participation in the War of the Pacific and their subsequent exclusion from national political life has been well told. Historians like Nelson Manrique, Mark Thurner, and especially Florencia Mallon have shown that indigenous peasants served as patriotic fighters in this devastating war, only to face brutal demobilization and racialized scorn after the fighting was over. As the dust settled and the bodies were cleared away, nonindigenous national authorities revised Peru's constitution to deny citizenship rights to the men and women they deemed ignorant and dangerous Indians.[5]

For the men and women living in the rural and predominantly indigenous district of Carhuanca, politics in the closing years of the nineteenth century and opening decades of the twentieth were defined by abuse exacted in a context of political neglect. During the Aristocratic Republic, Carhuanquinos' connections to national politics and politicians were more rhetorical than real, and regional authorities were accessible only to the district's wealthiest, most educated minority of men. What emerged, then, was a political culture in which local strongmen—called first *caudillos* and later *gamonales*—both amassed and subverted formal political authority, respecting or flouting official laws in accordance with their own interests. The resulting political order inside Carhuanca much resembled the ugly political worlds that González Prada and Clorinda Matto described: towns full of unpunished crime; class, racial, and gender exploitation; and violence. Yet González Prada's famous formulation that this political abuse was fostered by an alliance between national and local elites is flawed, for the Carhuanca case shows that local rural elites themselves suffered under—and protested against—the state's practices of exclusion, disregard, and neglect. Moreover, these rural strongmen fought against one another just as much as they exploited the poorer, more indigenous peasants in their midst.

Although Carhuanca's political culture was an "unruly order" far more unruly than it was ordered, it was by no means anomalous inside rural Peru.[6] Historian Lewis Taylor has described a "Hobbesian social climate" in Hualgayoc during the late nineteenth and early twentieth centuries, noting the excessive levels of violence, crime, and impunity.[7] Many Peruvians living during the Aristocratic Republic made similar judgments about their diverse regions.[8] Those judgments reflected the decrepit cast of the Peruvian state during the last years of the nineteenth century and first years of the twentieth. Crippled by the devastating war with Chile and economic ruin, and built on the racist and classist exclusion of indigenous campesinos, Peru hobbled into the 1920s operating on the premise of abandon.

CARHUANCA AND THE POLITICS OF ABANDON

Carhuanquinos' political engagements during the Aristocratic Republic played out inside three overlapping spheres: national, regional, and local. Looking first to the national, we can say that during these twenty-four years—and in sharp contrast to their experiences in the years that followed—Carhuanquinos had only limited connections with national politics. Although Carhuanquinos were conscripted to fight in the war against Chile, they did not form major guerrilla forces like those seen in provinces such as Huanta.[9] Indeed, Carhuanquinos' involvement in the war was so minimal that their participation receives scant mention in Carhuanca intellectuals' otherwise ample and detailed recollections of their district's history. Carhuanquinos' nonparticipation did not stem from any lack of patriotism or heroism but instead from the simple reality that eastern Ayacucho was not a major theater of the war. That minimal war involvement, though, meant that the national presidential struggles fought between Andrés Avelino Cáceres and Nicolás de Piérola were a matter of only small concern inside Carhuanca.

Carhuanquinos' engagement with national politics during the Aristocratic Republic first came to the fore with a 1909 election uprising, when supporters of opposing national congressional candidates came to blows. On May 25, 1909, Carhuanquinos watched as their district's local notables gathered to vote for departmental candidates seeking a seat in Peru's national congress. A fundamentally public affair, the elections took place at a voting table stationed in front of Carhuanca's town hall. Turning the very public electoral process into an equally public brawl, partisans of the two competing congressional candidates led their relatives, supporters, workers, and friends into verbal and then physical confrontation. Supporters of one candidate approached the town hall, led by a prominent district resident named Leóncio Cárdenas. All were armed with revolvers, carbines, slingshots, sticks, and daggers. Supporters of the other congressional candidate likewise neared the town hall, led by the local hacendados Benjamín and Miguel Carrasco. When the two groups of supporters met, they traded insults and then exchanged punches, stones, and bullets, and the battle bled out from the central plaza and town hall into the district's church and surrounding properties. By six that afternoon, three Carhuanquinos were dead, numerous homes were pillaged and burned, and countless bullets had been spent.[10]

While this uprising did connect with national political matters, triggered as it was by an election for national congressmen, the fight was as much about local animosities as it was about national politics. The conflict between the Carrasco and Cárdenas factions involved not only political differences but also disputes over land and the control of women. Paralleling interelite fights in other parts of early-twentieth-century Peru, the Carrasco–Cárdenas battle was a conflict between rural strongmen. The Carrascos were not themselves Carhuanquinos; natives of the neighboring province of Andahuaylas, they had come into Carhuanca in the late nineteenth century and used land purchases and illegal land seizures to establish two haciendas, Encuentro and Virán, in Carhuanca's fertile lower valley. Many Carhuanquinos living today remember the Carrascos as abusive hacendados who stole district land, mistreated and manipulated the campesinos who labored on their holdings, and stole Carhuanca's prettiest women from their suitors and even from their husbands.[11]

The Cárdenas family was only slightly more popular inside the district. Like the Carrascos, the Cárdenas family was not from Carhuanca but rather from Andahuaylas. And like the Carrascos, the Cárdenas family used its preexisting wealth to amass considerable amounts of land in Carhuanca, simultaneously assuming a prominent place in local politics. Although both the Carrasco and Cárdenas families had their share of enemies inside Carhuanca, their most bitter enemies were each other. Frequently fighting over the borders that divided their respective estates as well as over control of district government, the Carrascos and Cárdenases turned their enmity into a public uprising with the 1909 election. The very personal and highly local nature of their dispute is perhaps best revealed by the fact that three months after this clash, Benjamín and Miguel Carrasco's cousin Roberto was murdered, and the man widely thought responsible for the killing was Leóncio Cárdenas.[12]

It is too big an interpretive stretch to label the 1909 election skirmish an uprising rooted in national political sympathies. There is no written documentation that suggests strong party loyalties among either the Cárdenases or the Carrascos, and oral history testimonies cast the upheaval as a fight based on personal hatreds and angers. Which Carhuanquinos fought alongside which family—and, more crucially, *why* they fought alongside those families—is a question that finds no answer in the written or oral record. The historian can only guess that both the Carrascos and Leóncio Cárdenas drummed up support among those local notables and peasants most tightly connected to them through the bonds of patronage and friendship and among those who most hated the opposing faction. In the end, the 1909 uprising offers little insight into Carhuanquinos' ideas, attitudes, and opinions about national politics.

Those ideas and opinions about national politics and the Peruvian state did, however, find frequent expression in Carhuanquinos' protests and complaints. Carhuanquinos regularly invoked the national state in their letters and petitions, referencing the rights afforded them by the national constitution, behaviors outlawed by national legislation, and their status as citizens. Two indigenous Carhuanquinos cited their rights as citizens in a 1915 protest, for example, charging that Governor Francisco Allende was committing abuses "to the extreme of depriving us of our rights in a democratic country such as ours."[13] Their comment was not short of irony: As both men were illiterate, they were denied formal political participation in their "democratic" country.

Yet however ironic it was, this sort of complaint emerged repeatedly during the 1910s. An April 1917 protest from ten self-defined Indians and *varayocs* (customary indigenous authorities) showed the men seeking guarantees "using the rights extended to us by the Constitution of the State."[14] Similarly, three Carhuanquinos who labeled themselves "indigenous men" appeared before the Cangallo subprefect to denounce Carhuanca's governor for whipping, kicking, and beating them solely because they were varayocs. They also charged that instead of providing them the guarantees deserved by "a Peruvian citizen," the governor had imprisoned and tortured them.[15] Lastly, a December 1917 letter of protest showed Carhuanquinos demanding that their persons and interests "be protected from the most cruel and unheard of outrages and exactions of which we are victims, making use of our popular sovereignty and shielded by the constitutional laws to which all Peru's *pueblos* [towns] have a right."[16]

These spoken and written references to the national government and its legislation did not reflect a broad sense of inclusion or participation in national political life or the promotion of any sort of national political project. Instead, Carhuanquinos' words were little more than formulaic phrases used to compel provincial and departmental authorities into action on their behalf. Through their allusions to the law, the constitution, and the rights of citizens, Carhuanquinos and their scribes were mobilizing the only real capital they had with distant regional authorities: legal capital. As impoverished, disenfranchised, indigenous men and women, Carhuanquinos had few resources to use for political leverage other than the promises laid out in national legislation. However illusory and empty those promises were, Carhuanquinos still tried to use them to their benefit. They had little else to use.

While Carhuanquinos often used national legislation to try to protect themselves, many also believed themselves the victims of the national government's policies. This sense of victimization was especially sharp in relation to two elements of national rule, the military and taxes. Most Carhuanquinos staunchly rejected the national government's demand for their young men's military service. While national, regional, and sometimes even local authorities sometimes cast compulsory military participation as the duty of all Peruvian citizens, there was no doubt that conscription specifically targeted the indigenous population. Carhuanca's mayor explained in 1913 that he had selected Manuel Ochoa to conscript eligible Carhuanquino men because Ochoa was "an influential person among the Indians." The mayor also instructed the subprefect to order Carhuanca's governor to "notify the Indians" about conscription.[17] At the district level, then, it was clear that military service was for indigenous men, and indigenous men only.

Carhuanquinos' broad rejection of military service showed in their consistent opposition to conscription. In 1902, Carhuanca's governor discussed "the grave inconveniences we have always run into in the remission of conscripts," relaying that in the previous year armed attackers had liberated three conscripts being sent to Lima for service.[18] Flight from conscription was also a constant problem. The provincial subprefect explained in 1906 that all those men eligible for conscription "have hidden in the mountains, leaving only the elderly and the infirm in all the towns of my jurisdiction."[19] Similar problems continued in subsequent years. Carhuanca's authorities repeatedly informed the subprefect that conscripts refused to travel, that local varayocs refused orders to force the conscripts to travel, and that eligible conscripts had fled from the district. In 1913, Carhuanca's Governor Jacobo Marabitto explained that it was difficult to conscript men between twenty-one and twenty-five years old because "without exception, all have fled."[20] Some Carhuanquinos even tried to avoid the service by registering for conscription using a false name. Those unable to resist conscription sometimes fled after their incorporation into army ranks. The Carhuanquino Juan Mendoza Flores, for example, stood accused of desertion from army.[21] Beyond flight and desertion, there was also the option of revolt. Cangallo's subprefect relayed in 1917 that there had been an armed assault on Cangallo city with the end of freeing conscripts remitted from Carhuanca and Cangallo.[22] It is perhaps no surprise, then, that documents referencing conscription repeatedly show authorities using the word *capture* for recruits, likening the men to wayward chattel or criminals.[23]

Carhuanquinos had good reason to resist conscription. Military service meant time away from one's home, fields, and animals, as well as family, and conscripts were sometimes denied sufficient provisions and care while in the army. Nationally, campesinos in Piura complained bitterly about military conscription, resisting the draft and even freeing conscripts by force, and Puno campesinos listed conscription as foremost among their authorities' abusive actions.[24] Complaints from Carhuanquina mothers are especially useful for showing the difficulties conscription imposed. A Carhuanquina named Bicenta Espinoza wrote Cangallo's subprefect in December 1911, requesting that her son be released from military service. Espinoza explained that her son suffered from "incurable chronic illnesses," like rheumatism and epileptic attacks, and was missing his testicles. Espinoza added that she herself was poor, blind, and a widow, and thus needed her only son to remain by her side to support her. In a subsequent letter, Espinoza relayed that her son also suffered from leprosy and was liable to infect the other troops.[25] A Carhuanquina named Simona Balboa similarly protested that Carhuanca's lieutenant governor had conscripted her only son, even though the authority knew of her "lamentable circumstances of poverty" and her reliance on her son. She added that her son was also ill with tuberculosis and too young for the conscription and that the lieutenant governor had picked her son only because she had not bribed him.[26]

Carhuanquinos were often just as hesitant to pay national taxes as they were to participate in the military. The subprefect complained in 1892 that Carhuanca was notorious for its residents' reluctance to pay their taxes.[27] That reluctance threatened to morph into violent rebellion in November 1913. That month, Governor Jacobo Marabitto wrote the subprefect claiming that the subprefect's taxation orders had triggered outright revolt in Carhuanca. Marabitto alleged that when he informed Carhuanca's population that he would be taxing them, a number of indigenous Carhuanquinos appeared at his dispatch, refusing payment, insulting, and even threatening him. Invoking the specter of Indian tax rebellion, the governor alleged that many of Carhuanca's "Indians" went to Vilcashuamán the next day, meeting with one of the governor's longstanding enemies and agreeing to resist payment, rise up in rebellion, attack his dispatch, sack his home, kill him, and "commit a thousand crimes."[28] Though Governor Marabitto claimed that over 200 Carhuanquinos were in rebellion, there is no additional evidence to suggest that such a revolt actually occurred. But even if Marabitto's claims were exaggerated or even imaginary, the fact that this official was willing to make these charges suggests his confidence that higher authorities would find them believable. Carhuanquinos' well-known antipathy to taxes made the governor's claims seem credible.

Turning from national politics to regional matters, it is no exaggeration to say that regional government was largely nonexistent within the

grossly centralized makeup of the Peruvian state. There was no departmental governor, no departmental congress, and no real departmental bureaucracy. There was only a state-appointed prefect, a prefect-
appointed subprefect, and a departmental court system. Less than
ruling, these regional authorities supervised, receiving and reporting
news of local problems. Although these regional authorities had only
marginal powers of rule, Carhuanquinos still looked to them for assistance and intervention and still rued the neglect they suffered from
them. Carhuanquinos' sense of regional abandon was especially sharp
in the years before 1909, as their district formally belonged to the province of Lucanas. Separated from Lucanas's provincial capital by over
250 kilometers and the often uncrossable Río Pampas, Carhuanca was
extremely isolated from the regional authority responsible for it: the provincial subprefect.

This isolation fostered political neglect, as Lucanas subprefects
were rarely willing—or even able—to intervene in Carhuanquino politics. An 1890 letter from the Lucanas subprefect reflected this situation. Explaining that the Lucanas capital Puquio was separated from
Carhuanca "by a river that is almost impossible to cross" for lack of a
bridge and because the season's rains had swollen the river, the subprefect relayed that he had no means of communicating with Carhuanca
and requested that the Ayacucho prefect oblige the Cangallo subprefect
to assume temporary responsibility for the district.[29] The Lucanas subprefect likewise relayed in 1902 that strong rains interrupted his dispatch's communication with "isolated districts," especially Carhuanca,
as the Río Pampas separated it from Puquio.[30] Similarly, the subprefect
complained in 1907 that communication with Carhuanca was nearly
impossible because of the rainy season.[31]

Lucanas subprefects regularly admitted their failure to take needed
action regarding Carhuanca. One subprefect reported that he was unable to investigate the 1908 kidnapping of Carhuanca's newly appointed
governor as the district was so far away and Lucanas could not spare
any of its few gendarmes.[32] Another subprefect informed the prefect that
his office had received various complaints against Carhuanca's governor, Facundo Ochoa. But because of the "great distance" that existed
between Puquio and Carhuanca, it was impossible for him to investigate
these complaints personally.[33] The subprefect's words were not empty
excuses. Historian Alberto Flores Galindo has noted that because Peru's
nineteenth-century state was so weak, prefects regularly lamented the
lack of weapons, police, and reliable jails at their disposal.[34] Without
more resources, Lucanas subprefects could not pay close attention to
Carhuanca even if they wanted to. Carhuanca's isolation and abandon,

like the difficulty of rule from Lucanas, were so well known that the Cangallo subprefect actually recommended annexing the district to Cangallo as early as 1903.[35] Awareness, however, did not translate into action, and Carhuanca remained ruled (and unruled) from afar.

Only the bloody events of the May 1909 election uprising managed to temper Carhuanca's regional isolation. A group of campesinos from the small Carhuanca community of Ocopa drew connections between the perpetuation of violence inside Carhuanca and the district's distance from the Lucanas capital of Puquio. They charged that, since the May uprising, the "criminals" of the Cárdenas family had been committing "every class of crime, assaults, sackings, homicide, detention, and arson" and that these crimes were continuing in part because the "immense distance" between Carhuanca and Puquio had prevented Lucanas authorities from punishing the perpetrators.[36] The Lucanas subprefect agreed, admitting that "we are fully aware of the official condition in which the district of Carhuanca has found itself since the 25th of last May and that makes it indispensable to proceed energetically to avoid more victims." Yet he was unable to send gendarmes to the area because his subprefecture "absolutely lacks public forces."[37] Because of the May election uprising and these subsequent complaints, national authorities officially transferred Carhuanca to the province of Cangallo in November 1909.

A number of Carhuanquinos quickly applauded this transfer. They wrote their new subprefect in January 1910 to say that they were "celebrating the supreme good that providence has conceded us with the annexation of the district of Carhuanca to the province of Cangallo, whose administration is entrusted to your illustrious and just administration."[38] Carhuanquinos' enthusiastic perception of change did not last long. As early as April 1910, a number of men from the district complained that "in the more than three months that this district has belonged to Cangallo, our circumstances have not improved in the least. The same tyrant governs us, and we are in the same circumstances."[39] The signatories of a 1911 petition explained that because their previous governors had all been drunks or illiterates, their district had remained in a "deplorable" state of "backwardness." They also relayed that their sorry situation owed partly to the fact that "no provincial political authority has made a visit to this district."[40] That comment was telling, as it was this very provincial authority, the subprefect, who had the role of suggesting and ranking gubernatorial nominees for the prefect to select. Several Carhuanquinos also expressed frustration that the subprefect ignored their concerns.[41]

But even though they were unsatisfied with the Cangallo subprefect's level of attention, Carhuanquinos continued to demand that attention.

They wrote (or found someone to write) endless letters of protest to their subprefects, requesting guarantees and punitive action against their local authorities, their neighbors, and their family members. Having no police force readily accessible to them other than the unarmed varayocs, Carhuanquinos were totally dependent on subprefects to dispatch police to their district. With police so far away and often unavailable, men accused of serious crimes frequently enjoyed impunity, resisting arrest inside their district or simply fleeing the area before gendarmes ever even approached. Even when gendarmes did arrive, their presence was not always conducive to law enforcement. Many Carhuanquinos complained that gendarmes were allied with their local enemies and that the gendarmes themselves often beat, extorted, and stole from innocent campesinos.[42]

After Carhuanca's transfer to Cangallo province, Carhuanquinos' access to their subprefect grew differentiated across class lines. Wealthier Carhuanquinos had a substantially easier time speaking with subprefects than did their poorer neighbors, as direct verbal communication with the provincial authority required travel by horse or by foot to the city of Cangallo, along with time away from one's fields and animals. Only wealthier Carhuanquinos could afford such a sacrifice. A Carhuanquino named Mariano Cárdenas traveled to Cangallo to present a complaint to the subprefect in 1918. That trip, Cárdenas explained, entailed "abandoning my grain harvests to the great detriment of my interests," but he made that sacrifice to charge Carhuanca's governor with abuse of authority.[43] Carhuanquino Saturnino Balboa similarly appeared before Cangallo's subprefect in 1917 to denounce the "grave abuses and exactions" of the current tax collector. The trip to Cangallo was not easy for Balboa, who described himself as "suffering the rigors of my valetudinarian state" and "tired because of my advanced age."[44] Subprefects were in effect a more viable political resource for wealthier Carhuanquinos than for their poorer neighbors.

The regional court system did little to mitigate Carhuanquinos' political abandon. There is no doubt that Carhuanquinos recognized the court's potential; men and women initiated countless judicial cases against their local authorities, their neighbors, and their family members. With the help of local scribes or their district's justice of the peace, Carhuanquinos would submit written testimonies protesting their situations and occasionally appear in the Ayacucho court to testify in person. But, for all their efforts, Carhuanquinos' litigations consistently failed to bring meaningful changes into their district. Trials regularly dragged on for years—sometimes even for decades—without conclusion, denying victims justice and leaving perpetrators free to commit more crimes.

Worse still, courts did not always have the means to enforce their orders. Panfilo Cárdenas, for example, complained that the Carrascos were evading court orders for their arrest because they engaged in "the most punishable complicity with these pueblos' subaltern authorities to make a mockery of judicial orders."[45] Local strongmen were also prone to bullying witnesses. Panfilo Cárdenas complained to the Ayacucho judge that "the Carrasco brothers are exercising every class of pressure, pursuing witnesses" and impeding them from making statements.[46] Adolfo Carrasco, in turn, complained that Governor Facundo Ochoa and his allies mistreated witnesses with "cruelty and refined mercilessness" and that these men had "inhumanely battered" those who testified.[47] Bullying could also lead to false testimony. Carhuanquino Benjamín Hiyo refused to ratify his own signed written declaration, charging that Leóncio Cárdenas had drafted a statement of false and slanderous testimony and forced Hiyo—weakened by malaria—to sign it.[48]

Court inaction could also leave accused individuals languishing in prison for years without a conviction. One particularly egregious example was documented in a 1911 protest from Carhuanquinos Juan Zárate, Agripino Vasquez, Dionisio Gómez, and Jacinto Gamboa. Held in the Ayacucho prison for nearly two years without a trial, these men charged that the Carrasco brothers had both used and aggravated judicial disorder in Ayacucho's regional court to unduly prolong their stay in jail. These men asserted that the Carrascos had influenced the removal and replacement of judges on the Ayacucho court to paralyze the case against their enemies, leaving these men "without the remotest hope" that their case would be heard. They complained that, the previous year, their case had been left without a judge "for the hundredth time" and that the judicial process in Ayacucho was so irregular that no one worried about "the fate of the imprisoned." Finding their case yet again without a judge, they asserted that their situation "surpasses the limits of the tolerable."[49]

The courts also tended to reflect and reinforce Carhuanca's existing class divisions, as access to the regional judicial system—like access to regional authorities—varied according to wealth. The poorest Carhuanquinos could rarely afford to pay for the lawyers and scribes required for success in the system, nor could they easily afford to spend time away from their fields, animals, and families if they were required to give testimony in person. The strain of court participation on Carhuanca's poorest campesinos was suggested in a 1911 report from the gendarme Claudio Toledo. Toledo informed the prefect that on his very arrival in Carhuanca, "all of the Indians started to flee," knowing that the gendarme was in the district to gather up the witnesses called to testify in Ayacucho regarding the 1909 uprising.[50] More to the point, Carhuanquino Pastor Allende charged that he had been wrongly imprisoned for nearly three years and that his poverty alone kept him in jail. He charged that he was "without economic resources because they took even my money, and, without a defender who could orient me, I remain to this day in unjust and arbitrary imprisonment."[51]

Within this context of national and regional abandon, Carhuanquinos' local political world became defined by disorder and abuse. Crimes like theft, arson, battery, and even murder were both commonplace and regularly left unpunished, and they reached particular extremes following the 1909 election uprising. The chaos initiated with the 1909 election uprising continued not just for weeks or even months but for years. After the election skirmish, members of the Carrasco family repeatedly expressed concerns about their safety, informing provincial and departmental authorities that their lives were in danger. In 1916, the Carrascos' fears came to fruition. Gathering in a local home four hours before midnight, over a dozen Carhuanquinos made their final preparations for an attack on Adolfo and Miguel Carrasco. With some of the men dressed in disguise and some carrying revolvers, the men headed to the home of Adolfo Carrasco. Seeing Adolfo seated just inside his doorway, talking with his domestic servant, the men began to fire their guns. Both Carrasco and his servant fell to the ground, wounded, and their attackers hurried away, mistakenly believing their victims dead. From here, the attackers went to the home of Adolfo's brother, Miguel Carrasco. Finding Miguel's door shut, some of the men tried to force it open while others began to scale the walls. Finally making their way into the home, the men found Miguel Carrasco in his bed, readying for sleep. The attackers shot Miguel Carrasco, firing seven bullets into his body and killing him.[52]

These attacks on the Carrasco brothers pushed Carhuanca into an immediate political crisis. Word of the assaults spread quickly, drawing Carhuanquinos from their beds and into the district's streets. Someone began ringing the bell of Carhuanca's church, summoning people to the central plaza, and by seven the next morning over 200 Carhuanquinos had gathered in the plaza. Taking control of the situation, Carhuanca's governor and lieutenant governor ordered the assembled men and women into groups and sent them off to find members of the Allende and Cárdenas families, the presumed instigators of the attacks. The effort to capture these men brought chaos of its own, leaving several Carhuanquinos dead from ensuing gunfire, while countless homes and fields were destroyed in the wave of retributive violence that followed.[53]

That violence was considerable. The Allende family charged that dozens of community members attacked and pillaged their San Luis estate immediately after the murder. Paulino and María Allende testified that around 200 Carhuanquinos (most of whom they singled out by name) had invaded their holding, shouting "Pillage! Pillage! Pillage!"[54] The Allendes asserted that this mob of people entered both the family's home and its fields, stealing or destroying all they could before setting the estate ablaze. Davíd Carrasco, in turn, charged that Francisco and Pastor Allende stormed the Carrascos' two haciendas, Encuentro and Virán, accompanied by several other men, aiming to kill him and his workers, destroy the two estates' machinery, and burn the sugar cane fields. Similar assaults also occurred on the church-owned Champacancha estate.[55]

Violence also came in the form of physical personal attacks and even torture. The Carrasco family and their allies brutally beat and mistreated several Carhuanquinos thought linked to the Allendes. One such campesino charged that Adolfo Carrasco, the subprefect, and several other Carhuanquinos beat and tortured him before locking him in the district jail with neither food nor a bed. The campesino Edilberto Ortega similarly asserted that after these same men arrested him, they tied a rope around his waist and neck and hung him from the ceiling, keeping him suspended for four days. Ortega's wife, in turn, charged that these men tied her to a tree, binding her all the way from her neck to her feet, and tortured her there, keeping her bound for three days. There were also numerous reports that the Carrascos' workers attacked the Allendes' sympathizers with guns, clubs, and slingshots.[56]

Carhuanca's own authorities could do little to quell the violence. The district's communal indigenous authorities, the varayocs, were powerless to take action, as the district's local notables denied the varayocs access to the sort of firearms they themselves kept in their possession. Without firearms, varayocs were frequently unable to carry out their law enforcement duties against lawbreakers who were often armed. Carhuanca's local notables also undercut varayocs' authority through racist and classist denigration of the staff holders. Though varayocs commanded the respect of Carhuanca's impoverished indigenous majority—respect that accrued from the varayocs' position as heads of the civil-religious hierarchy—they did not win similar respect from the wealthier and whiter Carhuanquinos who held positions of state-sanctioned authority in the district. In April 1917, a number of Carhuanca varayocs protested to the subprefect, complaining that "we are victims of the authorities of our district." They charged that the governor and other authorities "committed every class of unspeakable abuses against us," making them perform unremunerated agricultural and domestic labor under the threat of imprisonment and fines.[57]

Carhuanca's state-sanctioned authorities—the governor, municipal mayor, and justice of the peace—rarely proved any better than varayocs at controlling crime. Indeed, Carhuanquinos saw their district authorities less as their defenders than as their victimizers, and complaints about authorities' abuses were legion. Charges against Carhuanca's authorities included allegations of unjust imprisonment, animal theft, economic exploitation, arson, and even kidnapping and torture. To give just a few of many examples: Several Carhuanquinos complained in 1910 that Governor Manuel Ochoa was committing innumerable abuses against those who "do not belong to his band," seizing their cattle, fining them, and even kidnapping them.[58] Another group of Carhuanquinos complained in 1913 that Governor Marabitto had been "perpetrating every class of exactions and abuses against individual liberty, mistreating and jailing honorable residents and married women." They charged that the governor had attacked their women to exact payment of the industrial contribution and that Marabitto was nothing more than a tool for those Carhuanquinos "who look at the pueblo's aboriginals as pariahs."[59] In 1917, Carhuanca's lieutenant governors Ignacio Herrera and Andrés Berrocal and the varayocs Lorenzo Morales and Manuel Chipana informed the subprefect that Governor Francisco Hiyo forced them to seize animals from Carhuanquinos without payment, forced them to do unremunerated manual labor for his private benefit, and even forced their wives into his service. To the protesters, Hiyo's behaviors amounted to an intolerable injustice.[60]

District authorities were also subject to manipulation and control by Carhuanca's gamonales. A Peruvianism, *gamonal* means "local strongman," but a more complete definition of *gamonal* comes with the 1929 words of Peruvian thinker Carlos Barreda, who wrote, "As you know, the name gamonal comes from *gamonito* or sucker, a short thick branch which grows close to the roots of the vine or other tree, and which absorbs without any effort the sap and nutritive elements which are needed by the grapes. Clearly, gamonal denotes useless individuals who exploit without restraint the life-force of the Indians."[61] Although many scholars treat the terms *gamonal* and *hacendado* as synonyms, this book makes it clear that not all gamonales were hacendados, and not all hacendados were gamonales.

Carhuanquinos regularly complained about gamonales' power over their district's authorities, calling those leaders gamonales' puppets and servile instruments. When the district's gamonales could not simply control district authorities, they often flouted those authorities' rule.

Governor Manuel Ochoa informed the subprefect in April 1910 that he had been unable to fulfill official orders to capture the Carrascos and their allies, as all were holed up on the Virán estate with guns, and his governorship did not have sufficient force to capture them.[62] Governor Pedro Bendezú, in turn, informed the subprefect that, without provincial assistance, he could not capture Juan Zárate and Fidel Gómez for their involvement in murder of Roberto Carrasco, as these men were "leaders of the rebelling gangs of this area."[63] Municipal agent Teófilo Cárdenas, by contrast, complained that Adolfo Carrasco—"better known as the Kaiser of Carhuanca"—had unjustly seized animals from several Carhuanquinos and that he was powerless to take action against the Carrascos.[64] Even when Carhuanca's authorities managed to arrest and jail local gamonales or their supporters, that victory was often short lived, as those imprisoned regularly broke out of jail. Perhaps the most extreme example of gamonales flouting authorities' rule came in 1908. Unwilling to accept the rule of the newly appointed Governor Agapito Gómez, Adolfo Carrasco kidnapped Gómez and held him prisoner in Andahuaylas.[65]

District authorities were not only abusive and easily manipulated; they were also often absent. While Carhuanca priest Father Luis Allende charged that "the Governors in these areas, isolated from the sentiments of civilization, are like monarchs, remaining in their posts year after year," a much more consistent problem was the perpetual *lack* of authorities in Carhuanca.[66] In March 1912, Governor Claudio Villar was not in Carhuanca; he had abandoned his post and the district and moved to Andahuaylas. The following November, the subprefect relayed that he had received numerous complaints from Carhuanquinos protesting that their district's lack of an authority allowed serious crimes to go unpunished. One month later, the subprefect again informed the prefect that Carhuanca remained without a governor and that Carhuanquinos repeatedly complained to him about that absence. The next month, the subprefect relayed that not only was there no governor, but Carhuanca's justice of the peace, lieutenant governor, and municipal agent were likewise neglecting their duties. Similar complaints of *acefalía* (leaderlessness) were frequent during these years.[67]

Carhuanquinos—both notables and their poorer neighbors—made exhaustive efforts to improve district political authority. They sent countless letters of complaint regarding existing authorities, made innumerable recommendations about who should hold positions of authority, and offered regular suggestions about what constituted effective political authority.[68] But those numerous letters should not distract us from the stark reality of Carhuanquinos' political disenfranchisement:

Carhuanca's governors were appointed by the Ayacucho prefect on the subprefect's recommendation, not elected by local residents, and Carhuanquinos' endless flood of correspondence supporting and protesting current and potential authorities played no significant role in deciding who did and did not hold formal power inside their district. Put bluntly, Carhuanquinos could talk all they wanted, but they had no real say.

Just as Carhuanquinos lacked the ability to choose and remove their district political authorities, they were also subject to the appointment of a second and distinct type of local authority: priests. Named to the parish by the Ayacucho bishop, Carhuanca's priests regularly assumed a prominent place in district politics. Priests' role in the 1909 and 1916 hostilities was clear. A priest named Father Mejía not only supervised the voting table in the 1909 elections, he also allowed the Carrasco band to use the district church for refuge once the fighting began. And when Father Mejía returned to Carhuanca months after the 1909 violence and his flight from the district, many Carhuanquinos protested with violence, even kidnapping and beating the governor to contest Mejía's return.[69] Priests likewise played a role in the 1916 violence. The men deemed responsible for killing Miguel Carrasco—Paulino and Armando Allende—were relatives of Carhuanca's former priest, Luis Allende.

Priests' political participation in the 1909 and 1916 conflicts was not unusual inside Carhuanca. Priests regularly took a prominent role in Carhuanquino politics, criticizing authorities and casting themselves as the best defenders of the local indigenous population. Writing the prefect about the events of the 1892 Virgin of Asunción festivities, Governor Pantaleón Quijana complained that Carhuanca's priest, Father Francisco Guerra, had flouted his rule, ordering and orchestrating the jailbreak of men imprisoned for harassing Carhuanca's lieutenant governor. Governor Quijana added that, in the days following the jailbreak, Father Guerra and his supporters paraded around the district each night, heavily armed and threatening to kill the governor.[70] Another example of priests' political interventions came in March 1907. Complaining to the Ayacucho prefect that Governor Quijana was reluctant to educate the district's indigenous population and should therefore be removed from power, Father Luis Allende informed the prefect that he himself shared the national government's goal of educating the youth "who will be the citizens of tomorrow and defenders of our national honor," added that he fought for good education and good teachers, and urged the prefect to appoint a governor who held such priorities.[71] Allende's careerist motives were unmistakable: He wanted the post of governor for himself. As the subprefect saw it, Allende's complaints against Quijana were unfounded, and his aim "undoubtedly, is to get an individual of his confidence into the governorship, with the end of fearlessly exploiting the inhabitants of Carhuanca and thus turning himself into the district's primary authority."[72] A third case of priests' political involvement came in May 1913. After Governor Jacobo Marabitto intervened in a disagreement between Father Mariano Romaní and a local schoolteacher, Father Romaní tried to rouse Carhuanquinos to revolt against the governor. Closing his mass with a sharp denunciation of the governor and later ringing the church's bells to summon Carhuanquinos to the plaza, Father Romaní and his followers actually attacked the town hall, fleeing Carhuanca when the rebellion fizzled.[73]

Priests' assumption of political power inside Carhuanca is not surprising. They were among the only literate men in the district, and they enjoyed more economic wealth than most of Carhuanca's other local notables, as they were among the few residents who had the capital to purchase lands in the late nineteenth century. Father Luis Allende, for example, became one of the district's largest landowners, acquiring the estate Ñeccercca and renaming it San Luis in his own honor. He then grew into one of Carhuanca's foremost local notables, amassing political and economic power that he used to his own private benefit. Father Allende was not the only Carhuanca priest to behave in this way. Father Julian Palomino, for example, purchased land from Carhuanquino Mariano Guillén in 1898. Priests accumulated money not only through the sale of lands but also through money lending. Father Julian Palomino noted in his will that he had managed to save 12,000 soles and that several Carhuanquinos owed money to him.[74] It also need be recognized that priests' wealth did not die with them: Many of Carhuanca's priests had children, despite church rules on priestly celibacy, and those children inherited their fathers' money. Father Luis Allende, for instance, shared his land and cash with his son, Francisco Allende. Francisco Allende then became one of the very few Carhuanquinos with enough resources to purchase lands outside the district, acquiring terrains in Huanta, in Andahuaylas, and in Huamanga province. Francisco Allende's son, Luis Allende Ayala, in turn, went on to become the most active land entrepreneur in Carhuanca, buying and selling terrain with startling frequency. The Allende example was not unique: A similar process occurred with Father Mariano Romaní and his son Crisóstomo.[75]

Priests' power extended beyond economic wealth. At one level, they enjoyed automatic authority and respect because of their profession, for religion without question mattered deeply to most Carhuanquinos. As an opponent of Father Luis Allende admitted, the priest "exercises more decisive influence than any other over the Indian mass, because

of the prestige inherent in his ministry."[76] Yet Carhuanca's priests were
rarely more upstanding in their behaviors than were district authorities.
Priests' abuses were commonplace and ranged from economic to social
misdeeds. Father Luis Allende was perhaps the district's most prominent
wayward priest, having come to Carhuanca only after church authorities transferred him out of the Huanta district of Luricocha because he
had committed gross economic abuses there.[77] Father Allende continued similar behaviors in Carhuanca, and in 1911 Carhuanca's municipal
mayor charged that he had received numerous complaints about Father
Allende's unjust economic demands—demands that were "making the
poor people cry."[78]

Other complaints against Allende included charges of animal theft
and even robbery of church ornaments. Father Allende's misbehavior
was indeed so bad that he was reprimanded and then suspended by his
prelate for economic abuses like charging *primicia* (tithe payments) and
seizing goods from the poor. But suspension did not stop Allende; the
priest actually continued charging the tithe after he had been removed
from his position as parish priest. Allende's successors were not considerably better behaved. Father Mariano Romaní faced charges of robbing
church coffers, habitual drunkenness, and rape. Similarly, Father Juan
Pablo Gutiérrez met accusations of attempted rape, battery, theft, and
disturbing the peace. One Carhuanquino even charged that the priest
was a nightly public nuisance, drunkenly shooting revolvers and harassing those who would not accompany him or sell him more alcohol.[79]

Such abusive priests were certainly not unique to Carhuanca. With
a growing shortage of priests at the end of the nineteenth century and
throughout the twentieth, the Catholic Church could not afford to remove abusive priests from duty and instead simply transferred them to
other parishes. Historian Jeffrey Klaiber has shown that there were also
concrete material motives driving priestly abuses. After the 1859 abolition of tithe payments, priests grew increasingly impoverished. Not only
did priests receive no state support, but they also had to pay taxes to
the state on all the sacraments they administered and on all the mar-
riages and funerals they performed. As a result, priests lived primarily
from the often exorbitant fees they exacted for their services and by acquiring, renting, and selling rural properties. Indeed, in Ayacucho, as in
many parts of Peru, priests became the main purchasers of land and the
Catholic Church one of the country's largest landowners.[80]

One did not, of course, require formal political or religious appointment to exercise authority and power inside Carhuanca. Local notables
influenced one another's choices and actions, just as they lobbied their
appointed authorities. Among the district's local notables, those with

the reputations of being gamonales carried that influence to a literal extreme, using weapons and physical brawn to push their local agendas. Men like the Carrascos, the Cárdenases, and the Allendes—all men who had migrated into the district with preexisting sources of wealth—held considerable influence inside Carhuanca not only because their wealth allowed them greater access to regional politicians and the courts but also because they could afford to buy guns to bully others and bring numerous men into their debt, whether as peons or as fictive kin relations. The combination of weapons and bodies allowed these men to dominate Carhuanca's politics.[81]

What emerged inside Carhuanca was a culture of impunity, a sense (more real than imagined) that the district's gamonales could quite literally get away with murder. This culture of impunity saw gamonales publicly celebrating their power and their armed strength, mocking attempts to control them—much like the Chumbivilcas gamonales Deborah Poole has studied.[82] Numerous Carhuanquinos complained that the Carrascos and their allies had evaded responsibility for their role in the 1909 uprising, using gunfire and assault to prevent their arrest. The Carrascos themselves made similar charges. Miguel Carrasco informed the subprefect in 1910 that his cousin Roberto's murderers remained free and were "triumphantly flaunting around in this town" even though there had been repeated orders for their arrest and remission to the Ayacucho jail.[83] Other Carhuanquinos made direct reference to such impunity. A lawyer for two Carhuanquinos charged that the Carrasco brothers were "potentates and hacendados who are outside the reaches of the power of justice, immune and privileged."[84] Many Carhuanquinos similarly complained that, immediately after Miguel Carrasco's murder, those responsible passed through Carhuanca's streets laughing, boasting, and firing their guns. One witness asserted that these men loudly boasted, "We have killed like men."[85] These complaints all suggest that Carhuanquinos lived inside a political order characterized by unpunished abuse. As one Carhuanquina phrased it, Adolfo Carrasco was committing grave abuses "as if there were no authority."[86] That political reality was a direct consequence of Carhuanca's abandon by regional and national authorities.

Gamonalismo grew relatively unchecked in Carhuanca for reasons of geography and land tenure patterns. Isolated from major departmental cities by physical distance and by a paucity of roads, Carhuanca became an ideal arena for the abuses of gamonalismo. Not only did local strongmen focus their political and economic energies on Carhuanca because they had no nearby cities toward which they could direct their ambitions, they were also able to enjoy impunity for their abuses and crimes because urban centers of authority were so very far away. Carhuanca's land tenure arrangements also allowed gamonalismo to flourish. With the entrance of relatively wealthy migrants into the district in the late nineteenth century, a process of land commoditization gained momentum in Carhuanca. Not bound by kinship or community ties and obligations, three sets of migrants—the Carrascos, the Cárdenases, and the Allendes—initiated Carhuanca's first substantial push of land commoditization, purchasing, selling, and purchasing land again, to their own private profit. Carhuanca-born campesinos soon entered the fray, with the Ochoa, Berrocal, and Quijana families taking active part in district land acquisition and resale by the first years of the twentieth century. There quickly emerged considerable class differentiation in Carhuanca, with wealthier, literate campesinos not only holding and acquiring more land and cash than their poorer neighbors but also gaining a monopoly on positions of formal authority in the district. Given these sharp economic and power differentials inside Carhuanca, a culture of intracommunity conflict and abuse soon developed, and gamonalismo flourished.

LURICOCHA COUNTERPOINT

The political exclusion Carhuanquinos faced was based on rule by abandon; but exclusion came in other shapes and guises, as the Luricocha example reveals. Luricocha—and the entire province of Huanta—began the Aristocratic Republic with an activist and politically engaged indigenous peasantry. Huanta campesinos had a long history of political engagement and cross-class, cross-race alliance, as Cecilia Méndez's work on Peru's early republican period has so ably demonstrated.[87] During the 1880s, Huanta's peasants fought the War of the Pacific alongside General Andrés Avelino Cáceres, Remigio Morales Bermúdez, and Luricocha hacendado Miguel Lazón. Huanta campesinos' efforts proved especially crucial between October 1883 and April 1885, when Chilean soldiers occupied Ayacucho and the collaborationist Iglesias government attempted to "pacify" the central and south-central sierra regions and subject the areas to its rule. The rural Quechua men who comprised the Huanta guerrilla forces were among the only Ayacuchanos who continued to resist both the occupation and the Iglesias regime. General Andrés Avelino Cáceres himself said that Huanta "is the only pueblo that has not allowed the invader to walk on its ground with impunity, but only after great efforts and over mountains of dead bodies."[88]

Like campesinos from across Huanta, Luricocha peasants continued their concerted political activism after the conclusion of the Chilean occupation, working to support General Cáceres once he assumed the presidency in 1886 and promoting pro-Cáceres (or *Cacerista*) political figures. Inside Huanta, the most important of those Caceristas was Miguel Lazón, owner of the Huayllay hacienda in Luricocha, a former subprefect and Cacerista general, and Huanta's representative in Peru's national congress. Lazón returned to Huanta from Lima in November 1889 to mobilize support for the Cacerista presidential candidate (and former Ayacucho prefect) Remigio Morales Bermúdez. Campesino support for Cacerismo, for the Morales Bermúdez candidacy, and for Miguel Lazón himself remained strong inside Huanta. One assessment of that strength came from Huanta's subprefect, who commented that campesinos from across Huanta were closely tied to Miguel Lazón "with whose party they are affiliated."[89]

When Lazón was murdered in January 1890 by his anti-Cacerista rival, the Huanta landlord Feliciano Urbina, Huanta campesinos began organizing to avenge Lazón's death. One Huantino recalled that, in the days following the murder, he saw countless people gathering together in the outskirts Huanta, all resolved to punish Lazón's murderers.[90] Every day, more and more campesinos arrived, carrying food, spears, and rifles. Huanta's subprefect reported that 3,000 campesinos had taken up arms to avenge Lazón's murder and that Urbina's sympathizers were preparing for an attack, digging trenches and parapets and occupying them with their rifles.[91] On the morning of January 24, 1890, thousands of campesinos stormed the town of Huanta. Hours of combat left many dead and many more wounded. Two days later, a number of campesinos burst into the church where Feliciano Urbina and several of his allies sought refuge, seizing Urbina and killing him soon thereafter. Urbina's death brought the uprising to a close, and most of the mobilized campesinos retreated to their home communities, leaving only 200 or so rebels in Huanta town.[92]

This uprising was driven by more than political sympathies alone. Campesinos from Luricocha and from across Huanta felt a deep loyalty to Miguel Lazón. Some of that loyalty came from strong personal affection for Lazón, as many campesinos were tied to the hacendado by the binds of paternalistic patron–client relationships. One witness testified that the mobilized campesinos had regarded Lazón as a father. This witness also relayed that Huayllay's guerrilla commanders wept over Lazón's death, telling him that they were "ready to die punishing their father's executioners."[93] Campesinos' loyalty to Lazón also stemmed from the man's direct leadership role in the War of the Pacific.[94] As one witness explained it, Huanta's peasants sought revenge for Lazón's murder as he "was the only one who, when the Chilean invasion of this department happened and the forces of General Iglesias pursued them and burned their homes, put himself at the head of them to lead them, in defense of their lives and properties."[95] Yet however noble campesinos' motives for their uprising were, most Huanta elites regarded the mobilized peasants as highly dangerous. The days preceding the seizure of Huanta brought these sentiments to the fore, as numerous Huanta authorities, hacendados, priests, and merchants voiced sharp and racially charged invective against Huanta's rural indigenous population. Eleven prominent Huantinos, including priests and local authorities, wrote the Ayacucho prefect to warn of looming chaos, charging that Huanta's campesinos were "barbarous men" who were "saturated with a satanic spirit of revenge."[96]

While Huanta's Cacerista campesinos escaped severe repression following their effort to avenge Lazón's death, their luck ran out in 1896. That year, Huanta peasants again mobilized in defense of Cacerismo and in alliance with the Lazón family, staging an uprising that soon became known as the Salt Tax Revolt. On the afternoon of September 27, 1896, approximately 500 Huanta campesinos appeared at the provincial subprefecture, asking the subprefect to abolish the new tax on salt and permit the circulation of the Bolivian currency. The subprefect informed the campesinos that such abolition was beyond his power but that he would discuss the matter with the Ayacucho prefect. The peasants retreated but returned less than one hour later, numbering between 6,000 and 10,000 men and armed with spears, sticks, slingshots, and rifles. These campesinos attacked the subprefecture, leading to a two-hour battle that resulted in the deaths of Subprefect Julian Abad and Municipal Mayor Odilón Vega. In the days that followed, over 4,000 campesinos remained in control of Huanta town.[97]

This uprising was only marginally about the new tax on salt. Much like the 1885 Atusparia uprising in Huaylas-Ancash discussed by historian Mark Thurner, the 1896 rebellion was more a challenge to the new post-Cacerista government's authority to impose a tax than a protest against the tax itself. Upset that Cáceres's opponent Piérola had won the violent 1895 battle for the presidency after President Remigio Morales Bermúdez's sudden death, Huanta campesinos protested against the new Piérola government by challenging its new taxation law. Proof of Cacerismo's place in this uprising came in testimony from numerous Huantinos. Following the revolt, many witnesses reported that Huanta campesinos had been demonstrating in favor of Cáceres in the weeks preceding the uprising.[98] Huanta's governor, for example, relayed that, prior to the seizure of Huanta, campesinos in communities throughout Huanta had been seen carrying out military exercises and yelling out *vivas* to General Cáceres, calling for his return to the presidency.[99] Equally telling, the men held responsible for orchestrating the uprising were prominent Caceristas. One witness went so far as to claim that the uprising amounted to a Cacerista-led "conspiracy against the government."[100]

Campesinos' longstanding support for the Cacerista Lazón family also propelled the revolt. Following the uprising, rumors and accusations circulated that Miguel Elías Lazón (son of the murdered Miguel Lazón) played a paramount role in the uprising. Several witnesses reported that campesinos' demands in the weeks preceding the uprising had included calls for Miguel Elías Lazón to serve as Huanta's subprefect, while other Huantinos claimed that the uprising had been organized by Miguel Elías Lazón and his siblings.[101] The Lima newspaper *El Comercio* echoed these charges, reporting that "the leader of the Indians is the son of Miguel Lazón, who died a few years ago."[102] Although Miguel Elías Lazón himself denied any role in orchestrating the 1896 rebellion, the force of the accusations against him show just how closely the Lazón family, Cacerismo, and Huanta campesinos remained allied in many elite Huantinos' minds.[103] Those perceptions terrified the region's pro-Piérola elites. One Huanta lawyer charged that the Lazón family was "pursuing by fire and blood a few honorable individuals not affiliated with Bermúdez's party, and this bloody hostility is responsible for the ruin and devastation of all the province, as well as the general flight of all its residents."[104]

These concerns were only magnified by Ayacucho elites' racist fears of Quechua campesinos. Their resulting rhetoric cast the uprising as a veritable race war. Ayacucho Prefect Pedro S. Portillo explained that, since the day of the uprising, "the Indian mass has remained the owner of said town, where they exhibit pillage and barbarity."[105] Huanta's governor similarly reported that "the Indians are the owners of the town of Huanta, where they show off their barbarity and triumphant savagery."[106] A group of prominent Huantinos even offered to fight against the "horde of lawless savages, opposed to civilization," explaining that they had to protect themselves against the "furor of the rebels."[107] The Ayacucho newspaper *El Debate*, in turn, charged that Huanta campesinos were "accustomed to robbery and killing, infatuated with an insolent spirit of insubordination."[108] Huantino elites' fears and charges resonated in Peru's capital. The Lima newspaper *El Comercio* echoed these charges, asserting that Huanta's troubles represented a "fight to the death between the savagery of communities and the population's civilized classes, which is necessary to defend, to the point of using extreme rigor if necessary."[109]

That extreme rigor came. Explaining Huanta's situation in dire tones, Ayacucho's prefect urged the national director of government to send 500 infantry troops and 150 cavalry into Huanta to reestablish order. Peru's Piérola government was quick to respond, dispatching Colonel Domingo J. Parra to Huanta with a military division of 800 men.[110] Domingo J. Parra's pacification mission lasted seven months, from the end of October 1896 until the end of May 1897. Over the course of those seven months, Parra's forces made three expeditions to capture members of the Lazón family. Troops occupied the Lazón family's homes and estates, sacking and burning their possessions and their fields. Troops under Parra's command also seized the deceased Miguel Lazón's daughters from their homes, taking them prisoner and placing them in the Ayacucho jail.[111]

Parra's sharpest violence was reserved for Huanta campesinos. Occupying the town of Huanta and then making expeditions into the districts of Luricocha, Huamanguilla, and other areas in Huanta, Parra exacted a brutal repression on peasants and their communities. Parra and his troops forced all campesinos they captured to surrender their weapons under threat of death, and he sentenced many of these captured men and women to death, imprisoning and then shooting them, solely on the suspicion of being a "rebel" or a "Cacerista." The executed campesinos included some of the most outstanding War of the Pacific guerrilla commanders. Parra and his troops also seized livestock from the communities they invaded, confiscating and then selling thousands of animals. Additionally, there were several reports of troops' indiscriminate rapes of women, young and old. Perhaps most devastating, Parra carried out *quintados* inside Huanta communities, forcing campesinos to line up in a row and then summarily executing every fifth person.[112]

Parra's campaign was neither quickly nor easily won, as his military forces encountered sharp resistance from Huanta campesinos. Parra reported that campesinos in one Huanta community attacked troops with gunfire and boulders rolled down from hillsides; residents of the Luricocha community of Huayllay did much the same. Parra reported that, in Huayllay, the "rebels resisted with a ferocious cruelty" and that, when his forces seized the pueblo, Huayllay *comuneros* (community members) burned their own homes down to prevent the soldiers from taking advantage of their refuge during the winter months.[113] Campesinos' attempts at self-defense, however, were largely futile; reports placed death totals as high as 5,000. One Huanta authority reported that Parra had wrought "extermination and devastation. Almost all the Indians' homes were burned, all of their cattle seized, and the persecutions, flagellation, and shootings carried out are even today remembered with horror."[114] In Domingo Parra's own words, "With the lesson they have received, they will moderate a bit their perverse inclinations."[115]

Parra's vengeful words proved sadly prescient. The impact of the Parra repression lasted not just for months, or even years, but for decades. For the two decades that followed the violence, Luricocha's campesinos and hacendados worked mostly just to rebuild their lives and recover from the psychological, physical, and economic trauma Parra created. Huanta's subprefect reported in 1903 that, since the 1896 pacification, the province was "convalescing and slowly developing," having been hurt in terms of capital and labor.[116] For Luricocha, the convalescence was slow indeed. Between 1897 and 1919, subprefects and governors relayed information about locust infestations, reticence toward military conscription, and campesino participation in infrastructure projects, but these official reports said almost nothing about Luricochanos' political efforts during the postrepression years. The reason for authorities' silence was simple: These men had little to report.[117]

The specter of the 1896 repression haunted Luricocha campesinos for decades. Unsympathetic Huanta authorities and landlords were quick to invoke the 1890 and 1896 uprisings when provincial campesinos made even humble requests for political reform; and, while campesinos' memories of the 1896 repression are largely absent from the documentary record, their actions spoke volumes. For most of the twentieth century, Luricocha campesinos eschewed the sort of oppositional and activist politics they had pursued during the 1800s. For these peasants, the risk of state repression remained close at hand, for while Domingo J. Parra and his military had come from Lima, those forces had staunch provincial and departmental allies. In the immediate aftermath of the repression, authorities, hacendados, and other elites throughout both the department of Ayacucho and the province of Huanta heralded the campaign's successful suppression of Huanta campesinos' political mobilizations. Subprefect Francisco Más asserted that the Parra repression had helped advance "the civilization and progress of this unfortunate province."[118] Members of the Pierolista Democratic Party held banquets to honor Parra's victory, and Parra supporters held a two-day celebration in Luricocha, complete with bullfights and a musical band. Huanta's mayor pinned a Gold Medal of Honor onto Parra's chest at a ceremony in Ayacucho, and Ayacucho's prefect reported in August 1897 that, thanks to Parra, "the department is enjoying complete tranquility."[119]

That "complete tranquility" lasted for decades. It was only with the 1919 start of the second Leguía administration that Luricochano politics revived, but this time campesinos largely abstained, leaving political radicalism and rebellion to hacendados and systematically choosing the safest, most staid paths of political action. That pattern held for most of the twentieth century. With the brief exception of participation in a 1969 uprising, most Luricocha campesinos stuck to an extremely cautious political course, avoiding almost any action that smacked of political radicalism or rebelliousness. The district's hacendados did not prove nearly so cautious. Spared from the worst violence of the Parra campaign and free from the crippling restraints of racism, Luricocha's hacendados had the luxury of pursuing politically radical paths. Not all Luricocha hacendados chose to follow those paths, but a sizeable number did. And, in so choosing, these landlords indirectly but unmistakably cast radical politics as their game, a game that indigenous peasants were not invited to play.

CONCLUSIONS: THE POLITICS OF ABANDON

"Peru today is a sick organism: wherever you poke your finger, pus erupts."[120] Such was the unhappy assessment Peruvian thinker Manuel González Prada made of his country in the late nineteenth century. By González Prada's analysis, the War of the Pacific had fostered an abusive partnership between Peru's coastal and sierra elites that allowed for the unmitigated exploitation of the country's rural indigenous majority.[121] Though such an alliance of elites did exist in some form, focus on that alliance alone shows only an incomplete picture of the political history of Peru's rural Andean populations during the Aristocratic Republic. Tracing out the political experiences of campesinos living in rural Ayacucho between 1895 and 1919 shows a much muddier picture of the parameters of authority, power, and contestation in the sierra.

While Luricocha campesinos faced violent exclusion from national politics, Carhuanquinos endured a political life defined largely by disenfranchisement and abuse. That experience of abuse was not sanctioned by a larger alliance between national and regional elites but instead was fostered by a situation of political neglect. Distant from both the departmental and provincial capitals and largely disconnected from regional markets, Carhuanca had only a weak connection to regional authorities and regional elites and still weaker connections to national authorities and elites. Isolated from both national and regional centers of power, Carhuanquinos suffered neglect from provincial and departmental authorities, compounding the disregard meted out by the national government. Within this context of larger political abandon, local politics much resembled the bleak political world Clorinda Matto painted in *Aves sin nido*. Carhuanca was a place filled with political, economic, and social abuse exacted by local authorities, notables, priests, and gamonales. The repercussions of that abuse stretched across the twentieth century, culminating in the violence of the Shining Path war. True to Don Hernán Carrillo's description, Carhuanca was a small town but a giant hell.

CHAPTER TWO

To Unify Those of Our Race

The Tawantinsuyo Movement in 1920s Ayacucho

Screaming from behind the doors of Carhuanca's jail, an indigenous campesino named Basilio Ochoa called for his supporters to free him from imprisonment.[1] As he made his urgent calls for rescue, Ochoa yelled that he had been jailed solely because he had defended Indian rights in Carhuanca and in Peru. When Ochoa's captors tried to transfer their prisoner to a provincial jail the very next day, they were attacked by hundreds of campesinos from communities in and around Carhuanca. The attackers were trying to liberate Ochoa, the local representative of Peru's Comité Pro-Derecho Indígena Tawantinsuyo (Tawantinsuyo Pro-Indian Rights Committee), an indigenous rights organization whose members coalesced into a national movement during the 1920s.[2] Explicitly valorizing indigenous identity and rights, the Tawantinsuyo movement proposed a revolutionary overhaul of the Peruvian nation-state, transforming the heretofore-reviled Indian into a Peruvian citizen equal to all others.

The Tawantinsuyo movement—named after the Quechua term for the Inka Empire—sought to end the extreme poverty, political exclusion, and sociocultural denigration that defined indigenous life inside Peru, and the movement attracted broad support in the departments of Cuzco, Puno, Arequipa, Ayacucho, Apurímac, Huancavelica, Junín, Ancash, Lima, La Libertad, Huánuco, Ica, and Piura. The Tawantinsuyo movement also coincided with and influenced a wave of rural mobilization throughout the country. By the middle of 1923, campesinos from across the sierra were invading haciendas, filing complaints, sending innumerable petitions, and sometimes rising up in violence. Huancavelica and Puno both saw major rebellions during the 1920s. The Department of Ayacucho, too, saw considerable violence, as campesinos in the provinces of La Mar and Cangallo staged extensive and bloody uprisings. The Tawantinsuyo movement and these concomitant rebellions proved so strong and popular that the government of President Augusto B. Leguía outlawed the Tawantinsuyo Committee in 1927.[3]

This chapter follows Tawantinsuyo Committee members inside and around Carhuanca, tracing the district's historical experience of the committee's emergence, activities, and fall. Carhuanca's indigenous peasants actively supported the Tawantinsuyo movement. They participated in meetings and protests and ultimately risked their lives for the movement, staging a massive uprising that ended only because of blanket military repression. If we adhere to a strict definition of the adjective *radical*—meaning of the root or roots; fundamental—then the Tawantinsuyo movement was among the most radical political movements of Peru's twentieth century. The movement sought a thorough overhaul of Peruvian social, economic, and political relationships, changing Peru into a country where the Indian would be as valued a citizen as a person with white skin. The Tawantinsuyo movement was also particularly significant because of its leadership and base of support. Within Carhuanca, the movement was led by two individuals who stood only tenuously within the ranks of local notables, while the movement's supporters were decidedly *not* local notables. These humble campesinos expressly challenged the power and domination of their "notable" peasant neighbors, both by threatening to kill "those who knew how to read and write" and by demanding access to literacy themselves. Not until the 1970s would there be another such concerted challenge to the power of local notables, a challenge that came in two very distinct forms: first from the Revolutionary Government of the Armed Forces and then from militants of the PCP-SL.

The radicalism, the popular composition, and the broad reach of the Tawantinsuyo movement show its unmistakable importance in Peru's twentieth-century political history. Yet the Tawantinsuyo Committee has received surprisingly little attention from historians. Beyond a handful of articles, theses, and book chapters, writing on the Tawantinsuyo Committee is scant.[4] The relative inattention to the Tawantinsuyo Committee appears particularly glaring when compared to the vast literature on Peruvian writer and activist José Carlos Mariátegui.[5] Although Mariátegui was certainly the best-known proponent of an *indigenista* socialism in the 1920s, he was not the only one. Campesinos affiliated with Tawantinsuyo likewise espoused a political discourse that melded class-based ideals with ideas about indigenous rights. But whereas Mariátegui's name barely registers in Ayacucho's archival or oral historical record of the 1920s, the Tawantinsuyo Committee had a profound impact on rural Ayacucho, inspiring indigenous campesinos and propelling them into action. The Tawantinsuyo Committee mattered to Leguía-era Ayacucho campesinos in a way that Mariátegui simply did not.

While historiographical attention to the Tawantinsuyo Committee has been minimal, the committee did become the subject of a significant historical debate with the publication of Marisol de la Cadena's brilliant book, *Indigenous Mestizos.* In her chapter on the Tawantinsuyo movement in 1920s Cuzco, de la Cadena challenges the notion that the Tawantinsuyo movement was a millenarian rebellion, an argument put forth by Peruvian historians like Wilfredo Kapsoli and Manuel Burga. De la Cadena rightly asserts that Tawantinsuyo was in no way a backward-looking mobilization seeking to reestablish a utopian Inka Empire. Instead, the Tawantinsuyo movement was a nationalist political effort that sought indigenous equality inside Peru. De la Cadena also critiques Kapsoli and Burga for uncritically accepting Cuzco elites' vision of the Tawantinsuyo movement as a violent, antistate rebellion, ignoring or dismissing Tawantinsuyo participants' assertions that theirs was a pacific, law-abiding effort. De la Cadena has solid evidence for the Cuzco case, and it is with good reason that she refers to the Cuzco Tawantinsuyo efforts as quotation-marked "rebellions" and as *alleged* rebellions.[6]

But what was true for Cuzco was not necessarily true for Peru, and here I break from de la Cadena's argument. What happened in Carhuanca was indeed a rebellion, without quotation marks or qualifiers. There is no question that Carhuanca's Tawantinsuyo supporters openly and actively defied the local authorities and military officials who sought to jail their leaders and quash their movement and all that it stood for. Just as significantly, Carhuanca campesinos' engagement with the Tawantinsuyo movement entailed a revolutionary embrace of racial and class equality. Tragically, neither the Tawantinsuyo movement nor its lessons endured past the 1920s.

TO UNIFY THOSE OF OUR RACE (I): THE COMITÉ
PRO-DERECHO INDÍGENA TAWANTINSUYO

Founded in Lima on June 16, 1920, the Comité Pro-Derecho Indígena Tawantinsuyo brought together relatively educated indigenous men (and some women) residing in the capital city to promote the rights of Peru's indigenous peoples and to press for comprehensive reform at the national, regional, and local levels. As the founders phrased it, they strove to "unify those of our race and make them aware of their political, economic and social rights."[7] At their very first meeting, committee members drafted a fourteen-point Declaration of Principles that stressed the protection of indigenous communities; defense against abusive authorities, priests, and gamonales; unification of indigenous peoples; Indians' moral and material improvement; solidarity with the working class; and the protection of indigenous laborers. Building a movement that was to reach into every corner of Peru, the committee drafted plans for a body of departmental delegates and provincial subdelegates. These delegates and subdelegates won their posts through election, voted for by indigenous men and women, and those committee members came together in several national congresses between 1920 and 1926.[8]

The Tawantinsuyo Committee had important antecedents in the early years of the twentieth century. One of those antecedents was an informal movement of indigenous campesinos from the southern department of Puno, remembered simply as "messengers." Beginning in the first years of the twentieth century, numerous Puneño campesinos journeyed to Lima to lodge protests before national authorities. The messengers invoked notions of a glorious indigenous past, citizenship, and nationalism that Tawantinsuyo Committee members repeated in later years.[9] Another important precursor to the Tawantinsuyo Committee was the Asociación Pro-Indígena. Founded by San Marcos University student Pedro Zulén, German immigrant Dora Mayer, and sociologist Joaquín Capelo, the Pro-Indian Association was a middle- and upper-class movement whose members saw themselves as allies of Indians but not as Indians themselves. Functional from 1909 to 1916, the association drew together a group of lawyers to defend indigenous peasants in civil and criminal cases, and it worked to inform campesinos of their constitutionally defined rights. The association also sent delegations to investigate abuses against indigenous campesinos throughout the country, reporting these abuses in Peruvian newspapers and in the association's own publications. The Asociación Pro-Indígena fed directly into the subsequent formation of the Tawantinsuyo Committee, as a few association members participated in the 1920 establishment of the Tawantinsuyo Committee. That committee soon transformed into a movement that proved tremendously more popular in both composition and size than its predecessors.[10]

The Tawantinsuyo Committee came to life at a propitious moment in time. During the early 1920s, there was increasing national interest in indigenous rights and culture in Peru, triggered by the messengers and the Asociación Pro-Indígena, as well as by major archeological discoveries of Inka ruins like Machu Picchu. This interest was by no means confined to Lima. Marisol de la Cadena has traced the rise of the middle-class *indigenista* movement in Cuzco, showing how Cuzco's urban intellectuals sought to remake Peru's national identity by glorifying its Inka past.[11] Nor was the indigenista movement solely the domain of middle-class intellectuals; Peruvian indigenism owed much to the actions and words of Puno campesinos involved in the 1915–1916 Rumi Maki rebellion. Led by a former army colonel, participants in this rebellion pledged to restore the Inka Empire.[12] Taking action against several Puno haciendas, the Rumi Maki uprising involved the participation of countless Puno campesinos. Although many elements of the Rumi Maki movement were likely more apocryphal than real, the uprising captured the attention and imagination of Peruvians across class and race boundaries. The movement established that men and women could use a discourse about the Inka to press for dramatic change.[13]

The early 1920s also saw considerable leftist activism and debate in Peru, spurred by international events like the 1910–1920 Mexican Revolution and by the 1917 Russian Revolution.[14] Inside Peru, numerous thinkers, activists, and workers began to engage the political philosophies of communism, socialism, and anarchism. The Tawantinsuyo Committee benefited as well from a relatively sympathetic national government. President Augusto B. Leguía had come to power just one year before, promising a *Patria Nueva*, a New Fatherland that would fully revamp Peru's antiquated political and economic systems. Because Leguía needed allies for his modernizing ends and backing against his oligarchic enemies, he sought supporters among Peru's middle and working classes and among indigenous peasants.

While Leguía's commitment to indigenous campesinos was based far more on political pragmatism than on actual concern about Indian rights, he did make a number of efforts to assist Peru's indigenous peoples. His new 1920 constitution officially recognized indigenous communities, and his government established the Bureau of Indian Affairs in 1921 to attend to indigenous complaints. The following year, Leguía created the *Patronato de la Raza Indígena* (Guardianship of the Indian Race) to protect indigenous campesinos by investigating their complaints, enforcing their rights, and aiding their education. Congruent with these efforts, President Leguía extended both recognition and support to the Tawantinsuyo Committee. A June 1920 letter from the Ministry of Development announced that it was officially recognizing the committee on the grounds that it was, "an institution of purely national character . . . that will bring great benefits to the indigenous race."[15]

Just as the Tawantinsuyo Committee impressed the Leguía government, the committee also inspired many indigenous campesinos. A fundamentally popular organization and movement, the Tawantinsuyo Committee was a primarily indigenous association loosely organized into branches that stretched out across the Peruvian sierra from the committee's headquarters in Lima. The first Tawantinsuyo Committee congress drew indigenous delegations from 145 sierra communities, and the Tawantinsuyo movement touched the lives of innumerable indigenous campesinos who heard the Tawantinsuyo Committee's proposals and demands discussed in their home communities. Those discussions were led by individuals who had attended the first congresses of the Comité Pro-Derecho Indígena Tawantinsuyo or who had received a copy of the committee's edict from relatives or friends. Additionally, thousands of copies of the Tawantinsuyo Committee's newspaper *El Tawantinsuyo* circulated throughout the central and southern sierra, left in train stations and distributed in rural districts.[16]

Inside the department of Ayacucho, the Tawantinsuyo movement attracted varying levels of popular support. The movement gained adherents in the province of Huanta and coalesced into a broad program of action and protest throughout much of the province of Cangallo. It was in the province of La Mar, however, where indigenous protest linked to the Tawantinsuyo movement grew into a massive rebellion. Many La Mar campesinos actively participated in the Tawantinsuyo Committee, and their ideas and actions informed a major uprising that melded a discourse of Inka revitalization with campesinos' anger at increased taxation, highway conscription, and the exploits of the La Mar hacendado and national congressional deputy Albino Añaños. The 1922–1923 La Mar rebellion drew active participation from thousands of La Mar campesinos, who staged huge rallies, seized provincial haciendas, and effectively gained control of much of the province. Violent from its outset, the La Mar rebellion ended in disaster. Campesinos' initial gains came at a tremendous cost, with hundreds of peasants killed during the protests and hacienda seizures, and those gains also proved fleeting. President Leguía answered the La Mar uprising with repression, sending in a military battalion whose soldiers razed peasant communities and executed hundreds of campesinos.[17] But while the La Mar rebellion was the most notorious uprising in 1920s Ayacucho, it was not the only one, as the Carhuanca case will show.

TO UNIFY THOSE OF OUR RACE (II): CARHUANCA

The first reports of Tawantinsuyo activity inside Carhuanca came in July 1923. The governor of a nearby district informed Cangallo Subprefect

Leóncio Cárdenas that two Carhuanquinos, Dionisio Fernández and
Basilio Ochoa, had forced campesinos from communities neighboring
the district of Carhuanca to attend a meeting under the threat of fines.
At that meeting, the indigenous campesinos Ochoa and Fernández explained that they were henceforth to be called commanders and that they
had won the legal suspension of all taxes on salt and alcohol, as well as
other rural taxes.[18] Further official reports soon followed, relaying that
Ochoa and Fernández had acquired an edict pertaining to the Tawantinsuyo Committee and reporting that the pair continued mobilizing indigenous peasants around Carhuanca, carrying out military exercises.
One of Carhuanca's oldest men, Don Isidro Durán, remembered hearing
much about such meetings inside Carhuanca and within the neighboring
community of Huallhua. Don Isidro told me that, at these assemblies,
those in attendance conducted military exercises, marched with their
own flags in their communities' central plazas, and listened while their
chosen leaders spoke out against the Leguía government. Particularly
important was the composition of these meetings. While the Tawantinsuyo leaders Fernández and Ochoa were situated tenuously within the
ranks of Carhuanca's local notables—Fernández because of his literacy,
Ochoa because of his family's prominence in the district—the vast majority of their supporters were humble indigenous campesinos.[19]

Shortly after these reports surfaced, a group of seven men—two
civil guard officers, Carhuanca's lieutenant governor, and four varayocs
from the district of Vilcashuamán—captured the Tawantinsuyo leaders
Fernández and Ochoa in Carhuanca. That capture, in turn, triggered outright rebellion. A military corporal named Mariano Berrocal reported
that, the day after the arrests, indigenous peasants from communities
surrounding Carhuanca acted on news of the capture, mobilizing in the
hills that overlooked Carhuanca. Corporal Berrocal added that "Ochoa
himself called out at the top of his lungs from inside Carhuanca's jail,
yelling that he was imprisoned because he defended indigenous tax pay-
ers and that he had gone to San Miguel to acquire an edict. He said that
because of this, he should be defended and rescued by the people."[20]

Corporal Berrocal and some fellow officers set off for Vilcashuamán
the next day, the prisoners Ochoa and Fernández in their custody. But,
as they headed out of Carhuanca, indigenous peasants from Carhuanca's
neighboring communities of Contay, Saurama, and Huallhua blocked
their path. Corporal Berrocal relayed—and no doubt exaggerated—that
a total of 500 campesinos had besieged them, trying to seize the captured Tawantinsuyo leaders Ochoa and Fernández and to kill the officers. Berrocal further explained that "they failed to snatch away the
prisoners only because of our resolve to carry out our commission. You

see, every time they neared us, we fired our guns, determined to die before giving up our prisoners."[21] The rebels finally withdrew toward Carhuanca, and the officers made their way to Vilcashuamán, where they placed the prisoners Ochoa and Fernández in jail.

Basilio Ochoa and Dionisio Fernández entered that Vilcashuamán jail on August 16, 1923. On or around that same day, waves of indigenous campesinos stormed Carhuanca. Rebels from the neighboring communities of Huallhua, Saurama, Contay, and Rayme Bajo and from Carhuanca itself raided the town. One Carhuanquino, himself accused of participation in the rebellion, testified about the siege. Speaking through a Quechua-language interpreter, this indigenous campesino told the court that "*montoneros* [armed fighters] composed of indigenous peasants from Huallhua and other communities invaded Carhuanca in the middle of last August and forced all the comuneros to rise up against the provincial authorities." This man further testified that the rebels had explained that because all fiscal obligations were now abolished no one should pay these taxes, threatening to punish those who disobeyed. Stating that the rebels numbered more than 2,000, this Carhuanca peasant protested that he was nothing more than an innocent bystander to the uprising.[22]

The uprising lasted for almost two full months, giving rise to the September murder of a Carhuanca teacher, Cirilo Patiño, and culminating with a major political meeting at Pampamarca, a section of land that divided Carhuanca district from the neighboring community of Huallhua. What happened at that meeting can only be imagined—the only documentary reference to it is court testimony that the rebels "went to the meeting in Pampamarca last October, making an agreement with the Morochucos."[23] If such an agreement did indeed happen, it signaled a broadening of the rebellion. Though the term *Morochucos* is the name commonly given to campesinos from the Pampa Cangallo district in central Cangallo, "Morochucos" implied something much more serious in this historical and political moment. By mid-1923, thousands of peasants from Pampa Cangallo had banded together under the leadership of a man named Juan de Dios Alarcón and popularly known as "Colonel Morochucos."[24] Speaking in late August 1923, the prefect of Ayacucho labeled Colonel Morochucos the "principal agitator of order in this province" and warned of the "tragic events" the man's efforts foretold.[25] So if Carhuanca rebels had in fact met and made an agreement with the Morochucos in Pampamarca, it is reasonable to guess that their local movement was about to expand considerably. But that expansion never happened. Repression came instead.

Subprefect Leóncio Cárdenas knew of Carhuanca's Tawantinsuyo movement well before it turned violent, receiving alarmist letters that warned of looming rebellion.[26] Subprefect Cárdenas took those warnings seriously, not least because he owned land in the district and his estranged wife and children all lived in Carhuanca. Calling for military intervention, Subprefect Cárdenas alerted Ayacucho's prefect, who in turn notified President Leguía about the uprising, and that alert soon brought nearly 100 soldiers from the Seventh Infantry battalion into Carhuanca and its outlying communities. Those soldiers arrived quickly, as their battalion was already stationed in Ayacucho, quashing similar uprisings across the department.[27]

Don Isidro Durán remembered the troops' arrival. Seven years old at the time, Durán saw the soldiers arrive in Carhuanca, and he watched as the rebels and their leaders fled into hiding. Confrontations occurred throughout the district, but the worst violence occurred in the community of Huallhua. When the troops entered Huallhua, rebels stood waiting for them, the men armed with sticks, slingshots, and stones, the women with ashes to fling at the soldiers. The soldiers fired warning shots into the air, but when the crowd did not disperse, the troops aimed their rifles at the rebels and fired, killing many. The soldiers then looted the peasants' homes and set them ablaze, stealing livestock and crops while the houses burned. Another Carhuanca octogenarian, Don Modesto Ramos, relayed that over twenty Huallhua campesinos died in the assault, a death toll other Carhuanquinos repeated. Those deaths brought a sudden end to the rebellion. In Don Modesto's words, "the people scattered and a great silence fell."[28]

However short lived, Carhuanca's Tawantinsuyo movement and consequent uprising represented an attempt to remake political, racial, and economic relations inside the district and inside Peru. At the national level, Carhuanca's Tawantinsuyo movement proclaimed full citizenship rights for all indigenous Peruvians. Tawantinsuyo supporters in Carhuanca and across Peru had made such nationalist claims to citizenship through a simple but radical move: They promoted the 1920 Peruvian Constitution. Adorned with the hand-drawn symbol of the Comité Central Pro-Derecho Indígena Tawantinsuyo, the twelve-page edict that Carhuanca Tawantinsuyo leaders Ochoa and Fernández read aloud to their followers was pointedly supportive of the existing national state and instructed Tawantinsuyo delegates to labor in defense of the "civic rights safeguarded by the state's constitution." The edict laid out the committee's fourteen principles and interspersed those principles with lengthy excerpts from the 1920 Peruvian Constitution. The document also called for the defense of indigenous communities, protection from abusive elites, indigenous unity, economic and social development, and solidarity with urban laboring classes. Those demands amounted to calls for a dramatic shift in the distribution of economic, political, and social power inside Peru. When Carhuanca's Tawantinsuyo leaders Basilio Ochoa and Dionisio Fernández testified in their own defense, they denied any role in inciting campesinos to violence. But they did not deny their relationship to the document, stressing that they "only" copied this edict and read it aloud to campesinos. That very transmission of ideas and arguments, however, was in itself a highly political act.[29]

Both in Carhuanca and across Peru, the Tawantinsuyo movement also addressed a widespread and debilitating problem: abusive local authorities. The twelve-page Tawantinsuyo edict outlined proposals for better government, instructing that "every Indian residing in whatever part of the republic can contribute to this committee's proposed work of regeneration, to the benefit of those of their race, by denouncing every type of abuse, whether committed by political or religious authorities or by gamonales." Additionally, Tawantinsuyo delegates were "required by duty to denounce any class of authorities or gamonales before the Central Committee" should those authorities attempt to displace indigenous peasants from their lands.[30] Such abuses were a very real problem. Misdeeds by authorities were in fact so egregious and so commonplace that the Leguía government actually contacted all department prefects in 1923, ordering them to respect and adhere to the law.[31]

Carhuanca's Tawantinsuyo sympathizers took the Tawantinsuyo directives against abusive authorities seriously, voicing strong opposition to their district officials. Carhuanca's Tawantinsuyo leader Basilio Ochoa was highly critical of Carhuanca's governor in the months preceding the August uprising. Governor Abraham Ochoa (not closely related to Basilio) complained to Subprefect Cárdenas in February 1923 that Basilio Ochoa and another man had threatened to kill him and that they "pass by my house late at night, firing shots and threatening my authority."[32] Shortly thereafter, Governor Abraham Ochoa again protested that a number of Basilio's supporters were "lying in wait near my dispatch, wanting to victimize me. They are mocking my authority, taking advantage of the fact that I do not have sufficient forces to send them to the city of Ayacucho."[33] Other humble Carhuanquinos echoed Basilio Ochoa's complaints about Governor Abraham Ochoa. Two Carhuanca varayocs traveled to Cangallo to denounce the governor before the subprefect. They charged that "Governor Ochoa took his gubernatorial post with the intention of using his authority to extort his subordinates and the community."[34] These varayocs asserted that the governor not only obligated them to do unremunerated agricultural work in his fields, but he also forced them to help his mistress in her kitchen. Should they fail to do the work, the governor fined them, imprisoned them, and/or beat them. Similar complaints against the governor followed from other district varayocs. While Abraham Ochoa had been replaced as governor shortly before Carhuanca's Tawantinsuyo uprising, his actions—like the actions of his predecessors—undoubtedly made the Tawantinsuyo movement seem even more appealing to Carhuanquinos. Not only did the movement promise to take action against abusive authorities like Abraham Ochoa, but the movement's local leader, Basilio Ochoa, had also been one of the governor's most outspoken critics.[35]

Memory also connects the uprising to anger at abusive authorities. Don Hernán Carrillo told me that the rebels of the 1920s rose up to kill "those who knew how to read and write."[36] An essay that Don Augusto Cárdenas—the aged son of Subprefect Leóncio Cárdenas—wrote in the early 1990s likewise asserted that "absurdly, the montoneros persecuted and executed those who 'knew how to read and write.'"[37] Here, to say "those who knew how to read and write" was to imply district and municipal authorities, for within Carhuanca—and across much of the sierra during the early twentieth century—literacy was often synonymous with formal political power. Several documents push this interpretation. Take, for example, this December 1922 letter from a handful of Carhuanquino elites: "The undersigned local notables of this town are taking this opportunity to speak respectfully on behalf of Santos Ochoa. The indicated Ochoa knows how to read and write . . . and has been chosen as a varayoc for the coming year. It is impossible that a person who can read and write should be named varayoc. Please be so kind as to name Ochoa lieutenant governor, a post to which he is much better suited."[38] Conversely, Carhuanquinos lacking literacy skills were barred (or quickly ousted) from district and municipal office. The functionally illiterate Tawantinsuyo leader Basilio Ochoa had himself twice been Carhuanca's governor, holding that post briefly in 1920 and again for a short time in 1921. But he lost his political posting precisely because of his limited literacy skills. Carhuanca teacher Cirilo Patiño racialized Basilio Ochoa's inability to read, repeatedly condemning Basilio and maligning him with the comment, "It should not be possible in a democratic and constitutional country like ours for animals like Basilio Ochoa . . . to govern districts."[39] Carhuanca's justice of the peace and lieutenant governor similarly called for Basilio Ochoa's ouster on the grounds of his near illiteracy.[40] These factors all suggest that if Carhuanca's Tawantinsuyo rebels wanted to kill "those who read and write," they wanted to kill local authorities.

But here we need be cautious, for just as literacy helped Tawantinsuyo rebels define their local enemies, literacy was also one of those rebels' central aspirations. An article in the committee's publication *El Tawantinsuyo* relayed that "we want to educate ourselves and our children. We need 'schools and more schools until the last corners of our *ayllus.*'"[41] Tawantinsuyo Committee members had many reasons for so prizing education. Most basically, indigenous campesinos valued education and literacy in their own right, desiring the ability to read and to write. At an economic level, literacy meant being able to personally inspect the contracts, land titles, and other legal documents that peppered rural life and thereby avoid being cheated or tricked into unwanted commitments. Literacy could even mean access to better-paying jobs where the ability to read and write was necessary. At a social level, literacy would allow indigenous campesinos to challenge the crippling constraints of racism. To be able to read and to write meant being able to communicate in Spanish, as bilingual Quechua-Spanish education was not attempted in Peru until the 1970s. And, at a political level, literacy remained the key to citizenship. As discussed in Chapter One, literacy—along with sex and age—was the determining factor for enfranchisement: Only those who could read and write were entitled to formal political participation through the vote. For all these reasons, Tawantinsuyo members made education a priority.

The apparent contradiction in Carhuanquino Tawantinsuyo participants' attitudes toward literacy was in fact no such thing. Tawantinsuyo campesinos esteemed literacy; what they despised was literate authorities' ability to abuse the illiterate campesinos in their midst. The solution to that abuse was twofold: Challenge local authorities and fight for universal literacy. As Tawantinsuyo Committee members explained at their first congress: "Before being bold it is necessary to be literate. . . . gamonales know that their regime will end the day the Indian knows how to read and write."[42] Moreover, because literacy remained the key to enfranchisement, the only way for indigenous campesinos to have any formal say in the election of national authorities—national authorities who in turn appointed departmental prefects, who then appointed provincial subprefects and district authorities—was to learn to read. Education was therefore critical to citizenship.

Carhuanca's Tawantinsuyo rebels showed their commitment to education through capital punishment: They killed the man who was denying local campesinos the very opportunity at the literacy they so prized, the teacher Cirilo Patiño. While he was still governor, Basilio Ochoa convened a public meeting of Carhuanquino authorities and the parents of schoolchildren to denounce Patiño, the teacher at Carhuanca's boys' school. Their consequent petition complained that Patiño "is failing to carry out even minimally the duties the state has bestowed on him." The document described the teacher as "absolutely ignorant, habitually drunk, scandalous, and an incorrigible criminal" and charged that he had convened school for only one single day in the months since he had been named its teacher. And, on that lone day of class, Patiño drunkenly attacked four students without cause. The petition's signatories asserted that Patiño's negligence was "gravely detrimental to the education of the area's children."[43] Although there were other reasons that Carhuanca's Tawantinsuyo rebels disliked Patiño—he was involved in a number of heated conflicts over land—his status as a derelict teacher made him an understandable target for Tawantinsuyo rebels.[44]

The Tawantinsuyo movement inside Carhuanca was not just about politics; it was also about economics. The first reports to Subprefect Cárdenas from Carhuanca's local notables and authorities cast taxation as the rebellion's primary cause, stating that Basilio Ochoa and Dionisio Fernández convened their meetings "to protest payment of the Rural and Industrial Contributions."[45] Huambalpa's governor gave a similar analysis, telling Subprefect Cárdenas that indigenous peasants from the communities that bordered Carhuanca "are rising up against all the authorities of this district and against our general population, on the pretext that all of the money from their tax contributions goes exclusively to our benefit."[46] Still another observer warned that Carhuanca's Tawantinsuyo leaders Ochoa and Fernández "have led Indians from these districts to believe that governmental orders have abolished taxes, contributions, et cetera. If these kinds of ideas spread among uncultured people, they could bring ill-fated consequences."[47]

Tax rebellions have a long history in Peru, as do historiographical arguments about those rebellions. Recent scholarship on Andean peasant politics has taken a sharp turn away from economic interpretations of the causes of peasant rebellion, and historians like Mark Thurner have pushed us to see how seeming "tax rebellions" often had more to do with issues of political legitimacy and the government's right to tax than with the burden of the taxes themselves.[48] This intellectual turn is both welcome and necessary insofar as it recognizes that rural peoples were guided as much by their minds as by their stomachs. But that turn should not be taken too far, as it remains true that economic constraints like taxes often mattered intensely for reasons as basic as survival. In the Carhuanca case, it is accurate to say that Tawantinsuyo rebels were gravely upset about taxes because the levies promised excessive financial strain. Given that the rebels were primarily subsistence farmers who struggled to gather any sort of surplus and had no ready access to cash, these levies represented a tremendous economic burden for already impoverished peasants. These same Carhuanca peasants had political concerns, too, believing that these taxes unfairly benefited abusive authorities, rather than the communities.[49]

A second economic matter driving Carhuanca's Tawantinsuyo rebels was land. In this regard, Carhuanquinos were far from unique. Across Peru's central and southern sierra, land regularly ranked as campesinos' primary concern. A government commission sent to investigate conditions in Puno in 1920, for instance, received an astonishing 7,080 complaints from campesinos of that department, and 86 percent of those complaints involved land. Similarly, members of the Cuzco board of the Patronato de la Raza Indígena noted that during the government body's first year of operation in Cuzco, the majority of complaints it received from campesinos regarded the usurpation of community lands.[50] Tawantinsuyo Committee founder Juan Hipólito Pévez even suggested that it was because of hacendados' violent actions against campesinos that the Tawantinsuyo movement proved so popular across the central and southern sierra.[51]

Although Carhuanquinos shared these preoccupations about land, the nature of their concerns differed from those of other areas. Whereas campesinos in departments like Puno, Cuzco, and Apurímac were battling against their hacendados, campesinos in Carhuanca were embroiled in land conflicts against one another. Accelerating a process that began in the late nineteenth century, Carhuanquinos continued to buy and sell one another's land in the first decades of the new century. Sales of small plots of land, usually around one-quarter hectare in size, grew more frequent during the 1920s. Some of these sales were driven by desperation: Tawantinsuyo leader Dionisio Fernández sold one-quarter hectare of land from his jail cell, selling the land to the very civil guard officer who had imprisoned him![52] Whether he needed the money to provide for his family, to pay his legal fees, or simply to appease the civil guard, Fernández's sale was likely compelled more by dire necessity than by desire. Other sales were driven by profit motives. The grandson of Carhuanca priest Father Luis Allende, a man himself named Luis Allende Ayala, began what would become his life-long pursuit of land entrepreneurship during the 1920s, buying and then quickly reselling land for his own profit. Both kinds of land transactions—those of desperation and those of accumulation—increased in frequency during the 1920s, generating tension between the poorer campesinos who had to sell their terrains and the wealthier campesinos who could amass land.[53] These class tensions factored into the angers driving Carhuanca's

Tawantinsuyo uprising, yet the larger land struggle at play in Carhuanca was a battle fought with the neighboring community, Huallhua.

Campesinos from Carhuanca and campesinos from Huallhua had long been in conflict over their borders, and that conflict had grown especially heated in the months preceding the uprising. Late in April 1923, Carhuanca's governor wrote to Subprefect Cárdenas, telling him about a recent confrontation between the neighboring communities. On the afternoon of April 22, the governor explained, he had traveled to Pampamarca—a small patch of land situated between Carhuanca and Huallhua—to divide and allot the communal terrain on Carhuanquinos' request. Carhuanquinos believed Pampamarca to be the property of their community, and they had the documents to prove it. Unfortunately, peasants from Huallhua believed they were the land's rightful owners, and they likewise had documents to back their claim. While the Pampamarca terrain was not particularly valuable from an economic standpoint—the dry, high-altitude land was good only for crops like potatoes and alfalfa—it symbolized the larger problem of intercommunity struggles for power and dominance. When Carhuanca's governor arrived at Pampamarca with a group of Carhuanquinos beside him, dozens of Huallhua campesinos were waiting there to meet them. Armed with slingshots and sticks, the Huallhua peasants insisted the land was theirs and refused to allow its division. Although the only casualties of this confrontation were two Carhuanca horses, campesinos from Carhuanca retaliated by seizing ten Huallhua horses as compensation, planning to auction off the animals and put the proceeds into communal coffers.[54]

Tensions ran extraordinarily high—as they still do today—and most Carhuanquinos who spoke to Alicia and me about the 1923 uprising asserted that the rebels were all from Huallhua and that they had invaded Carhuanca because of the Pampamarca conflict. They also stressed that Huallhua peasants had killed the teacher Cirilo Patiño because he once traveled to Pampamarca and read Carhuanca's land title aloud, asserting Carhuanquinos' legal right to the land before a crowd of Huallhua peasants. Don Ignacio Figueroa explained that the rebels "were just our neighbors. They wanted to appropriate Carhuanca's land. There was much jealousy. They wanted to take Carhuanca's land title away." When I asked Don Ignacio about Patiño's murder, he replied that Patiño "looked after the community's documents, its titles. It all happened because of Pampamarca, because of Huallhua-chica. Those people rose up against Carhuanca. They attacked and took Patiño at night, tying up his feet, tying up his hands. Savages."[55] Don Gregorio Escalante told a very similar story. Sitting inside his home with his wife and daughter looking on, Don Gregorio recounted, "I was born the very week the montoneros came. My dad told me that they were from Huallhua; they invaded Carhuanca. They came because of a teacher, Patiño, who always talked about Carhuanca's borders. And Huallhua, they just didn't like that, you see. They took the poor teacher from here, a bunch of them came, and they took the poor man away. And that's why Leóncio Cárdenas, Cangallo's subprefect, he sent all those gendarmes. . . . He sent them, and they killed those Huallhua montoneros."[56] Alicia and I heard this same tale over and over again, in interviews, in communal assemblies, and in meetings with the mayor.

There is no question that land conflicts between Carhuanca and Huallhua were heated during the mid-1920s. A number of Carhuanquinos wrote the subprefect in 1926, complaining that "for the last ten years, more or less, all the Indians from the hamlet Huallhua . . . have unduly appropriated a piece of land that belongs to the village of Carhuanca known as Pampamarca." The petition continued, stating that, "our land title proves that this piece of land is our property, since the time of our ancestors; it should not be possible for these irresponsible people to occupy the land any longer, since they already have enough land to cultivate." The letter concluded with a request, asking, "please be so kind as to notify Huallhua comuneros to abstain from harming our wretched district in this way."[57] Yet the overwhelming dominance of the land-motive memory clashes in confusing and troubling ways with the written documentary record of the 1923 uprising. Court documents about the uprising stress the Tawantinsuyo movement, and the letters and petitions that fill the subprefect's archive and the military archive make no reference to the role of Huallhua-Carhuanca hatreds or the fight over Pampamarca. Moreover, it is clear that the 1923 uprising involved campesinos from across the district of Carhuanca and not strictly from the neighboring community of Huallhua.[58]

The discrepancy between the documentary and oral historical records presents a methodological quandary. On the one hand, there is a tremendous amount of written documentation that casts the uprising as a rebellion linked to the Tawantinsuyo movement. Yet on the other hand, oral history scholars like Alessandro Portelli have shown the invaluable and myriad ways that oral histories can take scholars beyond mechanical facts and details, toward the larger meaning of the events under consideration. Similarly, Andeanist anthropologists Joanne Rappaport and Thomas Abercrombie have made a strong case for the parallel consideration of written and oral records, arguing that, even if local memories are somehow factually flawed, those flaws are revealing and meaningful in and of themselves. Significantly, other historians have noted a similar disconnect between written and oral historical sources regarding the Tawantinsuyo movement in other parts of Peru's sierra. Historian Manuel Burga noted that, as early as 1925, campesinos in Huancané, Puno were remembering the violence that had occurred there not as a product of the repression of the Tawantinsuyo Committee and its sympathizers but as an effort to stop indigenous campesinos from educating their children.[59]

For the Carhuanca case—as for the Huancané case that Manuel Burga studied—the disjuncture between the oral and written record represents far more than just a methodological dilemma. That disjuncture in fact allows us to see just how radical and even revolutionary the Tawantinsuyo movement actually was. If we take seriously the idea that forgetting is really only a special form of remembering, then we can ask why Carhuanquinos have so fully forgotten the Tawantinsuyo movement and so forcefully remembered the uprising as a conflict about land.[60] Explanations based on practicality jump to the fore. Memories must make some sort of sense to their owners, and to remember the 1923 uprising as a pro–indigenous rights movement would be to stretch the bounds of credulity. The Tawantinsuyo movement was the lone serious and concerted effort to valorize *indigenous* rights and demand *indigenous* national inclusion across the entire twentieth century, both in Carhuanca and in most of Peru. Though other Carhuanquinos and Peruvians in other historical moments would make similar demands for the rights and national inclusion of Quechua campesinos, they would not phrase those demands in ethnic terms. Instead, Carhuanquinos and Peruvians in later years and later decades used the language of class, speaking of indigenous campesinos as peasants and as workers but not as indigenous men and women.

That shift in language came partly as a result of Tawantinsuyo's repression and partly as one consequence of the rise of explicitly class-based political movements from the 1930s forward. Most crucially, the language of class helped Carhuanquinos make sense of their own daily lives. As their everyday experience was one of terrible abuse by individuals who looked and spoke very much like them, and whose most pronounced differences were ones of wealth, education, and access to formal positions of political authority, the notion of class conflict—of rich against poor, of local notables versus the humble—made intuitive sense to most Carhuanquinos. Part of the Tawantinsuyo movement's strength lay in its ability to articulate these local conflicts of class to issues of race and indigenous identity. But when that movement collapsed in the face of brutal military repression, only the ideas that most resonated with campesinos' everyday lives endured, and those ideas were ones of class.

Given Carhuanquinos' own shift toward class identification in the decades after the 1920s, it seems understandable that they remember the uprising not as a conflict about indigenous rights but as a conflict about land. That framing of the rebellion would make sense to the Carhuanquinos who lived through the uprising as children or heard about it from their elders, fitting their perceptions of themselves as peasants and of peasants' concerns as primarily material. The idea that Carhuanquinos would rise up to press for indigenous rights and indigenous inclusion, valorizing indigenous identity, culture, and concerns, would have been an idea so strikingly unusual in shape and content that it might seem nonsensical to those Carhuanquinos who had not lived through the movement as adults. What would make sense—what would be a possible memory—was an uprising that was about land, fought with the neighboring community of Huallhua over the still-contested terrain of Pampamarca.

Woven into this interpretation of contemporary Carhuanquino memory is the possibility that participants in the 1923 uprising did not readily share their Tawantinsuyo experiences with their young children, grandchildren, nieces, and nephews. Countless Carhuanquinos and their neighbors in surrounding communities invested their hopes and dreams in the Tawantinsuyo movement, and they risked their lives to make the movement's goals a reality. When that dream was quashed through military repression, the disappointment, the loss, and the sense of failure likely compelled silence.[61] It is also true that to speak of Tawantinsuyo's platforms and promise in the years immediately following the rebellion would have been dangerous. To celebrate the 1923 uprising as a pro–indigenous rights movement would be to hint at one's still unpunished involvement in a rebellion whose main participants—not only in Carhuanca but across Ayacucho and throughout Peru's sierra—had been tried in court or killed by the national military. To make such a hint would be particularly risky in Carhuanca, where the state had a terribly familiar face: that of Subprefect Leóncio Cárdenas. Carhuanquinos knew Subprefect Cárdenas personally; they knew he had ordered the military repression of the uprising, and they knew he could learn what Carhuanquinos were saying about the rebellion by simply contacting his children. Few people would risk the kind of incrimination that open remembrance of Tawantinsuyo could bring, least of all individuals who lacked financial resources, education, and powerful allies to protect themselves. It also makes sense, then, that local memory of Tawantinsuyo casts the uprising as one instigated not by Carhuanquinos but by outside enemies in the neighboring community of Huallhua.

Campesinos' need for protection seemed especially strong after the 1923 uprising, as Subprefect Leóncio Cárdenas's power inside Carhuanca did not dissipate following the 1923 repression; it instead grew stronger. The 1923 repression was soon overshadowed by another act of serious political violence that many blamed on Subprefect Cárdenas: the 1924 killing of Carhuanca's governor and his brother-in-law. On the last day of April 1924, three civil guards arrived in Carhuanca to arrest several Carhuanquinos wanted for their participation in the 1916 murder of the gamonal Miguel Carrasco. An argument between one of these three officers and Carhuanca's governor, Alejandro Zárate, quickly morphed into a bloody tussle involving dozens of Carhuanquinos. Punches flew, and gunshots soon followed, ultimately leaving Governor Zárate and his brother-in-law Benigno Palomino dead.[62]

Several distinct interpretations of *why* these murders happened emerged in the days, months, and years following the crime. Some Carhuanquinos saw the killings as a crime of passion, motivated by romantic love turned sour. Others believed the murders were a political crime, orchestrated to guarantee the impunity of Miguel Carrasco's killers. And still others cast the shootings as the consequence of community loyalties and hatreds. Carhuanquinos' understandings of the murders are interesting in and of themselves, but what matters most for our purposes here is the prominent role Subprefect Cárdenas played inside most of those understandings.

Mercedes Cisneros told Alicia and me about Subprefect Cárdenas's estranged wife: her great-aunt, Teófila Zárate. Mercedes described her aunt as a tall, refined woman who was very much a leader inside Carhuanca. "Another one of her stories," Mercedes began, "is that she was the wife of Cangallo's subprefect, Leóncio Cárdenas. . . . People say that she came here from Cangallo because her husband was a rascal (*pícaro*), and she didn't like that. So she escaped from Cangallo and came here, clutching her little children." After a while, Teófila became romantically involved with Benigno Palomino, and the couple had several children together. Mercedes's parents told her that Subprefect Cárdenas's feelings of marital betrayal led to the murders. "Trying to reclaim his children, and terribly disappointed, he ordered—he contracted—another person, Mariano Berrocal. And right here in the plaza, Berrocal shot Palomino, just after my aunt had given birth."[63] Adolfo Urbana shared a similar version of the murders, showing that this crime is remembered as one of passion, orchestrated by the civil guard Mariano Berrocal but ordered by Subprefect Leóncio Cárdenas.[64]

Other Carhuanquinos believed that Subprefect Leóncio Cárdenas had ordered the murders to ensure that those responsible for the 1916 killing of Miguel Carrasco remained unpunished. The Carhuanquina Dominga Cordero, mother of the just-shot Benigno Palomino, asserted that Subprefect Cárdenas had ordered the police to travel to Carhuanca "to facilitate the escape of Francisco Allende and of the other men responsible for the death of Don Miguel Carrasco, accused men who were facing capture in Carhuanca." To Dominga Cordero, the homicides were political assassinations carried out because Carhuanca's governor had arrested the men wanted for the 1916 murder. Charging that Subprefect Leóncio Cárdenas was the "unconditional protector" of the men accused of killing Miguel Carrasco, Dominga Cordero complained that "these men walk freely in Carhuanca, with the support of this authority." She added that, each time Subprefect Cárdenas visited Carhuanca, "these men are the first ones to go to his lodgings and welcome him." Cordero then argued that "this conduct makes it clear that my deceased son died at Berrocal's hands because he had carried out the Supreme Court's orders. . . . This was the motive for the commission of these homicides."[65]

There is no substantive evidence to support these accusations against Subprefect Leóncio Cárdenas; there are only the accusations themselves. Those accusations, however, suggest that Carhuanquinos saw the subprefect's power as unlimited, neither restrained by the law nor constrained by popular opinion. And as was true of Carhuanca's local authorities, the subprefect owed his position to the departmental prefect and not to the masses under his authority. The resulting lack of popular accountability fostered impunity, and many Carhuanquinos understandably felt they had no recourse against their subprefect and his actions. Dominga Cordero angrily complained, "I have not managed to find help of any kind in my wretched town, so terrorized by these crimes. Instead, I have met with indifference from everyone, most of all from the man entrusted with doing that mandated by law, Justice of the Peace Francisco Hiyo." She spoke of her difficulties in getting local investigators to do their jobs and her frustration over the trial's postponement. "During all of this, the assassins delight in their shameful impunity," Cordero lamented, adding that she, her daughter, and her nine orphaned grandchildren "only cry inconsolably at our misfortune. Things just cannot go on like this."[66] To Carhuanquinos like Dominga Cordero, Subprefect Leóncio Cárdenas could not only order an assassination without punishment, he could also guarantee impunity for the men who had carried out the killings. Many Carhuanquinos saw the subprefect as a powerful and aggressive incarnation of the state, believing that he killed his enemies and excused his allies' crimes. That vision, combined with knowledge of the subprefect's pointed opposition to the Tawantinsuyo movement, surely made open discussion of the repressed movement seem dangerous, if not deadly. It is no wonder, then, that Carhuanca's campesinos so thoroughly "forgot" Tawantinsuyo.

LURICOCHA COUNTERPOINT

Not every district in rural Ayacucho participated in the Tawantinsuyo movement; and, among those that did participate, the dynamics of involvement often differed substantially from one area to the next. Here, the district of Luricocha provides an important counterpoint to the Carhuanca case. While members of the Tawantinsuyo movement were present within Luricocha, their actions were strictly peaceful and accommodating of the Leguía government. It was instead a set of highly politicized district hacendados not affiliated with the Tawantinsuyo movement who waged an aggressive political campaign against President Leguía and his policies.

As in Carhuanca and across Peru, Luricocha members of the Comité Pro-Derecho Indígena Tawantinsuyo pressed for the rights of indigenous peasants and workers, meeting with men and women in their communities, penning letters to regional authorities, and asking President Leguía for help and support. While Luricocha's Tawantinsuyo delegates made many requests and had many dreams, their primary aims were twofold: to bring indigenous campesinos better education and better economic treatment. A 1925 letter to President Leguía showed these ends. Representing several communities in the district of Luricocha and the newly created district of Santillana, the indigenous campesinos Doroteo Silvera, Aniceto Carrasco, Nicanor Guerrero, and Salomé Pariona petitioned Peru's president for a number of guarantees. These men wrote, "In the name of the indigenous groups that constitute the Pro-Derecho Indígena Committees of the above listed towns . . . we have traveled to this capital city to implore you, Mister President, for . . . the construction of indigenous schools in our communities or *ayllus*." Arguing that there were more than 600 students in each of Huanta's districts who needed both regular and trade schools, these men asserted that Huanta's campesinos required schools "in order to educate ourselves, nurturing the heart and mind of our race, which groan under the gloom of ignorance." Though the lofty language probably came from their scribe, the men who signed the petition were all literate, and most certainly believed in the critical importance of education. Their next request showed as much: The men asked for Leguía's "fatherly aid," requesting that he "be so kind as to order the Ministry of Education to provide us with the appropriate quantity of books or primers necessary for the Indian spirit."[67]

Luricocha's four Tawantinsuyo representatives further urged the president to revise indigenous campesinos' economic obligations to the state. Like Tawantinsuyo activists elsewhere, they pressed President Leguía to reduce or abolish coca and salt levies, which "given our means, our misery, and our abandon, are excessive taxes."[68] By far the most impassioned economic request from Tawantinsuyo members in Luricocha was the demand that President Leguía abolish the 1920 Conscripción Vial Law. That law required all men aged eighteen to sixty years old to work six to twelve days per year on the construction of a national highway system, and it was a law from which all but indigenous men managed to win exemption. The vial's unremunerated labor took indigenous men away from their families and their fields and usually left the men underfed, overworked, and lonely. The committee members therefore asserted that the "Servicio Vial, twelve days of forced labor and hunger, is unjust and inhumane," and they asked President Leguía to suspend the law that was an "annihilator of the Indian's life."[69] These complaints—echoed by other indigenous peasants throughout Peru—went essentially unheard by the Leguía government. As the minister of public works reported, "The importance of our road building program will of necessity make inevitable the sacrifice of the lives of some Indians."[70]

Luricocha's Tawantinsuyo Committee members stated their goals in many different documents, and they worked hard to make these goals a reality, meeting with campesinos in their respective communities, traveling back and forth between Huanta and Lima, and writing numerous letters and petitions requesting material and political support. Yet, even though their message and requests resonated with indigenous campesinos' desires, Luricocha's Tawantinsuyo representatives found little district support for their efforts. Tawantinsuyo members' words and actions failed to garner much outright sympathy; committee members' petitions bore only their same few signatures and fingerprints, never those of campesinos not formally affiliated with the Tawantinsuyo Committee.[71] Moreover, Luricocha's Tawantinsuyo representatives never managed to build a broad and cohesive movement of the sort that shook Puno, Huancavelica, and the Ayacucho provinces of La Mar and Cangallo during this same time period. Even nervous provincial authorities made no mention of generalized support for committee members; they wrote extensively of Doroteo Silvera's travels between communities and his efforts to mobilize campesinos in both Luricocha and Santillana, but they reported no large meetings or protests. Those authorities were certainly looking for such protests. A number of Huanta elites requested, "We ask that the said Silvera be duly punished, obliging him to make guarantees to the state to avoid uprisings against the current regime. Otherwise, a situation will arise in which the people will rebel and the montoneros of yesteryear will reappear."[72] Had there been protests to report, Huanta's authorities certainly would have done so.

Luricocha campesinos' reticence to participate in the Tawantinsuyo movement was grounded in fear. Barely thirty years had passed since Domingo J. Parra's 1896 repression—a repression in which military forces razed several Huanta communities, destroying houses, burning fields, and killing thousands of peasants. Memories of those events were clearly on the minds of Huantino authorities. Like the men quoted above, Luricocha's mayor warned that political mobilization among the area's campesinos would result in "catastrophes and popular uprisings of Indians, and we will lament the same misfortunes suffered in the years 1890 and 1896."[73] The subprefect, in turn, noted that "Huanta has a very well-known history and reputation of being a battle-hardened province, and as such an Indian uprising here would be repeated enthusiastically in neighboring provinces."[74] These authorities also singled out Luricocha's Tawantinsuyo representatives as malicious and dangerous men. Huanta's subprefect argued that Silvera and his fellow committee member Nicanor Guerrero Oré "had the exclusive aim of exploiting other Indians, imbuing them with subversive ideas."[75] Others charged that "instead of letting Indians be united in solidarity with whites, he [Doroteo Silvera] is imbuing them with completely noxious ideas, and he is trying to separate us or, better said, make them hate us." These men warned that if Silvera remained free, Huanta's Indians would rise up "and try to kill us off like they did the time before."[76] Luricocha campesinos whose relatives, friends, and neighbors died as a direct result of the 1896 repression probably wanted to do all they could to assuage provincial authorities' concerns about a looming uprising. Shying away from participation in the Tawantinsuyo Committee served that purpose.

Although most Luricocha campesinos were unwilling to affix their signatures or thumbprints to Tawantinsuyo petitions and proved uninterested in supporting local committee members' protests against Luricocha authorities, they were prepared to make an indirect protest against one key Leguía policy, the highway conscription law. As early as January 1924, Luricocha's governor complained that, while in past weeks he had been able to send over 200 laborers, "this week, only fifteen workers from this district showed up for the Servicio Vial highway work." The governor blamed this "complete insubordination" on the activities of "a few bad elements" who came to Luricocha propagandizing against the Vial. The governor feared that if the subprefect did not intervene, he would be unable to send even a single Luricocha campesino to the highway labors of the coming week.[77] Huanta's subprefect voiced similar concerns, informing Ayacucho's prefect that the number of conscripted highway workers had fallen precipitously, particularly in Luricocha. The situation only worsened across the year 1924.[78]

Several Huanta authorities were quick to blame peasant noncompliance with the Conscripción Vial on Tawantinsuyo Committee members. In October 1924, Huanta authorities noted that Tawantinsuyo members were "stirring up the area's Indians, telling them not to participate in the Vial labor."[79] And, in January 1926, a group of Huanta notables, hacendados, and authorities charged that because Tawantinsuyo members had declared the area's campesinos "exempt from every obligation, such as the Law of Obligatory Service" there was now sharply diminished participation from Huanta campesinos in Vial highway labors.[80] The reality, however, is that Luricocha's Tawantinsuyo representatives were not the only—or even the first—Huantinos to urge indigenous peasants to abandon their Vial labors. Indeed, the primary reason why Luricocha's campesinos risked avoiding the Vial was because they were encouraged to do so by many district hacendados.[81]

A military officer reported that on the afternoon of October 14, 1923, the prominent Huanta landlords and professionals Max Gil, Mario and Luis Cárdenas, José M. Betalleluz, Guillermo Lama, and others held a public meeting in the city of Huanta to denounce the proposed State Coca Monopoly and protest against the Servicio Vial. These men were all part of a group named the "Liga de Defenza de los Derechos del Hombre"—the Rights of Man Defense League—and they had both organized and led the meeting. When six military officers arrived and told the assembled crowd to disperse, these relatively wealthy, non-Indian Huantinos urged a revolt, throwing stones and leading an attack that soon forced the officers to retreat. The officer blamed these elite men for the violence; the subprefect blamed them for the very opposition toward the Vial. Huanta's subprefect wrote, "I must inform you, Mr. Prefect, that the Indians have been completely peaceful and obedient with regard to the Vial law. Why, just last week 300 men participated in the labor. And if they participated in today's demonstration, it is only because of said instigators."[82]

The subprefect offered still more detail about the men and the Rights of Man Defense League. He explained that members of this group had physically attacked his predecessor and that they were collecting money from Huanta campesinos to help further their protests against the highway conscription and the coca monopoly. He even noted the difficulty of repressing the group, explaining, "I have not brought this fact to the attention of the Examining Magistrate (*Juez Instructor*) because he used to belong to this group."[83] What was this group? Members themselves offered an answer. Formally introducing themselves to Ayacucho's prefect in January 1923, members of the Rights of Man Defense League explained that "this nascent group does not pursue any political end. Instead, as its name suggests, its program of action grows from the sacred principles of solidarity and the defense of individual and collective rights." The men also provided the prefect a list of its forty-seven most senior members, a list that included priests, a pharmacist, an agronomist, lawyers, merchants, and hacendados. The group had an executive committee, a proworker commission, a complaint commission, a pro-Indian commission, a publicity commission, and district commissions for Luricocha, Santillana, and Huamanguilla.[84]

Members of this group regularly appeared in reports from police officers, the subprefect, and the prefect, stirring up trouble with their complaints against local, provincial, and national authorities and especially with their active opposition to the Conscripción Vial. Probably the most notorious of the League's members was Carlos La Torre, an agronomist, hacendado, and head of the Defense League's Luricocha Commission. In January 1924, Huanta's subprefect presented the prefect with a sharp denunciation of La Torre. He complained, "Mr. La Torre is one of the venal men who wish to see the Indians rise up and demand the repeal of this [Conscripción Vial] Law, the Coca Tax, and the State Alcohol Monopoly." The subprefect continued, charging that La Torre and his friends were engaging in dishonest politicking, falsely denouncing Luricocha's governor for abuse of authority and trying to incite the area's indigenous campesinos to rebel. According to the subprefect, La Torre even colluded with a low-level Luricocha authority to prevent the area's campesinos from fulfilling their highway conscription obligations. The subprefect also asserted that La Torre and his allies "traverse all the annexes of all the districts, declaring that the government wants to kill local cane and coca production so that foreigners can come to the country and have total control over the cultivation of these products."[85]

There were several reasons driving these elite Huantinos' opposition to President Leguía and his Conscripción Vial law. One explanation is money. Many members of the Rights of Man Defense League were prominent landlords who made their livelihood on the backs of campesino laborers. These men needed campesinos to plant, tend, harvest, and transport their crops for sale in provincial and national markets. If those peasants were out building highways for the president, they were not toiling in their landlords' fields. Economic self-interest also explains why these local elites opposed the proposed coca and cane alcohol taxes: As landlords and as merchants, these men made a good share of their money from the sale of these products and probably feared that the new taxes would cut into their profits. This was certainly the case for Luricocha hacendado Carlos La Torre, who earned a significant portion of his income from the sale of cane alcohol grown and processed on his Iribamba estate.[86]

Another explanation for these men's attitudes is political ambition. This explosion of hacendado politicking coincided with national congressional and presidential elections in which Supreme Court Justice Dr. Germán Leguía y Martínez was the lone candidate to challenge Leguía's continuing rule (a political risk that ultimately won the judge arrest and then exile on charges of fomenting revolution).[87] There was nothing coincidental about this overlap. The Huanta landlords who caused such a stir in late 1923 and early 1924 were waging a political campaign expressly directed against President Leguía. Not only did Defense League members promote Germán Leguía y Martínez's candidacy, they also made heated calls for the Leguía government's downfall. Those calls captured much attention (and outrage) in January 1924. Late that month, presidential sympathizers staged a large and peaceful rally in the city of Huanta, walking through the city's streets cheering President Leguía, Huanta's senator Pio Max Medina, and Huanta's National Deputy Manuel Jesús Urbina. Speaking before a crowd that numbered over 2,000, Huanta's mayor and the rally's other leaders called for the reelection of these three politicians. Problems began shortly after the rally came to an end. A military officer reported that, as the rally wound down, "a small group of inebriated men, mostly Indians, arrived at the corner of Comercio Street, led by Carlos La Torre and the Turk subject Juan Farach." The officer claimed that a third man then addressed the small crowd, speaking in the name of the Rights of Man Defense League and saying that "the government wants to kill off the coca and alcohol industries; that the Indians should swear to protest against such efforts and refuse to participate in road construction; and that they should spill their last drop of blood before obeying such mandates." Rights of Man Defense League members followed up this speech by calling for the government's downfall.[88]

Defense League members were just as interested in the congressional elections as the presidential ones; they wanted to see the ascension of one of their own ranks into Peru's Chamber of Deputies: Carlos La Torre. La Torre sought election to Peru's Chamber of Deputies as the representative for Huanta. Between October 1923 and January 1924, members of the Rights of Man Defense League made three nighttime appearances in the town of Luricocha, firing shots in the air and yelling out "vivas" to presidential candidate Germán Leguía y Martínez and to Carlos La Torre. On their fourth visit, the men came during the day. The mayor recounted that "they went all over the town, pressing people to join their protest against the coca tax and promoting La Torre's candidacy by casting him as the people's antitax savior."[89] Defense League members similarly voiced support for La Torre's congressional bid on the January 1924 day of the election rally.[90]

Significantly, the Luricocha and Huanta members of the Rights of Man Defense League did not regard indigenous campesinos as their political partners. These elite Huantinos saw themselves as the Indians' salvation, as great, enlightened men who would protect and redeem the uneducated and exploited natives. The Rights of Man Defense League did not include indigenous campesinos in its ranks, nor did its members push for indigenous enfranchisement. Put bluntly, these men wanted to rescue the Indians; they did not want to recognize them as equals. These elite men did not transcend the racism, sexism, and classism common to Peruvian men of their standing. Yet the force of these men's opposition to the Conscripción Vial was nonetheless reassuring to Luricocha's campesinos: Defense League opposition to the highway conscription was so vehement and so concerted that Luricocha's campesinos took a political risk and abstained from their hated Vial labors. Had Luricocha hacendados not offered campesinos their aggressive support on that front, it seems unlikely that district peasants would have protested against the Vial. The memories of 1896 were simply too fresh.

Although this tradition of energetic hacendado politics in Luricocha survived in later decades, the ideas and actions of Luricocha's Tawantinsuyo Committee did not. No longer in pressing need of political allies and alarmed by indigenous mobilizations across the country, President Leguía's government outlawed the Comité Pro-Derecho Indígena Tawantinsuyo in August 1927. The ban declared that the association "has no purpose of any sort and only exploits Indians" and that committee members were "ignorant people who do nothing more than create friction with regional authorities, obstructing and distorting the work of the government." Leguía's national decree banned both the Tawantinsuyo's Central Committee and its regional branches and instructed political authorities to ensure strict compliance with the ban.[91] Luricocha's authorities did not need to expend much effort to that end: The local branch of the Tawantinsuyo Committee was essentially defunct by early 1926. The committee's last official correspondences—or, at least, those that have survived in the archives—came in February 1926.[92] And months before Leguía's decree, local Tawantinsuyo leader

Doroteo Silvera had ceased identifying himself as a committee member. Writing to the subprefect in May 1927, Silvera identified himself only as an "indigenous resident of San José de Secce" before proceeding with his complaint about a neighbor. Silvera made no mention of the Tawantinsuyo Committee, no mention of his prominence in the district, and no mention of his past interactions with the subprefect. Tawantinsuyo had disappeared in Luricocha.[93]

TAWANTINSUYO RECONSIDERED

Ayacucho's rural indigenous men and women began silencing their own racial identity in the aftermath of the Tawantinsuyo movement's collapse, formulating a new, strictly class-based identity of peasant that interpreted local arrangements of power, wealth, social status, and abuse along economic rather than ethnic lines. Decades before the 1968–1980 Revolutionary Government of the Armed Forces officially reclassified "Indians" as "campesinos," Ayacucho's indigenous peasants relabeled themselves. Pushing past the heartbreaking disappointment of the Tawantinsuyo movement's repression and collapse, rural Ayacucho men and women found solace and new political direction in the idea of class. From the 1930s forward, Ayacucho campesinos embraced political projects that offered primarily class-based analyses, programs, and visions, stressing that inequalities based on wealth were the root of Peru's troubles and therefore the necessary focus for any solution.

The appeal of class was strong, and the Tawantinsuyo movement's language of indigenous rights remained absent—or nearly absent—for most of the rest of the twentieth century. Many scholars have commented on that apparent absence, contrasting it with the veritable explosion of indigenous-rights mobilizations in late-twentieth-century Bolivia and Ecuador.[94] While anthropologists like María Elena García and Shane Greene have critiqued these Andean comparisons, rightly cautioning against reductive portrayals of indigenous politics in Peru and reminding scholars about vibrant Amazonian mobilizations, it is nonetheless clear that many Quechua peasants in Peru remained wary of the label *indigenous* longer than did many of their South American neighbors.[95] Tawantinsuyo's suppression was a central factor in that wariness. Here, Don Modesto's words bear repeating. With the end of Tawantinsuyo, "the people scattered and a great silence fell."[96] On the matter of expressly *indigenous* rights, that silence long remained unbroken.

Tawantinsuyo's demise ultimately marked a sharp break in the course of rural Ayacucho's twentieth-century political history. Although notable and humble Carhuanquinos alike would continue to press for their political, economic, and social rights in the coming decades, they would do so in class rather than ethnic terms. The kind of radical equality that the Tawantinsuyo movement propounded and practiced disappeared; no other subsequent party or movement similarly melded attention to class and race. And until the 1970s, Tawantinsuyo was the only movement in twentieth-century Ayacucho peopled predominantly by peasants outside the ranks of local notables. Certainly, Tawantinsuyo's inclusiveness was not total; even though the committee's statement of principles referenced women, and even though some women participated inside the committee's ranks, Tawantinsuyo was an overwhelmingly male movement. Tawantinsuyo's disappearance nonetheless shut down a path toward meaningful equality and revolutionary change.

We Will No Longer Be Servile

Peasants, Populism, and APRA in 1930s Ayacucho

Tipping his hat and smiling, Don Marcelino Lizarbe told me, "I was an Aprista then. There were many Apristas here."[1] An elderly campesino from Carhuanca, Lizarbe shared with me his memories of APRA mobilization in the 1930s. Like many men and women in 1930s Peru, Lizarbe had believed that APRA (the American Popular Revolutionary Alliance) would bring about comprehensive economic, political, and social change. Such change seemed especially necessary in a national context of increasing urbanization and industrialization and in an international context of severe economic depression. A fundamentally populist party, APRA promised both socioeconomic justice and a national political transformation that would wrest power from the hands of the aristocracy and turn it over to the masses. Lizarbe's words invite a rethinking of the APRA's early history, as his comments run counter to two general assumptions about the party: that APRA's poor electoral showings in Peru's southern sierra reflected a regional paucity of sympathy for the party and that APRA held little appeal for rural indigenous peasants during the 1930s.[2]

As Peru's strongest and most enduring political party, APRA has received considerable attention from scholars. Yet while there are enough books about Aprismo to crowd many library shelves, much of this work is staunchly partisan in cast, celebrating or attacking the party and its founder, Víctor Raúl Haya de la Torre. And while Haya de la Torre's words, actions, and ideas have been documented and analyzed in impressive detail, only a few works have looked past APRA's leader to consider how the party emerged and operated in regions where Haya failed to tread.[3] As such, we still have only a fragmented knowledge of the party's history across Peru's many distinct regions, and we still lack a synthetic, historically grounded understanding of early APRA as a truly *national* party. This chapter begins the work of reconceptualizing APRA, situating Ayacucho's APRA in its comparative national context, and examining the party's emergence and popularity in Carhuanca. Inside Carhuanca, APRA drew sympathy and staunch support from the district's most powerful campesinos, who connected the party's national discourses to their local struggles for political power and land.

APRISMO IN PERU, APRISMO IN AYACUCHO

As was true of other populist and/or radical political parties like the Peruvian Communist Party and *Unión Revolucionaria* (Revolutionary Union), APRA's formal political role inside Peru began with the sudden end of Augusto B. Leguía's eleven-year presidency in 1930. Responding to widespread anti-Leguía sentiment and economic desperation triggered by global depression and financial crisis, the largely unknown army colonel Luis M. Sánchez Cerro led a military rebellion against President Leguía in August 1930.[4] Sánchez Cerro went on to head the Unión Revolucionaria party and win the presidency in the 1931 election, an election famous for its unprecedented inclusion of the working-class masses who were no longer disenfranchised by elitist property requirements. Although the electoral system still excluded the illiterate national majority, and while many Apristas made angry denunciations of electoral fraud, the 1931 elections were by far the broadest and most popular elections in the country's history to that date. Sánchez Cerro governed Peru with a mix of liberalized social legislation and conservative economic policies, ruling the country until his April 1933 assassination.[5]

The young man who shot President Sánchez Cerro was a partisan of APRA. Founded in the 1920s by middle-class Trujillo native Haya de la Torre, APRA espoused a broad political program emphasizing social justice and alliance between the middle and working classes. By the time of the 1931 elections, Haya had already established his popularity, having participated in the university reform efforts of the 1920s, in a 1923 protest for the separation of church and state (a protest that led to his exile), and in the popular universities. It was especially through these popular universities—informal classes that provided education, political instruction, and some social services, taught by progressive university students and attended by workers—that Haya built his ties to Lima's working and middle classes, and he retained those ties throughout his years in exile.[6]

Founding his APRA party in Mexico in 1924, Haya outlined a five-point political platform that called for resistance to North American imperialism, Latin America's political unity, the nationalization of private property and industry, the internationalization of the Panama Canal, and the alliance of the world's oppressed peoples. Haya returned from exile in the election year 1931 and began campaigning for the presidency, leading the APRA party his allies had launched inside Peru the previous year. Though Haya won the adulation of tens of thousands of men and women who crowded his rallies as he traveled from Piura down to Lima, he could not beat Sánchez Cerro. Haya's loss of the presidential election as well as his (largely unfounded) claims of electoral fraud triggered numerous political uprisings across Peru, uprisings that continued until Sánchez Cerro's successor President Benavides outlawed APRA in 1934.[7]

While APRA lost the 1931 election—and could not compete legally in elections for years to come—the party gained much more popular support in Peru's many regions than the rival Sánchezcerrista party, Unión Revolucionaria, or the newly emergent Peruvian Communist Party. With a highly developed party structure, regional flexibility, and creative political programs—crucial political assets that both the Communist Party and the Unión Revolucionaria lacked—APRA was able to win adherents throughout Peru. Strong Aprista movements emerged not only in Lima but also in Haya's home province of Trujillo on the northern coast, inside the northern department of Cajamarca, in the northern sierra province of Chachapoyas, in central sierra departments like Junín, and in southern sierra departments like Huancavelica and Ayacucho.

Inside Ayacucho, the Aprista movement focused on regional inclusion in the Peruvian nation-state. Under the leadership of Ayacucho lawyer and congressman Aristides Guillén, Ayacucho's Apristas pushed for regional political solidarity, action, and national recognition. In Ayacucho, as in other southern sierra departments, a stress on regional rights, decentralization, inclusion, and power defined Aprismo. A piece of Ayacucho Aprista propaganda pushed this point: "Ayacuchanos, we will no longer be servile! We will no longer be unworthy sons, tyrant's pupils! For Ayacucho's moral greatness and progress! Viva Peru! Viva Ayacucho!"[8]

Similar regionalist sentiment was present in other southern departments. Historian Jorge Basadre has deemed such broad anticentralist sentiment "the subversion of the provinces" and argued that "throughout the country, the flag of decentralization was propagated without resistance."[9] Apristas played a major role in this "provincial subversion." An Aprista named Luis Heysen, for example, organized the Regional Aprista Congress for Southern Peru in 1931. The congress's promoters actively advocated decentralization, and congress delegates deliberated how their regions' specific problems could be incorporated into the national party's program. APRA also promised an end to the sense of abandon and neglect common in the southern sierra, and that promise does much to explain the party's popularity.[10] While APRA never became the dominant political force in the southern sierra—Sánchez Cerro won significantly more votes than Haya de la Torre in the 1931 elections, and APRA consistently had its weakest electoral showings in the south—the party was nonetheless an important political actor in the south, and its stress on regional identity and decentralization help explain the party's power.[11]

Ayacucho's best-known branch of APRA was its base in the city of Ayacucho. Although APRA had been officially outlawed following President Sánchez Cerro's assassination, with its members jailed or forced into hiding, its publications shut down, and Aprista congressmen deported, Peru's Apristas continued their political activities unabated. Indeed, as historian Thomas Davies has argued, the repression actually unified the party and heightened feelings of party loyalty.[12] Apristas in Ayacucho were no exception. Following the example of the Trujillo Aprista activists, who launched a massive revolutionary uprising in 1932, urban Ayacucho Apristas started a rebellion in November 1934, seizing the prefecture, storming civil guard headquarters, and calling for national revolution.[13]

Although the Ayacucho rebellion intentionally coincided with other Aprista uprisings in Huanta, Lima, Huancayo, and Huancavelica, it was neither prolonged nor successful. As was true in Trujillo, military forces brutally and definitively quashed the uprising. After only four days of rebellion in the city of Ayacucho, infantry troops put an end to the uprising, and APRA was further repressed in the department and throughout Peru. With a brief interlude in 1936, the party would remain illegal until 1945. This facet of APRA's history is relatively common knowledge inside Ayacucho—university students have written theses on the 1934 urban uprising, senior citizens reminisce about the rebellion, and the local APRA branch still celebrates this 1934 "revolution."[14] Almost unknown inside the department is the fact that Aprismo existed not only in major departmental urban centers like Ayacucho and Huanta but in the department's peasant communities as well.

APRISMO IN CARHUANCA

Penning a letter to the Cangallo subprefect one March 1932 day, Carhuanca Governor Maximiliano García assured the subprefect that there was absolutely no Aprista activity and no Aprista propaganda within Carhuanca district.[15] Governor García's words may have been comforting, but they were hardly truthful given that he himself was one of the most prominent and militant Apristas in a district with a large Aprista presence. Those Carhuanca Apristas had been meeting and planning for several months before Governor García wrote his letter, but it was in the days, weeks, and months following his reassuring note to the subprefect that APRA activity came to dominate Carhuanca's political life.

Easter 1932 brought a political eruption in the district. During this holiest of Catholic holidays, Carhuanca's Apristas rallied before their district's city hall. District Apristas Pedro Félix Guillén, Miguel and Moises Estrada, Teobaldo García, Augusto Cárdenas, Lieutenant Governor Lázaro Gómez, Governor Maximiliano García, Municipal Mayor Dionisio Alfaro, and all of the district's varayocs denounced the subprefect's choice for a new Carhuanquino governor, Crisóstomo Romaní. Yelling at the very top of their lungs, the Apristas charged that Governor-Elect Romaní was unfit for the job, both because he was a *forastero* (a non-Carhuanquino migrant) and because he was a Sánchezcerrista. Municipal Mayor Moises Estrada added to the denunciation by proclaiming that, "as long as APRA exists in this town, no other party can rule."[16] APRA's dominance in Carhuanca would continue throughout the 1930s and into the 1940s and 1950s, winning the district a reputation as an Aprista stronghold.

Carhuanca's Apristas shared many common traits. Almost without exception, they were male, held at least a primary school education, owned multiple tracts of land, and had the social and cultural flexibility to sometimes self-identify as indigenous and sometimes as nonindigenous. Certainly, there were status differences among these Apristas. As the former subprefect's son, a large landowner, and the town's local teacher, the Aprista Augusto Cárdenas ranked higher on Carhuanca's informal socioeconomic ladder than, say, the Aprista Pedro Félix Guillén, a man who worked as the *mayordomo* (administrator) on the local Virán hacienda. But regardless of the differences of social and economic capital among Carhuanca's Apristas, it is nonetheless certain that these Aprista men were all among the town's wealthiest and most powerful campesinos. Such status was not unusual among Apristas in rural sierra communities.[17]

But while Carhuanca's Apristas ranked among their district's elite, they enjoyed no such status inside their country. Herein lay the fundamental attraction of APRA. Though Carhuanquinos and Andean campesinos in general had long been well aware of their race- and class-based exclusion from national political life and priority, that exclusion had grown considerably harder to ignore by the 1930s. The reason was migration. Migration had long been an economic necessity for many

Carhuanca peasants, and Lima was Carhuanquinos' favored destination. When I asked Don Emiliano Muñoz why he had left Carhuanca to work in Lima, his short answer said much: "Because of poverty, of course."[18] Carhuanquinos were hardly the only campesinos to make such migrations. From 1919 to 1931, around 65,000 men and women from across Peru moved to Lima; by 1931, recent rural migrants comprised almost 20 percent of Lima's total population. This sort of prolonged economic migration was regularly coupled with short trips to the capital city by peasants who wanted to lobby national politicians and bureaucrats.[19]

Growing connections with Lima through migration gave Carhuanquinos a painfully clear sense of their secondary status in their country because people who passed as de-Indianized mestizos in Carhuanca could not do the same in Lima and because the very relativity of economic relations that cast Carhuanquino elites as wealthy inside their district cast them as impoverished inside the nation's far richer capital city. Migrants themselves communicated that jarring realignment of racial and class status back to their home communities, either stating so directly on their return or by sending messages to that effect. APRA capitalized brilliantly on this onslaught of Lima migration. Not only did party leaders and members pledge to assist and empower the country's seemingly forgotten and abandoned masses, Apristas also lobbied on behalf of migrants and worked to extend them explicit political support.[20]

APRA's promise of national political inclusion reached Carhuanca through the words of migrants and through direct political propaganda. By way of their connections with Apristas in both Lima and the city of Ayacucho—including close ties with Ayacucho's Aprista leader Aristides Guillén Valdivia, owner of an hacienda near Carhuanca—Carhuanca's APRA sympathizers gained access to propaganda that pledged a realignment of national political power. Flyers and bulletins seized by authorities across Ayacucho show the kinds of ideas and demands Carhuanca's Apristas were most likely voicing and reading. An APRA booklet confiscated by police in the nearby city of Huancapi offered straightforward explanations of what APRA entailed. Addressed to the "Worker Citizen, Campesino Citizen," the booklet read:

WHAT IS THE APRISTA PARTY? It is a political party formed by the People (principally peasants and workers) to get involved and ensure the enforcement of their rights inside the Peruvian Nation. It is also known as the People's Party and the Popular Alliance [*Partido del Pueblo, Alianza Popular*].

WHO BELONGS TO THE APRISTA PARTY? All working citizens, regardless of their trade or activity (artisan, worker, farmer, merchant, clerk, professional), whose interests have never been defended by the Government.

WHO DOES NOT BELONG TO THE APRISTA PARTY? Peruvian citizens who have never worked, and who only by virtue of being ARISTOCRATS FROM LEADING AND UPSTANDING FAMILIES have spent the Nation's life and wealth at their pleasure. Among these PRINCIPAL FAMILIES there are also merchants, farmers, and professionals, but they are rich, powerful millionaires.

WHAT IS THE MAIN GOAL OF THE APRISTA PARTY? It is to meet the needs and realize the aspirations of this group of workers who form Peru's majority and whose legitimate interests have never been recognized by past governments. This main goal is called Social Justice.

FOR HOW MANY YEARS HAVE OTHER PARTIES RULED THE COUNTRY? Other parties have governed for 111 years, and during that time, they have lost wars; they have given away great tracts of our territory to neighboring countries; they have lent much money to rich countries, pawning our mines, railways, ports, and incomes. In contrast, they have never favored agriculture or industries. They have not built as many schools as we need. And above all, every time that the people have demanded something of the government, they have put those people in jail, deported them, or shot them.[21]

This document called for a radical transformation of power inside Peru, following the classic populist lines of an "us and them" ideology that promised to seize power from undeserving elites and turn it over to the deserving masses. Other materials confiscated in the city of Cangallo said much the same. Although there is no direct evidence proving that Carhuanca's Apristas acquired these particular flyers and booklets, various documents reference local Apristas' possession of party propaganda, and Carhuanquinos had multiple visits from Ayacucho Apristas who came to the district to advertise their party and its aims.[22] It is reasonable to assume, then, that Apristas in Carhuanca read, heard, and even espoused the kinds of claims seen in the above excerpt. Carhuanca's Apristas wanted what APRA sympathizers across Ayacucho and across Peru wanted: for APRA to rule Peru.

Carhuanca's Apristas fought the battle for national political power at the local level, trying to wrest control of their district from non-Aprista authorities. The Easter 1932 uprising described earlier was only one instance of a prolonged and often bloody fight for political domination of Carhuanca. Though the end of political control is hardly surprising, Carhuanquino Apristas' means to that end were rather more novel. Nationally, APRA benefited enormously from its leaders' and supporters' agility with political performance. From Haya de la Torre's days as a student leader heading up a massive 1923 demonstration in Lima against Peru's Sacred Heart consecration; to APRA's party symbols, songs, and salutes; and especially to the attempted and ultimately successful efforts

to assassinate President Sánchez Cerro, Apristas' audacity was one of
their strongest political assets. That audacity won them tremendous national political attention and put APRA at the very center of Peru's political imagination.

Apristas in Carhuanca made similar performances of and for
power. Carhuanquino Apristas' methods included a paper campaign:
They flooded the provincial subprefecture with inflammatory letters
and petitions denouncing their Sánchezcerrista governor Crisóstomo
Romaní and calling for Romaní's ouster. On the day of the Easter protest, nearly thirty Carhuanquinos sympathetic to or overtly allied with
APRA signed a petition calling for Romaní's removal. The signatories
charged that Romaní was an itinerant and a thief, who acted in con-
junction with local gamonales "accustomed to living at the expense of
the poor Indians and disturbing the public order."[23] Other letters soon
followed. A number of Carhuanquinos sympathetic to APRA and allied
with Carhuanca's most prominent Apristas composed a petition against
Governor Romaní, stating that the man was "a nasty character, who has
totally given himself over to the drink." They complained that Romaní
failed to carry out the obligations of his post, failed to follow his supe-
riors' orders, failed to respect the constitutionally defined rights of persons and property, and succeeded only in "affiliating himself with the
factions that divide this town."[24] Governor Romaní was well aware of
the many petitions against him. He complained to the subprefect about
"these ridiculous and malicious denunciations," asking his superior to
recognize that such false claims reflected nothing about his performance
as governor. Reminding the subprefect that Carhuanca was "full of opposing factions" that always acted against the authorities, Governor
Romaní asked the subprefect to pay no heed to "the eye-catching denunciations from Carhuanca's criminals."[25]

Aprista methods in Carhuanca also included daring denials of non-
Aprista authority. Governor Romaní complained in April 1932 that "this
town's Aprista group" was busily politicking and propagandizing against
him, telling the district's varayocs and lieutenant governors to ignore
all instructions from both himself and the subprefect on the grounds
that both of these authorities were about to be replaced. According to
Romaní, the Apristas asserted that the former governor and Aprista
Maximiliano García was bound to be reinstated as governor, and they
even tried to seize the town hall's archive on that pretext.[26]

Carhuanquino Apristas' most audacious denial of their political
opponents' authority took the form of jailbreaks. One June 1932 day,
Aprista Salomón Zárate approached Carhuanca's jail, frightened away
the varayoc who stood guarding the prison, and opened the jail's door

with his own duplicate key to free one of his local allies. The enraged Governor Romaní informed the subprefect that this was not the first time Zárate had committed such a jailbreak. "You see," Romaní stated, "he does this by habit."[27] Romaní's casting was not much of an exaggeration: Only eight months earlier, Salomón Zárate and a number of other Carhuanca Apristas had attacked the district jail and freed the Aprista Pedro Félix Guillén from the prison.[28] Such jailbreaks were not only highly practical, allowing district Apristas full liberty to continue politicking freely; they were also tremendously symbolic. Short of killing, imprisonment was a district authority's most powerful method for punishing local wrongdoers and/or political opponents. By perpetrating jailbreaks, Carhuanca's Apristas showed that they were politically stronger than the non-Aprista authorities who tried to persecute them, and they cast those local authorities as unable to control the very institution that best represented their power: the district jail.

Apristas' political performances had a definite gendered edge, promoting an image of radical masculinity. Certainly, Carhuanquino Apristas' jailbreaks, public displays of violence, and highly vocal protests fit a familiar image of swaggering and courageous rebels. But the district's Apristas also invoked gender matters directly, overtly stressing their own manliness and explicitly challenging the masculinity of non-Aprista authorities. A complaint from Governor Romaní reveals such a challenge. Governor Romaní relayed that on the afternoon of June 21, 1932, Aprista Salomón Zárate walked up to the governor's dispatch and spat out insults from the doorway. Boasting that he had freed a prisoner from jail "like a man," Zárate made threats against Governor Romaní's life and then left the dispatch. That afternoon passed into evening and then into night, and shortly after midnight Zárate and a group of his fellow Apristas went to Governor Romaní's home. These men fired shots from a revolver, yelled out "vivas" to APRA, and then charged Romaní's house. Bolting and then blocking his door from the inside, Governor Romaní did his best to stop the men from breaking down the door. He told the subprefect that "they kept yelling at me, saying that if I were really a man and really an authority, I would come out that instant and face them."[29] Carhuanca's Apristas deemed their bravery and audacity masculine and their governor's responses unmanly. Their casting had a larger national precedent. APRA's founder Haya de la Torre regularly emphasized virility, calling on Aprista men to be physically strong and healthy, and stressed a strong sense of male fraternity. As Haya phrased it, Apristas were "in the struggle, brothers; in suffering, brothers; in victory, brothers."[30]

With their letters, their denials of authority, and their violence, Carhuanca's Apristas got the end they so clearly wanted: control of the district. Governor Crisóstomo Romaní submitted his resignation in August 1932, asking the subprefect to install a military governor "who could show more zeal in administrating this damned town [*pueblo maldito*] whose inhabitants are a bunch of criminal bandits who do not and will not respect their governors."[31] After the subprefect refused Romaní's resignation, Governor Romaní simply abandoned his post and fled the district, tacitly leaving the governorship to his father-in-law Lucas Ochoa. Carhuanca's Apristas then penned yet another petition, beseeching the subprefect to name someone from their ranks to the gubernatorial post. Their request did not go unanswered. Aprista Pedro García became Carhuanca's new governor, and Salomón Zárate became the new municipal mayor.[32]

By the end of the 1930s, Apristas had realized political hegemony in Carhuanca. Although they did not maintain a consistent hold on district government, Apristas held positions of authority more often than not, leading Cangallo Subprefect Pedro C. Cárdenas to assert in 1937 that "Carhuanca is the center of Aprismo in this province."[33] And when non-Apristas won positions of power in Carhuanca, the town's Apristas worked hard to subvert their rivals' authority. Governor Inocencio Ochoa complained in 1937 that Aprista Pedro J. García and several varayocs were wandering throughout the town's streets, yelling out that García was the town's rightful governor and that all Carhuanquinos should gather the following Sunday, armed and ready, and oust Ochoa from the city hall. Apristas also wrote countless petitions to provincial and departmental authorities, launched numerous legal suits, and testified on one another's behalf, pushing their own material and political interests and fighting their political and personal enemies.[34]

Carhuanquino Apristas' main goal was the attainment of district political power, but they also led a much-remembered effort to acquire one of Carhuanca's only haciendas from its owner, the district priest Father Carlos M. Cárdenas. While Peruvian Apristas' relationship to the Catholic Church was tense during this era—tension that dated back to Haya's 1923 protest against the Sacred Heart Consecration and that led APRA's opponents to deride the party as anticlerical and anti-Catholic—Carhuanca's Apristas were driven less by ideology than by a nationwide trend in which peasant communities fought their local churches and hacendados for land.[35] Carhuanquino Apristas' leading role in their district's efforts to acquire the Hacienda Champacancha from its ecclesiastical owner further explains APRA's appeal in Peru's countryside. Such leadership on land issues was fairly common during the 1930s, both for Apristas and for members of other radical political parties.[36]

Carhuanquino efforts to acquire the Hacienda Champacancha began in 1933. Three district authorities traveled to Ayacucho city in March of that year, meeting with the Ayacucho bishop in an attempt to acquire the terrain from its religious owner, the Santa Clara Convent. Although the Champacancha hacienda did include some of Carhuanca's most fertile land, its importance was as much symbolic as it was economic. Many Carhuanquinos believed the Champacancha property essentially their own: They had long occupied and worked the land as tenants (*arrendatarios*) and subtenants (*subarrendatarios*), cultivating and harvesting the terrain that legally belonged to the Santa Clara Convent. While these tenants certainly relied on the fruit and corn they grew on Champacancha's lands, their dependence on the terrain was tempered by the fact that most tenants owned other plots of land throughout the district. In many ways, then, the fight for Champacancha was as much a matter of principle as it was of survival.

Carhuanca's Apristas headed the effort for the hacienda's acquisition. Men like Maximiliano García urged Champacancha's renters to forgo their rent payments and even uprooted the crops of the most loyal renters. Apristas also convened weekly meetings inside Carhuanca, bringing the district's campesinos together each and every Sunday to discuss the Champacancha acquisition. Those efforts, though, came to naught; in 1935, Carhuanquinos learned that the Santa Clara convent had already sold Champacancha in a secret sale. Worse still, Champacancha's new owner was himself a Carhuanquino: He was Carlos Cárdenas, the district's priest. Deeming Father Cárdenas a traitor and a scoundrel—one man remembered him as "Carhuanca's Judas"—Carhuanquinos began political and legal action against the priest.[37]

Arguing that Father Cárdenas had duped the Santa Clara nuns by wrongfully telling the sisters he had the permission of Carhuanca's campesinos for the purchase, the district's Apristas convened a public meeting and decided to take the matter to Ayacucho's prefect. Fifty Carhuanquino men left their families and their fields in May 1935 to make the long trip to the department capital. Apristas' leading role in this effort was certain.[38] Cangallo's subprefect complained that known Carhuanquino Apristas Pedro Félix Guillén, Dionisio Alfaro, Augusto Cárdenas (no relation to the priest), Inocencio Ochoa, Fidel Gómez, and Fidel García were "leading Carhuanca's Indians to believe that the Champacancha estate belongs to the community of Carhuanca," and many elderly Carhuanquinos alive today similarly remember these same men as the acquisition leaders.[39]

Advancing their protests to the national level of government, Carhuanquinos made appeals to the Bureau of Indian Affairs, winning a

1937 meeting with bureau staff. Carhuanquinos repeated their requests the following year, with Apristas Fidel Gómez and Salomón Zárate presenting a second appeal to the Bureau of Indian Affairs. Carhuanca Apristas worked hard to mobilize state support for the hacienda acquisition, but that support was not forthcoming.[40] When I asked one elderly Carhuanca Aprista if the state assisted with Champacancha's acquisition, his short answer revealed much: "The state? No, no, no. Only Carhuanquinos."[41] The state's intervention was actually counterproductive, as the Bureau of Indian Affairs ruled that, as long as Father Cárdenas remained Champacancha's legal owner, Carhuanca's campesinos would have to pay for usage of the hacienda's terrain, be it for crops or for pasture, and the Cangallo subprefect subsequently sent two civil guard officers to the district to ensure such payments.[42]

Although Carhuanca's Apristas headed the Champacancha acquisition efforts, many other non-Aprista Carhuanquinos actively participated in the struggle. Many district men and women, for example, refused to let Father Cárdenas sow a new crop. Believing that this obstruction would be less violent if women led the protest, Carhuanquina Teófila Zárate organized a group of district women to block the planting set to be done by hired laborers and protected by civil guards. One Carhuanquina relayed that "they say she went out in front, with the group of women. Señora Teófila was the one who headed the group, who led . . . They say that she stood out in front and threw stones [at the peons and civil guards], while the other women threw ashes. With those stones and ashes, they managed to untie the plows and remove them from the bulls, and they threw out all the seeds to make sure that they weren't sown. They say that the seeds lay there for a week, with the pigs eating them."[43]

Though such prominent female participation in land struggles had countless precedents and repetitions across Peru's Andes, that participation was nonetheless a transgression from expected gender roles. One Carhuanca woman who participated in the protest told the Ayacucho Supreme Court as much. The court interpreter translated this woman's Quechua words with the comment that "as a married woman, she does not normally leave her house to take part in fights, because her husband controls her and because she is always aware of her obligations."[44] That so many women were willing (and able) to engage in such transgressive public protest suggests how deeply the hacienda acquisition mattered to most Carhuanquinos; it mattered so much that they willingly defied gender conventions to increase the chances for acquisition. This particular example of direct land intervention on Champacancha by

Carhuanca campesinos was not an isolated case in the district. Similar actions took place in subsequent years, when numerous Carhuanquino men planted Champacancha's lands as though the terrain were their own. That illicit action angered the Cangallo subprefect, who charged that Carhuanquinos "do not know how to respect the mandates of legally constituted authorities. Carhuanca is a town that makes a mockery of every legal decree."[45]

Carhuanquinos complemented these illegal actions with a highly legalistic one: They hired a lawyer. Gathering up sparse financial resources, Carhuanquinos enlisted the services of an Ayacucho lawyer; with this lawyer's help, district campesinos made plans to purchase Champacancha from Father Cárdenas. Carhuanquino Apristas again took a leading role in the effort, collecting money from the community's campesinos, making an offer to the priest, and bringing the Bureau of Indian Affairs into the equation as an arbitrator. Carhuanca's Apristas took this step early on—shortly after Father Cárdenas's 1935 purchase—but disagreements over the hacienda's selling price slowed the process.[46]

The elderly Don Emiliano Muñoz explained Carhuanquinos' protracted negotiations with Father Cárdenas. Pounding the ground with his cane for emphasis, Don Emiliano told me, "We were in a lawsuit with this priest for five years. The whole community, for five years." The negotiations dragged on and on because Father Cárdenas kept demanding an unreasonable price for the land. "The community had to defend itself," Don Emiliano explained, "and so for five years, we were in a lawsuit. He had bought the land for 4,000 [*soles*], and we offered 8,000, we offered double. But he wanted 25,000!" When I asked how the sale finally happened, Don Emiliano threw back his head in laughter and explained. "We were in this lawsuit for five years. And at that time, Arcaparó, Alberto Arcaparó, was Ayacucho's senator. And this man said to Father Cárdenas, 'Listen, little priest, take the offer already! Otherwise, one of them is going to kill you. Only one person will kill you, and only one person will go to jail. The whole community won't go to jail!' And with that, he made up his mind."[47] On June 3, 1940, Father Carlos Cárdenas finally sold Champacancha to Carhuanca's campesinos, agreeing to the price of 8,139.18 soles.[48]

Although the Champacancha struggle seems very much a heroic communal narrative, it also carried a series of sharp political consequences. Most basically, the Champacancha purchase solidified Aprista control over Carhuanca. Apristas had led the acquisition effort, and they reaped the reward of local political support. But there were other, more problematic consequences of the purchase. Ironically, Carhuanquinos' united action to acquire Champacancha further divided the community. When the Champacancha acquisition was just getting underway, Carhuanca's governor described the district as a "little hell" where "antagonism, hatred, and malice reign."[49] Acquiring Champacancha broadened that hell.

Some of these newly exacerbated divides involved preexisting ties of family, work, and friendship: Those Carhuanquinos seemingly or actually allied with Father Cárdenas by virtue of their lineage, their profession, or their *compadrazgo* (fictive kinship) met hostility and exclusion from those angry at the priest. A few years after Champacancha's sale, Father Cárdenas complained that Carhuanca's legal representatives had allotted land only to their own friends and relatives, "leaving other comuneros without parcels of land, especially my father's relatives, even though they helped buy the land and should get part of the Champacancha estate."[50] Davíd Hiyo, in turn, charged that Carhuanquino Santos Cerón had levied false assault charges against him solely because Hiyo's father once worked as Father Cárdenas's Champacancha mayordomo. Hiyo testified that because of the Champacancha lawsuit "Carhuanca's comuneros have deemed us their enemies, going to the extreme of accusing us of crimes that neither I, nor my father, nor our relatives took part in."[51] Similarly, Davíd Hiyo's father Francisco complained that the town's leading Apristas had threatened to kill him, explaining that "this noxious crowd hates me only for the simple fact that I was friends with the priest Carlos Cárdenas."[52] Even Carhuanca's new priest suffered from his clerical association with Father Cárdenas. The pressure to dissociate oneself from Father Cárdenas was indeed so great that Cárdenas himself complained that his own brothers had "abandoned me when I was in mortal danger, when I had a frenzied lawsuit with comuneros of the district of Carhuanca," and he therefore disinherited his siblings when he composed his will.[53]

The greatest conflicts surrounding the Champacancha acquisition, however, involved money. Though Carhuanca's Aprista leaders cast the Champacancha acquisition as a communal struggle, Carhuanquinos divided the purchased estate in a highly individualistic way. Only those comuneros who paid twenty-five soles received a parcel of Champacancha land, and that was a sum of money only Carhuanca's wealthy peasants could afford to pay. When I asked Don Gregorio Escalante if he and his family participated in the effort to acquire Champacancha, his reply suggested such class divides. "Of course!" he answered. "Everyone did. The whole community. Well, those who had money did."[54]

There were also numerous complaints regarding financial fraud in relation to the hacienda purchase. A campesino named Gregorio Pacheco, for instance, complained that while he had paid Aprista leaders sixty

soles for parcels of Champacancha land, those leaders recorded his payment as a mere twenty soles. When pressed to explain the missing forty
soles, one district Aprista admitted the fraud but blamed it on a fellow
party member, a man who had conveniently left Carhuanca for Lima.[55]
Other fraud complaints soon emerged. Carhuanca's governor reported
in 1938 that he was receiving numerous visits from the district's indigenous campesinos, all complaining about the heavy financial contributions demanded by the local Apristas who had led the Champacancha
acquisition. When the governor investigated, he discovered that, while
those Aprista leaders had collected 7,080 soles, they had deposited only
3,500 soles in the community's account. That discovery led Subprefect
Cárdenas to file a lawsuit against four Apristas for misappropriation
of communal funds.[56] Similar complaints and charges of fraud relat-
ing to Champacancha continued well into the 1940s.[57] These conflicts
over money, communal land, and fraud showed how matters of class
deeply affected local debates about land tenure, rights, and control inside campesino communities during the 1930s.

The consequences of the Champacancha acquisition also stretched
into the realm of regional politics. Undermining the larger goals of
shared regional identity, regional solidarity, and regional political action that typified sierra Aprismo, Carhuanquino Apristas' efforts to
purchase Champacancha actually aggravated regional divides. These
regional fractures were both the cause and consequence of pejorative
labels, power struggles, and vindictive politicking. Driven by hostility to Aprismo, anger at Carhuanquinos' political independence, and
personal loyalties, Cangallo's subprefect Pedro C. Cárdenas regularly
derided Carhuanca. Subprefect Cárdenas (no relation to Father Carlos
Cárdenas) told the Ayacucho prefect that "Carhuanca is the center of
Aprismo in this province, as the majority of Carhuanquinos are thugs
and hoodlums."[58] Cárdenas used even sharper words in another letter.
He wrote that Carhuanca "is a district were the principle of authority is lax because three or four individuals . . . inculcate disobedience
against legally constituted authorities and keep the ignorant pueblo in
constant anguish." The subprefect continued, stating that "Carhuanca
is home to false apostles who exploit people's ignorance," and he recommended that the prefect "dictate drastic measures to put an end to the
resultant anomalous situation."[59] Rather than foster the kind of regional
solidarity and unified political action that Ayacucho Apristas so lauded,
Carhuanca's Aprista efforts further divided Cangallo province.

Although Carhuanquinos attempted to assert their political independence from the subprefect, the subprefect retained considerable power
over the district through his ability to nominate candidates for district

authority positions. Carhuanquinos were well aware of the subprefect's power in this regard and chafed against it. Such anger showed in relation to Carhuanquino governor Daniel Guillén Cárdenas. Many Carhuanquinos gathered in the home of the district justice of the peace in August 1937 to draw up a petition against their current governor, Daniel Guillén. These Carhuanquinos complained that, because Governor Guillén was both Father Carlos Cárdenas's cousin and the mayordomo of the Champacancha hacienda, he dutifully followed the priest's instructions to commit abuses inside the community. They charged that Governor Guillén therefore spoke out against the Champacancha effort, trying to demoralize those peasants seeking to acquire the hacienda. He also regularly stole eggs and hens, and he imprisoned his local opponents each and every day, charging the imprisoned fees for their "right" to occupy the jail. The Carhuanquinos who signed this petition had a simple explanation for Governor Guillén's hold on power: "He boasts that he will never lack while his cousin lives" because the priest "has much influence before the provincial subprefect."[60]

Carhuanquinos made similar complaints a few years later about their new governor, Primitivo Mayhua. Several comuneros signed a petition stating that Governor Mayhua had committed innumerable abuses and acts of extortion. Listing specific crimes of unwarranted fines, home invasion, theft, and even kidnapping, the signatories wrote that Governor Mayhua represented "gamonalismo incarnate." Worse still, they argued that Mayhua was "an ally of our adversary Carlos Cárdenas" and therefore incessantly tried to demoralize those campesinos attempting to acquire Champacancha. Again, the signatories blamed the Cangallo subprefect for their governor's appointment and power. The Carhuanquino signatories charged that Governor Mayhua "is sustained by Subprefect Pedro Crisólogo Cárdenas, who is his friend and was the *padrino* at his wedding."[61]

One last crucial political consequence of the Champacancha acquisition began in the capital city of Lima. Carhuanquino migrants resident in Lima played a major political and economic role in the Champacancha purchase and would continue to participate directly in their district's politics across the twentieth century. The economic importance of Carhuanquino migrants was well established by the 1930s. Just as migrants *into* the district had a profound impact on the area's economy during the late nineteenth century, with priests and wealthy landowners from Andahuaylas coming into the district and initiating the commoditization of district land, migration *out* of the district in the 1920s and 1930s (and beyond) had an equally strong economic impact on the district.

While out-migration meant the loss of migrants' labor on familial holdings, it often brought injections of cash into the district economy through migrants' financial remittances back to their communities. Out-migration also accelerated land sales inside Carhuanca. Individuals newly migrated from Carhuanca often sold their land to generate much-needed capital for their new urban lives, while well-established migrants often reinvested their earned capital by purchasing land in their home district. A Rayme Bajo campesina working in Ayacucho city as a seamstress and able only to speak Quechua, for example, sold a small portion of her land in 1938, probably to help support herself in the city.[62] The Lima migrant, Marcelino Quijana, in turn, sent his sisters money in 1929 so that they could secure the purchase of a half-hectare land plot and house for him. The increasing prominence of Carhuanquino land sales in the records of Ayacucho and Cangallo notaries during the 1930s suggests that land commoditization was only growing in frequency during this decade, and the increased rate of migration from the district offers a good explanation why.[63]

Migrants' economic impact was soon coupled with a political one. Though Carhuanquinos had begun migrating to Lima well before the 1930s, the Champacancha struggle fostered the emergence of a major political role in Carhuanca for Carhuanquinos living hundreds of kilometers away from their home district. Such a political role was commonplace. With the mass migration of sierra campesinos to Lima in the 1920s and 1930s, migrant clubs became ubiquitous in Lima, and club members regularly assisted their home communities.

To provide each other with some material assistance and a sense of belonging in a huge and often hostile city, Carhuanquino migrants formed a mutual aid society in 1921. Throughout the 1920s, the Mutualist Center of Carhuanca Town was a social organization above all else, allowing Carhuanquinos to meet up in a set locale and to celebrate important district holidays like the August 15 fiesta for Carhuanca's patron saint, the Virgin of Asunción. With the start of the Champacancha struggle, however, migrants gave a political bent to their existing economic and social activities. Finding their way to the Lima home of one Carhuanquino migrant, a number of Carhuanca men living and working in Lima gathered on March 16, 1936, to form a new migrant society, the Progressive Mutualist Society of Carhuanca Town and Annexes. The men who met that day drew up a thirty-two-point statement of purpose, outlining the group's makeup and the reasons for its existence. Naming a president, vice president, secretary general, treasurer, and seven other officials, the society founders pledged to organize a night school and male and female sports teams and to offer educational lectures. The last article of the society's statement of principles pledged to work for Champacancha's acquisition and ensure the just distribution of its terrain.[64]

Following through on this final pledge to aid the Champacancha acquisition, society members donated over 400 soles to the Champacancha purchase, sent letters and petitions to support the purchase effort, and gave moral and material aid to the Carhuanca peasants who traveled from Ayacucho to Lima to press for the hacienda's purchase.[65] The ties between this new migrant club and the struggle for Champacancha were so strong that many Carhuanquinos remember the two as mutually formative: The migrant club emerged precisely because of the effort to acquire Champacancha, and Champacancha ended up in Carhuanquino hands partly because of the migrant club's efforts. Don Emiliano Muñoz reflected on the close interconnection between the club and the acquisition. Explaining how Father Cárdenas purchased the hacienda and then charged Carhuanquinos for their customary uses of the land, Don Emiliano stated that "this is why the Lima residents formed the Mutualist Center. We all took the land together. Yes, miss. Yes."[66] Even Subprefect Pedro C. Cárdenas recognized the tight relationship between the Champacancha effort and the migrant society. He informed the prefect of the society's formation, urged his superior to refuse its existence, and charged that the society was nothing more than a group of troublemakers "who exploit the ignorance of Indians with deceptions about the acquisition of the Champacancha estate."[67]

The Progressive Mutualist Society's political efforts began with the Champacancha struggle, but those efforts by no means ended there. Society members repeatedly intervened on behalf of Carhuanquinos still living in Carhuanca, lobbying Lima-based authorities to take action against abuses inside the Ayacucho district. Society Secretary-General Pedro Gómez and President Manuel Pacheco, for example, protested to the minister of the state in October 1936. Speaking in the name of the society, the men reported that well-known gamonal Nicanor Carrasco and his henchmen had attacked and robbed Carhuanquino peasants Agapito Gutiérrez and Constantino Pérez. The society leaders then complained, "Mr. Minister, both comuneros presented their respective denunciations to the area's authorities, but they have yet to take action. As such, we appear before you to beseech you to bring justice for these poor and defenseless Indians."[68] Two years later, society members appeared before the director of indigenous affairs to lodge a complaint against Governor Primitivo Mayhua for abuse of authority.[69]

Although Carhuanca Apristas and Carhuanquino migrants formed an unusually strong political alliance, their efforts were nonetheless hindered by the frustrations of Peruvian political life. Only four years after the Champacancha purchase, Carhuanquinos were again complaining about the hacienda's former owner, Father Carlos Cárdenas. Aprista Salomón Zárate charged that the priest was unjustly collecting animals, crops, and cash from Carhuanquinos, all on the false pretext that he would use the proceeds to finance purchases for the district's church. The priest had also confiscated the entire church archive and kept it in his private possession, doling out information only to his allies. Because Father Cárdenas had denied two Carhuanca teenagers access to their birth certificates, the young men had been unable to enroll in high school.[70]

That Father Cárdenas could remain in Carhuanca after all his actions against the communal majority was no doubt frustrating to many Carhuanquinos. The fact that Ayacucho's bishop reinstated him as the district's priest just one year after Zárate filed the complaint described earlier was outrageous. On learning of the appointment, a group of Carhuanquinos penned a long letter of complaint. They wrote, "When we learned this painful news, the people came together and protested energetically, because said priest has the cruel and habitual sickness of vengefully retaliating against those who took active part in the Hacienda Champacancha conflict." They begged the subprefect to intervene and replace Cárdenas; and, although Cárdenas did indeed lose the position, he remained inside Carhuanca.[71]

Worse than Father Cárdenas's continuing presence was the continuing irresolution of the Champacancha struggle. Although Carhuanquinos attained legal rights to the land in 1940, the sudden death of the community's *personero* (legal representative) meant that fights over access to the estate continued unabated: Without the personero's record books, it was impossible for Carhuanca's authorities to know who had paid for how much land. In 1951, Carhuanquinos were still asking the national government to assist them in parceling up Champacancha. Another twenty years later, Champacancha's parceling *still* remained a pressing matter for Carhuanquinos; in 1971, district residents labeled the Champacancha division their district's primary problem.[72] For Carhuanquinos in Lima and in Carhuanca during the 1930s and beyond, life in Peru remained life in a state of abandon. Ayacuchanos writing in the newspaper *Sierra* objected to their department's political neglect, describing their department as "*Ayacucho siempre Abandonado,*" Ayacucho always abandoned.[73] Carhuanquino residents and migrants alike tried to fight that abandon, but they were ultimately unable to change it.

LURICOCHA COUNTERPOINT

Apristas' prominent place in Carhuanca politics was far from unique. Apristas were equally significant inside the district of Luricocha. But whereas Carhuanquino Apristas were relatively wealthy campesinos, Luricocha's Apristas were hacendados and middle-class professionals. Writing to Ayacucho's prefect just weeks after the 1934 Ayacucho and Huanta city uprisings, Luricocha Civil Guard Commander Eloy G. Espino cast his district as an Aprista haven. Espino told the prefect that Luricocha's "revolutionary Aprista leaders" had burned down his home and threatened to kill him and his family, all because of his energetic opposition to APRA. Espino also alleged that Luricochano Apristas were hoarding money, revolvers, and considerable amounts of ammunition as part of their plan to incite Luricocha campesinos to violent revolution. Not only did Commander Espino single out eight well-known Luricochanos, including Apolinario Fajardo, Aristides Flores, Carlos La Torre Cortez, Davíd Urbina, and José Salvatierra, as Apristas, he also he reported that numerous Aprista revolutionaries and leaders were hiding out on the Luricocha haciendas Iribamba and Huanchacc.[74]

Commander Espino's claims were no doubt exaggerated. He used those claims to demand his own reappointment as Luricocha's governor, having been demoted from that position four years earlier. Espino likely knew that the more heated his claims, the better his chance of winning the reappointment. Moreover, court documents prove that Espino had a long history of lying, of abusing his authority, and of slandering others.[75] Huanta's subprefect himself cast doubt on Espino's words, tempering Espino's claims in his own letter to the Ayacucho prefect. The subprefect stated that he saw absolutely no need to replace Luricocha's current governor and saw no sense in naming Espino to that position. Recommending against Espino's appointment, the subprefect wrote that, when Espino had previously been Luricocha's governor, "he committed a series of abuses and exactions, and those were the reasons why he was removed from the post." Further, on close investigation of the haciendas Iribamba and Huanchacc, the subprefect and his police officers found nothing: no fugitives and no weapons.[76]

Given Espino's careerist self-interest, his past history, and the subprefect's counterclaims, we must approach Espino's charges with much skepticism. Yet there was likely a basis of truth in Espino's political hyperbole. The subprefect reported that most of the Luricocha Aprista leaders whom Espino had named "are all fugitives and are being pursued with utmost effort." The subprefect added that both he and Luricocha's governor had already taken action against the two Aprista teachers whom Espino had denounced, and he noted that one of the named rebels had "direct and prominent participation in the revolutionary movement."[77] Later letters from other officials, political demonstrations, and Aprista propaganda all supported Espino's claims that Luricocha was home to a significant number of Apristas.

APRA's appeal to district authorities and hacendados might seem peculiar on first consideration. As they were among the wealthiest and most politically powerful individuals in Luricocha, these men were local elites rather than the impoverished and excluded masses APRA claimed to represent. The allure of Aprismo to such Luricochanos becomes considerably easier to understand with a shift of focus away from the local and toward the national: While such men were district elites, they often felt as ignored and as abandoned by national authorities as did their poorer neighbors. Such a sense of exclusion is reflected in the comment from one Ayacucho newspaper that dubbed the department's capital province to be "Huamanga, banished; Huamanga; forgotten; Huamanga, pitied."[78] Furthermore, Luricocha's Aprista hacendados were part of a long-standing tradition of politically engaged Huantino elites. And what was true of Luricocha's activist hacendados was true more generally across Ayacucho. An influential article by historians Luis Miguel Glave and Jaime Urrutia has shown that Ayacucho's provincial elites were often far from the stereotypical image of the exploitative feudal gamonal; these elites were instead an important sector of the Aprista party in the 1930s and advanced the notion of an Ayacuchano regional identity.[79]

It also need be recognized that the Luricocha Apristas whom Commander Espino named stood out not only because of their class but because of their gender as well. Nested within Espino's letter came a reference to a surprising group of Luricocha Apristas: women. Espino charged that the local teachers Miss Artemia Prado and Miss Vitaliana Medina aided and abetted the APRA movement and the district's Aprista leaders. Not only did these two women yell out "vivas" to APRA and call for the national government's downfall with "mueras," they also presented Luricocha's Aprista leaders with crowns and bouquets of flowers.[80] Whether Espino's comments were true, exaggerated, or apocryphal, there was indeed a significant female presence among Ayacucho's Apristas. There was a women's Aprista cell—the "célula femenina Aprista"—in the city of Ayacucho, and several Huanta city women faced arrest because of their public support for APRA.[81] Further, Ayacucho's female Apristas self-identified as an important and distinct group of APRA supporters, as APRA militants' loyal and suffering *compañeras* (partners or comrades). A piece of Aprista propaganda confiscated in Huanta stresses this point. Dotted with capitalized words, this tiny sheet of paper read:

Great causes are always nourished by GENEROUS BLOOD, and this time, the blood that has poured out from our fallen brothers in SAN LORENZO, TRUJILLO, HUARAZ, CAJAMARCA, SAN CRISTÓBAL, CUSCO, HUANCAVELICA, AND AYACUCHO is teaching us which route we must travel, tirelessly and resolutely. On this path, the APRISTA WOMAN knows that she must always be the honorable COMPAÑERA of party militants and of the struggle. As much in painful losses as in victory, she will always be at her brothers' side, arm in arm in this INCESSANT AND TENACIOUS struggle, a struggle that demands all of our efforts, all of our energy, and all of our sacrifices. . . . In this holy task, the APRISTA WOMAN marches reliably and radiantly on the precipitous route that leads toward the Conquest of SOCIAL JUSTICE, armed with the unbreakable FAITH that ONLY APRISMO WILL SAVE PERU.[82]

Some elite Luricocha women—like a handful of elite Luricocha men—believed that APRA was their country's lone salvation.

Although Ayacucho's hacendados and campesinos were too far removed from national and international capitalist markets to suffer the effects of global economic depression as severely as Peruvians living in the country's export-oriented center and coast, most Ayacuchanos still felt a pressing need for socioeconomic and political change. Luricocha's Apristas told their neighbors, relatives, and campesino tenants that APRA was the only possible rescue for their country, their department, and their district. Their actions inside Luricocha, however, were not nearly as exalted as their words. Luricochano Apristas spoke a lot, thought a lot, and met a lot, but they did not *do* a lot. Luricocha Apristas had only a brief spurt of activity during the 1934 rebellion: One Luricochano took active part in the 1934 Huanta city uprising, and two others simultaneously tried to capture Luricocha's mayor and seize control of the town. But after the rebellion's quick and brutal defeat, and APRA's more generalized repression nationally, Luricocha's Apristas limited their political efforts inside the district—and inside Huanta, Ayacucho, and Peru—to organizing and promoting their party.[83]

Luricochano Apristas' disinterest in continuing to pursue violent rebellion is easily understandable: The 1934 uprisings in Ayacucho city and Huanta city failed so miserably and were repressed so violently that continued pursuit of rebellion would have been foolhardy. But Luricocha's Apristas did not show much interest in nonviolent protest, either. They did not pen letters of political complaint, did not initiate court cases to push for social justice, did not mobilize the area's peasants to denounce local injustices, and did not visit local, regional, or national authorities to demand social, economic, or political change. Mostly, they just talked to each other. Official reports on Luricochano Apristas had little to denounce beyond the activists' party affiliation and political meetings, and though authorities called for careful surveillance of the Apristas' activities, their investigations uncovered little. Probably the most significant of Luricocha Apristas' actual actions was their participation in the Sociedad "Unión Obrera" de Huanta, the Huanta "Union with Workers" Society. Much like the Rights of Man Defense League of the 1920s, the Sociedad Unión Obrera brought together Huantino elites who wanted to assist and defend their province's impoverished masses. Indeed, several Luricochano Apristas in the Sociedad Unión Obrera had earlier belonged to the Rights of Man Defense League. Through the Sociedad Unión Obrera, Luricocha's Apristas lobbied for political change, but only in the most general of ways: denouncing injustice and calling for economic and social reforms. These Apristas did not, however, make any specific demands for change in Luricocha.[84]

The political disconnect between Luricocha hacendados and campesinos could hardly have been greater. While Luricocha's Aprista hacendados were strategizing about national politics, district campesinos were waging a localized struggle to improve their communities with better teachers, better priests, and better authorities. There is no evidence to suggest that Luricocha campesinos affiliated with APRA; there were no peasant signatures on Aprista petitions, no reports from provincial authorities documenting peasant participation in APRA activities, and no infusion of Aprista political language into campesinos' court testimonies or petitions.[85]

It is not especially surprising that Luricocha campesinos proved largely uninterested in Aprismo. The district's hacendado Apristas made no concerted effort to mobilize or even actively defend those peasants; economic self-interest and prejudices of race and class fueled such inactivity. Luricocha Apristas also included men pointedly despised by many Luricochano campesinos. District Aprista and former governor Aristides Flores was one such man. Back in 1929, two Luricocha campesinos denounced then-governor Flores to Ayacucho's prefect, claiming that the governor "has declared himself enemy of all the residents in his jurisdiction, and he keeps us in a state of constant alarm." The campesinos charged that Flores had subjected Luricochanos to arbitrary arrest and random acts of violence, "abusing our sad condition of being defenseless Indians."[86] That Governor Flores later became one of Luricocha's most vocal Apristas probably turned some Luricochano campesinos away from

APRA. The same can be said of Luricocha Aprista Apolinario Fajardo. Luricocha campesinos had levied many complaints against Fajardo during his tenure as district governor in the late 1920s, and Fajardo's later conversion to Aprismo probably soured many campesinos' attitude toward the party.[87]

Luricocha campesinos' lack of interest in Aprismo in no way reflected a paucity of political activity on their part. During the 1930s, district campesinos worked to remove an abusive governor from office, to win provincial support for their efforts to fight locusts, to improve provincial transportation, and to return an ousted priest to his position. Luricocha campesinos sent letters of protest; visited district, provincial, and department officials; and participated in lawsuits, all to better their lives and communities.[88] Luricocha campesinos' reticence to join the APRA by no means signaled a lack of interest in politics.

CONCLUSIONS

Decentralization was one of APRA's principal tenets, with the party calling for a more equitable distribution of power throughout the country. Suitably, then, scholarly understanding of APRA requires that we decenter our vision of the party to fully appreciate the party's regional diversity, complexity, and strength. While most scholars have focused on Aprismo in regions where the party enjoyed considerable electoral success—namely, the country's coastal and northern departments—this chapter shows that APRA also had a significant presence in southern sierra departments like Ayacucho, where its formal electoral showings were usually poor. Inside the rural Ayacucho district of Luricocha, Aprismo was the domain of politically active hacendados and teachers. Aprismo enjoyed a much broader base of support in Carhuanca, where a number of the district's wealthiest and most educated campesinos actively affiliated with the party. With the direct support of Carhuanquino migrants in Lima, the district's Apristas managed to purchase the Champacancha estate and established their own political hegemony in Carhuanca.

The history of Aprismo in 1930s Ayacucho foreshadows local experiences of the Shining Path War in surprising and revealing ways. Although we need to take much care in drawing such connections across time, steering past the obvious hazards of presentism and teleology, these linkages are too significant to ignore. Historian Lewis Taylor noted as much, commenting that the strong APRA tradition in Cajamarca shaped subsequent responses to the PCP-SL.[89] Within the department of Ayacucho, one crucial set of connections was familial: Many Ayacucho Senderistas were the sons and daughters of 1930s Apristas. Inside Carhuanca, at least four district partisans of the PCP-SL were the children of 1930s Aprista militants.[90] Inside Luricocha, leading Senderista Augusta La Torre was the granddaughter of district Aprista Carlos La Torre Cortez. Authorities raided the La Torre's Iribamba hacienda in 1931, looking for weapons and Aprista militants. Authorities raided that same hacienda again in 1970, arresting several founding members of the PCP-SL who were using the estate for training purposes. These family connections suggest that many 1930s Apristas shared their political hopes and frustrations with their children, leading several of those children to pursue a far more radical political path toward revolution.[91]

Aprismo's history in 1930s Ayacucho also had other, subtler, echoes in the 1980s. The passion and fervor with which Carhuanca's Apristas embraced their party identity and harassed their political rivals presaged Senderistas' political ardor and unwillingness to broker opposition. Carhuanquinos' eager embrace of the APRA also reveals that district residents embraced political parties as vehicles for change. That attitude continued in subsequent decades. Much the same was true of Luricocha's politically engaged hacendados. Luricocha campesinos' generalized disinterest in APRA, in turn, paralleled their broad rejection of the PCP-SL decades later. Although Luricocha's peasants may have sympathized with Aprismo's ideals and aims—as with those of Sendero—they were unwilling to involve themselves in a movement forcefully condemned by both regional and national authorities. When Ayacucho's Apristas proclaimed, "We will no longer be servile! We will no longer be unworthy sons, tyrant's pupils!" they were articulating a dream for change, equality, and inclusion that resonated strongly across the countryside. But as Luricocha campesinos' history makes clear, voicing that dream remained too dangerous for some.

CHAPTER FOUR

When the Ink Dries

The Politics of Literacy in Midcentury Ayacucho

With anger rising in her voice, seventy-nine-year-old Luciana Arauja explained, "There are many tinterillos, miss, who take advantage of the poor. Tinterillos who steal the homes of the poor. They can do this because they know how to read; they're teachers. They have everything, too. They have everything. It's because we're ignorant. They take advantage of that."[1] That September day in 2002, Luciana told Alicia and me of her then-current struggles with tinterillos, the shyster scribes who used forged documents and legal trickery to cheat her and other Carhuanquinos of their properties. Luciana was speaking of her contemporary problems, but her words seemed straight out of the mid-twentieth-century documents I had been reading in the Ayacucho archive. *Tinterillos*—a term literally meaning "men who use little inkwells"—were individuals who used the courts and the political system for their own material and social ends. They were men who used their literacy to compose or forge letters of protest, initiate court proceedings, and create fraudulent documents so that they might acquire more land, steal animals, impugn their local enemies, or escape imprisonment. Anger toward tinterillos represented just one component of Carhuanca's midcentury literacy politics, politics that entailed struggles over education and the uses (as well as the abuses) of that education. District campesinos fought for more and better schools, but they also expressed understandable anger at the unequal burden poorer peasants bore to build those schools. And while peasants valued literacy in general, they regularly voiced bitter complaints when their literate neighbors abused their education for personal gain.

   The Carhuanca example shows a deep and painful ambivalence toward literacy and education in rural Ayacucho of the 1940s and 1950s. This story of literacy politics has not been fully told. While scholars have done an excellent job of showing the myriad ways that campesinos fought for access to education—often against the wishes of the hacendados on whose land they labored—historians have not thoroughly explored the ways that schools and education angered campesinos, aggravating already troubling divides between richer and poorer peasants.[2] Marisol de la Cadena's book *Indigenous Mestizos* did much to complicate academic understandings of literacy in the Andes, showing how education serves as a coded language of race inside Peru. Anthropologist María Elena García's study *Making Indigenous Citizens* advanced the conversation, demonstrating how conflicts over bilingual education reflect continuing struggles over race, class, and citizenship in Peru's indigenous countryside.[3] This chapter goes further still, placing literacy politics at the very center of rural political life in midcentury Ayacucho.

READING POLITICS (I):
NATIONAL AND DEPARTMENTAL CONTEXTS

Carhuanca's midcentury literacy politics took place on a national, departmental, and local stage still very much defined by APRA. Inside Lima, Manuel Prado assumed the presidency the same year that World War II exploded in Europe, coming to power on an antifascist platform. Although the Prado government retained the official ban on APRA, his administration began a slow rapprochement with the party, releasing numerous Apristas from prison and tacitly allowing party members to organize. This quiet political reconciliation between the national government and APRA was greatly eased by APRA's rightward political shift. Prado rewarded APRA's increasing conservatism by legalizing the party in the run-up to the 1945 presidential elections. José Luis Bustamante y Rivero won those elections, heading up a left-leaning electoral coalition that included Apristas and Socialists, as well as Communists.

President Bustamante attempted to control APRA by co-opting it, governing in open alliance with Apristas. Bustamante's efforts were far from successful, however, for APRA was an increasingly complex and divided party. While some Aprista sectors inched ever further to the political right, others remained staunchly committed to leftist ideals. Those latter sectors launched a number of rebellions from 1945 onward, culminating in a massive uprising on October 3, 1948, in the coastal province of Callao. That October uprising drew together nearly 500 naval troops and 100 civilians, but it ended in disaster for the APRA.[4] President Bustamante outlawed APRA and ordered the arrests of party militants, leading to nearly 2,000 incarcerations. The anti-Aprista repression was strong, but it was not strong enough to satisfy Peruvian military generals. Judging Bustamante's actions to be too little, too late, military leaders under the direction of General Manuel Odría ousted Bustamante from power on October 29, 1948. The coup—known as the "Arequipa Revolution" in homage to its place of origin—brought still more arrests and repression, setting the political tone for the coming decade of the 1950s.[5]

While it was APRA's coastal sectors that captured the attention and ire of national authorities, the party also remained strong in much of rural and urban Ayacucho. In the months before Odría's Arequipa Revolution, the subprefects of Huanta and Cangallo alike offered repeated warnings about the continuing Aprista presence in their respective provinces.[6] APRA remained similarly dominant inside Carhuanca; indeed, the party actually grew stronger inside the district during the first years of the 1940s.[7] APRA even drew once-steadfast anti-Apristas like Luis Allende Ayala and Crisóstomo Romaní into its ranks. Yet when APRA fell back into national disrepute and illegality, several Carhuanquino Apristas were quick to denounce their membership in the party. Luis Allende made such a renunciation just prior to the 1948 military coup; numerous others did so shortly thereafter.[8] A telegram from several Carhuanquino notables to Peru's President, General Manuel A. Odría, was particularly telling. The telegram proclaimed, "We salute Your Excellency on the first anniversary of the restorative Arequipa Revolution, in which your sword put an end to internationalist sectarianism." The telegram described the "three years of misgovernment under the sway of Aprista politics" and stated the signatories' "unconditional support" for the new government. Those signatories included once-dedicated Apristas like Maximiliano García and Nicanor Cordero, along with fourteen other notables.[9] Carhuanca even established a local branch of the Odriísta Peruvian Restoration Party, as did districts throughout much of Ayacucho. But APRA by no means disappeared from Carhuanca. Even some of those who claimed loyalty to Odría and forswore APRA in their official communications continued to sympathize with the party. Nicanor Cordero, for example, pledged his opposition to the APRA around the same time that he passed through Carhuanca's streets yelling out vivas to that very same party.[10] Yet however important the twists and turns of APRA's political fate were during the 1940s and 1950s, they were overshadowed inside Carhuanca by a different sort of political struggle: conflicts over literacy.

READING POLITICS (II): CARHUANCA

Carhuanquinos' beliefs about education and literacy were riddled with ambiguities. Carhuanquinos craved education, but they often loathed the educated. Richer and poorer Carhuanquinos alike pressed for better schools and better teachers, yet they bitterly denounced those district residents who used education to their private advantage. Such attitudes were not examples of "contradictory consciousness." Carhuanquinos understood that the only way to escape the abuses of their neighbors was to acquire the tool of the abuser: education. Education was an instrument of both defense and offense, allowing Carhuanquinos to protect themselves and to acquire more material, political, and social power. As Ricardo Alvarado explained, "Educated men ruled in those times. Men who knew how to read. People would say, 'Oh, he's educated,' and he'd get whatever he wanted."[11]

It is no surprise, then, that notable and nonnotable Carhuanquinos alike repeatedly petitioned the state for better schools and better teachers. Back in January 1938, a number of Carhuanquinos gathered in a public assembly to denounce Mayor Pedro J. García's failure to proceed with school construction. The assembled men and women charged that "because of his lethargy and slovenliness, the construction of the boys' and girls' schools has yet to begin . . . even though we inhabitants have been ready to cooperate in said labor with all of our effort."[12] The signatories added that there was tremendous need for the construction of these schools, as some students were receiving classes in the public jail, while all the others studied in the central plaza. Carhuanquinos also pressured their fellow comuneros to cede their land and labor for the construction of a new school.[13] Members of Carhuanca's migrant society even took it upon themselves to make a significant donation to the district's boys' school, giving a flag and musical instruments for the school band.[14]

And just as they pressed for better schools, Carhuanquinos pushed for better teachers. In 1944, Governor Luis Allende Ayala complained that the main teacher of the boys' school had abandoned Carhuanca and that "the only teacher left for the large school population is the principal Climaco Gutiérrez, and he alone is insufficient for so many students. It is of utmost importance that you name another teacher; for, at the moment, Dionisio Alfaro has been proposed, and he is an individual who totally lacks a primary education and as such is unfit for the position."[15] Carhuanca authorities made more denunciations in the 1950s, complaining that the principal of the boys' school was habitually drunk and routinely negligent in his school duties.[16] Authorities were not the only ones to complain. The indigenous campesino Víctor Gómez made a formal complaint to the Ayacucho prefect about Odilia de Mayhua, a teacher in the Carhuanca girls' school. Trouble started when Gómez's young daughter and a schoolmate got into a squabble over a textbook they were forced to share. Gómez's wife went to the school the next day and asked Profesora de Mayhua to provide their daughter with a textbook of her own. The teacher responded to the request with violence, pulling the wife's hair, kicking and punching her, and "leaving her half dead." By Gómez's telling, such behavior was standard fare from the teacher. He complained that de Mayhua "doesn't teach anything, doesn't give out books to read, and she doesn't distribute the writing supplies ordered by the state." Worse still, she made her students "serve as domestics in her house."[17] Whatever the truth behind Gómez's charges, his heated complaints show Carhuanquinos' strong desire for better schoolteachers.

Carhuanquinos engaged in a public struggle for better schools and teachers, but they also made private familial efforts to educate their children. Many Carhuanquinos remember how their parents labored to educate them in the 1940s and 1950s, sacrificing their resources to allow their children to study. Enrique Canales explained that he started his studies in Carhuanca's school, although that school was clearly wanting. "There was a school here, but it was in the fields. The teachers didn't even know how to speak Spanish. We had to sit on the ground, and we wrote on agave leaves. The teacher came only when he wanted to; when he didn't want to, he didn't come. And what functionary was going to come from Cangallo to do an inspection? Never. It was a day and a half trip to get here! No, it was very difficult for us, very difficult to study."[18] Born into one of Carhuanca's wealthier peasant families, Enrique Canales was able to leave Carhuanca to study in Ayacucho. His parents were not desperate for his labor, and they had the resources to help support him in the city. "When I was studying in Ayacucho, for elementary school, it was a three-day trip. There was no highway. So a bunch of us boys went together, carrying our food; we arrived in Ayacucho. Then we had to look for a room we could rent. . . . We cooked with charcoal made from leaves. We'd take the leaves of certain trees, dry them, and then use them to cook."[19] Ricardo Alvarado was able to study in the Ayacucho secondary school Mariscal Cáceres, though such study was a strain for his family, given that his father had died while Ricardo was still a baby and his mother never remarried. When I asked if other Carhuanquinos studied alongside him at Mariscal Cáceres, Ricardo answered, "Only a few, because it was very hard in that time. . . . It was a sacrifice."[20]

Education was at once a common value and priority in Carhuanca. Yet however much Carhuanquinos shared the desire for education, their access to that education was sharply delimited by their socioeconomic position. Education was a sacrifice for Carhuanquinos, and although most Carhuanquino families were willing to make such a sacrifice, not many were actually *able* to. Only those families with an above-average quantity of livestock, productive lands, and access to cash were able to send their children to school. Without that wealth, parents could not afford to lose their children's labor in their fields, and they could not pay peons to substitute for their studying children. As Ricardo Alvarado explained, "Oh, how we suffered to study! Sometimes we didn't have money. Because we were peasants, it was hard."[21] Opportunities were also limited by place. Students in Carhuanca's elementary school came not only from Carhuanca but also from its annexes and from other districts because Carhuanca was one of the few towns whose school offered classes all the way up to fifth grade. Other nearby schools offered only first and maybe second grade.[22]

Access to education was also limited by sex: Boys and girls had separate schools, and the Carhuanca girls' school went only to the second grade. Worse still, many parents refused to permit their daughters to study at all. Juana Romero explained that her parents had never allowed her to study, telling her that she had to help in the kitchen and pasture the family's animals. "Why do you want to study?" they would ask her, "So you can send notes to your boyfriend?"[23] Only after she married in 1940 at the age of fifteen did Juana begin learning how to read, taught by her literate husband. Eugenia Alarcón told a similar story: "I studied first grade. I was raised by my grandmother, you see, and she said to me, 'My sheep and my cow are worth more than you! Why do you want to read? So you and your boyfriend can write each other letters?'"[24] Many Carhuanquinas in their sixties, seventies, and even eighties repeated similar stories to Alicia and me, often weeping as they did so.

Even if girls were fortunate enough to have parents or husbands willing to let them study, sex often drove them from their schools. Juana Romero told us that her husband had let her attend school and that "I was really smart, I was the school's standard-bearer. And I kept going until I got pregnant. I was embarrassed, so I left my studies."[25] Male teachers' sexual assault of female students was also a very real problem. One male Carhuanquino teacher working in the nearby community of Cochas was charged with raping a minor but found innocent by the court despite considerable evidence against him.[26] In addition, a few Carhuanca women told Alicia and me that one of the district's most prominent teachers had raped dozens of young female students and that many of those raped girls gave birth to children whom the teacher refused to recognize, despite his obvious physical resemblance to the children.[27]

The costs of education were high. Not only did families have to sacrifice to send their children to school, they also had to sacrifice to build the schools themselves. Schools required land on which they could be situated, but land was a precious commodity inside a subsistence-based peasant economy like Carhuanca's. Land that housed a school was land that could not produce crops. The fairest thing to do, then, was to put community-owned land toward the school, so that district residents would share the sacrifice of land equally. Such was the solution Carhuanquinos proposed in 1944; district residents donated a parcel of community-owned land to the Ministry of Education for the construction of a new school.[28] The need for school land nonetheless impinged on private ownership. A campesina named Fernanda Palomino felt compromised by the school construction. She complained that her small plot of land was next to the boys' school and that her neighbors were pressuring her to donate portions of her property for the school. Palomino explained she was simply too poor to give that land as a gift to the state without compensation.[29]

Labor for school construction proved even more controversial than land donation. National, regional, and district authorities alike expected local residents to volunteer their labor toward the construction of school buildings. That unremunerated labor came at a heavy cost; the time and energy peasants spent building a new school was time and energy they were not spending in their fields. Not surprisingly, then, school construction stalled at harvest time, and district authorities often complained about residents' unwillingness to volunteer their labor for school construction.[30] In October 1951, for example, Carhuanca Governor Honorato Hiyo urged the subprefect to intervene in the construction of the district's new boys' school. He asked the provincial authority to order the Carhuanquino brothers Teodor and Bonifacio Gómez to do carpentry labor for the school and to press district resident Francisco Melendres to make the tiles for the roof, as the governor's numerous orders had failed to spur Melendres into action.[31] What went unstated in these letters of complaint was the fact that Carhuanquinos bore the burdens and benefits of school construction unequally; the impoverished peasants who could least afford to expend their time and energy building schools were also the least likely to profit from those schools, unable to spare their children's labor in their fields. Schools were in effect built by the poorest peasants to educate the richest.

School construction was not the only field in which questions of literacy and labor collided. Literacy and labor were likewise at the core of Carhuanquino debates about varayocs, the traditional indigenous leaders who held the staff of authority. The unstated issue underlying these debates was race. Inside Peru, illiteracy was synonymous with Indianness; a similar racialization process was at work inside Carhuanca before, during, and after the 1940s and 1950s. Through that process, Carhuanquinos used literacy to decide which comuneros would be forced into the position of varayocs. In interview after interview, Carhuanquinos gave the same answer to my question of "which Carhuanquinos were varayocs?": illiterates. Those Carhuanquino men unable to read were the men forced into the varayoc role, while Carhuanquinos able to read escaped the duty. Emiliano Muñoz explained that he had never been a varayoc precisely because he knew how to read, and Enrique Canales asserted that the varayocs' disappearance owed to the rise in literacy rates. Canales explained that "varayocs were people who didn't know how to read or to write. They were uneducated (*ignorantes*). They were people who did not have the *libreta electoral* (electoral passbook). Now, most people know how to read and write. That's why they disappeared."[32] Documents cited in Chapter Two of this book support these memories: Only literate Carhuanquinos could become district authorities, and only illiterate campesinos could be varayocs.

Carhuanquinos' memories of the varayoc system are generally negative; they recall the system as one of unjust service. Those attitudes toward the varayoc system, however, were not universally shared across the Andes. Scholars of other Andean communities have celebrated the varayoc custom, casting the tradition as an example of indigenous cultural resistance and persistence. Following the perceptions and perspectives of their local informants, scholars like Roger Rasnake have argued that the varayoc system was a form of authority that simultaneously paralleled, complemented, and challenged colonial forms of rule, serving as a space where Quechua men could take much-deserved pride in their indigenous heritage. In addition, scholars like Billie Jean Isbell, Olga González-Castañeda, Miguel La Serna, and José Coronel have found evidence of considerable local support for the varayoc system in rural Ayacucho throughout much of the twentieth century.[33] Carhuanquinos living in the early decades of the twentieth century may well have seen the varayoc position as one of prestige and honor.

Certainly, some of that prestige did persist in the 1940s and 1950s, the last decades of the varayocs' existence in Carhuanca. Juana Romero told Alicia and me how varayocs from Carhuanca and from its annexes Rayme Bajo, Ocopa, Chilicruz, and Rayme Alto used to dominate the district's much-loved *Carnaval* festivities. Filling giant pots with cabbage, potatoes, *chuño* (dehydrated potatoes), broad beans, and meat, varayocs' wives and daughters prepared soup that they then served to comuneros from the entire district. Other varayocs' families prepared barrels and barrels of chicha, hauling the beer down from their homes and pouring it out for their neighbors and relatives. The food and drink were accompanied by entertainment.[34] Dressed in animal pelts, carrying large and colorful kerchiefs, singing and dancing while groups of co-muneros followed close behind, the district's varayocs would approach Carhuanca's central plaza for an *encuentro*, a showdown. As Enrique Canales put it, "Good and fed, good and drunk, good and noisy, they came to fight!"[35] Challenging one another in a contest mixing dance, stone throwing, and physical fighting, these men battled to see which varayoc was the strongest and the manliest. So doing, these men enjoyed a moment of real honor, respect, and glory inside Carhuanca.

That moment, however, was radically unlike varayocs' everyday lives and duties by the mid-twentieth century. By the 1940s and 1950s, varay-ocs were more like servants than authorities. In a 1945 letter, Governor Crisóstomo Romaní lamented the "reduced number" of eleven varay-ocs at his service, a number he deemed insufficient for the "construc-tion of public works and communal *faenas* like the repair of aqueducts, roads, small bridges, and various others."[36] In another case, members of Carhuanca's Catholic Brotherhood made a formal complaint to the migrant society in Lima, charging that Carhuanca's authorities were unjustly using the district's varayocs to labor in their fields and their homes. These Catholic brethren were not denouncing the general mis-use of varayocs' time and energy. They were instead insisting that the varayocs should be building Carhuanca's new church! The brethren felt they—not the secular authorities—should be the recipients of varayocs' unpaid labors.[37] The oral history record substantiates this portrait of varayoc duty. Juana Romero explained that the varayocs had existed primarily to serve the governor. They brought firewood to the gover-nor's home and hauled enormous ceramic barrels full of water from Carhuanca's spring to the governor's front door.[38]

On top of these duties, the varayocs had to give the governor two full days of their weekly labor. Each and every Thursday and Sunday for the yearlong duration of their varayoc duty, these men had to spend their entire day at the governor's door, waiting for his instructions and demands. Sometimes, the governor made the varayocs work in his fields; other times he sent them to Ayacucho or Cangallo city to deliver mes-sages. Walking for days on foot, the varayocs usually had only toasted corn, cheese, jerky, and coca to sustain them. Ricardo Alvarado remem-bered such abuses. He recalled that "the governor would say, '*Envarado* [varayoc]! Come here!' And he would make them sew, get salt, get seeds.

They had to get up first thing in the morning to do this. That was abusive. . . . They served for one year. The governor would send them to the city for any little thing. 'Listen, varayoc, go to Cangallo!' They'd get sent at any moment, poor little things. And they had to go, they had to."[39] Almost all of the Carhuanquinos whom Alicia and I interviewed told similar stories; if they were old enough to remember the varayocs, what they most recalled were the abuses.

Varayocs earned no salary, no material remuneration for their labor. All they received was the prestige of holding this important communal position. By the 1940s, most Carhuanquino varayocs judged that prestige as insufficient compensation for the material and moral abuse they suffered. When I asked Emiliano Muñoz if varayocs were generally happy with their post, he answered, "No, they complained a lot. The governor didn't let them work in their fields; they were like his servants. . . . The governor was like a king!"[40] And when I asked Ricardo Alvarado if varayocs protested their abuse, he answered, "Who could they complain to? When? The highest authorities were the worst abusers. There wasn't anyone the varayocs could complain to."[41] The written record, however, shows that Carhuanca's varayocs did complain. And they complained a lot. Complaints to Cangallo's subprefect from Carhuanquino varayocs and their literate allies led Subprefect Pedro C. Cárdenas to chastise the district's governors on several occasions. Subprefect Cárdenas wrote Carhuanca's civil guard commander in December 1944, instructing him to reprimand Carhuanca's governor for abusing the district's varayocs. He wrote, "My dispatch has learned that the envarados are not carrying out their official duties but instead are doing private labors on the governor's land. This is a punishable offense. I must inform you that the previous governor Allende was suspended from his duties for this same offense of using envarados to work his land, and my dispatch cannot tolerate such action, not even for one instant. Please inform the governor of this for the first and last time."[42] Just six months later, the subprefect repeated his command, having learned that Carhuanca's governor had lent varayocs' services to the district's civil guards. "Envarados cannot be at the civil guard's disposal," the subprefect wrote, "said envarados are only to serve each village's customs."[43]

Carhuanca's governors did not wholly ignore the subprefect's warnings. One governor protested that varayocs were "humble servants called to lend their aid in necessary cases of an official quality" and that "I do not abuse their kindness by requiring them to do every last sort of task."[44] But the district's successive governors did not change their behaviors, and the "humble" and "kind" Carhuanquinos forced into varayoc service did not readily consent to continuing abuse. Felix Peñaloza, for

example, complained to the Cangallo subprefect that Carhuanca's lieutenant governor and a civil guard officer were pressuring him to accept a varayoc position he did not want, as he knew such service would
jeopardize his already fragile health, his economic interests, and his
constitutionally defined right to refuse unremunerated varayoc service.
Charging that the lieutenant governor and the civil guard had already
imprisoned him for resisting this service, Peñaloza urged the subprefect
to intervene and guarantee his freedom.[45]

Aurelio Ochoa Huaraca made a similar complaint. Protesting to
Ayacucho's prefect in 1950, Ochoa charged that Carhuanca's governor
had abused his position of authority by naming Ochoa to the position of
head varayoc (*regidor de vara*). Ochoa argued that such posts had been
outlawed years ago because they infringed on individual liberty, unfairly
forcing individuals into unpaid labor service. By his telling, Carhuanca's
gamonales were "using the efforts of humble people and orphaned villages to wrongfully enrich themselves." Ochoa urged the prefect to protect his rights against the governor, fearing that, without such guarantees, the governor would simply imprison him until he accepted the post.
"By jailing me, he will make me accept the varayoc post, just as he has
always done with the humble Indians and inhabitants of our region. We
are forgotten by this country's laws, receive no respect whatsoever, and
are victim of every sort of taunt and lampoon by a few landholders who
today more than ever hold positions of authority in the district."[46]

Varayoc duty could even serve as a punishment. Sabino Soto, a self-
defined Indian from the Carhuanca community of Ocopa, denounced
Carhuanca Governor Nicanor Fernández for abuse of authority, extortion, and undue detention. Soto asserted that the governor had arrested
him without grounds, kept him imprisoned and incommunicado for two
days and nights, and then forced him into the duty of varayoc. Soto explained that while he would have been happy to assume that post had he
been asked and if his "situation were good," the duty was far too oner-
ous to assume given his status as an impoverished young man. To take
on the varayoc duty would require him to "leave his family without their
daily bread." By Soto's telling, his arrest, imprisonment, and the imposed
varayoc duty represented the governor's "ridiculous revenge" for his wife's
refusal to sell the governor a hammock.[47] By the late 1950s, varayoc service ended in Carhuanca. I have found no document describing its end,
nor met anyone who can remember exactly when or how it ended, but the
abuses of the duty are well documented and remembered.

Compounding quarrels over education and varayoc duty, literacy
politics in Carhuanca generated intense conflicts regarding tinterillos.
Tensions between richer and poorer Carhuanquinos regularly resulted in

complaints and lawsuits about land, animals, homes, and goods. Those tensions also pushed—and were pushed by—a specific "language of contention" that stressed differences of class.[48] Sometimes, campesinos phrased their complaints in the stark terms of class conflict. Epifanio Vásquez complained to the court that his accuser and his relatives were "influential in the town of Carhuanca, because they are rich and powerful men."[49] More often, though, Carhuanquinos utilized a specific label to criticize those local elites who abused their education, their wealth, and their political connections to take illegal advantage of their poor and illiterate neighbors: They called such men tinterillos.

Tinterillo was (and remains) a key insult inside Carhuanca, the label preferred over other racialized or class insults like *misti* (mestizo), *blanco* (white), *rico* (rich), or *instruido* (educated). Wealthy Carhuanquino peasants like Luis Allende Ayala, Dionisio Alfaro, Maximiliano García, Filomeno Morales, Teófilo Ochoa, and others all found themselves dubbed tinterillos at numerous points of their lives. Impoverished campesinos regularly invoked the label of tinterillo when they made complaints against their wealthier neighbors.[50] But poorer peasants were not the only ones to criticize tinterillos. Wealthier Carhuanquinos were just as likely to make such complaints. A group of Carhuanca authorities, for example, charged in 1955 that they were "always victims of frequent abuses . . . because the masses of this district have turned very rebellious under the direction of certain tinterillos who believe themselves masters of the pueblo."[51]

Tinterillos committed many wrongs in Carhuanca, ranging from political manipulations to economic abuses. To give a better sense of tinterillos' misdeeds, as well as local anger toward their behaviors, we can look at the examples of two particularly infamous district tinterillos, Crisóstomo Romaní and Primitivo Mayhua. First, Crisóstomo Romaní: The son of an Ayacucho priest assigned to Carhuanca's parish, Crisóstomo Romaní proved one of Carhuanca's most notorious tinterillos. Municipal Mayor Filomeno Morales complained about Romaní in November 1946, charging that Romaní had a terrible record and that "he dedicates himself exclusively to *tinterillada* and lives by sucking in this area's defenseless Indians." Morales asserted that Romaní had no occupation other than *tinterillaje*. "He doesn't have even a small piece of land and no assets of any sort to support himself and, as such, has to maintain himself through robbery, fraud, and slander, embroiling others in lawsuits and endangering the ignorant with court cases."[52] He also claimed that Romaní had already been expelled from three districts in Víctor Fajardo. There was much truth in Morales's assertions. Romaní had fled Carhuanca in the 1930s after he lost political power to the district's Apristas, and he took up residence in a number of different communities. His wife Victoria Ochoa told the court that comuneros in Tiquihua, Hualla, Canaria, and other communities had "thrown us out of their towns because of the countless abuses, robberies, frauds, and other punishable crimes that Crisóstomo Romaní committed daily."[53] Indeed, Tiquihua comuneros had held a public meeting to discuss Romaní's ouster from their community, drawing up a petition with two pages of signatures and labeling him a "black-handed tinterillo who . . . commits fraud and invents false documents to exploit the Indian masses."[54]

Carhuanca's police chief (*comandante del puesto*) Vicente Condori agreed with this depiction, stating that Romaní "loves to appear before justices of the peace or other authorities, presenting documents defending or denouncing others," presentations that often resulted in lawsuits. Romaní was, in the police chief's opinion, a "dangerous individual."[55] Romaní's reputation did not improve with time. In 1956, one Carhuanquino testified that "Crisóstomo Romaní is a tinterillo who earns his living by inciting the Indian masses."[56] And in 1957 Governor Germán Navarete cast Romaní as a "man of bad conduct and a terrible record," noting that Romaní was currently embroiled in a number of lawsuits with various Carhuanquinos for crimes like robbery, assault, and fraud. The governor added that Romaní had also "seized land from impoverished wretches, using fake papers that he made himself."[57] Romaní is also remembered by today's Carhuanquinos as a tinterillo. One Carhuanquino cast Romaní as a man who "loved being a tinterillo. Whatever happened, if there was a fight, he was right there, looking to get involved."[58]

Romaní's misdeeds took various forms. Many Carhuanquinos charged Romaní with crimes like cattle rustling and home invasion, but what was particularly frustrating about Romaní was his seeming ability to manipulate the authorities into believing that his victims were actually his victimizers. In 1947, Romaní traveled to the city of Ayacucho to levy serious accusations against police chief Vicente Condori before the department's prefect. Romaní claimed that the officer had forced him and his family to flee Carhuanca, threatening that "if we ever turned up in Carhuanca again, he would use his authority to detain us and punish us with torture."[59] Condori, however, saw a different motive behind Romaní's complaints. Explaining that Crisóstomo Romaní and another man had seized cattle belonging to the campesina Estefa Gómez, Condori had ordered Romaní to return the cows or face arrest. Condori explained to the prefect that Romaní's charges against him were false and owed only to this arrest order, and he charged that Romaní was not only a pernicious character but also "a known cattle rustler and dangerous tinterillo" who did his best to mislead higher authorities.[60] Numerous other cases revealed similar instances of Romaní's political deceptions.[61]

Romaní was also notorious for faking legal documents, usually by coercing others to sign such documents against their will. Sabino Soto initiated a lawsuit against Romaní, charging that the man had stormed into his home two hours after midnight on July 23, 1950, and forced him and his wife from their bed with the threat of physical violence. Romaní then dragged the pair to the home of Apolinaria Ochoa, forcing Soto to sign a document pledging to repay the seventy-two soles that Apolinaria had supposedly lent his wife the previous year. Though this loan had never happened, Soto affixed his signature to the fraudulent document, knowing that failure to do so would lead Romaní to beat him. In a similar case, three Carhuanquino authorities complained that Romaní had one of his civil guard allies threaten them at gunpoint, forcing them to sign a document denying Romaní's affiliation with APRA. That denial was plainly false given Romaní's recent affiliation with the party, but Romaní, the guard, and the coerced signatories all knew that such a document would help Romaní win release from prison.[62]

Romaní largely escaped punishment for his crimes. Though he was occasionally jailed, those incarcerations were both rare and short in duration. And though campesinos in other Ayacucho communities had managed to oust Romaní permanently from their districts, he remained a fixture inside Carhuanca (sometimes leaving but always returning) until his death. But Carhuanquinos did find a means to temper Romaní's impunity, a means against which Romaní's legal skills and documentary tricks were useless: witchcraft. Mayor Marcelino Guillén and district adviser Jesús Cárdenas penned a letter in January 1951, casting the Romaní family as the victims of sorcery. On Romaní's request, the authorities had visited his home and examined his gravely ill son, Teodomiro. Five months earlier, ten-year-old Teodomiro had fallen sick, complaining first of headaches, then of earaches. Next, the little boy's eyes swelled over, and he grew unable to eat, leaving him "a deaf/mute human skeleton." Interrogating both Romaní and the barely speaking child, the authorities determined that a campesino named León Ramírez—known popularly as a sorcerer (*brujo*)—had poisoned the boy. Ramírez had threatened the Romaní family with death following a dispute over land; he had been accused of similar poisonings in the past; and he had fed little Teodomiro a number of peaches, apples, and pieces of bread right before the boy fell ill.[63] Such supernatural tactics were really the only effective form of revenge poorer Carhuanquinos had at their disposal against a tinterillo like Romaní.

Although Romaní was a particularly egregious example of a
Carhuanquino tinterillo, he was certainly not the only one. Nor was
he the most hated. That dubious distinction fell instead to a man
named Primitivo Mayhua. Of the many Carhuanquinos whom Alicia
and I asked about Mayhua, only one came to Mayhua's defense. The
rest cast him as awful, stressing both his physical appearance and his
crimes. Many Carhuanquinos laughingly described Mayhua's ugliness,
remembering that his face was deeply scarred by pockmarks, that he
had only one good eye, and that he walked with a hunched back, loping
from side to side. Hernán Carrillo relayed that Mayhua was so excru-
ciatingly homely that strangers yelped at first sight of him, and many
Carhuanquinos remembered that Mayhua was so ugly that Carhuanca's
children labeled him a *ñakaq*, an Andean bogeyman said to slice people's throats. Wherever Mayhua walked, Carhuanquino boys and girls
would run away screaming, yelling out warnings of "Ñakaq! Ñakaq!
Ñakaq!"[64]

Lacking any formal school education, Mayhua taught himself to
read and to write, and he used his literacy to commit abuses. Many
Carhuanquinos recalled Mayhua's abuses inside the district, telling
of how he used fraudulent documents, lawsuits, and trickery to cheat
Carhuanca's poorest campesinos of their land. Ignacio Figueroa remembered Mayhua as "an abusive and opportunistic man; he wanted everything that he did not yet have. He even robbed old men, stealing their
cattle, their things, even taking their lands. . . . When he liked a piece of
land, he just took it, that's all."[65] Emiliano Muñoz remembered Mayhua
in much the same way, explaining that "he was really abusive. Especially
with the Indians. He'd steal their farmland; he'd even steal from his own
relatives, saying 'this belongs to my family.'"[66] Gregorio Escalante, in
turn, recalled that "at any moment, he'd kick the town's peasants. For
him, they were nobodies. And if they got mad at him, he'd seize their
land."[67] Most Carhuanquinos explained Mayhua's abuses in terms of his
literacy, stating that he used his ability to read and write to cheat illiterate campesinos out of their holdings. When I asked why Carhuanquinos
did not protest against Mayhua, Ignacio Figueroa explained that "most
people were illiterate, nothing more. And that's how Mayhua took advantage of them."[68]

The written record strongly supports Carhuanquinos' memories
of Mayhua and his crimes. Antonia Ochoa Vega took her complaints
against Primitivo Mayhua all the way to the national minister of government in 1949. Writing that Carhuanca was home to "a number of terrible individuals who are a danger to society, like terrorists," she outlined
Mayhua's crimes in detail. Doña Ochoa charged that Mayhua—"alias

Suwa Ñausa (blind thief)"—had not only robbed and swindled numerous Carhuanquino migrants residing in Lima but that he acted as a tinterillo inside Carhuanca, using legal slights of hand to dupe "poor Indians" out of their land. Further, she stressed that Mayhua acted in collusion with other Carhuanquino authorities like Luis Allende and Nicanor Cordero to "commit countless abuses against Carhuanca's Indians, mistreating defenseless women, uprooting their crops, and slandering honorable and innocent people."[69] Ochoa's strong words were not unwarranted. Dozens of campesinos filed lawsuits against Mayhua from the 1930s to the 1960s, accusing him of theft of land, crops, and animals.[70] Mayhua's crimes were so terrible, and so consistently unpunished, that the president and secretary general of the Carhuanquino migrant society petitioned the national minister of government to take action against Mayhua in 1955. The migrant society's petition charged that Primitivo Mayhua was an individual with a dreadful judicial and penal record. Claiming that Mayhua enjoyed considerable economic, social, and political influence, the migrant society stated that he "has committed and continues to commit a series of abuses and outrages against Carhuanca's defenseless inhabitants. Their only crime has been their opposition to this man's excesses, defending the tiny patrimony they inherited from their ancestors."[71]

Mayhua's crimes also included murder. Echoing references I had found in numerous documents, Hernán Carrillo told me that, at some point in the 1940s, Primitivo Mayhua decided to get married. The young woman he chose as his bride had no particular desire to marry the awful Mayhua, but after he fired his gun into the air and threatened to kill her, she acquiesced. Leading the woman into a church outside Carhuanca on Christmas day, Mayhua demanded that the priest marry them immediately. When the priest objected, stating that the couple first had to show necessary documents, Mayhua responded, "What documents? Damn you!" and shot the priest in the leg. Although that gunshot wound later became infected, and the priest died as a consequence, Mayhua managed to escape prolonged incarceration for the murder. After only three months in jail, Mayhua was able to use his political friendships and alliances to win release from prison.[72]

Not stopping with straightforward crimes like theft and murder, Mayhua waged legal and political battles against those Carhuanquinos unwilling to do his bidding. A campesino from Saurama added to the long list of complaints against Mayhua, charging that Mayhua dedicated himself to tinterillaje in Carhuanca and its outskirts, overlooking, hiding, and even encouraging crimes committed by those individuals tied to him and seeking revenge against each and every person he disliked.

This campesino charged that he was a victim of such vengeance. Having refused Mayhua's request that he become an *allegado* (tenant laborer) on Mayhua's land, the peasant was immediately faced with a groundless lawsuit in which Mayhua accused him of animal theft. The peasant wrote this letter of complaint from inside the Vilcashuamán jail, where he sat imprisoned for the fictitious theft.[73] A similar tale of Mayhua's vengeance came with his actions against Carhuanquino mayor Francisco Ruiz. Ruiz wrote to Carhuanca's migrant society in Lima, asking for help against Mayhua. He explained that Mayhua had falsified the birth certificate of one of his tenants, changing the tenant's date of birth so that he would win exemption from his obligatory military service. But when Mayor Ruiz refused to grant the exemption, knowing that the birth certificate was fraudulent, he received threats and then physical blows from Mayhua. Going further still, Mayhua drew up a petition to blame Ruiz for an imaginary case of arson and to demand his removal from power, and he then used both threats and bribes to get Carhuanquinos to sign the petition. Though the migrant society wrote a long letter of protest backing Ruiz, it was Mayhua who triumphed: Ayacucho's prefect removed Francisco Ruiz from his mayoral post in May 1955, replacing him with Germán Navarro, a man generally believed to be Mayhua's lackey.[74]

Primitivo Mayhua enjoyed impunity for his crimes. His thefts, frauds, and assaults went unpunished. He spent almost no time in prison, and he was actually handsomely rewarded by the state: Mayhua became a provincial inspector of Indian affairs in the 1950s and held that government post until his death. Many Carhuanquinos have blamed Mayhua's impunity on his political connections. The indigenous peasant Rosalino Vega made a formal complaint against Mayhua's impunity to Ayacucho's Supreme Court, charging that Carhuanca's governor and the district's police were intentionally ignoring court orders to arrest Mayhua, driven both by friendship and by their own collusion in Mayhua's activities.[75] Doña Ochoa's letter to the minister of government charged that Mayhua escaped imprisonment only because Cangallo Subprefect Pedro C. Cárdenas extended him both his friendship and his protection. She added that Mayhua's humble victims were too frightened to press charges against him "for fear that he would encourage those provincial authorities to mistreat them." Doña Ochoa ended her long letter with a strong plea for help: "I devotedly beg you, Mr. Minister, to put an end to the situation suffered by Carhuanca's Indians, its honorable residents, and its defenseless women, all victims of frightening abuses."[76] Interview testimony supported these written perceptions. When I asked if Mayhua spent much time in jail, Don Ignacio Figueroa answered, "No, no, no.

He didn't go to jail because he had his political advisers, his authorities. Some were from the province, others were from the department. He would bring these men sheep. It was bribery!"[77] Don Isidro Durán explained Mayhua's freedom from imprisonment with the comment that "Primitivo Mayhua was well connected to important politicians."[78] Others charged that Mayhua used the bonds of *compadrazgo* to his political advantage, making such ties with provincial and departmental authorities and then calling in political favors as his due.[79]

Though Primitivo Mayhua enjoyed impunity for his abuses, his abuses ultimately killed him. Through his work as Cangallo's regional inspector for Indian affairs, Mayhua won himself considerable hatred and resentment, usually linked to accusations of favoritism. Carhuanquino peasant Mariano Taipe wrote Lima's director general of Indian affairs in 1957 to complain about Mayhua, arguing that the inspector had taken a biased and unfair attitude toward Taipe's lawsuit over land, siding with Taipe's adversary because of kinship rather than facts. "Far from bothering to learn about the case, he has simply assumed jurisdiction, and his actions show not only a frank hostility to my rights but also a brazen partialness in favor of my opponent."[80] After years as Cangallo's inspector of Indian affairs, Mayhua was transferred to the same post in Lucanas. There, Mayhua continued his abusive ways, accepting bribes and privileging friendship over justice. Mayhua angered many Lucanas peasants, and his actions cost him his life. Adjudicating a border dispute between two Lucanas communities, Mayhua met with leaders from both communities and lent his full support to the leader clearly in the wrong. Unfortunately for Mayhua, the other leader was not only a victim of gross injustice but also a sorcerer. Furious at Mayhua for his misdeed, the victimized leader cast a spell on the inspector, who soon thereafter suffered a debilitating stroke. Although Mayhua sought treatment in Lima, the stroke ultimately killed him.[81] That campesinos' only recourse against a tinterillo like Mayhua—and like Crisóstomo Romaní—was sorcery suggests both campesinos' sense of powerlessness against such men in the official realm of courts and authorities, as well as a willingness to pursue extrajudicial solutions in a context of state neglect.

Tinterillos like Mayhua and Romaní caused much suffering inside Carhuanca, yet the very existence of tinterillos actually gave cohesion to Carhuanca as a community, providing a base level of unity. Had there been only one or two tinterillos inside Carhuanca, those men might themselves have become a focal point of communal solidarity, with campesinos uniting in opposition against them. But Carhuanca was home to many accused tinterillos, far more than just one or two, making such unity unlikely, if not impossible. There was, then, no simple conflict waged between all nonelite Carhuanquinos against all tinterillos but instead an unstable set of constantly changing alliances, where poor Carhuanquinos allied with a certain tinterillo in one moment and allied with his wealthy enemy in another. Similarly, local notables regularly battled among themselves, calling one another tinterillos and taking each other to court. Yet tinterillos' very omnipresence in Carhuanca did foster communal unity in two indirect but nonetheless crucial ways. First, given that their pueblo was so divided by fights and lawsuits between neighbors—fights aided and encouraged by shyster scribes—Carhuanquinos began to identify their district as a place defined by conflict and crippled by tinterillos. Whether wealthy or poor, more or less Indian, male or female, Carhuanquinos labeled their district a playground of tinterillos. Carhuanquinos in effect came to share a vision of their district as an area hurt by tinterillos. That vision was tantamount to a communal identity; it was an identity of communal victimization, but it was an identity all the same.

Second, tinterillos' abuses drove a shared language of contention inside Carhuanca. Carhuanquinos made *tinterillismo* the standard crutch of their arguments, using the term as a noun, a verb, and an adjective in their testimonies and petitions. Aparicio Cárdenas and Aniceto Vargas used such language throughout their November 1944 complaint to the subprefect, charging that Filomeno Morales and Sabino Morales "carried out *tinterillada*," describing the "abuse that the tinterillo Morales commits," and declaring that Filomeno was "skilled in tinterillada."[82] A number of Carhuanquinos affixed their signatures to a 1956 petition against Teófilo Ochoa, demanding that he renounce his claims to church lands, "having no grounds other than being a famous tinterillo accustomed to seizing others' holdings."[83] Luis Allende, in turn, blamed varayocs' disobedience on the fact that they had been "imbued by certain bad tinterillos who live in this town, like Pedro Félix Guillén, Teófilo Ochoa, and others."[84] Certainly, tinterillismo was a language used for fights, lawsuits, complaints, and insults, but the fact that all Carhuanquinos used that language suggests the ways that the discourse provided an ironic degree of communal unity, even though it was a language used to further local divides.

LURICOCHA COUNTERPOINT

Carhuanca's fights over education, literacy, and especially tinterillos were particularly strong. As Subprefect Pedro C. Cárdenas phrased it, "Carhuanca is one of the districts where inhabitants have dedicated themselves to tinterillismo in scandalous fashion."[85] The Luricocha case tempers the Carhuanca example, for while literacy politics were present in the district, they were often overshadowed by other pressing political concerns. In marked contrast to Carhuanca, for example, debates about varayoc service escape mention in Luricocha's documentary record, while oral history memories about the varayocs are largely positive.[86] Nor were debates about tinterillos as heated in Luricocha as they were in Carhuanca. I found only a handful of references to tinterillismo in Luricocha's prefectural and court records.[87] This is not to say that Luricocha was free from the sort of abuses that Carhuanquino tinterillos perpetrated; far from it. Indeed, complaints about economic, political, and social abuses and crimes emerged on a regular basis inside Luricocha. The near absence of the tinterillo discourse meant only that literacy was not the main gauge of power differentials inside Luricocha, a fact that is not especially surprising when we consider the major economic differences that separated district landlords from their campesino tenants.

Where literacy politics did loom large inside Luricocha was in relation to schools. Luricocha peasants dedicated a considerable amount of their time and their unremunerated labor to the construction of new schoolhouses. Campesinos in the Luricocha communities of Llanza and Ocana, for instance, invested their own money and labor in the construction of local schools, proceeding without any government assistance. *Sierra*'s Luricocha correspondent reported in 1948 that Llanza's "enthusiastic inhabitants" were building their own school, taking the initiative for the work in the face of a total lack of state and municipal support.[88] While hacendados in other parts of Peru actively impeded campesinos' access to education and schools, Luricocha landlords actually shared peasants' desire for more and better schools. Members of the hacienda-owning Ludeña family donated trumpets for the new Llanza school's musical band, and over 200 prominent Huantinos (both Luricochanos and others) petitioned Peru's president for a new girls' school in Huanta.[89] Certainly, there was occasional opposition to these construction efforts. A campesina named Gregoria Sánchez, for example, wrote Ayacucho's bishop in 1951, identifying herself as the tenant of the Chaquipata terrain, a property belonging to Luricocha's church. She explained that Luricocha's priest had unlawfully sold the terrain to Ocana's comuneros for the construction of a new school, and she complained that the area's campesinos had evicted her, chopping down her trees and destroying the rope fences that protected her holding.[90]

Luricochanos' concerns about education did not end with school buildings; district residents also pressed for better teachers. Campesinos in the Luricocha community of Huayllay fought a long and frustrating

battle against the teacher of their primary school, Delia León. Although
the character of Profesora León's transgressions escapes mention in the
documentary record, Huayllay peasants actively sought her removal from
their community. Those campesinos boycotted the school and forced
it to close for lack of students, and they repeatedly denounced Delia
León before Luricocha's governor, the regional education inspector, and
Huanta's subprefect between 1940 and 1941.[91] Huayllay campesinos'
complaints about Delia León were representative of a broader pattern of
dissatisfaction with rural teachers. Around this same time, campesinos
from the town of Luricocha levied complaints against the local teacher,
Alfredo Pacheco, and they complained in 1949 that the district's teachers worked only three or four days a week, abandoning their classrooms
for the city of Huanta.[92] Similarly, in 1958, Huayllay campesinos denounced their schoolteacher Lidia Girón to *Sierra*, complaining that she
had committed a series of abuses, like sending them to do her personal
errands, forcing them to purchase medicine from her, and selling text-
books provided by the state.[93]

　　To the degree that they struggled for better schools and better teachers,
Luricochanos engaged in literacy politics just as the men and women in
Carhuanca did. But Luricochanos had other political concerns that were
just as pressing as their desire for education. Luricocha campesinos, for
instance, also lobbied for better priests. In June 1940, a civil guard officer reported that over 200 indigenous campesinos from Luricocha had
presented themselves at the office of Huanta's subprefect, demanding
the restitution of their district's priest following the Ayacucho bishop's
decision to transfer the cleric out of his Luricocha parish.[94] Conversely, a
number of Luricocha campesinos wrote *Sierra* in 1949 to complain that
Luricocha's priest Father Marcial Ramírez was "not carrying out his sacred ministry." They charged that he was prioritizing his own breakfast
over morning mass, that he was clandestinely marrying couples, and
that he was charging enormous sums for his services.[95]

　　Party politics also remained vibrant in the district, if primarily among
Luricocha hacendados. Luricocha hacendado César Aibar continued to
be a leading member of APRA, heading up the Huanta branch of the
party. Aibar's brother, Santiago, and three other Huanta landlords, in
turn, pushed for the creation of a "Provincial Democratic Anti-Fascist
Committee" in 1942, following the lead of national Apristas eager to
distance themselves from the European fascists whom Apristas were often accused of resembling.[96] César Aibar also made a lengthy and impassioned plea for Huantinos to unite behind a single candidate for the 1945
congressional elections.[97] Aibar's motives were far from disinterested: He
himself was running as a candidate and faced tremendous competition

from a bevy of other contenders, including Luricocha hacendado Carlos La Torre Cortez.[98] These 1945 congressional elections soon morphed into a battle between provincial Apristas and anti-Apristas. Although APRA, the Peruvian Communist Party, the Peruvian Socialist Party, and others united in support of 1945 presidential candidate José Luis Bustamante y Rivero, that partnership was not replicated for the congressional elections. After the field of candidates was finally narrowed to just two, Huanta Apristas backed their party candidate Alejandro Carrillo while an amalgam of Peruvian Communist and Socialist Party members, along with centrist and rightist individuals staunchly opposed to APRA, endorsed Socialist Party candidate Oswaldo Regal. The 1945 congressional election struggle repeatedly degenerated into physical violence between Huanta Apristas and their opponents, and Regal's ultimate electoral victory did little to quell the animosity.[99]

Both Aprismo and anti-Aprismo remained strong inside Huanta long after the 1945 elections were over, and Luricochanos were prominent in those political currents. César Aibar and his brother Santiago continued their staunch devotion to APRA, while Luricocha landlord Carlos La Torre Cárdenas, son of Iribamba hacendado and 1945 congressional candidate Carlos La Torre Cortez, joined the Peruvian Communist Party.[100] La Torre Cárdenas was not the only Luricochano to join the PCP. Alfonso del Pozo, a self-described "conscious worker" and "working man" from Luricocha, announced in 1947 that he had joined the PCP. Vidal Cartolín Aguilar, another Luricocha man, likewise declared his membership in the PCP.[101]

Importantly, both del Pozo and Cartolín left APRA for the PCP. Del Pozo explained that while he had served as a secretary of discipline of the Luricocha Aprista Committee, he had lost faith in the party. He relayed that he had been one of the party's "fervent militants because I believed that it really was the party that fought for national independence, for sovereignty, and for the defense of democracy." Del Pozo continued on, stating that because APRA had gone against its own postulates, "wanting to sell our riches . . . to the North American imperialism that we once fought"; and because the party "tramples upon democracy with a Nazi-fascist ideology" he was quitting the party and joining the PCP, "defender of liberties and territorial integrity."[102] Vidal Cartolín Aguilar said much the same: "Convinced of the enormous betrayal that the Partido del Pueblo [APRA] is causing to sovereignty, territorial integrity and the democratic cause," he was leaving APRA for the PCP, "the party that defends national interests and integrity and has a precisely democratic line."[103]

Much invective passed back and forth between Luricocha Apristas and their Communist Party rivals, but the disputes between the parties and their sympathizers suddenly lost relevance in February 1949 when Huanta Apristas and Communists alike were rounded up by provincial authorities and placed in jail. Following orders from Peru's new military government under General Odría, Huanta's subprefect arrested Luricocha Aprista leaders Santiago, César, and Isidro Aibar, along with five other Huanta Apristas in February 1949. The subprefect also detained five alleged Huanta Communists, including one Luricochano. The arrests were for the men's political activities; as the subprefect phrased it, the arrested individuals were "carrying out secret activities to solidify sectarian forces."[104] Other arrests followed over the next few months, including the detention of Luricocha's Aprista secretary general, Manuel Flores Oré.[105] Those arrests were no small matter. These men remained imprisoned for several months, and conditions inside the jail were so poor that the detainees launched a protracted hunger strike.[106]

The Luricocha case injects an important dose of moderation into the discussion of literacy politics in midcentury Ayacucho. While struggles over education dominated the political lives of Carhuanquinos in the 1940s and 1950s, the Luricocha case shows that the same was not true throughout all of rural Ayacucho. Inside the district of Luricocha, literacy politics were often overshadowed by more conventional political struggles between parties, namely the APRA and the PCP. And while Luricocha had a number of active Communist Party members, Carhuanca apparently did not. If any Carhuanquinos joined the PCP in the 1940s or 1950s, they escaped the notice of ever-watchful authorities. Yet although the content of political involvement varied between rural Ayacucho districts, the *fact* of political involvement was the same.

CONCLUSION

Just after six on a July 1959 morning, Carhuanca's schoolhouse began to burn. The fire destroyed the school, and authorities suspected arson.[107] While the person or persons responsible for the fire were never discovered, we can easily imagine the mixed feelings Carhuanquinos held as they watched the school burn down. Some might have felt terrible sadness, knowing that the fire represented yet another obstacle to the education for which they fought so hard. Others might have felt a grim satisfaction, feeling that the school's destruction marked a form of revenge against the wealthier residents of the district who misused their literacy to the detriment of their poorer neighbors. Many Carhuanquinos likely felt a contradictory mix of both emotions, given that they held painfully ambiguous feelings about the uses and abuses of education.

Carhuanquinos' experience of literacy politics shifts our understanding of Andean men and women's attitudes toward education. Certainly, Carhuanca's residents struggled for better schools and better teachers, as earlier literature has demonstrated. But Carhuanquinos also felt a palpable anger toward the educated, believing themselves unfairly victimized by tinterillos and unduly subjected to varayoc duties on the grounds of illiteracy. Such ambiguous feelings were by no means limited to the 1940s and 1950s. Tawantinsuyo rebels of the 1920s pressed for education at the exact same time that they pledged to kill "those who knew how to read and write." Later chapters will show that such ambivalence continued through the 1960s and 1970s as well. Most of those who joined the PCP-SL had their first exposure to the party in high school or university settings, but the very first targets of their violence were precisely the local notables who shared Senderistas' privileged access to education. The ink remained fresh in Ayacucho's literacy politics long after the 1940s and 1950s ended.

CHAPTER FIVE

The Last Will Be First

Trotskyism and Popular Action in the Belaúnde Years

New Ideas
New Men
NEW METHODS
BELAÚNDE '62
PRESIDENT!

Written on the front door of a Carhuanquino home, this small piece of election propaganda reflected the heady cast of politics in 1960s Peru.[1] Throughout the country, Peruvians from different social classes and divergent political sympathies made calls for national socioeconomic transformation, convinced that fundamental change was as much necessary as it was welcome. With a national context of unchecked poverty and severe economic inequality, and an international context that cast radical reform as the sole alternative to revolution, many Peruvians saw the 1960s as a time for political experimentation and pointed socioeconomic transitions. They believed their country required new ideas, new men, and new methods of rule. Cuba's 1959 revolution gave particular urgency to this belief. Knowledge that a group of young, poorly armed, idealistic guerrillas had managed to wrest national power from an oligarchic dictator made a tremendous political impact inside Peru. Fearful that persisting rural and urban poverty would lead to the sort of violent revolutionary upheaval seen in Cuba, many members of Peru's urban professional classes and the military began demanding the kind of socioeconomic reforms heralded by U.S. President John F. Kennedy's Alliance for Progress. The Cuban Revolution represented something entirely different for many young political activists inside Peru: a dream. Joining together in dozens of different left-wing parties, thousands of young Peruvians prepared their own plans for a national revolution along Cuban lines. Peruvian reformers and revolutionaries alike saw the Cuban experience foreshadowed in their own country by the actions of campesinos across the central and southern Andes. During the closing years of the 1950s and into the early 1960s, rural men and women from the sierra began to unionize and stake claims to hacienda lands through protests, strikes, and the direct seizure of land. Sierra campesinos' rural activism pushed both reformers and revolutionaries to race toward change.

This chapter considers how Carhuanca campesinos approached the promise and possibility of fundamental socioeconomic transformation, living within a national and departmental context of considerable rural political activism. Unlike their neighbors in other departments, other Ayacucho provinces, and even other nearby districts, Carhuanquinos largely abstained from this torrent of rural political activism. Although Carhuanca did have a number of prominent Trotskyist leaders and activists, these young people had only limited influence inside the district. The Carhuanquinos who affiliated themselves with Trotskyism straddled the divide between Carhuanca's wealthiest peasants and the humbler district masses, coming from families that had long sought—but never quite managed—to ensconce themselves within the ranks of the district's local notables. These young revolutionaries' ineffectiveness, however, stemmed less from their local class and race positions than from the rigidity of their political visions, long-standing local enmities, and their overt hostility toward Catholicism. Trotskyists inside Carhuanca were also overshadowed by district partisans of Fernando Belaúnde Terry's Acción Popular Party, partisans who were almost without exception local notables.

The political roads taken by Carhuanquinos show the centrality of reformism to indigenous campesinos' lives in this otherwise revolutionary historical moment. Richer and poorer Carhuanquinos alike were inspired by President Belaúnde, his promises for political and economic progress, and his civic action programs. While not all Carhuanquinos sympathized with Belaúnde, his programs, or his district representatives, all found their lives profoundly affected (for better and for worse) by his presidency. Although campesinos in Carhuanca saw Belaúnde's presidency as a chance for meaningful political and economic transformation, their hopes were ultimately squashed. Carhuanca's wealthier campesinos quickly appropriated Belaúnde's principles and programs for their own ends, using the guise of "Popular Cooperation" to force their poorer neighbors into unremunerated and largely despised labor relationships. In the end, Belaúnde's promises for comprehensive reform came to naught, his promises of national inclusion for the country's impoverished indigenous peoples proved illusory, and his civic action programs left communities more deeply divided than ever.

REFORMS AND REVOLUTIONS:

NATIONAL AND REGIONAL CONTEXTS

Proclaiming "Land or Death!" in petitions, letters, and demonstrations, campesinos in the Cuzco province of La Convención gained national and then international attention with their efforts to claim ownership of the hacienda land they labored. Organizing in a peasant federation in 1958, these rural men and women began withholding payments from their hacendados, laboring hacienda land as though they were its owners rather than just tenants; they even began seizing hacienda property. With their land recuperation efforts already well underway, three La Convención campesinos invited a young Trotskyist labor organizer to participate in their struggle. That young activist was Hugo Blanco Galdós, a man who quickly gained fame as a Peruvian version of Fidel Castro, the leader of Cuba's revolution. Between his 1958 entrance into the La Convención Valley and his May 1963 arrest, Blanco and La Convención campesinos seized dozens of provincial haciendas, using force to defend themselves and their tacit agrarian reform from the military. Many Peruvians believed that these events signaled the coming of popular revolution in the country.[2]

Events in La Convención and the accompanying threat of revolutionary war made agrarian reform a national political priority. Motions for land redistribution legislation had emerged as early as 1956, but it was with the 1962 presidential candidacy of the young architect Fernando Belaúnde Terry that agrarian reform seemed imminent.[3] Yet when the votes were counted following the 1962 election, Belaúnde ranked second behind the now overtly conservative Aprista candidate, Haya de la Torre. Although Haya had beaten Belaúnde, he had not won the one-third of the popular vote required by Peruvian electoral law, leaving the presidency to be decided by Peru's Congress. Fearing that congressmen would select Haya and thereby forestall reformist legislation, progressive military officers alleged electoral fraud and assumed control of the country. These officers ruled Peru for one year, carrying out an initial agrarian reform and overseeing a second presidential election that Belaúnde won.

There is no question that Belaúnde's promises and approach represented a new turn in Peruvian politics. Unlike the aristocratic presidents who had ruled Peru throughout most of its republican history, Belaúnde

offered a truly national mandate for change, promising reforms meaningful not only to those living on the coast but also to the men and
women living in the long-ignored sierra and jungle. Belaúnde's actions
were even more telling than his words. Campaigning as no other previous Peruvian presidential candidate had, Belaúnde actually traveled
to the sierra, visiting dozens of highland communities and speaking
directly with rural men and women. Traveling by truck and by horse,
Belaúnde paid an unprecedented level of political attention to historically neglected indigenous campesinos. Belaúnde commented on sierra
peasants' abandon and promised to end it. In his words, "The provinces
cannot be governed, like colonies, by remote control from the center—a
method which is not only inefficient but which offends the honor and
sensibility of regions which my opponents have not deigned to visit."[4]
Not only did Belaúnde's words and physical presence promise the very
kind of decentralization and regional attention that had made APRA so
popular in the sierra during the 1930s and 1940s, those words and his
presence also promised the sort of direct personal relationship between
a national leader and "the people" that is the hallmark of populism. As
Belaúnde phrased it, "I go out to meet the people, to give ear to their
complaints and hopes. I do not wait idly at home for them to knock on
my door: I seek them out wherever they live, on the coast, in the sierra,
or the jungle."[5]

Belaúnde also cast campesinos as partners in his political program,
laying out plans for civic action campaigns, dubbed Cooperación Popular,
that would have rural men and women participate directly in Peru's ref-
ormation, combining their labor with the state's material resources to
build local infrastructure. Popular Cooperation projects included things
like reforestation efforts, the building of new schools, and especially road
construction. Though many of his contemporaries criticized Belaúnde for
his quixotic fixation on building a highway through the jungle, it need
be recognized that Belaúnde's presidential campaign promised to transform the structure of Peruvian economics, politics, and society. Similarly,
while scholars like Stefano Varese have rightly argued that Belaúnde's
jungle colonization schemes and military actions imperiled indigenous
Asháninka communities, it is nonetheless true that Belaúnde's populist
platforms promised a level of national inclusion to Andean peasants that
was unprecedented in the twentieth century.[6] It is not surprising, then,
that Belaúnde so inspired many Ayacucho campesinos.

Following Belaúnde's election, campesinos throughout the sierra began recuperating hacienda land. Many of these campesinos had joined
together in peasant unions and federations, and an estimated 300,000
campesinos seized nearly 400 haciendas between 1963 and 1964.[7] While

these campesinos believed Belaúnde was allied with them and committed to agrarian reform, he soon showed his rigid opposition to extralegal rural mobilization. The president authorized special assault troops to take repressive action against invading campesinos, repelling their land seizures by force. The military's actions came at a heavy cost; by the time Belaúnde's agrarian reform bill finally passed—seriously weakened by congressional modifications—over 300 campesinos had been killed.[8]

While Belaúnde and Acción Popular pledged national transformation through legalistic reform, other Peruvians had a different sort of transformation in mind. Inspired by the astonishing success of the guerrillas who seized control of Cuba in 1959, many young Peruvians grew determined to make popular revolution happen in their own country. Organizing in dozens of distinct left-wing parties with affiliations that ranged from Leninist to Trotskyist, Stalinist to Maoist, these young men and women discussed, debated, and plotted their path to revolution.[9] Beginning in June 1965, three separate guerrilla fronts launched uprisings aiming to bring the kind of revolutionary change seen in Cuba.[10] That revolution did not happen, for Belaúnde showed even less interest in negotiating with the guerrillas than he did with land-seizing campesinos. Within six months of their initial revolutionary actions, all three guerrilla fronts had fallen. The guerrillas' fall came partly as a consequence of their failure to coordinate their operations and in part because of their considerable isolation from the campesinos whom they claimed to be leading. But it was repression by the Peruvian military that was most responsible for the guerrillas' demise. Shock troops waged battles against the guerrillas, while air force planes bombed villages with conventional explosives and napalm, continuing their attack until winning military victory in January 1966. Although the military campaign was brief, the devastation it wrought was enormous: An estimated 8,000 men and women died during the repression, and 19,000 hectares of land were burned.[11] The revolutionary moment had passed.

While the department of Ayacucho witnessed fewer land invasions and hacienda seizures than seen in sierra departments like Junín, Pasco, and Cuzco, many Ayacucho campesinos did engage in processes of organization and mobilization similar to those occurring in other departments. Gathering together for five days of deliberation, campesinos from communities across Ayacucho met in Huamanga in June 1963 to establish the Federación de Campesinos de Ayacucho (Ayacucho Peasant Federation). Forty-five delegates from eighteen communities and haciendas participated in the congress, electing Trotskyist activist and POR-T (Trotskyist Revolutionary Workers Party) member Antonio Cartolín as the federation's president.[12]

During the five days of their congress, the campesinos in attendance agreed on a lengthy plan of action. Among their many resolutions, they pledged to create and arm "peasant militias," self-defense associations that would "protect the peasantry from the crimes of gamonales and government massacres."[13] They demanded material support like seeds, fertilizers, tools, and tractors for peasant communities. They agreed to push for the unionization of all hacienda laborers and demand the immediate nationalization of the foreign-owned International Petroleum Company. And they resolved to press the national government for an immediate amnesty of all rural activists jailed for their political efforts. The most prominent of their many demands, though, was for a "revolutionary agrarian reform" that would end the hacienda system and "deliver land to those who work it."[14] Participants at the congress agreed to encourage campesino land invasions, cease all labor services for hacendados, and abolish all payments and debts owed to hacendados. As they phrased it, "Nobody will give us land if we do not take it with our own hands."[15]

Although the congress made demands of Belaúnde, Federation President Antonio Cartolín was as opposed to the Acción Popular government as his fellow Trotskyist Hugo Blanco. Cartolín told the Trotskyist newspaper *Obrero y Campesino* that "authentic agrarian reform will not be accomplished by this or any other capitalist government."[16] Defining agrarian reform as "taking haciendas away from gamonales, without paying them a cent of indemnity, and delivering them to the peasants and communities who work them, without charge," Cartolín followed the Peruvian Trotskyist line and asserted that peasants themselves would bring about the reform through their own direct action: "We campesinos ourselves will do this. Better said, we are already doing this, through the occupation of land. . . . Land or Death! Venceremos! This is the slogan of Hugo Blanco, and we peasants of Peru have all made it our own."[17]

Assessing the Ayacucho Peasant Federation's work several months after its founding, Cartolín announced an upcoming Second Departmental Peasant Congress.[18] That 1964 congress never happened. Accused first of "intellectually authoring" an attack on two civil guards at the Huanta hacienda Huaynacancha in August 1963, Cartolín soon found himself imprisoned for promoting a violent land seizure in the Apurímac community of Ongoy.[19] With its President Cartolín and its Vice President Máximo Molina both jailed for their involvement in the Ongoy uprising, the Ayacucho Peasant Federation crumbled. Cartolín and Molina retained their leadership positions for several years thereafter; but, working from their distant Arequipa jail, they could do little more than compose political letters and tracts calling for the formation of a revolutionary party. Without its leaders, the Ayacucho Peasant Federation essentially disappeared and remained absent until the Velasco years.[20]

Events at the provincial level closely paralleled those at the departmental one, as Cangallo saw a burst of campesino organizing at the outset of the 1960s. Established in 1959, the Cangallo Provincial Campesino Federation planned its first convention for March 1962. Composing and distributing a flyer addressed to Cangallo's campesinos—specifically naming all of the many communities and annexes inside the district— the provincial federation's leadership committee urged the province's campesinos to attend the convention. The federation's flyer was uncompromisingly militant, asserting anger at socioeconomic abuses and making aggressive demands for change:

For more than 400 years, we have been eagerly awaiting the dawn of justice. Enough is enough. For more than four centuries, we have been suffering the flagellation of barbaric injustice. Enough is enough. We are still living the tragic misery of our lives, cheated and deceived by those who represent bastard interests. Enough is enough. The latifundista gentlemen continue to enrich themselves, exploiting our sweat and the wealth of our land, a docility imposed by the imperialist master of the North who is plundering all of Latin America.

Explaining that congress participants would denounce such abuses and search for a solution, the flyer exhorted Cangallo campesinos to attend. The flyer closed with the words: "For Justice, Land, and Liberty! For Cangallo's Student-Worker-Campesino Front! For the recovery of our Petroleum! For the solidary Provincial Union of Cangallo! For Agrarian Reform! . . . . LAND OR DEATH!"[21]

Though Cangallo's campesinos received their invitations, the convention did not take place; Cangallo's subprefect forbade it. Less than one week before the convention was to begin, Subprefect Edilberto Huamani complained that "the Indians of Pomacocha, invoking false motives of betterment and with purely demagogic ends of a political character, are trying to organize the first convention of campesinos of the Province of Cangallo."[22] He therefore resolved to prohibit any and all campesino assemblies, congresses, or meetings on the Pomacocha estate, the designated site of the convention. Subprefect Huamani's concerns stemmed from two sources. The first source was the hacienda Pomacocha itself. Owned by the same Santa Clara convent that had held Carhuanca's Champacancha hacienda, Pomacocha became Ayacucho's equivalent of Cuzco's La Convención. Campesinos who labored on the hacienda had made early moves to acquire the property, forming a peasant association in 1948 and soliciting the national government to expropriate the hacienda. Organizing in the "Unión Campesina de Pomacocha" in

1959, campesinos on the hacienda resolved to withhold all rent payments, to refuse the provision of their labor services to the convent, and to deny the authority of the hacienda's administrator. Beginning in 1960, Pomacocha campesinos started seizing portions of the hacienda's lands, overtaking the entire property and ousting its administrator in October of that year. Less than two weeks before the scheduled convention, Subprefect Huamani warned that "this subprefecture is aware that on the hacienda Pomacocha, meetings of more than 100 to 200 people are continually taking place, meetings in which agreements are made to stir up the province's Indian masses and create violent excesses." Shortly thereafter, Subprefect Huamani prohibited the convention.[23]

The other source of Subprefect Huamani's concern was Manuel Llamojha Mitma, secretary general of the Cangallo Peasant Federation. A campesino activist from Concepción, Cangallo, Llamojha Mitma was well known to the subprefect and to authorities throughout the province. Since the 1940s, Cangallo hacendados had attempted to check Llamojha's efforts to organize the province's campesinos, initiating numerous—often frivolous—lawsuits against him. Dubbing Llamojha a "communist leader" and the "principal organizer of the Indian masses," Subprefect Huamani shared Cangallo hacendados' concerns about the campesino leader.[24] However reactionary, the subprefect's fears about Llamojha's politics were not completely unfounded. Llamojha ran as a congressional candidate in the 1962 elections, representing the revolutionary Frente de Liberación Nacional (FLN). By 1963, Llamojha had become secretary general of the Confederación Campesina del Perú (CCP). Much later, he joined the Shining Path.[25] Cangallo authorities' concerns about Pomacocha and about Llamojha persisted throughout the 1960s. In his 1965 report to the general director of government and municipalities, Cangallo's subprefect relayed that

. . . there is an individual named MANUEL LLAMOCCA MITMA [*sic*] born and residing in the district of Concepción, Cangallo, who is a communist partisan. Currently a member of the National Confederation of Peruvian Peasants, he regularly makes visits to the districts with the end of agitating the masses to carry out invasions. He also is actively involved with those of the communist tendency who reside on the Hacienda Pomacocha.[26]

The subprefect's charges were highly exaggerated; neither Llamojha nor Pomacocha campesinos were planning an armed struggle or instigating communist subversion. Yet the subprefect's provocative charges were themselves suggestive of a provincial context of considerable rural political activism, energy, and fear. It was within that context that Carhuanca's campesinos lived, argued, and acted.

CARHUANCA:

THE PROMISE AND PRACTICE OF PROGRESS

Although its local impact was slight, Peru's revolutionary left had an unmistakable presence inside Carhuanca. Carhuanquino Pedro Prado was a leader of the left-wing Federation of Students at the Universidad Nacional San Cristóbal de Huamanga (FUSCH) and spent a year in prison for his suspected affiliation with the MIR (the Movement of the Revolutionary Left), the party that launched two of the 1965 guerrilla uprisings. One Carhuanca-born schoolteacher belonged to the Stalinist branch of the Peruvian Communist Party, while Cipriano Meneses and Gothardo Guillén joined the Trotskyist POR-T. These two men were not the district's only Trotskyists. Gothardo's father, Pedro Félix Guillén, served as secretary of campesino affairs in the Trotskyist-controlled Ayacucho Peasant Federation, and Gothardo's cousin Antonio Cartolín Guillén served as that federation's president and as a central-committee member of the Trotskyist POR-T. Cartolín was without doubt the most important Trotskyist in the entire department of Ayacucho as well as the department's most prominent campesino leader, and he was a Carhuanquino.[27]

While Cartolín held a tremendously prominent place inside Ayacucho politics, organizing and mobilizing the department's campesinos, rallying in favor of Trotskyist platforms, and publicly pushing his party's revolutionary demands, he was at best a limited presence inside Carhuanca. Many Carhuanquinos living today do not remember him; only his relatives and men of his generation speak of him with familiarity. Cartolín's inconspicuous status in Carhuanquinos' historical memory stems from the simple reality that Cartolín did very little inside the district. Documentary references to Cartolín's local political efforts are confined to a set of September 1961 telegrams from Carhuanca Governor Davíd Hiyo. Warning Cangallo's subprefect that "Communist politics are reaching Carhuanca," Governor Hiyo asserted that leftist activities were "stirring up the district," and he requested support from the subprefect's office.[28] Hiyo telegrammed the subprefect again the next day, charging that the "communists" Gothardo Guillén and Antonio Cartolín had thrown stones and insults at Primitivo Mayhua's house.[29] A few days after the attack on Mayhua's house, Guillén and Cartolín interrupted a local Acción Popular rally, leading a band of instrument-playing students to the public meeting and disrupting the gathering. That same night, the two men stoned the town hall.[30] Beyond these few scattered incidents, Cartolín is essentially absent from Carhuanca's documentary record.

It was instead Cartolín's cousin, Gothardo Guillén, who proved Carhuanca's most prominent leftist. As early as 1961, Carhuanquino authorities were petitioning Ayacucho's prefect to arrest Guillén on the grounds that he had been uttering "Soviet phrases" inside the district.[31] Carhuanca's governor testified in 1965 that Gothardo Guillén, his brother Agustín, and their father, Pedro Félix Guillén, "have turned into sociopolitical delinquents, as communists and terrorists, imperiling various citizens with this communist propaganda."[32] Carhuanca's mayor similarly complained that Gothardo Guillén and his father "seem to be communist propagandists, operating with terrorism just as the leaders of said sectarian party operate."[33] On another occasion, the district governor complained that Gothardo Guillén was actively promoting "communist propaganda" and threatening to kill the district's parish priest, mayor, governor, and others.[34]

Although the accusation of communism was unquestionably a strategic language of slander inside Carhuanca—with individuals regularly employing the label "communist" to win authorities' intervention against their local enemies—it is certain that Gothardo Guillén's revolutionary political sympathies were real. Cipriano Meneses remembered how both he and Gothardo had sympathized with Trotskyism and felt "ready for world revolution."[35] Cipriano Meneses acted on his sympathies in the countryside: He participated in the land invasions taking place in Huamanguilla, Huanta. His friend Gothardo, in contrast, made the classroom his priority. Gothardo Guillén worked as a teacher at the elementary school in Cocha, a community located thirty kilometers away from Carhuanca in the district of Huambalpa, and he quickly became the subject of complaints from Cocha authorities and many parents of Cocha schoolchildren. Those complaints alleged that Gothardo "taught students not to believe in God's existence, taught against the Catholic religion and against the principle of authority in general, to the extreme of not respecting their own parents."[36] Carhuanca's priest, Father Quintin Arrieta, later testified that Cocha campesinos had informed him that Gothardo "was not fulfilling his duties as a teacher but instead was agitating students, teaching them that God does not exist and that the bishop and priests cheat the pueblo with the aim of exploiting their ignorance."[37] Arrieta also relayed that a police investigation had revealed that Gothardo Guillén was a communist and that he used his classroom as a forum to teach children communist principles and to disbelieve in God, the Virgin, and the saints.

While Gothardo Guillén, his father, his cousin Antonio Cartolín, and his friend Cipriano Meneses all worked to introduce Trotskyism into Carhuanca, and although the district did have other leftist activists like

the Stalinist schoolteacher and the MIR activist Pedro Prado, revolutionary politics made only a slight impact on 1960s Carhuanca. These men
did not win a broad base of support in the district, nor did they lead any
significant local mobilizations. These Carhuanquino leftists failed to ac-
complish much of anything inside their district partly because they too
narrowly conceptualized Peruvian peasant struggles as a fight between
campesinos and hacendados. Antonio Cartolín, for example, defined
agrarian reform strictly as "taking haciendas away from gamonales,
without paying them a cent of indemnity, and delivering them to the
peasants and communities who work them, without charge."[38] By that
definition, Carhuanquinos had already realized agrarian reform back in
1940 when they purchased the Champacancha hacienda. Cartolín's vision certainly applied to the thousands of campesinos invading hacienda
lands across Peru, but that vision did not apply to Carhuanca; having
no hacienda, Carhuanca's reality just did not fit the Trotskyist mold.
Nowhere in Cartolín's writings or speeches did there appear an agenda
for activists or campesinos working and living outside the domination of
haciendas. Cartolín and his fellow leftists saw hacendados as the problem and their eviction as the solution, leaving no room in their platforms
and programs for other rural realities. Carhuanquinos, then, did not
embrace Trotskyism because it had almost nothing to offer them.

Local hatreds likewise checked Trotskyism's appeal inside Carhuanca.
Within the district, there was an unmistakable connection between
Trotskyism and the Guillén family. The Guillén family, though, had
been notorious inside Carhuanca long before its members began promoting Trotskyism. Pedro Félix Guillén struggled throughout his life
to enter the ranks of Carhuanca's local notables, waging endless (and
fruitless) challenges for official positions of authority and regularly petitioning the court for access to lands he believed his enemies had stolen
from him. Guillén was also one of the district's most prominent Apristas
in the 1930s and 1940s, leading Carhuanquinos' efforts to acquire the
Champacancha hacienda. Some Carhuanquinos saw Guillén as a local
hero, dubbing him "Papacha Guillén" because of his commitment to socioeconomic change for Carhuanca.[39] But while he was adored by some
Carhuanquinos, Pedro Félix Guillén was despised by many others. That
sentiment often extended to his son, Gothardo. Interestingly, enmity toward the Guilléns transcended the boundaries of Carhuanca's notable/
nonnotable divide. One elderly Carhuanquino remembered Pedro Félix
Guillén without fondness. "He was a thief, *caramba*! He was the ac-
complice of thieves."[40] Another Carhuanquino recalled that Pedro Félix
Guillén and Luis Allende Ayala had a prolonged fight over the terrain
Ñecercca. This man explained that "Lucho Allende gave an *arriendo*

[land lease] to the Martínez family from Ayacucho. So, Guillén started to fight with Manuel Martínez, and during this fight, Martínez took off part of Guillén's nose!" "With a machete?" I asked. "He bit it off!" came the reply. This Carhuanquino added, "How ugly, eh? He was left with a hole! His whole nose! This man walked around with a little piece of paper over his nose. That's the father of Gothardo Guillén . . . People with bad habits, they think they're powerful. They think they're brought up better than the rest of us, that they're more capable than the rest of us. The whole family has the same face!"[41] A Carhuanquino of quite humble origin said of Pedro Félix Guillén, "I have heard bad things about him. Maybe it's just bad information, but even down in the valley, they always said he was a bad man. . . . People said that he killed a man named Rojas, killed him in the river."[42] Commentaries on Guilléns within the documentary record offer much the same perspective on these men. Father Arrieta cast Pedro Félix Guillén as a "villainous communist leader" and repeated the charges that Guillén had murdered two men and thrown both of their bodies into the Río Pampas.[43]

Still another reason for Trotskyism's limited appeal in Carhuanca centers on religion. Through various actions and incidents, Pedro Félix and Gothardo Guillén cast Catholicism, the Catholic Church, and particularly priests as their political enemies. That enmity had long roots: Pedro Félix Guillén had led Carhuanca's struggle to acquire the Champacancha estate from its ecclesiastical owner, Father Carlos Cárdenas, and his bitter land conflict with Luis Allende Ayala had its origin when Allende Ayala's grandfather Father Luis Allende purchased the terrain Ñeccercca (renaming it San Luis) that Guillén steadfastly insisted was his own. Moreover, as a Carhuanquino whose ancestors were all Carhuanquinos, Pedro Félix Guillén surely felt resentment against the ecclesiastical migrants who came into the district and acquired the large tracts of land and local authority that Guillén himself coveted but never quite attained. His bitter rivalry with the Allende and Romaní families, both of priestly in-migrant origins, suggests as much. Trotskyism's atheistic dictates only added to Pedro Félix Guillén's indignation against Carhuanca's priests. District priest Quintin Arrieta repeatedly denounced the Guilléns for their atheism, complaining that Gothardo Guillén had interrupted holy services by barging into the church during mass, wearing a hat and mocking religion. Arrieta also claimed that Gothardo had physically assaulted the priest who preceded him in Carhuanca. Father Arrieta even denounced Gothardo Guillén before Ayacucho's bishop.[44]

The conflict between the Guillén family and the Catholic Church climaxed in April 1965, when Pedro Félix and Gothardo Guillén assaulted

Father Arrieta. The commander of Carhuanca's civil guard post reported that Father Quintin Arrieta had appeared before him on April 15, 1965, to denounce the Guilléns for assault. The priest reported that on April 13 at 10 p.m., he had left the presbytery to carry out a mass. Father Arrieta relayed that, as he passed by the tower of the old church, the two Guilléns appeared suddenly, armed with sticks and stones. Father Arrieta claimed that Pedro Félix Guillén brutally beat him and then said, "You miserable cleric. I'm going to kill you because you have denounced my son Gothardo Guillén Gómez before the bishop's dispatch." Arrieta also charged that when Pedro Félix Guillén attacked him, Guillén had said, "This is the reward you get for all your preaching against communism."[45] One Carhuanca woman remembered the attack. This woman told me that Pedro Félix Guillén had been in her mother's store that day, drinking chicha. When he saw the priest Quintin Arrieta pass, the drunken Pedro Félix Guillén started hurling insults at the priest and then rushed at him. Seemingly from nowhere, Gothardo appeared and grabbed the ends of the white scarf draped around the priest's neck and pulled, trying to strangle the cleric. That scarf, though, ripped in two, "as though it had been cut by scissors," and the priest was able to escape.[46] Gothardo fled and later asserted that he had not even been in Carhuanca that day. Pedro Félix Guillén, in turn, willingly took the blame for his son.[47]

In this violent conflict between the Guilléns and Father Arrieta, most Carhuanquinos took the side of the priest. A number of Carhuanquino notables penned a letter to Ayacucho's prefect, denouncing the attack on Father Arrieta and countering the many accusations Pedro Félix Guillén had made against the priest. Their letter asserted that "we vigorously protest the denigrating statements made by the criminal Pedro Félix Guillén who stated that, 'our priest is an immoral drunkard.' These are unfounded statements of a fanatical communist, criminal, cattle rustler, pseudo-sorcerer, pseudo-*curandero* [medicine man], and immoral man." They closed their letter with the comment that "Pedro Félix Guillén and his sons Gothardo and Agustín Guillén are eternal enemies of priests and of religion because they are communists."[48]

There were clear class sentiments driving such denunciations; many of Carhuanca's wealthier campesinos thought Pedro Félix Guillén an upstart campesino: He had labored as a mayordomo on the Carrasco haciendas in the early decades of the twentieth century, he initiated countless (unsuccessful) land lawsuits against Carhuanca's most successful land entrepreneur Luis Allende Ayala, and he constantly (if unsuccessfully) sought positions of district authority. Carhuanca's local notables did not want to grant Pedro Félix Guillén inclusion in their ranks, and their alliance with Father Arrieta reflected that stance. Yet Carhuanquino anger at Pedro Félix Guillén is not reducible to class sentiment alone; several poorer Carhuanquinos also testified against the Guilléns at the ensuing trial for the attack on Father Arrieta.[49] The best explanation for those poorer campesinos' anger is religion: They were incensed at the Guilléns' attack on the Catholic Church and its local representative. Though many of these poorer Carhuanquinos may have agreed with Trotskyism's calls for socioeconomic and political justice, most were decidedly less sympathetic toward its local emissaries the Guilléns and their anti-Catholic stances.

While the Guilléns' actions and their Trotskyist philosophy certainly caught many Carhuanquinos' attention, Acción Popular loomed much larger in their lives. The first local documentary references to the party came in August 1961, when the governor of a nearby district complained that two men had appeared in his town, seeking signatures of support for Acción Popular. He did not know their names, but he knew their plans: They were headed for Carhuanca. Within a few months, Acción Popular had gained a strong base of support inside Carhuanca, and the 1962 presidential elections saw much propagandizing in favor of Fernando Belaúnde Terry. Nominated into power by sympathetic authorities at the provincial and departmental levels, Acción Popular took control of Carhuanca's district government in the latter half of the 1960s. Acción Popular thereby became the first party to break Aprista dominance inside Carhuanca.[50]

Carhuanca's Acción Popular sympathizers found their leader in Luis Allende Ayala, the man who was the foremost enemy of Pedro Félix Guillén. Many comuneros saw in Allende the very embodiment of the progress Belaúnde's party promised. Describing the long-dead Allende with much fondness, Hernán Carrillo remembered the man as a dark-skinned, Quechua-speaking peasant who had no more than a single year of elementary education. But Allende, by Don Hernán's telling, bettered himself through hard work and sacrifice. He struggled to educate himself, studying the Bible, the dictionary, and Cervantes's *Don Quijote*. Allende also labored diligently on his land, transforming his San Luis holding into a successful and productive terrain. He proved himself a model campesino and an exemplary authority, winning the esteem of many and gathering an astonishing 150 godchildren over the span of his life.[51] Ricardo Alvarado recalled that Allende "had an orange plantation, you see. After that, he dedicated himself to vegetable cultivation. He was a hard-working campesino. Other campesinos were lazy by contrast. He worked hard."[52] Now, as previous chapters have shown, not all Carhuanquinos held such a view of Luis Allende Ayala. Many of the area's campesinos saw Allende as a tinterillo and gamonal who used his literacy and his positions of authority to cheat poorer comuneros of their land and who ruthlessly exploited the labor of the district's varayocs. Additionally, by the 1940s, Luis Allende had become the most active land entrepreneur in the district, routinely buying and selling Carhuanca land.[53] But whether campesinos admired or despised him, all would concur that Allende was one of Carhuanca's wealthiest campesinos, and his wealth represented the sort of prosperity that his Acción Popular party promised.

Carhuanca's Acción Popular party centered its activities on the most basic of Fernando Belaúnde Terry's many visions: progress. An ideal as hard to define as it was to achieve, progress meant things like infrastructure, education, and sanitation to Carhuanca's Acción Popular supporters. Rufina Enciso served as one of the first Acción Popular authorities in Carhuanca, working as the district's lieutenant governor. She explained that she and the other Acción Popular authorities had fought hard for progress. "After we became authorities, we thought: first, the highway. Second, urbanization. We have to urbanize the people. Third, drinkable water. After that, a high school." Enciso talked at length about Carhuanquinos' 1967 meeting with President Fernando Belaúnde Terry—a meeting treated in the following pages—and she attributed Carhuanca's advances with electricity, education, and infrastructure to him. "Thanks to him, he gave us these things, and we progressed."[54] Local school teacher Alonso Chuchón repeated the same discourse of progress in the Ayacucho newspaper *Paladín*, requesting that Carhuanquinos residing in Ayacucho and Lima make financial donations for the district's public infrastructure projects, "so that such works can result in material and educational progress in the struggle between misery and disgrace."[55]

Although Acción Popular's promise of progress had broad appeal, the practice of progress affected Carhuanquinos unequally: Wealthier campesinos benefited far more than did their poorer neighbors. Conflicts over public works projects made this difference especially clear. While Acción Popular—and its public works program, Cooperación Popular—celebrated notions of common labors for the common good, a disproportionate share of that supposedly common burden fell on Carhuanca's poorest, most Indian, and least powerful campesinos. District comuneros from the community of Saurama, for example, demanded remuneration for their participation in local school construction efforts, participation that their community authorities argued should be provided voluntarily. Those authorities explained to the subprefect that "the subsidy given to said town by the Ministry of Education is only for the purchase of certain materials. The personal labors of the community are understood to be acts of cooperation with the supreme government's National School Construction Plan." These authorities therefore asked the subprefect to sanction protesting Saurama comuneros for their "destructive attitude toward works that serve the common good."[56]

Similar problems emerged regarding Carhuanca's elderly population. Fabian Estrada Pérez complained to Cangallo's subprefect in 1966, asking for guarantees on behalf of his elderly parents. Although Carhuanca's authorities had previously excused his parents' participation in communal labors because of their advanced age, requesting only economic collaboration, the current authorities were insisting that seniors take part in communal manual labors.[57] Teodocio Quijana made similar complaints two years later, asking Ayacucho's prefect to extend protection to his aged father. Explaining that his sixty-five-year-old father was "sickly and of fragile health because of his elderly condition," Quijana charged that Carhuanca's mayor and governor had made excessive demands of his father. "Without taking into consideration my father's delicate health, they are requiring him to participate in public works like the construction of highways, roads, irrigation channels, and schools. . . . By being forced to attend these works, he has been close to death's door." Quijana further asserted that when his father refused to participate in these labors, the district's mayor and governor punished him by seizing his possessions and animals, appropriating the goods for themselves. Quijana complained that, by so doing, these authorities were "taking advantage of the ignorance of this pueblo's residents, on the pretext that they are carrying out work for the public good."[58]

Carhuanca's authorities usually paid such complaints little heed, justifying their demands for unpaid labor through references to the Belaúnde government's platforms and to indigenous custom. Not only did Mayor Luis Allende Ayala minimize Teodocio Quijana's concerns about his father, but he also used the cover of indigenous culture and tradition to excuse Carhuanquino authorities' excessive labor demands. Allende, for example, asserted that while he did indeed oblige participation in public works projects, such participation "conformed to the established customs of the pueblo that have existed since times of yore." He further explained that the area's comuneros were required to maintain roads and irrigation channels and that "by custom, all comuneros work together through the *faena* system, all for works that serve the common good."[59] With such a comment, Allende was not only using indigenous culture to justify the exploitation of indigenous labor, he was also echoing President Belaúnde himself. As Belaúnde phrased it during a campaign visit to Apurímac, "The people have been deprived of their ancient right to elect leaders. They have been humiliated by the rule of strangers, cheated of their property and their meager income. But of one thing they could not be robbed, namely their traditions. They have gone on building roads, schools, churches."[60]

The public works project that most aggravated class and race tensions inside Carhuanca was the project closest to President Fernando Belaúnde Terry's heart: highway construction. Talk of building a highway into Carhuanca turned serious late in 1961, when a group of Carhuanquino local notables founded the Comité Pro-Carretera Vilcashuamán-Carhuanca. With Don Moises Ochoa Guillén—a former air force pilot, a former district authority, and a prominent local intellectual—serving as president of the highway committee and Carhuanca teacher Alonso Chuchón serving as vice president, the highway committee convened a general assembly in Carhuanca in December 1961. The committee members who led that meeting soon asserted that the highway's construction required two sources of support, financial support from the national government and unremunerated labor from Carhuanca's campesinos. Glossing this unpaid physical labor with the patriotic language of the Belaúnde campaign, highway committee members stressed that they would build the highway through "civic action" and requested that the national government provide them with tools, explosives, and civil guards to oversee the labor.[61]

The highway committee made President Belaúnde's programs their own. Writing a letter to the Ayacucho newspaper *Paladín* in February 1968, highway committee vice president Alonso Chuchón explained that "in collaboration with the authorities and through the efforts of Popular Cooperation, we have used civic action to build a further three kilometers of highway, linking up with the nine kilometers built in 1964." He asserted that the highway "will bring material, spiritual, and educational progress" and called on Carhuanquino migrants to help fund the effort. As he phrased it, "Carhuanquinos, your hometown needs you!"[62]

For many of Carhuanca's wealthier local notables, the highway construction effort represented a moment of local, regional, and national glory. Highway construction committee members and district authorities traveled to Vilcashuamán with picks and shovels to inaugurate the labor symbolically, snapping photographs to remember and celebrate their effort. When the construction effort stalled because workers lacked machinery like a tractor and because workers themselves were in short supply, Carhuanca's local notables took a dramatic step: They traveled to Lima to solicit President Belaúnde's help. Carhuanca's authorities went to Lima in March 1967, meeting with Belaúnde to request tractors for the construction effort.[63]

Although sierra campesinos had a long tradition of voyaging to Lima to seek support from national authorities, Carhuanca's local notables felt their trip particularly impressive. Rufina Enciso was serving as Carhuanca's lieutenant governor at the time, and she told Alicia and me how she, Alonso Chuchón, and Luis Allende Ayala had traveled to Lima to seek Belaúnde's support. She explained how they finally won a meeting with Belaúnde himself. "We went down to the golden room, and we talked there. 'All, all, all of Carhuanca is completely abandoned. It's an ancient district, and there is nothing there,' we said. We made him see that." Enciso recalled that, after their meeting, President Belaúnde accompanied the three Carhuanquino authorities out of the meeting room to greet the many Carhuanquino migrants who had accompanied their district authorities to the Presidential Palace. "It was so exciting, *caramba*! We achieved everything through this meeting, and Carhuanca progressed." Showing Alicia and me photos of Luis Allende Ayala shaking hands with Belaúnde, Encisco explained that "it was the first time this class of people had presented themselves to him. Never, ever before had such people met with the president."[64] Because of this meeting, Carhuanca received a tractor from the national government, and the completed highway reached Carhuanca in 1971.[65]

While many of Carhuanca's local notables share Doña Rufina Encisco's proud remembrance of the highway construction effort and the meeting with President Belaúnde, poorer Carhuanquinos were largely opposed to the construction. Some of that steadfast opposition involved fear of the outside. One district resident recalled that Carhuanquinos had gathered in a public assembly underneath the central plaza's huge cedar tree and voiced their opposition to the highway. This man remembered comuneros saying, "No! We must not make this highway. Because when the highway comes, thieves are going to come. And they are going to steal our daughters, our wives, our possessions!"[66] Another Carhuanquino recalled that the highway's opponents feared the road would "bring hunger," as it would allow robbers easy access to Carhuanquinos' crops and animals. Other comuneros feared that the highway would damage their croplands, worrying that the road would pass directly across their holdings.[67] Without question, the biggest concern among poorer Carhuanquinos was the construction labor itself. The work was unpaid labor to be done exclusively by Carhuanca's poorest campesinos, individuals who could least afford to be away from their fields and who could least afford to provide for their own subsistence while away from home. Rufina Encisco remembered how these workers suffered, and her patronizing recollections reveal Carhuanca's deep class divides: "The comuneros, poor little things. Without any money, without anything, they went to work. What could we use to pay them? What could we pay? We didn't even have any money to pay them, poor little things."[68]

Poorer Carhuanquinos' opposition to the unpaid highway labor substantially slowed construction efforts. A group of Carhuanca authorities, residents, and highway committee members penned a letter to the minister of state in June 1964, explaining that, while district comuneros had agreed in two general assemblies "to work with patriotic action" in the construction of the Vilcashuamán–Carhuanca highway, the majority had not complied with their promises. Complaining that only 170 of the 456 laborers had carried out their required week of labor, the letter's signatories requested that the minister provide guarantees to ensure "compliance with our agreements from the sluggish ones who are refusing to attend said labor, as this is a work for the common good and the progress of the pueblo who find themselves in an area far removed from the department capital and isolated from the benefits that civilization brings."[69] The civil guard ultimately provided those guarantees: Guards went from house to house, collecting laborers for the highway. If the designated campesinos refused to comply, the guards imprisoned them in Carhuanca's jail.[70]

Acción Popular's programs generated other conflicts as well, including a sudden surge of antagonism among district communities. Taking a markedly different cast from the campesino–hacendado struggles occurring throughout Peru's central and southern sierra, Carhuanquinos' land conflicts were fought between neighboring communities. The 1960s saw comuneros from Carhuanca's multiple communities push for legal recognition of their communities and particularly of their borders. That push was impelled by the upsurge in national attention to campesinos' land rights, President Belaúnde's support for campesino community recognition, and especially by the fear that neighboring communities could and would encroach on their lands. Comuneros in the district capital worked for Carhuanca's recognition as a *comunidad indígena* in this decade, agreeing to work to this end at a public assembly in September 1962. That assembly named Moises Ochoa Guillén the *gestor* (administrator) of the recognition process and appointed Cecilio Morales and Moises Aguilar as his assistants.[71] Recognition, though, did not come quickly. Three years later, Ochoa Guillén wrote the Bureau of Indian Affairs, asserting that, "the recognition of our community is urgent and indispensable."[72] This delay produced considerable alarm inside Carhuanca, as some Carhuanquinos were well aware that neighboring communities were winning recognition while Carhuanca lagged behind. Ramón Palomino spoke of the recognition process, explaining that "I was worried about the community. It was the year 1964, and Cangallo was recognized as an Indian . . . community. Rayme Alto was getting recognized. And here I was, you see, a *muchacho*, and my pueblo had yet to be recognized."[73] It was not until July 1967 that Carhuanca won its official recognition as an indigenous community.[74] Carhuanquinos' efforts to win community recognition were part of a broad trend among Peru's sierra campesinos. With the Belaúnde government encouraging such recognition efforts, the number of legally recognized rural communities jumped. In the department of Puno, for example, only thirty-eight communities won legal recognition between the 1920s and early 1960s, but 107 communities won such recognition between 1964 and 1968.[75]

These struggles for community recognition, like arguments over public works projects and highway construction, show that Acción Popular affected Carhuanquinos' lives far more than did Trotskyism or any other revolutionary leftist politics in the 1960s. But Acción Popular's power in Carhuanca was not a testament to its popularity with Carhuanquinos. It need be remembered that Carhuanca's men and women—like campesinos throughout Peru—lived under a political system defined largely by the absence of democracy. Although President Belaúnde reintroduced municipal elections into Peru in 1963, those elections did not resolve long-standing problems with local authorities. Historian José Tamayo has argued that, in Cuzco, these municipal elections "left the local government of the 'notables' behind"; but, in Carhuanca, these elections did no such thing. Local notables continued to dominate district office, and Carhuanquinos' dissatisfaction with those appointed authorities surfaced repeatedly in their letters and petitions.[76]

Democracy's absence was perhaps most glaring with regard to Carhuanca's Acción Popular lieutenant governor, Rufina Enciso. Unpopular because of her gender, because of her wealth, and because of her arrogance, Enciso quickly became one of Carhuanca's most hated authorities. Many Carhuanquinos remember how Enciso enforced her commands with a *verga*, a whip fashioned from a bull's penis.[77] Her use of that whip in many ways likened her targets to animals, offering an unspoken racial commentary on her own self-identified whiteness and nonelite Carhuanquinos' Indianness. At the exact same time, the female authority's punitive use of a bull's penis gendered her authority as masculine. One elderly Carhuanquino laughingly recalled that "she used to walk around with a whip! She always used to carry a verga! And caramba! She used that thing to manage the community. . . . *Carajo*! We were all afraid of her!"[78] Another Carhuanquina remembered that Enciso "ordered people to build the highway. She walked around with her whip, and the community obeyed her. She whipped the comuneros who did the highway work, so they took her whip away and threw it in the ravine."[79] Even Enciso herself remembers how she enforced her rule through fear, arguing that her position as a woman demanded as much. Enciso told Alicia and me that "they said, 'What is a woman going to do? How is it possible that they appointed a woman when we have never seen a female authority? What is this? What is this?' But my sign, I'm a Leo, and I have a Leo's character, valiant, I frightened everyone." She also explained to us that she was very strict and serious as an authority and that she ruled with both "*cariño* [affection] and rigor" because if an authority rules only with affection, the people will grievously misbehave. She remembered, "They were so afraid of me!" and she recalled how, when she investigated complaints of wrongdoing, Carhuanquinos would flee in fear, screaming "Aaaaaaayyy! Here she comes!"[80] Though Carhuanquinos feared and loathed Enciso, they had no real recourse against her. She even managed to evade the one departmental investigation that ensued against her, convincing investigators that Carhuanquinos' complaints about her use of a two-meter-long *verga* had to be false, as no bull could possibly have had a penis two meters in length. The investigators quickly dismissed all charges against Enciso.[81] Though the Enciso example is perhaps as extreme as it is strange, it very clearly demonstrates that Acción Popular's prominence and power inside Carhuanca must not be mistaken for popularity.

LURICOCHA COUNTERPOINT

Carhuanca's 1960s history of leftist revolutionaries and staid Belaundista reformers was mirrored inside Luricocha, but the reflection was a distorted one: Whereas Carhuanca's Belaúnde advocates were the district's most affluent and powerful campesinos, the president's staunchest supporters in Luricocha were relatively humble peasants. And while Carhuanca's Trotskyists, Maoists, and Stalinists stood just outside the ranks of local notables, Luricocha's most radical leftists were hacendados. Luricocha's hacendados, however, were a deeply divided class, and those divides showed in their politics. Just as some district hacendados moved to the extremes of the political left, others crept further and further to the right. These landlords' political conservatism grew in direct correlation to increasing peasant activism within the province of Huanta. Fearing that they would lose their land and their power to peasants, such hacendados pushed anticommunism to the fore of their political lives.

Viewed from today's vantage point, Luricocha's most significant 1960s leftists were those of the La Torre family. Carlos La Torre Cárdenas—

son of 1920s activist and Iribamba hacendado Carlos La Torre Cortez—joined the Peruvian Communist Party (PCP) at some point in the 1940s or 1950s, and he remained active in the Ayacucho branch of the party throughout the 1960s and 1970s.[82] Dividing his time between the Iribamba estate, which he inherited together with his brother Luis, and the city of Ayacucho, where he worked as a public employee, La Torre Cárdenas opted for the pro-Soviet PCP-Unidad on the PCP's 1964 split into pro-Soviet and pro-China factions. While La Torre Cárdenas never ascended into the highest ranks of his party, he did make one highly consequential political acquaintance: He befriended Abimael Guzmán Reynoso, the man who would go on to found the Shining Path in 1970. Shortly after Guzmán's 1962 appointment to the Universidad Nacional San Cristóbal de Huamanga, the Arequipa native sought out La Torre Cárdenas because of their joint membership in the presplit PCP. Guzmán and La Torre Cárdenas became fast friends and fast comrades; La Torre Cárdenas and his wife Delia Carrasco regularly invited Guzmán into their Ayacucho home for social visits and to talk politics.[83]

It was on one of those visits that La Torre Cárdenas and his wife introduced Guzmán to their young daughter, Augusta. Augusta shared her father's interests in politics, joining the PCP in 1962 when she was seventeen years old. Guzmán and Augusta soon became romantically involved, and the couple wed in 1964. That same year, both Augusta and Abimael Guzmán joined the pro-China PCP-Bandera Roja (Red Flag), and they traveled to China the following year for training in a Chinese military school. On their return to Ayacucho, Augusta and Abimael dedicated themselves to Maoist politics. Augusta La Torre Carrasco's political abilities and experience, along with her link to Guzmán, led her to assume the second highest post in the PCP-SL from 1980 until her 1988 death.[84]

These Maoist connections are fascinating in retrospect; in the context of 1960s Huanta, however, Maoists and Maoism were far less prominent than Trotskyists and Trotskyism. While Maoists remained concentrated in the urban center of Huamanga, Trotskyists loomed large in the 1963 founding congress of the Federation of Huanta Campesinos. That congress was a massive political event that brought together over 4,000 indigenous campesinos from eighty haciendas and communities across the province. During the four days of the congress, the campesinos in attendance elected the peasant federation's leadership committee and discussed a broad range of issues. While congress participants agreed on a variety of resolutions—extending all the way from guarantees for unimpeded peasant unionization, to the creation of technical training schools in peasant communities, to the construction of homes for orphaned children and the elderly—agrarian reform was their primary concern. Present for the congress, Ayacucho federation president Antonio Cartolín told the newspaper *Obrero y Campesino* that "the congress called for immediate and total agrarian reform, without indemnity payments to gamonales and without cost to communities and campesinos, according to the principle that land should belong to those who work it."[85]

The central figure at the Huanta congress was the provincial federation's secretary general, Jesús Soto Porras. A wealthy campesino residing in the city of Huanta, Jesús Soto was sympathetic to Trotskyism and its mandates, although he did not formally affiliate with the POR-T.[86] During the first years of the 1960s, Soto became the *gestor* (administrator) of the northern Huanta community Qachir and headed comuneros' efforts to acquire the local hacienda. Not limiting his work to Qachir, Soto became involved in campesino–landlord battles throughout the province, traveling to different Huanta haciendas to meet with peasants, offer them legal advice, and encourage their efforts against their landlords. Huanta campesinos, in turn, actively sought out Soto's assistance, traveling to his home in the provincial capital to solicit his advice and support. Valentín Quintero, a Huanta Aprista and urban storeowner, remembered that "Soto walked from hacienda to hacienda" promoting agrarian reform. Quintero recalled that "his house was like a lawyer's office. Everyone from the *alturas* (Huanta highlands) came there, and he oriented them in what they had to do."[87]

The provincial prominence of Trotskyists in general, and of Jesús Soto in particular, combined with the increasing number of Huanta land invasions, triggered a variety of reactions from Luricocha hacendados. Aprista hacendado César Aibar expressed some sympathy toward the idea of agrarian reform. A campesino who had been a tenant on Aibar's Pampay I hacienda recalled that Aibar gathered all his tenants together in a meeting, urging them to press for recognition as a community and donating hacienda land for a school. Aibar even advanced the cause of agrarian reform, explaining the process to campesinos and parceling up his lands for sale to these men and women.[88] Though this campesino's fond recollection of the hacendado Aibar is surely softened by nostalgia, his assertions are supported by documentary evidence. Aibar and several other Huanta hacendados proclaimed that "all political parties and all men of good will are ready to carry the agrarian reform forward." There was, however, a catch. Aibar and his fellow hacendados sought an agrarian reform that would compensate landowners, believing such a law a preferable alternative to the land invasions that would leave hacendados without remuneration for their lands. As the hacendados' communiqué phrased it, "we do not believe that invasions are the best path, because these do not drive anything and they serve no purpose. We believe that this movement of agitating the Indian masses is destined to create an environment for communizing our country." The letter added that "the invasion of our lands does not constitute an act of justice, but rather of injustice, because it deprives us of our livelihoods and reduces our families to misery and creates a new source of economic and social conflicts."[89] The memo closed with an assertion of willingness to cooperate with the Belaúnde government's agrarian reform.

Other Luricocha and Huanta hacendados were decidedly less generous in their assessments of Soto and the issue of agrarian reform. Huanta landlords José Arguedas Pérez and Eduardo La Torre Tello denounced Soto to Huanta's subprefect in January 1963, complaining that Soto was a "propagandist of international communism, who has made the province of Huanta the center of his operations and whose activities are gravely endangering the social order and public peace." They charged that Soto advocated the violent dispossession of hacendados from their estates, theft of hacendados' crops, and the appropriation of hacendados' cattle. The two hacendados also charged that Soto "makes the Indians believe that with the triumph of the Communist Party, lands will be delivered to peasants freely and without any obligation."[90] Hacendados throughout the province made similarly panicked complaints about Soto to Huanta authorities.[91] Although these hacendados' inflammatory claims were grossly exaggerated and reflected more their desperation for military intervention than an accurate description of Jesús Soto's activities or political sympathies, their exaggerations do much to show the conservative political turn of many landlords during the 1960s.

Hacendados in Luricocha need not have worried, for peasants in the district abstained from radical action against their landlords. Although some Luricocha campesinos participated in the Huanta peasant federation's congress, and although some urged their relatives and neighbors to claim hacienda land for themselves, the district saw no hacienda seizures of the kind occurring elsewhere in the province.[92] Luricochanos' abstention from the land recuperation movement of the 1960s reflected neither their disinterest in land ownership nor an uncomplicated devotion to their hacendados. That generalized abstention was instead a product of their commitment to legalism and to faith in President Fernando Belaúnde Terry's Acción Popular program.

The best example of Luricocha campesinos' strong preference for legalism occurred on the Huayllay hacienda. In November 1963, four Huayllay campesinos—two of whom had migrated to Lima and were

back in Huayllay for a visit—convened a meeting of the hacienda's tenants. At that meeting, these four campesinos pressed their neighbors
to take direct, violent action against the hacienda's owners, the Cavero
brothers. Reading out a letter to President Fernando Belaúnde Terry
penned by the leaders of Huayllay's Limeño migrant club, these four
campesinos detailed the Cavero hacendados' abuses. The letter relayed
that the Caveros impeded Huayllay campesinos' access to education,
forced campesinos to work for a substandard wage, and obliged campesinos to transport the hacendados' crops and fertilize their lands without
compensation. The letter continued on, stating that the Caveros forced
campesina women to provide unpaid domestic services, forced tenants
to take care of their cattle and assume full responsibility for lost animals, and used corporal punishment against tenants. After outlining still
more abuses, the letter closed with the request that President Belaúnde
expropriate the hacienda and deliver it to Huayllay's comuneros. Once
they finished reading and translating the letter into Quechua for the assembled campesinos, the four Huayllay men pushed their neighbors to
take aggressive action against the Cavero hacendados: They urged their
fellow comuneros to kill the Caveros and claim the hacienda as their
own.[93]

These plans did not come to fruition. Not only did Huayllay campesinos reject the four men's plans to kill the Cavero hacendados and seize
the hacienda, a number of comuneros actually denounced the meeting's leaders and their murderous plan to the civil guard. Huayllay
campesinos' unwillingness to seize the Caveros' lands did not reflect
their feelings toward the hacendados, nor to hacienda service. Huayllay
campesinos living today remember the Caveros with disdain, and most
enthusiastically embraced the Velasco government's expropriation of the
hacendados' property. Indeed, one of the peasants who denounced the
meeting leaders to the authorities was the very same individual who led
Huayllay's efforts to acquire the Caveros' hacienda under the Velasco
agrarian reform of the 1970s. Comuneros' reluctance to appropriate the
Caveros' property instead came from their insistence on legalism and
their faith in President Belaúnde Terry. Huayllay comuneros likely saw
the hacienda's seizure as dependent on the Caveros' murder—the meeting's leaders certainly suggested as much—and the area's campesinos
were unwilling to commit that violence. That unwillingness emerged in
part because Huayllay's campesinos had already seen just how seriously
Huanta's authorities proceeded in relation to antihacendado violence.
Only four months before the November meeting, civil guard officers had
questioned numerous Huayllay campesinos about an alleged attack on
the hacendado Abelardo Cavero by one of the leaders of the November

meeting. Civil guard officers interrogated numerous Huayllay campesinos about the attack, and while all denied the veracity of Cavero's charges, the very act of questioning was in and of itself a probable deterrent to subsequent violence against the hacendados. Seeing how diligently the civil guard responded to a scuffle, many Huayllay comuneros likely feared how those guards would respond to a double homicide.[94]

Huayllay's campesinos were also staunch in their allegiance to President Belaúnde. The Huayllay migrant society letter to President Belaúnde Terry reflected comuneros' belief in their close relationship with Peru's new leader. The letter read, "In this hour that you, Mr. President, have signaled with the noble scream of a man who wants to redeem forgotten pueblos. . . . THE LAST WILL BE FIRST." Repeating back to Belaúnde his promise that the "land is not of those who hold it, but of those who make it carry out its economic destiny," the letter requested that the president expropriate the Caveros' hacienda.[95] Similar expressions of confidence in Belaúnde came from Huayllay comuneros who petitioned government ministries and agencies for assistance. Huayllay's lieutenant governor, justice of the peace, and municipal agent, for example, lobbied President Belaúnde and the Cooperación Popular program for shovels, hoes, explosives, machinery, and technical direction to complete a highway into Huayllay.[96] Huayllay campesinos constructed President Belaúnde as their ally and their partner, and genuine belief in that calculated construction explains why most Huayllay comuneros proved reluctant to invade the area's haciendas: They thought President Belaúnde would help them win that land legally and peacefully.

Huayllay campesinos were not the only Luricocha peasants to favor legalism over the direct seizure of land. After Pampay II hacendados Eliseo and Juan Mavila claimed that local campesinos had physically attacked them and usurped portions of their land, Pampay II campesinos forcefully asserted their innocence to departmental authorities. In a letter to Ayacucho's prefect, Pampay II campesinos cast themselves as "men who have lived from our honorable work with the sweat of our brows, have never thought of such an invasion; we do not even know what the word implies."[97] The letter's signatories also stressed that the Mavilas had repeatedly frustrated campesinos' fully legal efforts to purchase the hacienda.[98] As was true of Huayllay campesinos, these Pampay II comuneros cast President Belaúnde as their political ally, arguing that the prefect should extend his support to them, as the Belaúnde government had both promised and demanded such support. As they phrased it, "Such realities will not be possible now that we have a Supreme Government that has made social justice its principal bastion and to which we campesinos owe our gratitude."[99]

Committed to legalism and eager to ally with President Fernando Belaúnde Terry, campesinos in Luricocha communities eschewed the revolutionary left's calls for direct action and the seizing of hacienda lands. Rural men and women in communities like Huayllay, Pampay I, and Pampay II were instead prepared to wait for President Belaúnde's promised legal reforms. What is perhaps most surprising is just how long Luricocha campesinos were willing to wait. As late as 1967, district campesinos still regarded Belaúnde as their ally, traveling all the way to Lima to meet with the president in the hopes that he would personally overturn a new provincial land tax.[100] Unfortunately, Belaúnde refused to intervene in that tax case, just as he failed to introduce any meaningful reform into Luricocha. Although Belaúnde passed a limited agrarian reform bill in 1964, that legislation did not affect any Luricocha haciendas. The only Acción Popular promises that Luricocha peasants saw fulfilled were Cooperación Popular's civic action infrastructure projects. Luricocha's campesinos received material support for highway and school construction, providing their own labor for the projects. And much like what transpired in Carhuanca, the civic action scheme produced heated conflicts inside the district's communities, as more privileged authorities expected and demanded that their less powerful neighbors participate in extensive unremunerated labor efforts. Those poorer neighbors, in turn, often protested and refused to participate.[101] Luricocha campesinos appreciated the potential of President Belaúnde, Acción Popular, and Cooperación Popular, but the experience of Belaúnde's rule ultimately proved disappointing. When progressive military officers under the leadership of General Juan Velasco Alvarado ousted Belaúnde from power in 1968, Luricochanos—like Carhuanquinos—made no protest in Belaúnde's support.

CONCLUSIONS

Although President Belaúnde's promises, his Acción Popular party, and his Cooperación Popular program dominated rural Ayacuchanos' lives, the Belaúnde presidency has received decidedly less academic attention than the reforms and programs of the 1968–1980 Revolutionary Government of the Armed Forces. While books and articles on the military government and its reforms are almost too numerous to count, studies specifically devoted to the Belaúnde presidency are scant.[102] This lopsided attention is understandable, given that the military government's reforms were far more comprehensive and radical than those of Belaúnde. Nonetheless, the Belaúnde years need to be taken seriously as a key moment in Peruvian political history. It was with Belaúnde that campesinos in Carhuanca, and throughout the central and southern sierra, had their first real sense of twentieth-century national political inclusion and attention. The Revolutionary Government of the Armed Forces would extend that sense tremendously, but the sentiment began under Belaúnde. Similarly, it was during the Belaúnde presidency that campesinos first confronted the choice between reform and revolution, a choice that anthropologist Linda Seligmann argues was central to the Velasco years.[103]

By recasting the first Belaúnde presidency as a key historical period in which campesinos saw the Peruvian president as their ally and themselves as partners in a push for national socioeconomic change, we can better understand the character of rural men and women's political dreams in the second half of Peru's twentieth century. Certainly, these men and women were eager for agrarian reform, but they were also longing for recognition as citizens worthy of presidential attention and capable of contributing to the nation's progress. Despite the initial promise of the Belaúnde presidency, that recognition failed to materialize. Belaúnde became too mired in congressional power struggles to enact the transformations he had pledged, and his Cooperación Popular program perpetuated and exacerbated longstanding abuses inside rural communities. Graver still, district representatives of Belaúnde's Acción Popular party often proved to be more like old-style gamonales than they did agents of progressive change. And as we will see in the next two chapters, their misdeeds did not go unpunished: Acción Popular authorities were among the very first individuals killed by PCP-SL militants inside Carhuanca. Ayacuchanos had thought Belaúnde's new ideas, new men, and new methods would bring the socioeconomic and political change they so needed and wanted. That change did not come, making the new military government's promises and programs seem all the more urgent.

CHAPTER SIX

Unfinished Revolutions

Ayacucho and the Revolutionary Government of the Armed Forces, 1968–1978

On a January day in 1983, Don Luis Allende Ayala shuffled around Carhuanca's central plaza on his knees, begging forgiveness for his many abuses. Luis Allende was not acting of his own accord; young Carhuanquinos affiliated with the Shining Path had taken Allende from his home at gunpoint and then forced him to kneel and circle the plaza. These Carhuanquinos then shot Allende, instructing all onlookers to leave his body untouched. That order purposefully denied Allende the dignity of burial and transformed his corpse into a warning to others. Similar executions soon followed. Over the next weeks, months, and years, PCP-SL militants assassinated Carhuanca notables Alonso Chuchón, Alejandro Quijano, and Vitalicia Cárdenas. Other local notables, including Rufina Enciso, Augusto Cárdenas, and Erasmo Berrocal among numerous others, survived certain execution only because they escaped the district.[1]

These assassinations marked a bloody and extreme form of what Carhuanquinos had long been demanding: decisive action against abusive local notables. Wealthier and poorer Carhuanquinos alike had sought such action from provincial, departmental, and national officials since the first years of the twentieth century. And for a brief moment in the early 1970s, it appeared that such action was finally about to happen. In 1968, military generals under the leadership of General Juan Velasco Alvarado ousted President Fernando Belaúnde Terry from power and established the Revolutionary Government of the Armed Forces. This regime brought unprecedented government attention to Carhuanca, reversing the long-standing governmental practice of abandon. The Revolutionary Government of the Armed Forces pledged to overhaul local political, economic, and social relations by bringing average campesinos to power in place of the local notables who had so long abused their positions of authority in the district. But before Carhuanca's humble campesinos could begin consolidating their grasp on local political authority, the Revolutionary Government of the Armed Forces backtracked on its reforms and announced its retreat from power. That retreat ushered in a new and devastating phase of politics inside Carhuanca and inside Peru, a period in which militants of the Peruvian Communist Party–Shining Path used brutal violence to oust local notables from power, an ouster that the military government's reforms had promised—but failed—to carry out.

This chapter traces Carhuanquinos' history between 1968 and 1978, one of the most tumultuous and important periods in Peru's republican history. Under General Velasco, the military government introduced a series of progressive reforms, including a comprehensive agrarian reform project, an educational reform, and several economic reforms intended to develop autonomous rather than export-oriented financial growth. Although the military government under Velasco enjoyed tremendous popular support at the outset of its rule, nationwide unrest, disappointment with the reforms, fissures within the military, and economic decline led to Velasco's removal by General Francisco Morales Bermúdez in 1975. This "second phase" of the military government slowed and even reversed some of the Velasco reforms and prepared Peru for a return to electoral democracy in 1980. Discussion of the final two years of military rule, from 1978 to 1980, is reserved for the next chapter.

NATIONAL AND REGIONAL CONTEXTS

Peru's Revolutionary Government of the Armed Forces is best known for its sweeping agrarian reform initiative, a program that accomplished a massive redistribution of land inside Peru. The Revolutionary Government's political reforms have received far less popular and academic attention; but, in districts like Carhuanca, it was those reforms that proved most consequential. The core of these political reforms was participation: The Revolutionary Government sought to incorporate the country's masses into a "social democracy of full participation" by providing humble men and women the chance to take part in the work of governance, extending opportunities for engagement with responsive government agencies, and tackling the perennial problem of abusive local authorities. Here, the bureaucratic agency SINAMOS was a key vehicle of political change. SINAMOS, an organization whose acronym stood for the National System of Support for Social Mobilization but could be read literally as "Without Masters (*sin amos*)," served to educate and orient the population. SINAMOS representatives traveled throughout Peru, visiting communities and towns to inform Peruvians about the military government's reforms.[2]

Along with SINAMOS, the Campesino Community Statute was another crucial instrument of political reform. This law initiated a transformation of traditional structures of rule inside rural communities by introducing popularly elected Administration and Vigilance Councils and a General Assembly of community members, by restricting community membership to full-time residents who made their living exclusively in agriculture, and by restructuring land ownership along communal lines. SINAMOS and the Campesino Community Statute, along with the changes they generated, were not without problems; they sparked both confusion and sharp conflict. But the most devastating shortcoming of these reform efforts was their impermanence. The very political changes that Ayacucho's campesinos had so long been demanding proved fleeting, slowed and then stopped by the military government's "second phase" and the return to democratic rule in 1980. Before laws like the Campesino Community Statute and agencies like SINAMOS had a chance to remake national, regional, and local political relationships, the military government was gone.

The military government's plans for political change appealed to campesinos across Ayacucho, as many peasants longed for action against abusive district authorities. A May 1970 assembly organized by the Ayacucho Agrarian Federation and attended by campesino delegates from Huamanga, Huanta, Cangallo, Fajardo, and La Mar placed the problem of abusive authorities at the very center of its conclusions. The Agrarian Federation president asserted that "governors and mayors were not proceeding as they should," and four of the assembly's five final recommendations addressed the issue of abusive authorities.[3] The military government's reforms promised to rectify these problems of district rule but ultimately failed on that count. PCP-SL militants then took it upon themselves to rid rural zones of abusive local notables, using murder instead of reform. The Truth and Reconciliation Commission found that many campesinos across eastern Cangallo allied with the PCP-SL to win revenge against the wealthier and more powerful members of their communities, people like mayors, governors, and justices of the peace, who were impoverished by national standards but wealthy and powerful by local ones.[4]

FROM ABANDON TO ATTENTION: CARHUANCA

Heralding a sharp reversal in the Peruvian state's long-standing practice of neglect, SINAMOS representatives traveled to Carhuanca in May 1971 to collect Carhuanquinos' opinions about their district's needs. Carhuanca residents—local notables and nonnotables alike—responded enthusiastically. Over 300 men and women from the district gathered to discuss their concerns with those government representatives. Carhuanquinos' primary demand reflected their long-standing neglect by the state: They asked that the government bring a final conclusion to the Champacancha issue. Champacancha was the ex-hacienda once owned by the Santa Clara convent that Carhuanquinos had struggled to purchase in the 1930s.[5] While Champacancha's sale became official in 1940, the government had never clarified the estate's frustratingly ambiguous status. Purchased under the community's name, Champacancha was neither officially private property nor officially communal land. Many Carhuanquinos wanted the land divided out among the over 500 Carhuanquinos who had participated in the estate's purchase, while many others felt the land belonged to the community and should be held communally. Although Carhuanquinos had repeatedly solicited state intervention regarding the estate, government officials had never provided a final decision on the matter.[6] The presence of the SINAMOS representatives that May 1971 day suggested that a long-overdue resolution was coming.

The May 1971 visit by SINAMOS representatives was not an isolated occasion. SINAMOS representatives repeatedly visited the district to give talks and training sessions and to discuss Carhuanca's problems. Additionally, SINAMOS regularly invited a select number of Carhuanquinos to take part in its training sessions in other parts of the province, the department, and even the country.[7] SINAMOS's engagement with Carhuanquinos brought the kind of national inclusion, attention, and participation that district residents had long been denied. Many Carhuanquinos saw SINAMOS as an ally, a partner, and a resource for improving district life. Members of the Huamanga-based mutual aid society, the "Association of Comunero Sons and Daughters of Carhuanca," solicited SINAMOS's presence for a 1972 meeting in Carhuanca, explaining that SINAMOS's attendance would "awaken social sentiment."[8] Even Carhuanquino Trotskyist Antonio Cartolín embraced SINAMOS. Pardoned from his prison sentence by the Velasco government, Cartolín resumed his post as secretary general of the Ayacucho Campesino Federation and accepted a paid position inside SINAMOS.[9]

Such a choice was not unusual; numerous prominent Peruvian leftists
assumed posts within the military government.[10] Perhaps the best proof
of SINAMOS's impact on Carhuanca comes from the individuals whose
power the institution most threatened: local notables. Carhuanca's
wealthiest residents regularly denounced SINAMOS and its representatives, slandering them in an effort to diminish SINAMOS's influence. As
Community President Edilberto Hiyo informed a SINAMOS representative, several Carhuanca notables "always make propaganda against
you, asserting that you are a crazy communist."[11]

Given the unprecedented level of attention and support from the national government, there emerged a climate of reform inside Carhuanca,
wherein many distinct groups of Carhuanquinos pushed for the betterment of their respective communities. Unlike the 1960s efforts of
Carhuanca's Acción Popular authorities, these reformist efforts were advanced and supported by a diverse group of campesinos, rather than just
the district's wealthier, de-Indianized local notables. Rayme Bajo authorities and residents, for example, petitioned the subprefect in September
1973 soliciting support for "the betterment of the pueblo." They wrote
that, "due to the constant enthusiasm that exists in our community,"
they had carried out a number of public works to "achieve progress and
triumph in every aspect of improvements."[12] Other Carhuanquinos took
similarly progressive steps. Forming an "Association of Comunero Sons
and Daughters of Carhuanca," Carhuanca migrants in urban Ayacucho
pressed for things like a new mayor for Carhuanca, potable water, and
reforestation projects.[13] Not since the Tawantinsuyo movement had
there been a similar amount of truly popular political participation inside Carhuanca.

The military government's reforms not only pledged to overhaul political relationships between Carhuanca district and the national state, those
reforms also promised a dramatic transformation of political authority
inside the district. With the military government's reforms, it seemed
that power was finally going to shift out of the hands of Carhuanca's
notoriously abusive local notables and into the hands of the more impoverished, more indigenous Carhuanquino majority. The government's
introduction of the Administration and Vigilance Councils was central
to that shift. The Administration and Vigilance Councils would finally
allow for local democracy, instituting new local authorities who would
be popularly elected, not appointed. Just as crucially, all adult comuneros, regardless of sex or literacy, had the right to vote.[14] Enrique Canales
remembered how Carhuanca's local notables dreaded the prospect of
losing control of the district, and he recalled how the Administration
and Vigilance Council president and his supporters prepared a flyer that

called for popular participation in upcoming communal elections.[15] The leaflet explained that in those elections "poor comuneros and campesinos will end up victorious," defeating "rich, exploitative comuneros."[16] The flyer included a hand-drawn picture of a poncho-clad campesino depositing his vote in a ballot box, and it urged Carhuanca peasants to bring "COMUNRUNAS TO POWER," melding the Spanish word for "common" with the Quechua term for "people." The flyer also asserted that it was "indispensable to give our community new leaders capable of successfully confronting the pueblo's problems. Promoting new groups of leaders is nothing more nor less than injecting fresh blood into the community of Carhuanca." Tellingly, the flyer also referenced the local notables who threatened the election's success. The flyer insisted that interference from "certain elements of those local power groups in decline and partisans of the 'dissolution' of the community" must be prevented, as it was certain that they were going to try to impede the election.[17]

The Administration and Vigilance Councils were only the start of the military government's challenge to local notables' power. Throughout the 1970s, Carhuanquinos levied heated complaints against their district authorities, complaining about those authorities' words, actions, and inactions.[18] Such complaints against abusive authorities were certainly not new inside Carhuanca. As previous chapters have shown, efforts to check abusive behaviors by authorities were constant throughout Carhuanca's twentieth-century history. But, in the 1970s, it seemed that provincial and departmental authorities were finally taking Carhuanquinos' complaints against their local notables seriously, paying attention to the charges and promising action against the offenders.[19]

Cangallo's subprefect Carlos Mújica, for example, made numerous complaints about the province's justices of the peace, repeatedly singling out Luis Allende Ayala as a notorious example of an abusive authority. Subprefect Mújica reported that Cangallo was home to many justices of the peace who were "acting against the humble people of the countryside, as in earlier times, and with counterrevolutionary tendencies, among others Luis Allende of Carhuanca."[20] On another occasion, the subprefect charged that he had received many complaints from campesinos who asserted that Allende impeded them from planting their lands and even ousted them from their properties. Arguing that Allende was "acting against the Revolutionary Government's postulates," the subprefect dubbed Allende a "counterrevolutionary."[21] At still another point, the subprefect charged that Allende had misappropriated almost 20,000 soles during his 1967–1970 tenure as Carhuanca's mayor, and the Cangallo Land Court judge filed a complaint against Allende for judicial interference and usurpation of court authority.[22] Given that Luis Allende had long been the subject of heated complaints from Carhuanquinos and had just as long been reappointed to power by provincial and departmental authorities, these condemnations against Allende from superior authorities were striking. The condemnations suggested that real, meaningful action against abusive authorities was finally going to occur.

Carhuanca's humbler men and women also capitalized on government sympathy to strike out against one particularly powerful group of local notables: teachers. Teachers had long wielded considerable political, economic, and social authority inside Carhuanca. Not only did they earn a salary from the state, their literacy situated them squarely within the district's small privileged elite, just as their role as educators imbued them with social capital and power. Not surprisingly, then, teachers had long been among Carhuanca's most powerful, and most hated, local notables. Back in the 1920s, the teacher Cirilo Patiño had lost his life because of his abuses of power. From the 1930s forward, Augusto Cárdenas, the son of former subprefect Leóncio Cárdenas, had been both a schoolteacher and a prominent local Aprista. Alonso Chuchón, in turn, was both a schoolteacher and one of Carhuanca's wealthiest men, owning a home large enough to serve as a local motel.

Much of the literature on the PCP-SL has focused on teachers as the primary transmitters of Maoist thought and Senderista plans into rural communities, and the next chapter will show that this casting is fundamentally accurate. Yet a focus on Maoist teachers alone gives only a partial vision of schoolteachers and their role during the Velasco years. For while many young educators were indeed sympathizers or even partisans of the PCP-SL, members of an older generation of schoolteachers still employed during the 1970s were often among the most politically conservative members of rural communities. Like their younger and more radical counterparts, these older teachers often objected to the military government and its reforms. But unlike their younger counterparts, who thought the military government unduly staid and even reactionary, older teachers often thought the government far too radical and too leftist, knowing that the regime threatened their power and status.

Those older teachers had good reason to worry. Numerous Carhuanquinos seized on the military government's support to challenge teachers' power inside the district. Carhuanca's humbler men and women repeatedly denounced the district's teachers by criticizing their commitment to teaching, to the military government, and to the district's progress. SINAMOS representatives who visited Carhuanca in May 1971 reported that Carhuanquinos believed teachers to be their community's second biggest problem, preceded only by the Champacancha division. Carhuanca comuneros reiterated their antiteacher complaints just a few months later, demanding the removal of all the teachers working in Carhuanca's elementary school.[23] At a February 1972 public assembly in Carhuanca's plaza, district comuneros repeated their demand to replace all the teachers at Carhuanca's school. Those Carhuanquinos present at the meeting complained that, because most of the school's teachers were themselves from the district, they dedicated more time to their agricultural labors than to teaching. They also complained that the teachers "do not serve the pueblo in anything" and that they were "trying to sabotage the efforts of the president of the community."[24]

Humbler Carhuanquinos had more than just the government's sympathy to support their actions against older teachers; they also had the government's legislation. Here, the military government's Education Reform law was of only minimal importance. That law called for the creation of new school districts, broadened access to education, introduced bilingual education and other curriculum changes, and implemented new teaching practices. Within Carhuanca, the Education Reform led to the reorganization of district school administration and the opening of the district's first secondary school in 1977.[25] But when it came to average Carhuanquinos' challenges against teachers' power, the Campesino Community Statute proved far more consequential than did the Education Reform.

The Campesino Community Statute directly threatened the majority of Carhuanca's older schoolteachers. Although most of the district's teachers were from Carhuanca and had deep familial roots in the district, their very profession as teachers disqualified them from comunero status and all the perquisites that status brought. By the letter of the Campesino Community Statute, only those men and women who earned their living from the land, and not from their work as state employees, qualified as community members. Only community members, in turn, had the right to hold land inside Carhuanca, as it was an official Campesino Community.[26] Many poorer Carhuanquinos were quick to seize on this change, confronting those teachers who had long dominated the district. Two Carhuanca comuneros challenged the teacher Erasmo Berrocal, a member of one of Carhuanca's leading families and a major landholder in the district. These two campesinos complained that Berrocal was trying to seize their landholding, and they argued that, as a teacher, Berrocal was not a comunero and therefore had no right to acquire land inside the community. Numerous others similarly accused Berrocal of holding communal lands in usufruct, of taking control of large extensions of district land, and of illegally distributing communal land among his godchildren. Crucially, all of these complaints stressed that the Campesino Community Statute prohibited such actions by state employees like teachers.[27]

The principal of Carhuanca's boys' school, Alonso Chuchón, similarly found his economic and political status under attack. Two Carhuanca sisters, the illiterate campesina María Ochoa and Victoria Ochoa (the estranged wife of Crisóstomo Romaní), claimed that Chuchón was making illegal claims to their land, and they mobilized Chuchón's status as a teacher against him. On the urging of these sisters and the Administration and Vigilance Council President Edilberto Hiyo, the head of the Ayacucho Ministry of Agriculture and Campesino Communities office visited Carhuanca in June 1971 and notified Chuchón to desist in his land acquisition efforts.[28] After a protracted battle, the Ochoa sisters ultimately won government intervention in their case. The head of Campesino Communities instructed the Ayacucho land court to suspend Chuchón's judicial effort to acquire the land.[29]

The Campesino Community Statute also promised a gradual but nonetheless radical equalization of wealth inside the district. According to the statute, comuneros who owned private plots at the time of the statute's institution were allowed to retain their usufruct rights to their plots, provided that those holdings did not exceed the legally defined "family-sized unit." Control of land in excess of that defined amount was to revert to the community. No communal land could be sold, no new usufruct rights could be established, and existing usufruct rights could not be inherited. As such, on a comunero's death, his or her land would return to the community for collective exploitation. Within a generation, then, private property would cease to exist inside the district, and all comuneros would have equal access to equal amounts of land. Carhuanca's long-standing divides of wealth—divides that separated rich peasants from poor ones and notables from the humble majority—would slowly disappear.

Predictably, Carhuanca's teachers and other local notables were both terrified and outraged by the Campesino Community Statute. Enrique Canales remembered local notables' heated opposition to the law. He explained that "the educated people here in Carhuanca didn't like it. . . . The titles say that on being considered a campesino community, one doesn't leave one's will and testament. Instead, you leave your land for the community, at the hands of the communal authority, so that the communal authority will give it to another person who needs it. This didn't suit the educated people either."[30] Adolfo Urbana similarly recalled that the district's wealthiest residents feared that Carhuanca's status as a campesino community would lead to the communalization of their private plots of land.[31]

Local notables' opposition to the Campesino Community Statute was so heated that a number of them actually proposed Carhuanca's dissolution as a campesino community. Late in May 1972, a group of Carhuanquinos led by the school principal Alonso Chuchón, Governor Néstor Cordero, and Mayor Nicanor Cordero petitioned the minister of agriculture and the head of Campesino Communities to dissolve Carhuanca as a campesino community and to dismantle its communal government. They charged that the Administration and Vigilance Council had brought only "negative results" and that, for that reason, they "seek the extinction or dissolution of the Carhuanca Campesino Community."[32] These notables' fear and anger suggests just how much change the military government's reforms promised (and threatened) to bring.

We should not overstate the promise of the military government's reforms; those reforms did have serious limitations that compromised their effectiveness. Carhuanca's tumultuous history of local conflict by no means ended with the ascension of the military government. In many ways, those disputes actually got worse. Much of this conflict surrounded the issue of agrarian reform. Like many districts throughout rural Peru, Carhuanca was not a direct beneficiary of the military government's agrarian reform. Because Carhuanquinos had purchased the Champacancha estate in 1940, their district was no longer home to the kinds of haciendas that the military government expropriated in other parts of Peru. But even though areas like Carhuanca were not formally included in the military government's agrarian reform project, that reform still greatly affected local land tenure relationships. Old land conflicts between Carhuanca's various communities, between neighbors, and within Carhuanca families flared up, while new land fights erupted.[33]

Such conflicts between and within communities and families were of course nothing new. Across the entire twentieth century, land fights had been a constant in Carhuanca life. Two factors did, however, set the conflicts of the 1970s apart from previous land tensions. First, there were new expectations of government intervention and support for the protagonists. Evidence of such expectation is found in Carhuanquinos' quick and repeated appropriation of the military government's language. Velasco's agrarian reform law pledged to restore land to those peasants who worked it, and Carhuanca men and women regularly mobilized that pledge to bolster their land claims. One example came with Cecilio Rojas's 1975 complaint about his plot of land, Mocchayocc. Rojas directly invoked government discourse, asserting that he sought protection of his possession in concordance "with the postulates of the Peruvian

Revolution that 'land is for those who work it.'"[34] Other similar examples were legion.[35] These conflicts were also different from earlier ones because government support actually *was* often forthcoming. Unlike the lawsuits of previous decades that regularly dragged on for decades and decades without resolution, there were frequent rulings in these cases as well as the official termination of long-unresolved conflicts from earlier decades.[36] While welcome, that decisive government action regarding land claims gave added urgency to long-standing fights over land.

Reinvigorated conflicts over land were rendered still more troubling because of the apparent contradictions within the military government's land laws. How, for example, was land supposed to go to its tiller if all land inside a community was to be held communally, as the Campesino Community Statute dictated? Nowhere was that contradiction more problematic than in the Champacancha case. While many Carhuanquinos wanted the land divided among its original purchasers, many others believed the land was now official community property because of the Campesino Community Statute. Edilberto Hiyo was one such man. Hiyo wrote the director of the Department of Communities in 1971 to contest the Carhuanquino mayor's complaint that he was refusing to distribute Champacancha lands. Hiyo charged that the mayor's complaint was "completely false in all its parts, as the articles contained in the Statute of Peru's Campesino Communities terminally prohibit the division and fragmentation of communal lands."[37] Though a few Carhuanquinos tried to stake out a conciliatory arrangement that would parcel out land to purchasers but retain some sections for communal use, Carhuanca comuneros remained divided.[38] To this day, the Champacancha lands remain in dispute. Although Carhuanquinos favoring collectivization of the land had the Campesino Community Statute on their side, government officials were reluctant to enforce that statute's rules.[39] The contradictions among different laws, like the contradictions between a given law's stipulations and its application, generated considerable frustration and anger inside Carhuanca. Those contradictions also impeded the path of meaningful and permanent reform within the district, and within Peru, limiting how much change the military government could actually bring about.

The limits, contradictions, and shortcomings of the Revolutionary Government's reforms were significant, but the gravest shortcoming of those government reforms was their impermanence. Through SINAMOS, the Campesino Community Statute, and concerted government criticism of abusive local authorities, it seemed that Peru's national government was finally set to take dramatic action against the political, economic, and social injustices that had plagued Carhuanca across the twentieth century. The military government's reforms promised to reduce and eventually eradicate the inequalities between notables and nonnotables that had fostered the abuses inherent in gamonalismo. But the Revolutionary Government of the Armed Forces withdrew from power before its promised actions came to fruition. From February 1977, when the military government called for the election of a Constitutional Assembly, the Revolutionary Government of the Armed Forces slowly retreated from power, a retreat that was finalized with the 1980 presidential elections. During that three-year withdrawal, the military government provided less and less support for its more progressive reforms, slowly bringing them to an unceremonious end. By the time the military formally stepped down from power, Carhuanca's local notables were poised to regain their hold on district authority.

Tellingly, the PCP-SL's earliest actions inside Carhuanca targeted those very same local notables. The first Carhuanquino whom the PCP-SL attacked was Luis Allende Ayala, the same abusive authority whom military government officials had deemed "counterrevolutionary" and criticized for his mistreatment of humble district peasants. PCP-SL militants soon targeted other notorious district authorities. One of those authorities was longtime authority Honorato Hiyo, father of the far more progressive Velasco sympathizer Edilberto Hiyo. One elderly Carhuanca woman remembered, "Honorato Hiyo, he was rude. He was an authority, judge, governor. He was rude and arrogant."[40] For that reason, the woman explained, Senderistas killed him. Another woman explained the reason for Mayor Alejandro Quijana's death, stating, "Alejandro Quijana was mayor. The state had sent seeds for the poor and the elderly, but he didn't want to give the seeds to them, and he kept them. He didn't distribute them. Because of that, they entered his house at night and took him out. They gave the community everything that he had been keeping from them, even broad beans."[41] One Carhuanquino who was himself a local notable and an authority in the 1960s had a different perspective on the PCP-SL's first murders. He said, "They killed Luis Allende. They killed Mayor Alejandro Quijana. After that, they killed Alonso Chuchón. They killed only the best people."[42]

These local notables had long abused their positions of authority to appropriate land and acquire wealth at their poorer neighbors' expense, and many Carhuanquinos explain Senderistas' actions by referencing notables' misdeeds. Several Carhuanquinos blamed Luis Allende's abuses of his poorer neighbors for his death. One Carhuanquino relayed that Allende "was a humble man, but he always fought with others because he gave only two soles to work on his land . . . The *terrucos* (terrorists) killed him for that."[43] Another Carhuanquina recalled that "when animals entered onto his land, he made their owners do work for him. They had to make chicha, grind wheat. He charged for pasture rights. The people complained because of that, because he was bad, and they took him from his house by day, and they killed him."[44] There is no doubt that Allende was Carhuanca's most active land entrepreneur. From the 1930s through the 1970s, Allende bought and sold more Carhuanca terrains than any other district comunero. His purchases and sales embittered many Carhuanquinos; many asserted that his purchases and sales were based on falsified documentation and theft. Many others resented the way Allende's land deals took advantage of and exacerbated Carhuanquinos' poverty.[45] The notarized words of one Carhuanquino were telling: He feared he would "be victimized by Don Luis Allende Ayala who uses every means possible to appropriate these pieces of land."[46] It is probably no accident that many district residents suspect this particular Carhuanquino's son of having ordered Luis Allende's murder.

Luis Allende was not an isolated example. PCP-SL militants killed the wealthy teacher Alonso Chuchón for much the same reason, while Erasmo Berrocal and Rufina Enciso escaped death only by fleeing the district.[47] Many Carhuanquinos similarly attribute Vitalicia Cárdenas's death to her land greed. As the daughter of Cangallo's former subprefect Leóncio Cárdenas and the sister of prominent schoolteacher Augusto Cárdenas, Vitalicia managed to acquire a significant amount of land inside the district. Like Allende, Vitalicia was also involved in numerous land conflicts, and she also was notoriously protective of her land's borders.[48] One Carhuanca woman told Alicia and me that Vitalicia Cárdenas was "*muy mala*" (very bad) and that she guarded her land jealously, punishing anyone whose animals strayed onto her land to pasture or who themselves wandered onto her property to collect firewood. By this woman's telling, Senderistas killed Vitalicia Cárdenas for such behavior, punishing an abusive landholder in a way that the military government's reforms had not.[49]

Although PCP-SL militants' first actions represented a violent completion of the military government's failed reforms, it needs to be stressed that those militants had no sympathy for the military government itself. Senderistas' discourse deemed the Revolutionary Government of the Armed Forces authoritarian and reactionary, and their war sought to destroy the very state that the military government had tried to build. Senderistas' disdain for the military government is apparent from the fact that the PCP-SL's early targets in Carhuanca included the men most sympathetic to the Revolutionary Government of the Armed Forces. Don Edilberto Hiyo, the first president of the Administration and Vigilance

Council, received early and repeated threats from Sendero and ultimately fled to Lima to save his own life. Adolfo Urbana, a government-employed school inspector, a speaker at many SINAMOS training sessions, and a staunch supporter of the Velasco regime, was likewise singled out for attack. Faced with multiple death threats from the late 1970s onward, Urbana fled Carhuanca for Lima shortly after the PCP-SL declared its "People's War."[50]

LURICOCHA COUNTERPOINT

Luricochanos' experience of military government reform differed enormously from that of Carhuanquinos. Whereas Carhuanca was essentially untouched by the agrarian reform law, that same law brought dramatic changes into Luricocha. Yet, for all their differences, one central point remains true of both districts: PCP-SL militants found their entry point into local life through a bloody completion of the work the Revolutionary Government had promised, but ultimately failed, to do. This point is a contentious one, as proved sadly clear to me during my brief interview with Pampay campesino Lucio Arroyo. Jumping up from his place beside me, Don Lucio punched his hands to his hips and abruptly ended our interview. He raised his voice to say, "That's all, *gringa*!" and then hurriedly ushered my friend Reina Vargas and me out of his home in the rural Luricocha community of Pampay. Don Lucio, Reina, and I had been talking about the military government's agrarian reform, and I had been asking pointed questions about Luricocha campesinos' opposition to elements of the agrarian reform law. Don Lucio's sudden termination of our conversation was as unsettling as it was unexpected, and once outside his home I bewilderedly asked Reina what I had done, what I had said to so upset the man. Reina shrugged and told me I had been "*tocando carne*," sticking my finger in a still-open wound. I had asked one too many questions about the local conflicts generated and exacerbated by the Velasco reforms.[51]

Don Lucio's sharp reaction to my questions about the local impact of the agrarian reform was one I encountered repeatedly during my interviews in Luricocha. Campesino after campesino in the Luricocha communities of Huayllay and Pampay adhered to a specific script about President Velasco and his reforms, calling Velasco the man who had liberated them from slavery and citing the agrarian reform as the instrument of their salvation. When I questioned that perspective with documents detailing the problems of the military government's reforms, I met opposition. My fruitful interviews with an elderly Huayllay campesino, for example, came to an end once I began asking specific questions about local conflicts generated by Velasco's administrative and economic reforms. This man who had been so very eager to tell me of Huayllay's hacendados, the community's official recognition, and even Huayllay's colonial past essentially ended our research relationship after I shared several photocopied documents that challenged his romantic portrayal of the Velasco years in Huayllay. This man never again sat down to speak with me; he instead regularly postponed or cancelled our scheduled conversations.[52] When I showed these same documents to another Huayllay campesino, this second man conceded that the reforms had generated local strife, but he then stressed that Huayllay's comuneros had quickly transcended that conflict and had been united ever since.[53] Another example of formulaic responses came when I interviewed a Pampay campesino about Velasco's agrarian reform. This man spoke at length of the frustrations and failures of the agrarian production cooperative created by Velasco's agrarian reform but then insisted that "Velasco liberated us. He gave us our liberty from the *patrones*. We have been free ever since the agrarian reform happened."[54]

The best explanation for these responses came from my friend Reina. My questions about the Revolutionary Government's reforms were "touching an open wound," treading on subject matter that was still too sensitive to probe. That wound had two sources. One source is loss: By presenting me with a strictly heroic portrait of the military government, campesinos in Luricocha were mourning and honoring the one government that had sided with them and promised them thoroughgoing change. Facing the past, campesinos' recollections are full of painful nostalgia for the years preceding the horror of the Shining Path War. Facing the future, these memories serve as morality tales, describing what an ideal government should be and glossing over the very serious problems generated by that government's reforms.[55] The other source of this wound is remorse: Shining Path militants took full advantage of the conflicts generated and aggravated by the military government's reforms, and their first actions included a twisted completion of those reforms through violence. That troubling and uncomfortable connection between the military's reforms and Shining Path violence—between the reforms that promised so much good and the violence that brought such unrelenting horror—compels silence.

Ironically, for all their warm recollections of the military government, Luricocha campesinos actually had a violent introduction to the Revolutionary Government of the Armed Forces and its reforms. The first military government reform to affect their lives was a law Luricochanos greeted with almost universal anger: Decree Law 006-69.

Promulgated in March 1969, this law required secondary students to pay for any course they had failed and needed to repeat. The obligatory payment was 100 soles a month, a hefty sum for most campesino families. Protests against this law grew steadily and ultimately turned violent in June 1969. On the 21st of that month, thousands of campesinos stormed Huanta's central plaza. Civil guards responded first with tear gas, then with bullets.[56] Lucio Arroyo was among the wounded; he was shot in the foot and remains disabled to this day.[57] Pampay campesino Silvio Medina recalled that "the police started to shoot at us with bullets. And the people only had stones, slingshots and stones, nothing more." By the end of the day, eighteen campesinos were dead, and sixty-six were wounded.[58]

To Luricocha Maoists like Augusta La Torre and her husband Abimael Guzmán, the 1969 education uprising showed the revolutionary potential of Huanta campesinos.[59] The uprising, however, meant something entirely different to most Luricocha and Huanta peasants. To the province's campesinos, the uprising was primarily about their friendship and political alliance with a young Huanta lawyer named Mario Cavalcanti. That alliance had begun back in 1967, when several Huanta campesinos traveled to Lima to seek exoneration from a new property tax. Cavalcanti explained that "a commission of campesino leaders came to Lima, but they didn't know how to enter the palace . . . so they looked for me."[60] Cavalcanti returned home to Huanta soon thereafter, and he made repeated visits to various Huanta communities to assist campesinos with their legal troubles. Those communities included haciendas in Luricocha district. Lucio Arroyo remembered that Cavalcanti "always, always came. And before, we used to have a meeting every eight days, all the community, all the members."[61] Pampay campesino Silvio Medina similarly recalled Cavalcanti's relationship with Huanta campesinos, stating: "He was our defender."[62]

Cavalcanti formalized that role of "defender" when he became the legal adviser to the Association of Campesinos of Huanta Province. In that post, Cavalcanti represented approximately 8,000 Huanta campesinos on a number of issues, organizing meetings and speaking with provincial authorities about matters like irrigation, highway construction, and education issues, among others. Cavalcanti's role as legal adviser grew even more important with the emergence of protests over Decree Law 006-69. By April, the Huanta Campesino Association formed the Sole Committee for the Struggle for Free Education to protest against the law. Similar protests against the law were occurring throughout the country, but mobilization against the law was strongest in Huamanga and in Huanta.[63] Protest against the law escalated in June 1969, when a group of Huanta secondary students were expelled from their school for refusing to pay the fees demanded by Decree Law 006. A student protest and clash with police followed the expulsion, and Huanta high school students declared themselves on indefinite strike. Mario Cavalcanti played a prominent role in these protests, helping convene informational meetings about the law and discussing the legislation with the Huanta subprefect and Ayacucho prefect.[64]

The protests reached their bloody climax because police arrested Mario Cavalcanti and two other protest leaders, flying them to Lima. Shortly thereafter, a group of Huanta campesinos took the subprefect hostage in reaction to Cavalcanti's arrest. With the subprefect's capture, a Huanta civil guard sergeant sent an urgent telegram to Ayacucho, warning that Huanta's civil guard required immediate reinforcements or the entire town would "disappear."[65] Those reinforcements arrived on the same day that hundreds of Huanta campesinos streamed into Huanta city for an emergency meeting convened by the Sole Committee. Lucio Arroyo told me, "We went there, for a meeting. Everyone, everyone. Not just Pampay, not just Llanza. All of Huanta."[66] Silvio Medina nodded when I asked him if he had attended the protest. "Yes, I went," he said. "The whole highway was full. People from everyplace went, more from here went."[67]

Importantly, many Luricocha campesinos remember the uprising more as their defense of Mario Cavalcanti than as a protest over the education law. Lucio Arroyo spoke in detail of Cavalcanti and recalled the protest over what he called "Decree 006"—but his recollections were less clear over the substance of that decree. "This, it was 006. It was about water, they wanted to shut it off. We don't remember anymore, not anymore. We've forgotten. It was about water." Don Lucio nodded and agreed when I suggested the decree was about education rather than water, but he again stressed what was most important: Cavalcanti himself. "The people had listened to him, they had seen how it would be, and then he was arrested, and they were attached to him. Not just this community, but the whole community of Huanta. . . . All of us, all of us. Every last one of us was with him."[68] Silvio Medina's recollection of the protest likewise emphasized Cavalcanti.[69]

The 1969 uprising marked an ironic start to the Revolutionary Government's tenure, for while Luricocha and Huanta campesinos vigorously protested the military government's education law and Cavalcanti's arrest, their opposition to the military government was not long lasting. Agrarian reform was the reason. The Revolutionary Government of the Armed Forces enacted one of Latin America's most comprehensive agrarian reform projects just days after the education riots.[70] Within Luricocha, the agrarian reform brought about tremendous changes in land tenure. Many of those changes occurred with the establishment of one of Ayacucho's six Agrarian Production Cooperatives (CAPs), the CAP Gervasio Santillana. The CAP Gervasio Santillana came into official existence in June 1973 and ultimately included nineteen former haciendas, 157 members, and a total of the 2,952 hectares of land.[71] Although the vast majority of Luricochanos were thrilled about the idea of agrarian reform, the practice of reform was often frustrating and even maddening. This was especially true for those campesinos affected by the CAP Gervasio Santillana.

Many of the Luricocha campesinos included in the CAP Gervasio Santillana quickly came to resent the cooperative itself. Imposed by military government leaders who wanted to increase rural productivity by replicating communist countries' experiments with large-scale collective agriculture, agrarian production cooperatives held little appeal for most sierra campesinos, who had long cultivated land in individual parcels. Because of peasants' general preference for individual over collective production, the CAP Gervasio Santillana triggered conflicts linked to questions of ownership and profit. Many CAP Gervasio Santillana members, for example, believed that urban functionaries were taking advantage of them, transporting their products to Lima without first weighing them so as to shortchange cooperative members on the resulting profit.[72] There were also heated conflicts about ownership rights. Four days before Christmas 1975, the CAP Gervasio Santillana's director, a Cuzco agronomist named Ezequiel Pantani, traveled to Pampay to collect wheat and garbanzo seeds from cooperative members. The seed collection was a matter of much contention, as many Pampay campesinos felt that the seeds should remain in their possession and not go to the cooperative. When Pantani finally received the seeds from the CAP's council members, a group of ten campesinos attacked his truck, hurling stones at the vehicle while others climbed in and unloaded the seeds from the vehicle.[73]

Another problem with the CAP involved the question of autonomy. For many campesinos, agrarian reform was supposed to entail freedom from an hacendado's orders and obligations, but the CAP brought no such freedom. Each CAP had a director—usually a professional technician with a degree in agronomy or veterinary medicine—selected by the Ministry of Agriculture, and those directors made decisions and gave orders much like the hacendados of times past. Many members of the CAP Gervasio Santillana resented cooperative director Ezequiel Pantani for this very reason. One group of CAP members, for example, charged that Pantani mismanaged the cooperative's production and marketing. These men went so far as to assert that Pantani "commits abuses with the members of the very same cooperative, making them work for free."[74] Even those fond of the CAP's director bristled at the requirements imposed on them. Silvio Medina recalled that "it was annoying. At any moment, they could call on us and we had to go to a meeting. So, we lost time. Sometimes the meetings didn't even happen."[75]

The CAP also generated considerable tensions between members. Most of these conflicts were waged between the member-elected Administration and Vigilance Council and the cooperative's rank and file. A number of cooperative members denounced the campesinos who comprised the Administration and Vigilance Council, accusing them of being nothing more than Director Pantani's "accomplices."[76] Those leaders themselves regularly criticized their fellow cooperative members. In 1975, the CAP's Administration Council president and secretary charged that the cooperative members Víctor Aliendres Ñaupa and José Teodoro Quispe Cusichi were flouting their responsibilities. Not only had these two men failed to participate in their obligatory irrigation duties, they had also given "insolent" responses to the Administration Council's work directives. The Administration Council president and secretary therefore asked the subprefect to inflict "the most drastic punishment that your dispatch would contemplate."[77] These conflicts among cooperative members carried serious consequences as members could demand the ouster of their neighbors from the CAP. The CAP Gervasio Santillana's members agreed to do just that, ousting the CAP member Elías Mallqui Cárdenas from the cooperative for "failing to carry out the duties contingent on him as a beneficiary of the agrarian reform."[78] Such expulsion was no small matter; Mallqui held approximately two hectares of land, and following his ouster that land was to be cultivated by other members of the cooperative.

The CAP Gervasio Santillana generated equally serious conflicts between those campesinos who belonged to the cooperative and those who did not. Campesinos from the Luricocha community of Coraceros complained that agrarian reform functionaries had repeatedly pressured them to join the cooperative, even though the cooperative was an administrative and economic failure. They charged that the functionaries had coerced, manipulated, and even lied to them, trying to get them to join the cooperative. Campesinos from this same community also complained that, while they alone had constructed and maintained an irrigation canal, cooperative members were unjustly claiming preferential rights to the use of the water.[79]

Tensions between cooperative members and nonmembers were especially heated over the matter of pasture rights. Most of the men and women who belonged to the CAP Gervasio Santillana believed that they should have exclusive right to the cooperative's pasture lands. They, after all, were the ones who labored the cooperative's lands, and they were the ones responsible for paying off the cooperative's debts. If campesinos who did not belong to the cooperative wanted to pasture their animals on cooperative land, they should have to pay for that privilege and be held responsible for any damages incurred to crop land. To enforce the CAP's exclusive pasture rights, the cooperative's president rounded up all foreign cattle in March 1977, corralling all animals found on cooperative land that did not belong to CAP members. Nonmembers from communities surrounding the cooperative were then informed that they would have to pay a fee to win their animals' release.[80] Campesinos who did not belong to the CAP were quick to protest the roundup, deeming such pasturing fees a vestige of hacienda times. These nonmembers petitioned the Ayacucho prefect immediately after the roundup, stating, "We consider these actions typical counterrevolutionary acts, given that they want to revive customs already superseded."[81]

Anger at the CAP Gervasio Santillana provided PCP-SL militants with an entry point into Luricocha life. Plagued by these conflicts, by theft, and by the outflow of labor to jungle plantations, the CAP's production faltered, and the CAP Gervasio Santillana began to collapse. The 1978 death of Director Pantani pushed the cooperative toward its ultimate demise. Transporting the cooperative's wheat and potato yields to Lima, Pantani died when his truck overturned. Don Silvio saw Pantani's death as the end of the CAP Gervasio Santillana. "He died. And with that, the cooperative ended. After that, there were others, but they just were not like him."[82] The CAP faltered badly, and many members formally petitioned for their community's formal separation from the cooperative. Yet the CAP Gervasio Santillana hobbled on into the early 1980s.[83] Here, PCP-SL militants found an opportunity. Recognizing the anger and frustration that the military government's agrarian cooperatives had created, PCP-SL militants dubbed the agrarian reform a new form of feudalism and demanded the breakup of the CAP Gervasio Santillana's lands. Shining Path rebels then divided and distributed some of the cooperative's lands themselves.[84]

Similar opportunities for PCP-SL militants arose from the conflicts that ensued inside Luricocha campesino communities distant from the CAP Gervasio Santillana. Although the military government favored cooperatives for land redistribution, it did sometimes distribute lands to campesino communities. Such was the case in the Luricocha community of Huayllay. Agrarian reform officials adjudicated the Huayllay hacienda and delivered it to the area's campesinos in January 1973.[85] The hacienda's expropriation was of monumental importance to Huayllay campesinos; many of the community's campesinos remember that expropriation as the moment they were delivered from slavery. Just as critical and consequential as the disappearance of the hacienda was the August 1975 transformation of Huayllay into an official campesino community, structured and ruled in accordance with the military government's Campesino Community Statute.[86]

While Huayllay's campesinos voted unanimously to accept its change into an official campesino community, not all comuneros eagerly endorsed the stipulations of the Campesino Community Statute. As in Carhuanca, the notion of communal land proved particularly controversial. One Huayllay campesina complained that her opposition to the incorporation of her land plot into Huayllay's communal holdings led the community's authorities to insult, threaten, and rob her and to uproot her crops. Charging that Huayllay's authorities were trying to "appropriate the goods of every poor family," this woman requested that the subprefect guarantee her safety.[87] A peasant named Casiano Inga, in turn, made a formal complaint against Huayllay's new communal authorities. Inga charged that these men had been extorting Huayllay's comuneros, obliging them to donate large quantities of barley for the planting of communal lands. By Inga's telling, those comuneros who refused to provide the barley were subject to aggression and abuses from Huayllay's new authorities.[88]

These reform-generated conflicts were significant; but, as was true in the Carhuanca case, the military government's greatest shortcoming in Huayllay was its impermanence. One Huayllay man brought this problem of impermanence to the foreground, a campesino named Máximo Ayala. Much like the abusive local notables who populated Carhuanca but were comparatively rare in Luricocha, Ayala was a relatively wealthy campesino who dominated positions of appointed authority in Huayllay prior to the 1970s. One Huayllay man recalled that Ayala was a *malo* (a bad man) who always tried to take advantage of comuneros, while another comunero told me that Ayala was a "semi-gamonal" and a tinterillo who had long monopolized authority positions in Huayllay. "His whole life, he was an authority, justice of the peace," this man told me of Ayala, "he never wanted to leave that post."[89] Not surprisingly, Ayala struggled to retain his privilege by fighting the military government's reforms. As one comunero speaking in 1975 phrased it, Ayala was "opposed to the current revolutionary process and the Annex of Huayllay's progress."[90]

Ayala proved a steadfast opponent of the military government, its reforms, and its local supporters in Huayllay. Ayala, for example, worked against the agrarian reform, fearing that his own large land plot would be subject to expropriation. One Huayllay campesino told me that Ayala "didn't want the reform. He spoke against it. He basically spoke against the government."[91] Several Huayllay campesinos reported that Ayala tried to organize Huayllay comuneros against the agrarian reform, visiting their homes at night to denounce the reform. Ayala not only fought the military government's reforms, he also attacked the government's local supporters. Repeatedly denouncing Huayllay's new communal authorities as communists, Ayala made numerous complaints against the community's leaders. Ayala's charges were especially sharp against Huayllay's teacher, Aniceto Cisneros, a man closely allied with both the community's authorities and the Velasco government. Ayala made a formal legal complaint against Cisneros in 1975, asserting that Cisneros had "adopted a dangerous and hateful role," as the leader of Huayllay's campesinos.[92] Ayala also physically assaulted one Huayllay authority, threatening to do the same to others.[93]

Huayllay's communal authorities and comuneros looked to the state for assistance against Ayala, and they were quick to receive the support they sought. Writing Huanta's subprefect in July 1973, a group of Huayllay campesinos charged that Ayala had been appointed to his post as justice of the peace with neither the consent nor even the knowledge of the community, manipulating his relationship with the governor of Luricocha to win the post. Listing Ayala's misdeeds, they asked the subprefect to replace him. Comuneros and authorities made similar complaints to the subprefect again in August 1975. State officials were quick to attend to the campesinos' complaints. The regional agrarian reform office responded immediately to the Huayllay petition, instructing Ayala to abstain from harassing schoolchildren's parents.[94] The Luricocha civil guard proved similarly sympathetic. After Huayllay's authorities imprisoned Ayala in the community's jail for being "contrary to the community's progress," civil guard officers interrogated Ayala and chastised him for his counterrevolutionary actions. Following the interrogation, the civil guard officer put Ayala into the subprefect's custody, noting that he had been "detected as an instigator contrary to the agrarian reform and an agitator of the Community of Huayllay Annex."[95]

Just as significant as the military government's quick and decisive response was the fact that the government's decided support for campesinos was unmistakably fleeting. By the time the Morales Bermúdez government was organizing its departure from national power, Máximo Ayala had returned to a position of formal authority inside Huayllay, serving as justice of the peace. Comuneros' frustration with Ayala was evident from Ayala's own complaints. In March 1979, Ayala wrote the subprefect to complain about protests by Huayllay's lieutenant governor and four others, men who had been the most enthusiastic supporters of the Velasco reforms inside Huayllay. Ayala alleged that these men entered into his office drunk and then verbally harassed him. But, safely returned to his position of power, Ayala responded to this challenge simply by informing the subprefect and asking the provincial leader to appoint a different lieutenant governor.[96]

Parallelling the process in Carhuanca, PCP-SL militants gained a foothold inside Huayllay by taking their own action against Ayala. One Huayllay man remembered how UNSCH students had come into Huayllay twice before the violence, talking to comuneros one by one. Speaking in Quechua, the students would inquire about all the community's authorities, asking, "What is he like? Is he a bad man? Is he abusive?" The students then compiled a "blacklist" of all the bad individuals inside Huayllay, later killing the individuals on the list. When PCP-SL militants came into Huayllay and asked comuneros who in their community was abusive, many campesinos pointed to Máximo Ayala. Placed on the PCP-SL's local blacklist, Ayala was soon murdered by Senderistas. "They knew who were the bad ones and who were the good ones," one Huayllay man explained. "They took him [Ayala] from his house and killed him. Yes. He was mediocre . . . You can say he was a bad sort." The man continued on, telling me, "The subversives realized this, through others. They asked. And if a person was bad they liquidated him, whether he was an authority or not."[97] By killing Ayala, PCP-SL militants achieved what the military government had promised but ultimately failed to do: They permanently removed Huayllay's most-hated authority from power.

CONCLUSIONS

Hustling President Fernando Belaúnde Terry out of the Presidential Palace in October 1968, General Juan Velasco Alvarado and other members of the Revolutionary Government of the Armed Forces began a reformist experiment that sought to overhaul the structure of Peru's economy, society, and political system.[98] While the military government's reforms in Ayacucho were limited in comparison to its efforts in other parts of the country, those reforms nonetheless had an enormous impact on the Ayacucho countryside. The military's program—and particularly its agrarian reform and Campesino Community Statute—began a fundamental transformation of political and economic relationships throughout rural Ayacucho. For campesinos living in the district of Luricocha, the mili-

tary government's expropriation of area haciendas and creation of a production cooperative brought major changes in the nature of land tenure
and labor for rural men and women. For campesinos in Carhuanca, the
agrarian reform and Campesino Community Statute changed Carhuanquinos' notions of land ownership, even though the military government
made no active interventions in the district. And for campesinos in both
Luricocha and Carhuanca, the military government's reforms started to
recast the character of local authority, enfranchising all adult campesinos and putting sharp limits on the power of local notables.

Several scholars have argued that the military government's agrarian reform facilitated the rise of the PCP-SL. Anthropologist Linda
Seligmann has shown how the agrarian reform created and aggravated
fissures in rural Cuzco, generating new political conflicts by radically
rearranging relationships between campesinos, the state, regional elites,
and community authorities. These power rearrangements fostered painful splits and arguments that strengthened Sendero enormously, as
PCP-SL radicals capitalized on campesinos' frustration with the state,
with intermediaries, and with each other. Florencia Mallon, in turn,
has made compelling arguments about how the agrarian reform's grave
shortcomings in Andahuaylas soured campesino leaders' attitudes toward the military government. Not only did the agrarian reform in
Andahuaylas proceed much too slowly for eager campesinos and their
leaders in the leftist Vanguardia Revolucionaria party, but the military
government also brutally repressed local efforts to speed the agrarian
reform through the seizure of Andahuaylas haciendas. The military government's actions left some campesinos and many of their Vanguardia
Revolucionaria leaders convinced that the only way to win fundamental
change was to destroy the state rather than engage it. More recently,
Ponciano del Pino has asserted that some Huanta campesinos saw the
agrarian reform as an attack on long-standing moral and social systems,
while others used the reform to push themselves into positions of greater
authority and power. The ensuing tensions translated into political violence during the 1980s.[99]

The Luricocha and Carhuanca cases show yet another relationship
between the military government and the PCP-SL. Although PCP-SL
militants were determined to destroy the Peruvian state and construct a
new utopian society from the ruins, many of their earliest actions were
continuations—albeit far more radical and violent ones—of the military
government's reforms. Senderistas' first actions in Luricocha included
the dissolution of an agrarian cooperative in favor of a more direct distribution of land to the tiller. Ironically, that action was very much in
the spirit of the military government's initial agrarian reform promises.

PCP-SL militants also eliminated an old-style authority and gamonal in the Luricocha community of Huayllay, the very sort of power figure that the military government's Campesino Community Statute had promised to remove from power.

In Carhuanca, PCP-SL militants similarly attacked the local notables whom the military government had pledged to oust from authority positions. In addition, PCP-SL militants attacked the very same older generation of schoolteachers that the military government's reforms promised but failed to sanction. Sadly, Senderistas' actions proved poor consolation for the military government's shortcomings. Fetishizing violence and brokering no opposition, PCP-SL militants brought trauma, death, and suffering that grossly overshadowed the disappointments of the Velasco years. It is hardly surprising, then, that Ayacucho campesinos remember the Revolutionary Government of the Armed Forces with such uncomplicated fondness. Those years of change were far, far better than the decade of horror that followed, and the connection between the military government's failures and Shining Path's early actions has left an open wound on Ayacucho's rural indigenous communities that remains too painful to touch.

CHAPTER SEVEN

Abandoned Again

1978 Onward

Lowering her voice and leaning in toward me, a Carhuanca woman tilted her head in the direction of a district schoolteacher. "He walks around now, pretending his hands are clean," this woman whispered, "but they're not."[1] This Carhuanquina angrily told me of the man's prior affiliation with Shining Path, and then she spoke of other Carhuanca-born schoolteachers who had joined the PCP-SL and died fighting that party's 1980–1992 war. I heard many such accusations against the living, and many such remembrances of the dead, during my time in Carhuanca. Many spoke to me of the Carhuanquino schoolteachers who orchestrated the PCP-SL's takeover of the district and of the district students who followed their Senderista schoolteachers into the war. Teachers and students loom large in Carhuanquinos' discussions of the Shining Path, as they do in most academic accounts of the party and its war.[2]

This chapter pays close attention to teachers and students, but these pages also consider the responsibility borne by state actors. Velasco's ouster and the military government's decision to transition Peru back to civilian government marked the resumption of the politics of abandon for Carhuanca. In response to student assaults on police posts in 1978, departmental officials withdrew police forces from eastern Cangallo, purposefully removing the one institution that might have been able to take early action against PCP-SL militants. Departmental and national authorities then ignored the increasingly dire protests of citizens in Carhuanca and other eastern Cangallo districts during the remaining years of the 1970s. Those departmental and national authorities also paid little heed to the official warnings and pleas of Cangallo's own subprefect, who made ever more desperate calls for the police's return. The 1978 police withdrawal directly facilitated the rise of PCP-SL militants inside eastern Cangallo districts, including Carhuanca. Those PCP-SL militants were primarily teachers and their students.

While the narrative of Senderista teachers and students is a familiar one, the story of abandon has not been told. The need for such a telling becomes clear when we consider former military president Francisco Morales Bermúdez's testimony to the Truth and Reconciliation Commission. Morales Bermúdez stated that "determined elements of Sendero were detected as persons of a certain tendency, but in no moment (in 1979 and in 1980) was there any intelligence information that said, 'careful, we have a problem here.' There was never, ever anything like this."[3] President Morales was mistaken; those warnings and cries were present and ever louder from late 1978 onward. Departmental and national authorities simply chose not to listen.

THE RETURN OF ABANDON

Peru's Revolutionary Government of the Armed Forces began its retreat from power in 1977, announcing plans for a Constitutional Assembly to draft a new constitution for the country. While the military government was mapping the return of electoral democracy, men and women affiliated with the PCP-SL were finalizing their own political plans. Abimael Guzmán had formed the PCP-SL in 1970; and, from the moment of its formation, the PCP-SL was closely linked with university students at the Universidad Nacional San Cristóbal de Huamanga (UNSCH), where Guzmán was a professor in the Faculty of Education.[4] There were considerable connections linking Guzmán, the PCP-SL, and the province of Cangallo. At the UNSCH, students from Cangallo were especially prominent in both the Faculty of Education and in the university in general, second only to students from Huamanga province in numerical presence.[5] On graduation, many of those Cangallo-born education students joined the national teachers' union, the Sindicato Único de Trabajadores en la Educación del Perú (Sole Union of Peruvian Education Workers, or SUTEP).

Nationally, SUTEP had proven a strong and radically leftist union from the time of its 1972 formation. The union's radicalism was perhaps best shown by the denunciations it received from the military government. President Velasco charged that "extremists of the worst kind are involved in SUTEP. . . . Here the choice is clear, either the revolution or SUTEP. They want to overthrow the government. Well, let them try if they can, and take the consequences."[6] The military government also denied SUTEP official legal recognition until 1978 and even tried to cripple SUTEP by creating a rival, progovernment teachers' union.[7]

The military's antipathy toward SUTEP was reciprocated in kind; the union was an outspoken critic of the military government, and it enforced that criticism with action, declaring repeated strikes and work stoppages across the 1970s.[8] SUTEP teachers went on strike in 1978, demanding a 100 percent salary increase, the reinstatement of teachers fired or transferred for their union activities, and SUTEP's legal recognition. This strike lasted a full eighty days. Teachers again went on strike in 1979, angry at the government's failure to meet its promises. This second strike lasted 118 days.[9]

The Cangallo branch of SUTEP, the SUTE-Cangallo or SUTEC, was just as radical as the national union. From the outset of the 1970s, SUTEC was led by Maoists, and teachers affiliated with SUTEC became the key disseminators of PCP-SL ideology and programs in Cangallo.[10] By the last years of the 1970s, SUTEC participation in the national teacher strikes of 1978 and 1979 won the provincial union official condemnation for its political extremism and influence.[11] Cangallo Subprefect Jaime Escalante, for example, accused SUTEC teachers of creating antigovernment reaction within campesino communities, grassroots organizations, and among students just to win support for their 1979 strike. The subprefect even asserted that teachers were planning to carry out acts of sabotage, such as blocking highways and burning bridges. The subprefect also claimed that SUTEC teachers were distributing inflammatory flyers, making graffiti, and cutting telephone lines. Although provincial and departmental authorities took action against SUTEC members, removing Cangallo's mayor from power because of his affiliation with SUTEC and suspending some teachers because of their antigovernment activities, SUTEC remained at the center of antigovernment protest and leftist organizing inside Cangallo.[12]

Teachers' protests inside Cangallo were matched by student actions. On the afternoon of November 9, 1978, secondary school students from the city of Cangallo abandoned their classes and as many as 400 of them gathered in Cangallo's central plaza to launch a student strike in protest against the military government's new "grade twelve" law. That law raised the lowest passing grade for any course from eleven to twelve, an increase in standards that many students, parents, and teachers thought unacceptable. Streaming out from the plaza and into the streets, Cangallo secondary students shouted slogans like, "Twelve, No. Eleven, Yes" and "We want to study." Holding rocks in their hands and shouting protests, students approached the civil guard headquarters. Police threw tear gas at the students, students replied with rocks, and the police answered with bullets. Firing into the air and then into the crowd to disperse the demonstrators, police gunfire killed two students.[13]

Less than two weeks later, a second major student strike occurred in the province of Cangallo, this one in the district of Vischongo. On the morning of November 20, Vischongo secondary students met in the district's soccer stadium and agreed to strike in protest against the new grade twelve law and the deaths of the striking Cangallo students. Vischongo's civil guards were quick to intervene, throwing tear gas at the gathered students and immediately taking three students into custody, beating them with clubs, kicks, and punches as they made the arrests. The violence soon spread, with protesters cutting the district's telephone lines and hurling stones at the district's civil guard post. As in the city of Cangallo, guards responded with tear gas and bullets, but no deaths resulted in Vischongo. The Cangallo and Vischongo strikes triggered an immediate radicalization of politics throughout Cangallo province and particularly in the eastern districts of Vischongo, Vilcashuamán, Huambalpa, and Carhuanca. Subsequent student strikes followed in Vilcashuamán and in Carhuanca. As a consequence of these violent strikes, the Ayacucho civil guard command ordered the withdrawal of all civil guards from the districts of Vischongo, Vilcashuamán, Huambalpa, and Carhuanca.[14]

That withdrawal proved one of the worst administrative decisions in Ayacucho's twentieth-century history, as Senderistas throughout eastern Cangallo took the 1978 police retreat as their opportunity to finalize their preparations for war. But this withdrawal was not simply a matter of poor administrative judgment. Instead, it reflected the painful historical reality of eastern Cangallo's political abandon. Rather than expend the energy, resources, and bodies needed to confront the area's increasingly volatile mobilizations, departmental and national officials simply turned away, taking their police officers with them. And, despite the increasingly desperate pleas of provincial residents and even the provincial subprefect, departmental and national officials steadfastly refused to return the police forces. Without the police, PCP-SL militants were able to prepare openly and actively for war.

The immediate aftermath of the police withdrawal saw an explosion of Maoist organizing in the eastern Cangallo districts of Vilcashuamán, Vischongo, and Huambalpa. Explaining that rumors abounded regarding a planned sacking of Cangallo city to protest the student deaths, Subprefect Escalante informed the Ayacucho prefect that the atmosphere in Cangallo province was extremely tense and warned that there was a profusion of leftist leaders residing in several Cangallo communities. Other provincial authorities made repeated complaints regarding the burst of propaganda inside Cangallo, propaganda that included graffiti calls to abstain from the Constitutional Assembly elections and to take up armed struggle to seize control of the national government. The sub-prefect's concerns about leftist—and particularly Maoist—parties grew panicked in March 1979. He commented that, since the November 1978 strikes, Cangallo had become a "conflictive province," home to many acts of violence.[15]

At the end of April 1979, the subprefect filed reports of a growing "infiltration of communists into campesino communities."[16] Relaying that there was a "proliferation of revolutionary groups" in the districts of Vilcashuamán, Vischongo, Huambalpa, and Carhuanca, the subpre-fect explained that these groups were taking advantage of the police absence and forming their own counterrevolutionary communal police forces. The subprefect also warned that the leftist Frente de Defensa del Pueblo (People's Defense Front) was convening ever larger and ever more frequent meetings in numerous campesino communities, forging plans to sack the city of Cangallo and carry out a campesino strike to block the weekly market activities.[17] The subprefect repeated similar claims about looming campesino strikes, the planned sacking of Cangallo, and leftist activities that June and again in July.[18]

It was in July 1979 that Subprefect Escalante first made a specific warning about Sendero Luminoso. Escalante relayed that he had proof of the "existence of elements addicted to parties of the left, quite espe-cially students of the Huamanga University. They are introducing them-selves into the heart of their communities and elections, with aims to create reactions and protests to the various economic measures dictated by the government." Escalante added that SUTEC remained strong and was "continuing to carry out counterrevolutionary activities, given that its leaders are of the PCP band and of the political group existing in Ayacucho, Sendero Luminoso."[19] In October 1979, Escalante wrote that the lack of police presence in Carhuanca, Vilcashuamán, and Vischongo, as well as in Huambalpa, had allowed for the "appearance of people of terrorist tendencies" in these districts.[20]

The civil guard's withdrawal from Vilcashuamán, Huambalpa, Vischongo, and Carhuanca greatly eased the PCP-SL's growth in these districts. It needs to be said that Subprefect Escalante made numerous and increasingly dire calls for the civil guard's return—calls to which de-partmental and national authorities paid no heed. Almost immediately after the civil guard's retreat from Vilcashuamán in November 1978, Subprefect Escalante relayed that the district's population was pressing for the guards' return, fearing for their own security. In February and again in March 1979, Subprefect Escalante explained to the Ayacucho prefect that the police absence in Vilcashuamán, Vischongo, and Car-huanca was impeding the transmission of documents and judicial orders, and he urged for the reestablishment of the police posts.[21] In July 1979, Escalante told the prefect that, because of the continuing frequency of strikes and robberies in the districts of Vilcashuamán, Vischongo, and Carhuanca, he was soliciting the reestablishment of police service in said districts.[22]

Subprefect Escalante's calls for the return of police detachments turned desperate by August 1979. He informed the prefect, "As your Dispatch is already amply aware, since the withdrawal of police service from the districts of Vischongo, Vilcashuamán, and Carhuanca, shameful activities have been occurring, due to politicized persons intruding in the various grassroots organizations."[23] Subprefect Escalante charged that these "politicized persons" were instigating the three districts' residents to carry out acts of sabotage and massive protests against the government. Escalante added that, in Carhuanca, teachers and comuneros were protesting against the 1980 general elections. Escalante asserted that "these maddening acts are occurring in light of the absence of police service within this zone, where politicized elements of leftist tendency have proliferated," and he added that these leftists were assuming key posts within the three districts' local organizations, making the reestablishment of police service absolutely necessary.[24]

Cangallo's subprefect was not the only official warning of grave political activities afoot in the region. Peruvian journalist Gustavo Gorriti has uncovered numerous intelligence reports voicing similar concerns from 1977 forward. A March 1977 navy intelligence service report documented military exercises conducted by the "Communist Party of José Carlos Mariátegui," and a December 1978 report from the civil guard's Central Intelligence Office reported that the PCP-SL had decided to "culminate and lay the groundwork for armed struggle to begin."[25] Other reports commented on plans for the "establishment of a liberated zone" in Pomacocha and about the presence of "subversive organizations and guerrilla training camps" in Vilcashuamán, Vischongo, Pomacocha, and Chito.[26] Though numerous, these reports triggered no action. The police did not return to the zone, and PCP-SL militants were able to develop, launch, and fight their so-called People's War. It was political abandon that allowed those militants to flourish unchecked.

ABANDON IN CARHUANCA

Carhuanca's experience of the years 1978 and 1979 paralleled the provincial history outlined in the preceding section. Several Carhuanca men and women became early and active participants in the PCP-SL, and most of these early PCP-SL militants were young schoolteachers. Kimberly Theidon's study *Entre prójimos* reveals that a strikingly similar pattern held throughout the provinces of Cangallo and Víctor Fajardo.[27] Although teachers in Carhuanca—and Carhuanquino teachers working outside their district—were hardly all leftists, let alone Senderistas, there were a number of Carhuanca teachers who did indeed belong to the PCP-SL. Exactly why these Carhuanquino schoolteachers joined the PCP-SL is impossible to know; all of the individuals whom I describe below are either dead or unwilling to share their personal histories with me. These men and women probably joined the PCP-SL in part because of their exposure to Abimael Guzmán and other radical UNSCH faculty, in part because of their participation in Maoist student groups, and in part because of their affiliation with the Maoist-dominated Cangallo teachers' union, SUTEC. But, as is clear from their actions, many of these schoolteachers were also drawn to the PCP-SL because of their anger at the abuses and crimes of Carhuanca's local notables.

One of the first Carhuanquinos to join the PCP-SL was Pedro Prado, a teacher employed in central Cangallo. Pedro Prado was a Carhuanca-born man who had been imprisoned in the 1960s for suspected involvement with the MIR, the Movement of the Revolutionary Left. Prado taught at a school in central Cangallo, and he was also a key figure in SUTEC, serving as SUTEC's very first secretary general. As SUTEC's secretary general, Prado won repeated condemnation from provincial and departmental authorities. Cangallo's subprefect denounced Prado for "inciting members of the teaching profession to commit reprehensible acts with a marked antirevolutionary tendency."[28] At a 1974 seminar organized by SINAMOS, government representatives complained that Prado was a "SUTEC militant" and that he "openly attacked the Revolutionary Government."[29]

Those charges were not unwarranted. During a speech at the large funeral for the two Cangallo students killed in the November 1978 clash with police, Prado voiced the kind of sharp antigovernment invective that typified radical Maoist thought of the era. Prado charged that the Revolutionary Government of the Armed Forces was responsible for popular hunger and misery and that its representatives were exploiters, "irrational animals," and assassins. Explaining that he was paid by the pueblo and not by the state, Prado promised that "one day there will be peace and liberty where there do not exist oppressed nor oppressors."[30] That Prado's words resembled Senderista discourse of the 1980s was no accident; he was already a member of the PCP-SL. Prado had joined Sendero Luminoso at the UNSCH, where he studied in the Education Faculty and had PCP-SL founder Abimael Guzmán as a professor.[31]

Pedro Prado was one of Carhuanca's first PCP-SL members, but others soon followed. Like Prado, most of Carhuanca's earliest Senderistas were teachers, and many of them had studied at the UNSCH. Saturno Najarro was one of these men. Born in the late 1950s, Najarro studied education at the UNSCH and taught in the Vilcashuamán community of Huallhua and then in Carhuanca at the outset of the 1980s. Saturno and his brother joined the PCP-SL; and, from 1982 onward, Saturno Najarro was the PCP-SL's political commander in Carhuanca. Remembered in Carhuanca as "*el cojo*" ("the cripple"), Saturno was born into one of the district's poorer families; no Najarro had ever filled the ranks of Carhuanca's local notables. Membership in the PCP-SL not only provided Saturno Najarro and his brother the opportunity for the sort of local political power that their family had long been denied; that membership also allowed them to seek violent retribution against the Carhuanca notables who had long monopolized such power.

Carhuanquinos offered me several explanations for Saturno Najarro's membership in the PCP-SL. One Carhuanquino told me that Saturno was an unwanted child, born physically sound but disabled by his mother's repeated beatings. Because of this treatment, the interviewee explained, Najarro "made Mao his God."[32] More Carhuanquinos blamed Najarro's UNSCH studies for his entrance into the PCP-SL's ranks. When I asked one Carhuanquino if Najarro had been rebellious as a youngster, this man shook his head and instead blamed Abimael Guzmán. This man relayed that Guzmán "fanaticized all those students, he convinced them. They were ignorant *muchachos*, youngsters, of campesino parents."[33] The most telling comment Alicia and I heard about Najarro came from one woman who blamed Najarro's mother for his political radicalism. This interviewee told us that Najarro's mother had loudly and proudly proclaimed, "I raised my son to make the pueblo of Carhuanca tremble."[34] Apocryphal or not, that memory suggests the centrality of local hatreds and conflicts to the decision to join Shining Path.

Another of Carhuanca's PCP-SL leaders was Reynaldo Barrientos García, son of Carhuanca schoolteacher Francisco Barrientos. Like Najarro, Reynaldo Barrientos had studied education at the UNSCH and was employed as a teacher in Carhuanca. And, like Najarro, Barrientos was joined in the PCP-SL by two of his siblings; his sister Magda and brother Carlos both became Senderista militants inside Carhuanca. When I asked one man who had been a secondary school student in Carhuanca in the late 1970s and early 1980s if he remembered Reynaldo Barrientos, this man replied, "Yes, he was a high school teacher. He came and began to organize the teachers. And then, after organizing among teachers, he started with the students."[35] Another Carhuanquino

recalled that Barrientos was "one of the members of the terrorist organization. Those men were organizing in the pueblos around Carhuanca
over the question of terrorism, of Sendero Luminoso."[36]

It is worth noting that Reynaldo's father, Francisco, had been subject
to many complaints and lawsuits from several of the district's local notables and had himself been active in the district's APRA party during
the 1940s.[37] Those actions against his father may well have encouraged
Reynaldo's sympathies for the PCP SL, as that party pledged decisive
action against abusive gamonales. Additionally, Reynaldo himself had
previously solicited intervention from SINAMOS against the unethical
actions of the priest Quintin Arrieta, but that legalistic route of cooperation with the government had resulted only in disappointment.[38] Six
short years after his attempt to use legal channels to realize change,
Barrientos was calling for the obliteration of the military government,
deriding local government supporters as "yellows," and threatening to
kill those Carhuanquinos with whom he had once sought SINAMOS's
support.[39]

There is one last teacher whom Carhuanquinos regularly associate
with the PCP-SL, a man whom I will call Edgar. I have withheld Edgar's
actual name because he—unlike Pedro Prado, the Najarro brothers, and
the Barrientos siblings—actually survived the years of civil war and is
alive today. Although Edgar was not one of the Senderista leaders who
commanded Carhuanca during its years as a "liberated zone," many
Carhuanquinos told me of this man's ties to Sendero. I regularly asked
Carhuanquinos about Edgar's father, a man never quite included in the
ranks of the district's local notables and never allotted a position of formal authority but prominent nonetheless for his numerous lawsuits and
petitions against the area's wealthiest campesinos, as well as his early
affiliation with APRA. One elderly Carhuanca man remembered that
Edgar's father had been "a little bit vivo, a little thief, a tinterillo. They
say his sons are the same way, because one of his sons was a *terruco*
[terrorist]."[40] Several others told me that Edgar had only recently been
released from El Frontón prison—the primary jail for Senderistas and
suspected Senderistas—as had his son and wife. Another man told me
how difficult it was to have Edgar living in Carhuanca once again: "It's
hard, miss. He's thinking . . . He's figuring out how to annihilate us,
how to do something. He's never left the political behind."[41]

But if Edgar did indeed belong to the PCP-SL, his trajectory toward the party differed from Carhuanca Senderistas like the Najarro
brothers and the Barrientos siblings. For one, Edgar did not study at
the UNSCH; he had studied only up to the final years of secondary
school and gained employ with that education and participation in a

government-sponsored teacher-training program, as was common for rural teachers. Edgar was also of an older generation than the Najarros and the Barrientos siblings; he had been born in the early 1940s and had been teaching in and around Carhuanca since the 1960s. Additionally, Edgar began Maoist propagandizing in Carhuanca well before other PCP-SL militants started organizing in Carhuanca. As early as 1972, some of Edgar's local enemies accused him and another man "of being communists and of carrying out a campaign about the Revolutionary Government of the Armed Forces."[42] Edgar was also accused of pasting flyers around Carhuanca that denounced local authorities, the owners of local transport services, two agrarian reform functionaries, and Carhuanca school principal Alonso Chuchón. One of those flyers ended with the calls, "Justice for the poor and needy! Unity, tenacious struggle against hunger, misery, and oppression!"[43] In 1976, Edgar was deemed responsible for painting bright red graffiti around Carhuanca, graffiti with leftist commentary like: "VIVA PEKING," "THE PUEBLO IS NOT BEING HEARD," "UNITY AND STRUGGLE," and "THE PUEBLO WILL NOT BE DECEIVED."[44] Although an eyewitness saw Edgar skulking around the district with a can of paint in hand the very night before the graffiti appeared, the civil guard finally decided that Edgar's guilt could not be proven.[45]

I do not know for certain where Edgar's political sympathies lay. Many Carhuanquinos were reluctant to speak at length about any of the district's surviving Maoists because of their understandable fears of retribution. As one elderly Carhuanca man said in response to my question about Senderistas, "There were a lot of them, miss, but I can't tell you who they were. They might come by night and get me."[46] My own efforts to speak with Edgar similarly came to naught. In our first and only conversation, Edgar angrily accused me of being a CIA agent, a Senderista, and Lori Berenson, the American woman jailed for her involvement with the Túpac Amaru Revolutionary Movement. As no Carhuanquinos gave me specific details of Edgar's actions within the PCP-SL—unlike what they told me of Pedro Prado, the Najarros, and the Barrientos siblings— it is quite possible that Edgar never actually belonged to Sendero. What is certain, however, is that he cultivated enemies among Carhuanca's authorities and many parents of schoolchildren. Throughout the 1970s, parents and authorities filed complaints against Edgar for everything from absenteeism from his school, to the rape of a schoolgirl, to showing up drunk for communal assemblies, to trying to "incite the people to disorder and to not participate in communal works."[47]

The Edgar example is instructive. His case suggests some of the personal reasons that rural schoolteachers may have been drawn to the

PCP-SL. Excluded from the district's formal hierarchies of power, Edgar and especially his father had consistently fought for inclusion in the ranks of district authority, repeatedly proposing their own candidacies for mayor or governor and repeatedly failing due partly to scorn from local notables. Edgar's father—like Reynaldo Barrientos's dad—had joined APRA to fight against those notables; Edgar chose a more radical path toward power by (likely) affiliating with the PCP-SL. Much the same was true for the Barrientos, Najarro, and Prado examples; those families never ranked among Carhuanca's formal authorities or local notables. Edgar and his family were also excluded from the class of rich campesinos, trying always to acquire more land and defend their own properties and regularly losing literal ground to the district's local notables. The same applied for the Barrientos, Najarro, and Prado families. Taking the Edgar example into consideration also helps further explain why local notables like Luis Allende Ayala, Alonso Chuchón, and Alejandro Quijana were among PCP-SL militants' first targets: They were from the very kind of politically powerful and wealthy families that men like Edgar and his father had been envying and fighting all their lives. These Senderista teachers had been born and raised in a district ravaged by the unchecked abuses of local notables, and these teachers found in the PCP-SL a party that promised to take definitive punitive action against such abusive strongmen.

As was true throughout eastern Cangallo, Carhuanca's Senderista teachers took the police withdrawal as an invitation to radicalize their mobilization. The very day of the civil guards' retreat from Carhuanca, Saturno Najarro climbed up into the bell tower of Carhuanca's church and began clanging the steeple bell. Yelling out vivas to the student strike and celebrating the police withdrawal, Najarro captured the attention of the many Carhuanquinos who gathered in the central plaza on the church bell's summons.[48] Although the PCP-SL would not launch its People's War until well over a year later, the November 1978 day when Najarro rang the church bell stands out in many Carhuanquinos' memory as the day that Senderistas began their rapid ascent to power in the district. One man recalled the police withdrawal, telling Alicia and me, "Those leaders of Sendero Luminoso took advantage of this opportunity to enter into the pueblo."[49] A Carhuanquina similarly recalled that, on the day the police withdrew, Najarro stood on the embankment next to the church and told everyone that the police withdrawal was a great victory, and he gave instructions on what Carhuanquinos should and should not do. Soon thereafter, this woman recalled, Najarro and his allies made a list of which Carhuanquinos were with them and which were against them, and they later used that list to decide whom to kill.[50]

From November 1978 onward, the handful of Senderista teachers in Carhuanca brought other PCP-SL activists into the district from Huamanga and from Vilcashuamán; they convened local meetings, started new grassroots organizations, and launched the notorious "popular schools" inside the district.[51] Those "popular schools" were clandestine study groups where selected students were indoctrinated with PCP-SL plans and programs and trained militarily for the coming war. The former principal of a Vilcashuamán school told the Peruvian Truth and Reconciliation Commission, "Sendero selected the smartest students to indoctrinate, the leaders who could best influence their classmates," and those students then went out into the countryside to organize campesinos.[52] Each popular school had around fifteen students for every teacher; and, once a child had agreed to participate, attendance at the popular school became mandatory. One Carhuanca man explained that, well before 1980, "the youth were already studying, teachers had come here working. In the general assembly, they would say 'Mao, Mao.'"[53]

Carhuanca students proved especially interested in the PCP-SL's program. A Chilicruz man who had himself been a student in Carhuanca's secondary school shortly after its 1977 opening remembered that "all the students were involved, were participants in this movement."[54] Inside Carhuanca's popular schools, teachers taught Mao's "red book" and instructed students on how to use guns and dynamite. One Carhuanca couple told Alicia and me that their sixteen-year-old son had entered Sendero's ranks, learning to use a rifle and carrying out military exercises, all on his teachers' instruction.[55] In addition, a man who had been a student during the late 1970s recalled that "all the students left, they went here, they went there, and some to this day have not returned, because they have a lot of ties, grave ones, to the violence."[56]

Carhuanca's PCP-SL teachers and their student followers soon spread their political efforts out from the classroom and into the larger district. The Cangallo subprefect charged that, in Carhuanca, "always the same teachers, with the support of communities, have carried out various meetings, where they have attacked the government and . . . they make calls against the 1980 general elections."[57] In August 1979, Reynaldo Barrientos led a group of secondary and university students through Carhuanca's streets yelling "Down with the government! Down with the Yellows! Down with the electioneers!" That same night, Barrientos cut the district's telephone lines, stealing fifteen meters of cable and effectively blocking Carhuanca's communication with other communities and authorities.[58] On another occasion, Barrientos stormed a neighborhood civic action meeting, arguing that the meeting's leaders were interested only in their own personal advancement. Still another time, Barrientos protested the end of the 1979 teachers' strike by gathering sympathetic teachers from the district's annexes and holding a demonstration in Carhuanca's central plaza. At that protest, Barrientos and his allies sharply denounced the "yellow" teachers who had returned to work. These protests were also accompanied by death threats against Carhuanquinos who had supported the military government.[59]

The politics of abandon greatly facilitated Carhuanquino Senderistas' success, as departmental authorities left local complaints against PCP-SL militants unanswered. Those complaints were numerous. Two Carhuanca campesinas, for instance, formally denounced Reynaldo Barrientos in October 1979 for "inciting the masses against the physical integrity of the complainants and against their patrimony."[60] Another protest came from Carhuanca's governor, Cecilio Morales, and the head of Carhuanca's Post and Telegraph Office, Juan Zárate Vega. Both men filed a complaint with the prefect against Barrientos in August 1979, relaying that Barrientos and his followers had verbally attacked the government and cut the area's telephone lines. Governor Morales and Zárate charged that "said interruption had been planned by a group of subversives headed by said agitator," and they urged the prefect and the police to punish all those involved.[61] Further complaints came from Adolfo Urbana, who repeatedly denounced Barrientos to provincial authorities.[62] These Carhuanquinos sought help against PCP-SL militants in the months preceding the party's declaration of war, but that help did not come. As had occurred so many times across the twentieth century, Carhuanquinos sought the aid of state actors to fight local crimes and abuses, and they sought that aid in vain. Departmental and national officials failed to intervene, and that disregard ultimately allowed the PCP-SL to gain full control of Carhuanca for two entire years.

LURICOCHA COUNTERPOINT

Carhuanquinos regularly made accusations against the living and dead, pointing fingers at those neighbors who had supported or even joined the PCP-SL. My conversations in Luricocha could not have been more different. Campesinos in Huayllay, Pampay, and Luricocha town spoke of Senderistas strictly as outsiders, as nameless university students and unknown terrucos. This uniform casting of PCP-SL militants as strangers bristled against the knowledge I had acquired from other sources, for it is clear that some Luricochanos did indeed participate in the PCP-SL's ranks. The most notorious example is, of course, Augusta La Torre, who served as the PCP-SL's second-in-command until her 1988 death. Luri-cochanos who testified before the Truth and Reconciliation Commission also named a handful of district residents who supported the PCP-SL, likewise noting that some youth from Huayllay and Pampay were forced to enter the PCP-SL's ranks.[63]

The contradiction between the oral histories I collected and the evidence of Luricochano participation in the PCP-SL was in some ways a reflection of the limits of my oral history research in the district. My time in Luricocha communities was far too brief for me to build the kind of friendship and trust that necessarily precede confessions (or even accusations) of local participation in, or sympathy for, the PCP-SL. Even the Truth Commission interviews failed to generate detailed discussions about Luricochano participation in the PCP-SL's ranks. Individuals who testified generally preferred to speak about their resistance to Sendero and the suffering they experienced because of the war.[64] This generalized reticence to speak of Luricochano participation in the PCP-SL, and to stress the presence of outsiders in the party's ranks, reflected a larger process of reconciliation at work inside the district. By portraying Senderistas as outsiders, Luricocha campesinos were attempting to heal fissures in their communities, to rebuild and reconcile after years of bloody and destructive war.[65] But Luricochanos' memories of Senderistas as outsiders also reflects the reality that most of the PCP-SL militants who entered Luricocha *were* from outside the district, some from other parts of Huanta, more from other parts of Ayacucho. The predominance of outsiders among Luricocha Senderistas was not accidental; it reflected the PCP-SL's failure to mobilize a significant number of Luricochanos into local leadership positions and the party's inability to attract a substantial number of Luricocha peasants into its ranks.

Inspired both by the 1969 education riots and by Huanta's long-standing notoriety as a place of rebellion and resistance, PCP-SL leaders like Abimael Guzmán, Augusta La Torre, Osmán Morote, and Antonio Díaz Martínez deemed Huanta the ideal locale for beginning their trek toward popular war. That choice was all the more appealing because the La Torre family's Iribamba hacienda in Luricocha provided an excellent location for political organizing and training. Guzmán and Augusta La Torre regularly traveled to Iribamba in the late 1960s and into 1970, often accompanied by fellow members of their nascent Shining Path party.[66] These repeated trips to Iribamba soon raised the suspicions of local authorities, and in June 1970 police raided the hacienda. That raid led to the arrests of several PCP-SL militants, including Guzmán and Osmán Morote, charged on the grounds of subverting the agrarian reform.[67]

The 1970 arrests on the Iribamba estate led to the PCP-SL's prolonged absence from Luricocha. It was only in 1976 that PCP-SL sympathizers resumed cautious mobilization efforts in Huanta, sending activists into the area by using established contacts with UNSCH students and rural schoolteachers. Restricting their provincial efforts to the districts of Huanta, Luricocha, and Iguaín, Senderistas would visit district communities in groups of three, lodging in the homes of high school and occasionally university students and helping out with agricultural chores.[68] Becoming more active and vocal as the 1970s drew to a close, PCP-SL militants had assumed a fairly prominent posture in Luricocha by 1978. The area where those militants were most active was the La Torre's Iribamba estate, where members of the PCP-SL established one of the party's first military training schools.[69] Augusta La Torre herself made an appearance in the district around this time, presenting herself at the Luricocha El Carmen hacienda of her aunt Adriana Cárdenas and her uncle Eduardo Spatz. The visit was political rather than social: La Torre asked if she could purchase her uncle's sizeable gun collection. He pointedly refused.[70]

My interviews—like those of the Truth Commission—only hinted at this presence of the PCP-SL. One Huayllay man told me that the first PCP-SL militants to come to the community arrived before the violence. He told me that these people were *universitarios* (university students) who spoke with the area's comuneros and drew up a "blacklist" of the abusive people in the community. The people on that list were the PCP-SL's first targets.[71] The Luricochanos who spoke before the Truth Commission offered similar recollections. One woman recalled that Senderistas began appearing in 1979 in Huayllay, and she remembered people telling her that these individuals came to raise the consciousness of community members.[72] Another witness recalled that the Iribamba estate was home to nighttime meetings by workers who gathered "to plan and develop subversive actions."[73] One Truth Commission interview also suggested a deeper story of anger and betrayal. One witness testified that an entire Luricocha family "walked with Sendero Luminoso" after losing a land lawsuit to the witness's family.[74] Such testimony, however, was the exception. Most of the individuals with whom I spoke, like most of the Truth Commission interviewees, emphasized the unfamiliarity of Senderistas, their own rejection of the PCP-SL, and their patriotic participation in the ranks of the rondas campesinas. Those testimonies fit inside the larger story of twentieth-century Luricochano politics. Whereas district hacendados were eager participants in the ranks of that century's various parties and movements, indigenous peasants favored a

far more staid course of political action along with repeated expressions
of loyalty to the Peruvian state.

EPILOGUE: THE 1980S AND BEYOND

Inside the district of Carhuanca and across eastern Cangallo, the politics of abandon enabled the PCP-SL's domination of Cangallo's political scene. Anger at that abandon drew many to the Shining Path, and
that abandon itself facilitated the PCP-SL's progress as the withdrawal
of police forces from eastern Cangallo and state officials' steadfast refusal to return those forces allowed the PCP-SL to mobilize practically
unchecked. Abandon also conditioned the PCP-SL's first actions inside
the district. Ruling Carhuanca as a "liberated zone" from 1982 until
1984, PCP-SL members under the local political command of Saturno
Najarro took up residence in the district's city hall and exacted brutal
punishments against the authorities and notables who had long enjoyed
impunity for their abuses and misdeeds.

Here, the obvious needs stating: There was nothing liberating about
life in the "liberated zone" of Carhuanca.[75] Beyond assassinating local
notables, Carhuanca's PCP-SL militants dominated Carhuanquinos'
daily lives and actions. Najarro and his fellow militants governed though
a "Popular Committee" made up of representatives of smaller "generated organisms" like the Poor Campesino Movement, the Popular Youth
Movement, the Popular Women's Movement, the Popular Children's
Movement, and the Popular Intellectual Movement. Membership in
these committees was forced, not voluntary. Those individuals who
proved most active and sympathetic to the PCP-SL from these various
groups became part of the PCP-SL's militias. The militias carried out the
duties of the police in the district. From the ranks of militia members,
the most enthusiastic entered the PCP-SL's Popular Army as guerrillas
and patrolled the "liberated zones."[76]

Whatever initial sympathies Carhuanquinos had for the PCP-SL
militants who brought decisive and irreversible punishments to abusive
local notables, those sympathies slowly vanished as PCP-SL militants
proved even more abusive and cruel than the notables whom they had
ousted from district power. Faced with the PCP-SL's continuing violence
and authoritarian command over the district, many Carhuanquinos decided to flee for Lima. As one woman explained, "When the terrucos
came, everyone escaped. Even the priests. Everyone."[77] One of the few
Carhuanquinos who remained in the district told Alicia and me, "Oh,
pretty *madrecita. Caramba.* There was almost nobody here."[78] Those

Carhuanquinos who remained were mostly so old and/or impoverished that flight to Lima was simply not an option. A ninety-year-old man remembered agonizing over the decision, recalling how he asked himself, "'What are we going to do? Where are we going to take our things? What are we going to do? We are going to die here.' Saying this, we stayed."[79] A ninety-three-year-old woman, in turn, recalled that "a girl about your age came to my home and said to me, 'Are you going to leave or not? If not, I'm going to barbecue you! I'm going to throw this bomb at you.' She was holding something big in her hand. . . . What a time! Those were terrible times."[80]

Although those Carhuanquinos who remained in the district lived under Senderista command, their actions were compelled far more by force than by political desire. Senderistas organized district residents into committees like the Poor Campesino Movement, and Carhuanquinos had to participate in daily formations and military exercises. As one elderly Carhuanca man remembered, "They obligated us, group by group. Two years they were in control. They lived in the city hall. It was like their barracks. . . . They had us under their feet."[81] The same man recalled that "almost daily, they made us say vivas. They were calling on us, and we, *caramba*, we were scared."[82] A middle-aged Carhuanquina named Patricia Quispe remembered being forced to nominate one of her fellow Carhuanquinos for a district leadership position. When Patricia reluctantly chose a neighbor, that neighbor retaliated by nominating Patricia for a parallel position. It was in this way that Patricia—an incredibly sweet, soft-spoken woman in her sixties whose gentleness moved both Alicia and me—became a district PCP-SL commander.[83]

Forced into participation with Sendero, Carhuanquinos had little choice but to follow PCP-SL militants' orders. One Carhuanquino man remembered arguing with the PCP-SL militants. He questioned local Senderistas' claims that they were going to seize the presidential palace in Lima and gain control of the country. "I protested. 'How are you going to enter the palace when it is under the control of more civilized people?' That's what I asked."[84] Though brave, such challenges were extremely rare. Most of the Carhuanquinos who remained in the district accepted the PCP-SL because they were too frightened to object. Their fear was well grounded, as Sendero militants often killed their opponents. When Alicia asked an elderly Carhuanca woman why no one protested against the Senderistas, the woman replied, "What could you do? Those compañeros would shoot you."[85] Another aged Carhuanquino told us, "When the terrucos came, they made us stand in formation. They told us, 'If you side with us, the police will never come.' We had to say yes. If we had said no, they would have killed us. That's how we spent this saddest life."[86] Still another man who lived in Carhuanca during these years told the Peruvian newsmagazine *Equis X* that PCP-SL militants "execute not only 'traitors' but 'snitches' too. But I have seen, in reality, that they kill those who oppose them. Sure, they accuse them of being 'snitches,' but this is just a pretext. They accuse everyone who opposes SL of being 'snitches.' They also kill the hecklers. They call them 'cockroaches,' and they say, 'we have to destroy these cockroaches.'"[87]

Carhuanca's civil war experience changed dramatically in 1984 when shock troops from Lima (*sinchis*) arrived in the district. An elderly Carhuanca man explained that the Virgin María de Asunción had appeared inside the government palace in Lima and beseeched the president for help. This man told us, "Mamacha Asunta stood before the president and said, 'Señor, they have killed almost all of my sons, they are killing my sons. Give us some troops to pacify everything.' After saying that, she disappeared . . . So the president gave orders, because the Virgin Asunta had told him about Carhuanca. Because of that, four or five helicopters came."[88] Those helicopters were full of troops who quickly brought an end to PCP-SL rule of the district, asserting military rule through the use of terror and violence.

Tragically, the troops' arrival did not mean an end to Carhuanquinos' suffering. One elderly Carhuanquino remembered, "We had to fight with the sinchis. The sinchis were thieves of the first order, and they took all of us to the plaza . . . they took all of our valuables by force, breaking into our homes house by house." This man recalled that sinchis brutally mistreated Carhuanquinos. "They whipped us like Christ. Those wretches, those wretches."[89] Although these soldiers regained control of Carhuanca, it was not until the late 1990s and early years of the 2000s that Carhuanquino refugees began returning to the district. The PCP-SL's civil war had sputtered to an end, thanks to President Alberto Fujimori's 1992 capture of PCP-SL founder Abimael Guzmán and the valiant efforts of the peasant-staffed rondas campesinas. Far from liberation, the PCP-SL had brought only violence, devastation, and ruin to Carhuanca, to Ayacucho, and to Peru.

Conclusion

☽

Shifting his rifles as he stood to leave, Don Isaac Escobar repeated his earlier words to me. "Those were years of crying, miss. Crying, crying, crying."[1] Many share Don Isaac's memory of the Shining Path's 1980–1992 People's War. Seventeen thousand Peruvians appeared before Peru's Truth and Reconciliation Commission, and their testimonies document the appalling horror of the civil war, detailing forced disappearances, arbitrary executions, assassinations, kidnapping, sexual violence, torture, violence against children, and mass internal displacement. It was a civil war that both begs and defies explanation.

There are no easy answers for how and why the Shining Path emerged and waged its devastating war. But in tracing the eighty-five years of rural political history that prefaced the insurgency, we can see a certain logic behind the seemingly illogical course of events that played out in Ayacucho's countryside during the first years of the 1980s. War first came to the district of Luricocha through the choices and actions of Augusta La Torre, daughter of a prominent hacendado family. Augusta La Torre embodied a district tradition of politically engaged, activist hacendados. Her grandfather was a founding member of the anti-Leguía Rights of Man Defense League, a candidate for Chamber of Deputies, and (briefly) a member of the APRA. Her father, in turn, was a member of the pro-Soviet wing of the Peruvian Communist Party. The La Torres were broadly representative of Luricocha hacendados—a group of landowners who readily engaged in party politics across the twentieth century. Luricocha hacendados filled the ranks of the district's APRA party and the Peruvian Communist Party, implicitly casting party politics in the district as a landlords' game.

Although a small number of Luricocha campesinos joined Augusta La Torre inside the Shining Path, most Luricocha peasants rejected the PCP-SL and allied with military forces to defend their communities against the Maoist rebels. These campesinos' political trajectories had long historical precedents. From the 1920s forward, most Luricocha campesinos eschewed radical political movements in favor of reformist actions to improve their communities. Few Luricocha men and women joined the Tawantinsuyo Movement; fewer still joined the APRA or the Trotskyist Revolutionary Workers Party. Instead, Luricocha's indigenous campesinos lobbied, quietly but steadily, for better teachers, responsible priests, and better treatment from local authorities. Luricocha peasants also stressed their loyalty to the Peruvian state, voicing their support for President Belaúnde in the 1960s, President Velasco in the early 1970s, and, ultimately, for the armed forces sent to battle Shining Path militants.

Shining Path militants gained a much firmer foothold in the district of Carhuanca than they did in Luricocha. Here, too, the past offers explanations. Throughout the twentieth century, both wealthier and poorer Carhuanca peasants affiliated themselves with diverse political movements and parties. As such, joining a political party like the PCP-SL was not an unusual course of action inside Carhuanca. Without question, the PCP-SL was far more extreme and far more violent than any of the parties and movements that preceded it inside Carhuanca. But even the PCP-SL's use of absolutist violence had significant historical motives. PCP-SL militants' first victims inside Carhuanca included local notables like Luis Allende Ayala, Vitalicia Cárdenas, and Honorato Hiyo. These local notables and their relatives routinely abused their local positions of power for material gain, generating tremendous suffering among their neighbors. Carhuanquinos had long denounced these notables' misdeeds; bitter complaints against these local elites stretch back to the closing years of the nineteenth century. But Carhuanquinos' letters of protest, verbal complaints, and court testimonies had little effect in a context of government abandon.

From the 1920s forward, Carhuanca men and women embraced political movements, motivated partly by a desire to challenge the district's local notables. Many indigenous Carhuanquinos joined the Tawantinsuyo movement in the 1920s, believing that their mobilization could end the tyranny of "those who could read and write." Decades later, a handful of other Carhuanquinos hoped Trotskyist mobilization would finally remove these notables from power. Still other Carhuanquinos looked the Campesino Community Statute in the 1970s to end the abuses of district elites, but those notables remained firmly in power. Only the bloody, extremist violence of local Senderistas ended the reign of these local elites. Although most Carhuanquinos were horrified by PCP-SL militants' exceptionally cruel methods, they understood exactly why these notables died.

The PCP-SL's actions in Carhuanca were anything but unique. Throughout Ayacucho and across much of rural Peru, Senderistas targeted abusive local notables for assassination. Scholars of the PCP-SL have long known about those killings, and anthropologists like Ronald Berg and Billie Jean Isbell have established that these brutal punishments won Senderistas the initial support of many indigenous campesinos.[2] This study historicizes that support. Decades of bitter frustration over local notables' criminal impunity and the palpable inability to check those notables' crimes make campesinos' approval of Senderista assassinations comprehensible.

Taken together, the eighty-five years of history examined in this book suggest that the Shining Path's People's War was a period of both historical continuity and historical rupture. To borrow Steve J. Stern's notion, the PCP-SL operated both "within" and "against" history.[3] Echoing military theorist Carl von Clausewitz's famous assertion that "war is the continuation of politics by other means," this book demonstrates that the PCP-SL's armed struggle was a continuation of political efforts and actions that stretched across the twentieth century.[4] Like the Tawantinsuyo movement, Aprismo, Trotskyism, and even Acción Popular and Velasquismo, the PCP-SL advanced a political project designed to fundamentally remake the Peruvian nation-state and transform political, economic, and social relations inside the country.

Yet just as the PCP-SL and its armed struggle represented historical continuity, the party and its violence also generated historical rupture. The PCP-SL's war brought a level of violence and terror unmatched in Peru's twentieth century. The destruction, fear, and trauma unleashed by the PCP-SL's armed struggle far surpassed the violence associated with any of the other twentieth-century movements treated in this book, and in this sense the PCP-SL and its war marked a sharp historical break with earlier political mobilizations. This rupture was largely a consequence of the PCP-SL's method. The Shining Path argued that change could come only through the complete and total annihilation of the state. To achieve that end, PCP-SL militants planned to gain control of the countryside and then overtake Peru's urban centers and state government. When Shining Path revolutionaries met local opposition to their plan, they usually responded with extreme force. This political method sharply differentiated the PCP-SL from its predecessors. The Tawantinsuyo movement, Acción Popular, and Velasquismo all made campesino cooperation with the state central to their programs; the PCP-SL looked instead to destroy the state. And while Apristas of the 1930s, like Trotskyists of the 1960s, professed and practiced the need for a revolutionary overthrow of the national government, at no moment did those activists become major aggressors against the civilian population. So while the PCP-SL's ends were not wholly unlike those of its political predecessors, its means of extreme and gratuitous violence were sharply different from those employed before.

To argue that the Shining Path was nested inside Peru's rural political history is to invite controversy. Many Peruvians angrily rejected the Truth and Reconciliation Commission's decision to label the PCP-SL a political party rather than a terrorist organization, feeling that the party label gave the Shining Path grossly unwarranted historical and political legitimacy.[5] While that anger is understandable, it should not prevent us from seeing the important historical continuities that marked Peru's twentieth-century political history. Across the twentieth century, Peruvians dreamed, labored, and fought to transform their country. They developed a series of political projects that were exceptionally creative, innovative, and unique. But while conditions and structures shifted slightly from one decade to the next, terrible poverty, political neglect, and racism consistently devastated twentieth-century Peru. Continuity overwhelmed rupture.

Sifting through the eighty-five years of history that preceded the Shining Path's People's War, it is impossible to miss the centrality of politics to rural Ayacucho life.[6] Politics permeated campesinos' daily affairs, shaping their decisions, their actions, and their dreams. Inside Carhuanca, politics took the shape of participation in movements and parties, including the PCP-SL. Inside Luricocha, politics had a different cast. Most Luricocha campesinos shunned formal party involvement, leaving such overt political participation to their landlords and instead using letters and visits to local authorities to advance reformist goals. Luricochanos' efforts to improve their lives and communities accommodated elites insofar as they rarely presented a direct challenge to existing socioeconomic systems and power structures, yet those efforts were resistant in that they expressed discontent with the conditions of rural life.[7] Crucially, Luricocha campesinos' actions and inactions must be understood as political undertakings. The decision to shy away from radical movements like the PCP-SL was a highly political move, and campesinos' professions of loyalty to the state represented strategic efforts to better the social and economic conditions of Luricocha communities.

Recognizing the Shining Path's divergent fortunes in the countryside raises an immediate question: Why did the PCP-SL's success vary so dramatically from place to place? Differences in land tenure systems might seem an obvious answer, particularly given that haciendas dominated Luricocha while peasant smallholdings predominated in Carhuanca. Such a formulation would certainly reinforce the 1960s-era formulation

that independent smallholders like those in Carhuanca were more politically radical than hacienda peasants like those in Luricocha.[8] But a
focus on land tenure systems alone is insufficient, for the simple reason
that Sendero's fortunes in other parts of Peru's sierra followed an entirely opposite pattern, succeeding on haciendas and failing in communities. Historian Nelson Manrique has shown that, inside Junín, PCP-SL
militants had little success inside autonomous communities like those of
Alto Cunas; it was instead in areas long dominated by haciendas that
Sendero gained a strong foothold.[9]

The contrast between the Junín and Ayacucho cases is plain: Senderistas
had little success inside the autonomous communities Manrique studied,
whereas those militants gained control of the communities I studied. And
just as the PCP-SL had early success in the Junín haciendas Manrique
examined, Luricocha's hacienda campesinos forcefully rejected Sendero.
It seems clear, then, that the PCP-SL's fortunes in the Andean countryside
did not correspond to patterns of land tenure. But nor were Senderistas'
early victories and losses wholly random. The Carhuanca and Luricocha
cases suggest that PCP-SL militants fared best in those areas rife with
sharp internal conflict, abusive authorities, and gamonalismo. Manrique's
findings support this assertion; he simply found those conditions in hacienda areas. My assertion also meshes well with historian Miguel
La Serna's recent work. La Serna makes the compelling argument that
Sendero flourished in areas where local injustice ran rampant; community
members supported the PCP-SL in the hopes that the party would bring
long-overdue punishment to local actors who had consistently violated
accepted standards of conduct inside the community. Where communal
systems of authority and justice remained strong and effective, however,
community members largely rejected the PCP-SL.[10]

Luricochanos' and Carhuanquinos' distinct political paths also came
as a consequence of their divergent experiences of state rule. Luricocha
peasants' staid, accommodationist trajectory was largely a by-product
of state violence. Terrorized and victimized by the 1896 repression,
Luricocha campesinos subsequently eschewed involvement in the sort
of radical movements that incurred the wrath of state actors. Fear was
central to Luricocha peasants' rejection of twentieth-century political
parties, and fear helps explain why campesinos chose a seemingly safe
political course of requesting local reforms and professing loyalty to the
Peruvian state. But loyalism ultimately spared indigenous Luricocha
peasants no suffering. State military forces were quick to repress the
1969 education protests, and they blanketed Huanta with violence
during the 1980s, acting on the tragically ironic and highly racialized
misconception that Huanta campesinos were eager converts to the PCP-
SL's cause. Rule by reaction endured across the twentieth century.

Carhuanquinos' political trajectory was likewise shaped by their experience of state rule. So remote from departmental centers of power,
Carhuanquinos made near constant use of the court system and flooded
provincial, departmental, and even national authorities with letters and
petitions. So doing, Carhuanquinos were trying to win official attention
and intervention from state actors who usually offered little more than
callous neglect in response. For Carhuanca, the realities of state abandon produced a political environment where tinterillismo flourished,
and that abandon allowed the abuses of local notables and gamonales to
remain largely unchecked. Knowing that state actors would do little to
rectify local injustices, many Carhuanquinos turned to political movements and parties in the hopes that such activist political involvement
might finally bring change.

The change that Carhuanquinos sought was simultaneously local and
national in scope. Members of the Tawantinsuyo movement pressed for
change inside their communities, pushing for better schools, better authorities, more just labor practices, and fairer taxation. But Tawantinsuyo
members also wanted to transform the place of the Indian worker inside
Peru, making the indigenous laborer a full citizen with rights equal to
any other. The same can be said of participation in APRA. Carhuanca's
Apristas directed their energies toward local matters like controlling
district authority positions and acquiring the Champacancha hacienda.
But these Apristas were also engaged in a larger national movement
that sought to wrest power from the oligarchy and bring socioeconomic
justice to the country. Much the same was true of affiliation with the
PCP-SL. Senderistas sought to punish the local notables and gamonales
who had caused so much suffering inside Carhuanca, but these PCP-SL
militants were also partaking in a larger struggle to raze the Peruvian
state and usher in Maoist utopia.

There is nothing unusual about this mixture of local and national
concerns. Most campesinos understood that the everyday horrors of racial and class oppression inside their communities were connected to
larger problems in their province, their department, and their country.
When they challenged local problems, they confronted an entire system of inequality and injustice. As Eric Wolf commented in his classic
work *Peasant Wars of the Twentieth Century*, "Peasants rise to redress
wrong; but the inequities against which they rebel are but, in turn, pa-
rochial manifestations of great social dislocations. Thus rebellion issues
easily into revolution, massive movements to transform the social structure as a whole. The battlefield becomes society itself."[11]

Politics certainly brought Carhuanca residents a kind of national inclusion that tempered the district's isolation—an inclusion premised on

shared party membership in organizations that included Peruvians from the country's many different regions. Admittedly, there was much regional political variation. Lima Aprismo, Trujillo Aprismo, Chachapoyas Aprismo, and Ayacucho Aprismo, for example, were all distinct political movements, with disparate agendas, varying levels of popularity, and different groups of partisans. At the same time, though, each of these movements was an *Aprista* movement, sharing the same name, the same national leader, and the same basic principles of social justice and popular inclusion. Political parties gave Peru coherence as a nation-state that the exclusionary government did not. But recognition as partisans was not tantamount to recognition as citizens, and Carhuanca residents—like other rural Ayacuchanos—still longed for the attention and concrete assistance of government authorities.

Acknowledgment of the centrality of politics in Ayacucho campesinos' lives undercuts two influential arguments about the PCP-SL. The first of those arguments comes from Peruvian scholar Carlos Iván Degregori. Degregori asserted that campesinos' long subjugation to gamonal abuses conditioned peasants to accept PCP-SL militants as just another political boss and led campesinos to tolerate Sendero's domination, just as they had long tolerated gamonal mistreatments. Degregori wrote, "In an environment where rural gamonalismo, although in shambles, still provided codes of domination and subordination, in a region without a strong network of new peasant organizations and with a weakly developed market, in an area that did not have the opportunity to explore the democratic spaces that opened up in other parts of the country after the 1980 municipal elections, the peasants seemed disposed to accept a new patrón and even accept his punishment."[12] The Carhuanca case sharply contradicts Degregori's assertion. Carhuanquinos' long historical record of fighting their abusive authorities and denouncing gamonalismo suggests that they never surrendered to "codes of domination and subordination." In addition, it was not because Carhuanquinos were "disposed to accept a new patrón" that the PCP-SL gained its initial stronghold in the district. Instead, the PCP-SL advanced because Senderistas took decisive punitive action against the very gamonales and authorities whose abuses Carhuanquinos had repeatedly and unsuccessfully contested.

The second argument maintains that the PCP-SL floundered in areas where other political parties and organizations were well established, while it flourished in locales that lacked a history of strong political engagement.[13] In an early but significant consideration of Sendero, Degregori asserted that the PCP-SL capitalized on campesinos' political inexperience, noting that the party proved strongest in areas with a "weak tradition of modern organization."[14] Ronald Berg offered a variation of this same argument, asserting that Senderistas encountered much opposition in rural areas with long histories of independent political organization and action.[15] This study shows the limits of such an argument. Many Carhuanca campesinos with extensive political experience found the PCP-SL and its program appealing. Indeed, campesinos' frustrations with the shortcomings of their earlier political experiments and affiliations led many of them to embrace the PCP-SL and its program of action.

Just as the eighty-five years of rural Ayacucho history treated in this book reveal the centrality of politics to peasants' lives, those eighty-five years of history also expose the enduring impact of anti-Indianism on rural Andean life. By *anti-Indianism*, I mean two entwined systems: a system of beliefs that cast indigenous peoples as broadly inferior to nonindigenous mestizos and whites and a system of practices that exploited indigenous labor and land to bolster nonindigenous wealth. Through a careful and honest consideration of anti-Indianism's hold on the Andean countryside, we can better understand the origins and process of the Shining Path's People's War. The horror of that war was felt unequally across Peruvian civil society; the race and class dimensions of the civil war violence are nothing less than shocking. Seven out of every ten of the 69,000 dead were indigenous, and nearly six out of ten were rural agricultural workers. It was PCP-SL militants who were responsible for the majority of these deaths, killing more individuals than military and paramilitary forces combined.[16]

It is difficult to understand how and why PCP-SL rebels could show such callous disdain for the very same humble peoples they claimed to be defending. Deborah Poole and Gerardo Rénique have offered one explanation, arguing that PCP-SL militants' Maoist ideology and rigidly class-based political vision contributed to their scorn for all things indigenous.[17] Marisol de la Cadena, in turn, situates Senderistas' racial sentiments inside a long history of provincial intellectual thought.[18] This study, like de la Cadena's work, shows that PCP-SL rebels' bloody disregard for the Indian was not historically unusual. One of this book's most troubling findings is that a seemingly nineteenth-century conceptualization of "the Indian problem"—an ideology that cast indigenous peoples as ignorant, uncivilized, unfit for citizenship, and detrimental to national progress—persisted throughout the twentieth century. Similarly, practices of Indian labor exploitation, land theft, and servitude remained strong during much of the twentieth century.

Regional authorities in Ayacucho derided indigenous campesinos as "backward Indians" and regularly invoked the specter of race war. Huanta landlords and authorities conscripted indigenous campesinos for highway construction while Indian-labored lands provided the basis of hacendados' wealth. These anti-Indian ideologies, structures, and practices also penetrated down to the very marrow of Ayacucho society, metastasizing inside indigenous communities themselves. Within Carhuanca, self-defined local notables regularly scorned their poorer neighbors as "ignorant Indians," ruthlessly exploited their labor and land, and actively denied these poorer Carhuanquinos the opportunity for formal political participation.

Such exclusions and exploitations were made on the formal grounds of illiteracy, but the substance of the matter was race. Although Carhuanca's local notables were seen as indigenous in a national context, they self-defined as "not Indian" at the local level. This dual racial identity was on display for me during my time in Carhuanca. Wealthy Carhuanquinos whose trouble with the Spanish language and whose phenotype seemed to cast them as indigenous regularly stressed that they were not Indian and not of the "Carhuanca race." These local notables' dual racial identity also appeared historically. Standing inside the Presidential Palace in 1967, Carhuanquino governor Luis Allende Ayala seemed unmistakably Indian. He barely reached President Fernando Belaúnde Terry's shoulder, and his dark skin and Andean features contrasted against the president's more European traits. President Belaúnde even made direct reference to Allende's Indianness, asking the governor how to say "viva" in Quechua.[19] Yet, inside Carhuanca, Luis Allende was not Indian. He listed his race as mestizo or *trigüeño* (wheat-colored) on court documents; he cast himself as a "local notable" rather than "indígena" on petitions; and he crassly abused Indian labor while stealing campesinos' land.

While it is upsetting that disdain of the Indian infected indigenous communities, it is altogether tragic that the campesinos who fought most actively to bring social, political, and economic justice to Peru were often the very same people who reproduced anti-Indian prejudice and exploitation inside their very own indigenous communities. Apristas in 1930s Carhuanca, for example, pushed for a radical remaking of the Peruvian nation-state to bring about a more equitable distribution of wealth and power in the country. Yet these same men regularly stood accused of land theft, tinterillismo, abuse of authority, and gamonalismo inside their home district, denounced by their poorer, more Indian neighbors. Similarly, Acción Popular's most enthusiastic representatives in Carhuanca echoed President Belaúnde's calls for progress, modernity, and development, promising the vindication of Peru's poorest people. Yet those same Acción Popular authorities pursued their progressive goals on the backs of Carhuanca's humblest residents, forcing them into unremunerated labor on local infrastructure projects. As one impoverished Carhuanquino bitterly summarized the situation, "The authorities talk, talk, talk, but they do nothing except fuck us over. Authorities exist only to fuck Carhuanquinos. That's how it has always been."[20]

PCP-SL militants took action against Carhuanca's traditionally abusive local notables, killing long-time authorities like Luis Allende, Alonso Chuchón, and Alejandro Quijana. But those Senderistas ultimately replicated the abusive disdain they had punished, using violence and the threat of violence to coerce impoverished, indigenous Carhuanquinos to do their bidding and to provide their sustenance. It seems that Carhuanca's twentieth-century political activists were caught in the quicksand of anti-Indianism; the harder they struggled to end national abuses against destitute indigenous communities, the deeper they sank into perpetuating those abuses at the local level.

It is neither easy nor pleasant to acknowledge the strength of anti-Indianism inside rural Andean communities. My first encounter with former Carhuanca mayor Mariana Gálvez is telling in this regard. Speaking at a 2001 conference in Huamanga, Mariana remarked that she was Carhuanquina and that, as an impoverished, forgotten district, Carhuanca truly represented "Perú profundo."[21] With her long, red fingernails, flashy jewelry, and derogatory remarks about Carhuanca's poorest campesinos, the self-proclaimed "Mayor Mariana" hardly seemed to be what historian Jorge Basadre had in mind when he described "Perú profundo," the authentic Andean heart of the Peruvian nation-state. Yet the research and writing of this book has shown me that Mariana—a bitterly reviled authority inside the district—was just as much a part of Carhuanca as was Juana Romero, the incredibly sweet, elderly, monolingual campesina who read my coca leaves and sang beautiful songs about the Virgin de Asunción. Both had long family histories in the district, and both women had lived, worked, and raised families there. Likewise, the hated gamonal and tinterillo Primitivo Mayhua was just as much a Carhuanquino as Emiliano Muñoz, the warm and thoughtful octogenarian whom Alicia and I especially loved visiting. It is tempting to close our eyes to abusive and even loathsome individuals like Mariana Gálvez and Primitivo Mayhua and pay full academic attention only to those persons who embody all that is special and wonderful about *lo andino*.[22] But such selective vision would do a fundamental disservice to both our readers and to the people we write about, disregarding the shocking realities and troubles that Andean men and women faced—and still face—inside their home districts each and every day. It is only by taking a relentlessly unromantic approach in the consideration of rural indigenous life, seeing and writing with both eyes wide open, that we can understand both the emergence of the Shining Path and the troubling process of its war.

Notes

INTRODUCTION

1. Like most of the interviewee names in this book, "Isaac Escobar" is a pseudonym. All pseudonyms are followed by an asterisk in the footnotes. Interview with Isaac Escobar* (May 21, 2001).

2. Comisión de la Verdad y Reconciliación (CVR), *Informe Final: (Perú, 1980–2000)* (Lima: Universidad Nacional Mayor de San Marcos, 2004). Available at: www.cverdad.org.pe

3. Popular and government observers added the party's longstanding slogan "For the Shining Path of Mariátegui" to its name to distinguish it from the numerous other branches of the Peruvian Communist Party. For the sake of clarity, this book likewise adopts the qualifier "Sendero Luminoso" or "Shining Path."

4. A thoughtful overview of the literature on the PCP-SL appears in Lewis Taylor, *Shining Path: Guerrilla War in Peru's Northern Highlands, 1980–1997* (Liverpool, UK: Liverpool University Press, 2006), 1–46.

5. A critique of early North American literature on the PCP-SL appeared in Deborah Poole and Gerardo Rénique, "The New Chroniclers of Peru: U.S. Scholars and Their 'Shining Path' of Peasant Rebellion," *Bulletin of Latin American Research* 10:2 (1991): 133–191.

6. A number of excellent studies emerged in the aftermath of the war. Works' specific to the department of Ayacucho include Cecilia Méndez, *The Plebeian Republic: The Huanta Rebellion and the Making of the Peruvian State, 1820–1850* (Durham, NC: Duke University Press, 2005); Núria Sala i Vila, *Selva y Andes: Ayacucho, 1780–1929, historia de una región en la encrucijada* (Madrid: Consejo Superior de Investigaciones Científicas Instituto de Historia, 2001); Kimberly Theidon, *Entre prójimos: el conflicto armado interno y la política de la reconciliación en el Perú* (Lima: Instituto de Estudios Peruanos, 2004); Miguel La Serna, "The Corner of the Living: Local Power Relations and Indigenous Perceptions in Ayacucho, Peru, 1940–1983" (Ph.D. Dissertation,

University of California–San Diego, 2008); Wendy Coxshall, "From the Peruvian Reconciliation Commission to Ethnography: Narrative, Relatedness, and Silence," *PoLar: Political and Legal Anthropology Review* 28:2 (November 2005), 203–222; Jonathan Ritter, "A River of Blood: Music, Memory and Violence in Ayacucho, Peru" (Ph.D. Dissertation, University of California–Los Angeles, 2006); Ponciano del Pino, "'En busca del gobierno': Comunidad, política y la producción de la memoria y los silencios en Ayacucho, Perú, siglo XX" (Ph.D. Dissertation, University of Wisconsin–Madison, 2008); Caroline Yezer, "Anxious Citizenship: Insecurity, Apocalypse and War Memories in Peru's Andes" (Ph.D. Dissertation, Duke University, 2007); Olga González-Castañeda, "Unveiling the Secrets of War in the Peruvian Andes" (Ph.D. Dissertation, Columbia University, 2006); Arthur Scarritt, "The Rattle of Burnt Bread: Indigenous Immobilization and Land Loss in the Peruvian Highlands, 1982–2003" (Ph.D. Dissertation, University of Wisconsin–Madison, 2006).

7. Steve J. Stern, "Beyond Enigma: An Agenda for Interpreting Shining Path and Peru, 1980–1995," in *Shining and Other Paths: War and Society in Peru, 1980–1995*, edited by Steve J. Stern (Durham, NC: Duke University Press, 1998), 8.

8. Carlos Iván Degregori, "The Origins and Logic of Shining Path: Two Views," in *Shining Path of Peru*, 2nd ed., edited by David Scott Palmer (New York: St. Martin's Press, 1994), 59.

9. Iván Hinojosa, "On Poor Relations and the Nouveau Riche: Shining Path and the Radical Peruvian Left," in *Shining and Other Paths: War and Society in Peru, 1980–1995*, edited by Steve J. Stern (Durham, NC: Duke University Press, 1998), 60–83.

10. Marisol de la Cadena, "From Race to Class: Insurgent Intellectuals *de provincia* in Peru, 1910–1970," in *Shining and Other Paths: War and Society in Peru, 1980–1995*, edited by Steve J. Stern (Durham, NC: Duke University Press, 1998), 22–59.

11. Florencia Mallon, *Peasant and Nation: The Making of Postcolonial Mexico and Peru* (Berkeley: University of California Press, 1995), 310–311.

12. Taylor, *Shining Path*, 63–80.

13. Del Pino, "En busca del Gobierno"; Theidon, *Entre prójimos*; Yezer, "Anxious Citizenship." Other important discussions of postwar memories appear in Paulo Drinot, "For Whom the Eye Cries: Memory, Monumentality, and the Ontologies of Violence in Peru," *Journal of Latin American Cultural Studies* 18:1 (Mar. 2009): 15–32; Cynthia Milton, "At the Edge of the Peruvian Truth Commission: Alternative Paths to Recounting the Past," *Radical History Review* 98 (May 2007): 3–33.

14. Statistical analysis of Ayacucho's poverty appears in Carlos Iván Degregori *Sendero Luminoso: I. Los hondos y mortales desencuentros* (Lima: IEP Documento de Trabajo, 1985), 7–17.

15. Since 1984, Carhuanca has belonged to the newly created province of Vilcashuamán.

16. Perú, *Censo nacional de población y ocupación, 1940, Vol. 6 Departamentos: Ica, Huancavelica, Ayacucho* (Lima: Dirección de Estadística, 1944), 5.

17. Those easternmost Cangallo districts are Huambalpa, Vilcashuamán, Vischongo, and Saurama, districts that today join with Carhuanca to form the province of Vilcashuamán.

18. CVR, *Informe Final*, Volume IV, Capítulo (Cap). 1.1, 40.

19. Ibid.

20. Kimberly Theidon likewise offers a comparative discussion of districts in Huanta and Cangallo (as well as Víctor Fajardo). She, too, noticed a palpable difference in the character of campesino political engagement between these areas. See *Entre prójimos*, 35.

21. Perú, *Censo nacional de población y ocupación, 1940, Vol. 6,* 5.

22. José R. Ruiz Fowler, *Monografía histórico-geográfica del departamento de Ayacucho* (Lima: Imprenta Torres Aguirre, 1924), 183.

23. CVR, *Informe Final*, Vol. IV, Cap. 1.1, 18–20.

24. For more on the rondas campesinas, see Orin Starn, "Villagers at Arms: War and Counterrevolution in the Central-South Andes," in *Shining and Other Paths: War and Society in Peru, 1980–1995*, edited by Steve J. Stern (Durham, NC: Duke University Press, 1998), 224–260.

25. Kimberly Theidon, *Entre prójimos*, 36; Ponciano del Pino, "En busca del gobierno."

26. Mallon, *Peasant and Nation*; Méndez, *The Plebeian Republic*; Mark Thurner, *From Two Republics to One Divided: Contradictions of Postcolonial Nationmaking in Andean Peru* (Durham, NC: Duke University Press, 1997); Charles Walker, *Smoldering Ashes: Cuzco and the Creation of Republican Peru, 1780–1840* (Durham, NC: Duke University Press, 1999).

27. Marc Becker, *Indians and Leftists in the Making of Ecuador's Modern Indigenous Movements* (Durham, NC: Duke University Press, 2008); Laura Gotkowitz, *A Revolution for Our Rights: Indigenous Struggles for Land and Justice in Bolivia, 1880–1952* (Durham, NC: Duke University Press, 2007).

28. See, for example, the story "Ayacucho Siempre Abandonado" in the migrant newspaper *Sierra* (Primera Quincena [PQ] Apr. 1947), 2.

29. Aaron Bobrow-Strain, *Intimate Enemies: Landowners, Power, and Violence in Chiapas* (Durham, NC: Duke University Press, 2007).

30. Cecilia Méndez, "The Power of Naming, or the Construction of Ethnic and National Identities in Peru: Myth, History, and the Iquichanos," *Past and Present* 171 (May 2001): 138. See also Méndez, *The Plebeian Republic*.

31. Interview with Hernán Carrillo* (Feb. 17, 2003).

32. Interview with Rufina Encisco* (Mar. 14, 2003).

33. Interview with Faustino Carrera* (Oct. 5, 2003).

34. Archivo Regional de Ayacucho (ARA), Corte Superior de Justicia (CSJ) Cangallo, legajo (leg). 8, expediente (exped.) 1409 (testimony of Manuela Quijana: Nov. 11, 1948).

35. ARA, Subprefectura Cangallo (SC) Caja 5 (Dec. 23, 1940).

36. Marisol de la Cadena, *Indigenous Mestizos: The Politics of Race and Culture in Cuzco, 1919–1991* (Durham, NC: Duke University Press, 2000).

37. Mallon, *Peasant and Nation*.

38. For reflection on Peru's education myth, see María Elena García, *Making Indigenous Citizens: Identities, Education and Multicultural Development in Peru* (Stanford, CA: Stanford University Press, 2005).

CHAPTER ONE

1. Interview with Hernán Carrillo* (Feb. 17, 2003).
2. Clorinda Matto de Turner, *Aves sin nido* (Caracas: Biblioteca Ayacucho, 1994), 32. (Originally published in 1889).
3. Manuel González Prada, *Páginas libres; Horas de lucha* (Caracas: Biblioteca Ayacucho, 1985), 343.
4. Manuel Burga and Alberto Flores Galindo, *Apogeo y crisis de la República Aristocrática: oligarquía, aprismo y comunismo en el Perú, 1895–1932* (Lima: Ediciones Rikchay Perú, 1980).
5. Mallon, *Peasant and Nation*; Thurner, *From Two Republics*; Nelson Manrique, *Las guerrillas indígenas en la Guerra con Chile: campesinado y nación* (Lima: Centro de Investigación y Capacitación, 1981).
6. My comment about Carhuanca's "unruly order" borrows from the title of Deborah Poole, ed., *Unruly Order: Violence, Power and Cultural Identity in the High Provinces of Southern Peru* (Boulder, CO: Westview Press, 1994).
7. Lewis Taylor, *Bandits and Politics in Peru: Landlord and Peasant Violence in Hualgayoc, 1900–30* (Cambridge, UK: Center of Latin American Studies University of Cambridge, 1987), 74.
8. Rosalind Gow, "Yawar Mayu: Revolution in the Southern Andes, 1860–1980" (Ph.D. Dissertation, University of Wisconsin-Madison, 1981), 93; Alberto Flores Galindo, *Buscando un Inca: identidad y utopía en los Andes*, 4th ed. (Lima: Editorial Horizonte, 1994), 244.
9. Archivo Histórico Militar (AHM), Leg. 1879, Caja 6 ("Decreto": Mar. 23, 1879); AHM, Leg. 1885, Caja 11 (letter from Remigio Morales Bermúdez: Dec. 20, 1884).
10. Interview with Isidro Durán* (Mar. 14, 2003); ARA, CSJ Leg. 337, Cuad. 25 (testimony of Leóncio Cárdenas: Jan. 28, 1911).
11. ARA, CSJ Leg. 337, Cuad. 25 (testimony of Leóncio Cárdenas: Jan. 28, 1911; testimony of Facundo Ochoa: Mar. 10, 1911; testimony of Pánfilo Cárdenas: Sept. 29, 1911). Interviews with Hernán Carrillo* (Feb. 17, 2003); Emiliano Muñoz* (Oct. 5, 2003); Isidro Durán* (Mar. 14, 2003); Ignacio Figueroa* (Sept. 23, 2003).
12. ARA, CSJ Leg. 337, Cuad. 25 (testimony of Leóncio Cárdenas: Jan. 28, 1911; testimony of Facundo Ochoa: Mar. 10, 1911; testimony of Pánfilo Cárdenas: Sept. 29, 1911). For similar interelite fights elsewhere in Peru, see Flores, *Buscando un Inca*, 243; Alejandro Diez Hurtado, *Comunes y haciendas: procesos de comunalización en la Sierra de Piura (siglos XVIII al XX)* (Piura, Peru: CIPCA, 1998), 152.
13. ARA, Subprefectura Cangallo (SC), Caja 37 (Oficios de Carhuanca (OCar) 1937: Apr. 26, 1915).
14. ARA, SC Caja 49 (OCar 1917: Apr. 25, 1917).

15. ARA, SC Caja 49 (OCar 1917: June 11, 1917).

16. ARA, SC Caja 25 (OCar 1918: Feb. 16, 1918).

17. ARA, SC Caja 11 (OCar 1913: Dec. 27, 1913). Details of compulsory military service appear in Thomas Davies, *Indian Integration in Peru: A Half-Century of Experience, 1900–1948* (Lincoln: University of Nebraska Press, 1974), 46.

18. ARA, Prefectura (Pref.) Leg. 27 (Oficios de la Subprefectura de Lucanas [OSL]: Dec. 20, 1902).

19. ARA, Pref. Leg. 99 (OSL: Nov. 24, 1906).

20. ARA, SC Caja 11 (OCar 1913: Nov. 11, 1913).

21. ARA, Pref. Leg. 100 (Oficios recibido de la guardia nacional y la guardia civil [OGNGC]: Oct. 6, 1912.

22. ARA, Pref. Leg. 100 (OGNGC: Jan. 3, 1917).

23. ARA, Pref. Leg. 27 (OSL: Dec. 20, 1902); ARA, Pref. Leg. 100 (OGNGC: Mar. 24, 1913; Nov. 12, 1913; Jan. 3, 1917); ARA, SC Caja 9 (OCar 1911: Dec. 1, 1911, Dec. 7, 1911).

24. Diez Hurtado, *Comunes y haciendas*, 158; Davies, *Indian Integration*, 49.

25. ARA, SC Caja 9 (OCar 1911: Dec. 4, 1911). (Both letters have the same date.)

26. ARA, SC Caja 24 (OCar: Sept. 5, 1911.)

27. ARA, Pref. Leg. 26 (OSL: July 22, 1892).

28. ARA, SC Caja 11 (OCar 1913: Nov. 21, 1913).

29. ARA, Pref. Leg. 26 (OSL: Feb. 27, 1890).

30. ARA, Pref. Leg. 27 (OSL: Jan. 16, 1902).

31. ARA, Pref. Leg. 27 (OSL: Apr. 7, 1907).

32. ARA, Pref. Leg. 27 (OSL: June 1, 1908).

33. ARA, Pref. Leg. 28 (OSL: Oct. 14, 1909).

34. Flores, *Buscando un Inca*, 243. See also Carlos Aguirre, *The Criminals of Lima and Their Worlds: The Prison Experience, 1850–1935* (Durham, NC: Duke University Press, 2005), 66–68.

35. ARA, Pref. Leg. 27 (OSL: May 14, 1903).

36. ARA, SC Caja 55 (OCar 1910: Feb. 25, 1910).

37. ARA, Pref. Leg. 28 (OSL: May 31, 1909).

38. ARA, SC Caja 55 (OCar 1910: Jan. 15, 1910); ARA, Pref. Leg. 28 (OSL: Nov. 22, 1909).

39. ARA, SC Caja 50 (OCar 1910: Apr. 30, 1910).

40. ARA, SC Caja 9 (OCar 1911: Nov. 29, 1911).

41. ARA, Pref. Leg. 18 (OSC: Jan. 7, 1918); ARA, SC Caja 25 (OCar 1918: Feb. 25, 1918).

42. ARA, SC Caja 18 (OCar 1918: Mar. 9, 1918); ARA, SC Caja 49 (OCar 1917: May 13, 1917; June 24, 1917); ARA, SC Caja 25 (OCar 1918: May 9, 1918; Apr. 23, 1918); ARA, Pref. Leg. 17 (OSC: Apr. 8, 1912).

43. ARA, SC Caja 25 (OCar 1918: Feb. 20, 1918).

44. ARA, SC Caja 49 (OCar 1917: Dec. 11, 1917).

45. ARA, CSJ Leg. 337, Cuad. 25 (testimony of Panfilo Cárdenas: Sept. 29, 1911).

46. Ibid.

47. ARA, SC Caja 49 (OCar 1917: Dec. 11, 1917).

48. ARA, SC Caja 49 (OCar 1917: Sept. 18, 1917).

49. ARA, CSJ Leg. 342, Cuad. 7 (letter of complaint by Juan Zárate, Agripino Vásquez, et al.: Apr. 18, 1913).

50. ARA, SC Caja 9 (OCar: Dec. 21, 1911).

51. ARA, CSJ Leg. 350, Cuad. 10 (testimony of Pastor Allende: Aug. 8, 1919).

52. ARA, CSJ Leg. 362, Cuad. 7 (passim: case initiated Oct. 29, 1915); ARA, CSJ Leg. 351, Cuad. 2 (passim: case initiated Jan. 8, 1916); ARA, CSJ Leg. 351, Cuad. 1 (testimony of Paulino and María Allende and Ciriaco Ochoa: Mar. 24, 1916).

53. Ibid.

54. ARA, CSJ Leg. 351, Cuad. 1 (testimony of Paulino and María Allende and Ciriaco Ochoa: Mar. 24, 1916).

55. ARA, CSJ Leg. 350, Cuad. 10 (testimony of Davíd Carrasco: Dec. 22, 1916).

56. ARA, CSJ Leg. 348, Cuad. 10 (respective testimonies of Toribio Balboa, Edilberto Ortega, and Francisca Mendívil: Mar. 24, 1916).

57. ARA, SC Caja 49 (OCar 1917: Apr. 25, 1917).

58. ARA, SC Caja 50 (OCar 1910: Apr. 30, 1910).

59. ARA, SC Caja 11 (OCar 1913: Oct. 23, 1913).

60. ARA, Pref. Leg. 18 (OSC: undated 1917 document signed by Ignacio Herrera, Andrés Berrocal, Lorenzo Morales, and Manuel Chipana).

61. Flores, *Buscando un Inca*, 102.

62. ARA, SC Caja 55 (OCar 1910: Apr. 27, 1910).

63. ARA, SC Caja 55 (OCar 1910: illegible date, letter from Governor Pedro Bendezú).

64. ARA, SC Caja 49 (OCar: May 2, 1917).

65. ARA, Pref. Leg. 99 (OGNGC: June 1, 1908).

66. ARA, Pref. Leg. 27 (OSL: Mar. 17, 1907).

67. ARA, Pref. Leg. 17 (OSC: Oct. 10, 1912; Nov. 1, 1912; Dec. 6, 1912; Jan. 21, 1913); ARA, Pref. Leg. 19 (OSC: Mar. 24, 1915); ARA, SC Caja 11 (OCar 1913: Sept. 22, 1913).

68. ARA, Pref. Leg. 27 (OSL: Jan. 10, 1908); ARA, Pref. Leg. 18 (OSC: Nov. 8, 1917); ARA, SC Caja 49 (OCar 1917: Sept. 12, 1917).

69. ARA, SC Caja 55 (OCar 1910: July 22, 1910).

70. ARA, Pref. Leg. 26 (OSL: Aug. 20, 1892; Aug. 25, 1892).

71. ARA, Pref. Leg. 27 (OSL: Mar. 17, 1907).

72. ARA, Pref. Leg. 27 (OSL: Apr. 8, 1907).

73. ARA, SC Caja 11 (OCar 1913: May 24, 1913; May 28, 1913; June 1, 1913).

74. ARA, Notary Bruno Medina, Leg. 170 folio (fol.) 694 (May 20, 1898); ARA, Notary Bruno Medina, Leg. 266 fol. 45 (Feb. 21, 1903).

75. ARA, Notary Celso Bustios, Leg. 221 fol. 567 (Feb. 2, 1916); ARA, Fuero Comun (FC) Leg. 86 exped. 12; ARA, Notary Francisco Mavila, Leg. 451

libro 2 fol. 385 (Nov. 27, 1928); ARA, Notary Saturnino Bedoya, Leg. 276, libro 1 fol. 750 (Feb. 9, 1912); ARA, Notary Saturnino Bedoya, Leg. 276 libro 1 fol. 2024 (Dec. 27, 1912); ARA, Notary Juan Cabrera, Escrituras Imperfectas "A" fol. 15, (May 1, 1912); ARA, Notary Bruno Medina, Leg. 168 fol. 353 (June 13, 1896).

76. ARA, Pref. Leg. 27 (OSL: Apr. 7, 1907).

77. ARA, Pref. Leg. 10 (OSH: Nov. 23, 1889; Feb. 26, 1890).

78. ARA, SC Caja 55 (OCar 1910: Mar. 28, 1910).

79. ARA, SC Caja 11 (OCar 1913: May 9, 1913; May 15, 1913; May 27, 1913; June 25, 1913; Sept. 24, 1913; Sept. 29, 1913); ARA, SC Caja 3 (Oficios de la Prefectura: Apr. 30, 1913); ARA, SC Caja 37 (OCar 1915: Apr. 15, 1915; Apr. 21, 1915).

80. Jeffrey Klaiber, *The Catholic Church in Peru, 1821–1985: A Social History* (Washington, DC: Catholic University of America Press, 1992), 47–49, 71.

81. The first Carhuanquino usage of the word *gamonal* that I have found was in ARA, SC Caja 49 (Sept. 13, 1917).

82. Deborah Poole, "Performance, Domination and Identity in the *Tierras Bravas* of Chumbivilcas (Cusco)," in *Unruly Order: Violence, Power, and Cultural Identity in the High Provinces of Southern Peru*, edited by Deborah Poole (Boulder, CO: Westview Press, 1994), 104–107.

83. ARA, SC Caja 55 (OCar 1910: Dec. 16, 1910).

84. ARA, CSJ Leg. 337, Cuad. 25 (testimony of Ildefonso Santa Cruz: Jan. 28, 1911).

85. ARA, CSJ Leg. 362, Cuad. 7 (testimony of Inocencio Negri: Oct. 29, 1915).

86. ARA, SC Caja 49 (OCar 1917: July 4, 1917).

87. Méndez, *The Plebeian Republic.*

88. Quoted in Luis E. Cavero, *Monografía de la Provincia de Huanta,* vol. 1 (Lima: n.p., 1953), 258. For information on Huanta guerrillas, see AHM, Leg. 1885, Caja 11 (letter from Remigio Morales Bermúdez: Feb. 20, 1885); AHM, Leg. 1884, Caja 8 (letter from Remigio Morales Bermúdez: Nov. 17, 1884); AHM, Leg. 1885, Caja 3 (letter from Pedro Más: Jan. 6, 1885); AHM, Leg. 1879 Caja 6 ("Decreto": Mar. 23, 1879); Archivo Público de la Biblioteca Nacional (APBN), Manuscript D3969 (May 20, 1886); APBN, Archivo Cáceres, Caja 52 (June 20, 1881); ARA, CSJ Leg. 267, Cuad. 18 (testimony of Lino Castro: June 3, 1891).

89. ARA, Pref. Leg. 10 (OSH: Jan. 16, 1890).

90. ARA, CSJ Leg. 267, Cuad. 18 (testimony of Víctor Bustamente: June 3, 1891).

91. *Eco del Pueblo* (Feb. 15, 1890), 49.

92. ARA, CSJ Leg. 267, Cuad. 18 (passim: case initiated June 3, 1891); ARA, Pref. Leg. 10 (OSH: Jan. 20, 1890; Jan. 21, 1890; Jan. 26, 1890; Jan. 30, 1890; Feb. 10, 1890).

93. ARA, CSJ Leg. 267, Cuad. 18 (testimony of Víctor Bustamente: June 3, 1891).

94. Ibid.

95. ARA, CSJ Leg. 267, Cuad. 18 (testimony of Apolinario Ancho: June 3, 1891).

96. *Eco del Pueblo* (Feb. 15, 1890), 49.

97. *El Debate* (Oct. 9, 1896), quoted in Juan José del Pino, *Las Sublevaciones indígenas de Huanta* (Ayacucho: n.p., 1955), 125–128; AHM, Leg. 1896, Caja 8 (letter from Ramón Guillén, José and Antonio Arangüena, and Davíd Cabrera: Oct. 2, 1896); AHM, Leg. 1896, Caja 8 (letter from Pedro Portillo: Oct. 2, 1896). An influential study of the Salt Tax Revolt appears in Patrick Husson's *De la guerra a la rebelión (Huanta, siglo XIX)* (Cuzco: Centro de Estudios Regionales Andinos "Bartolomé de las Casas," 1992).

98. ARA, CSJ Leg. 293, Cuad. 3 (testimony of Santos Anaya: Nov. 26, 1898); ARA, CSJ Leg. 294, Cuad. 16 (testimony of Félix Torres: Sept. 5, 1896).

99. *El Debate* (Oct. 9, 1896), quoted in del Pino, *Sublevaciones indígenas*, 126.

100. ARA, CSJ Leg. 294, Cuad. 16 (testimony of José Bustios: Sept. 5, 1896).

101. ARA, CSJ Leg. 294, Cuad. 16 (testimony of Policarpo Arce: Sept. 5, 1896; testimony of Félix Torres: Sept. 5, 1896).

102. *El Comercio* (Oct. 5, 1896), quoted in del Pino, *Sublevaciones indígenas*, 131.

103. *La Voz del Centro* (Sept. 28, 1896), quoted in del Pino, *Sublevaciones indígenas*, 124.

104. ARA, CSJ Leg. 265, Cuad. 10 (testimony of Acencio Bondinel: Jan. 30, 1890).

105. *El Debate* (Oct. 9, 1896), quoted in del Pino, *Sublevaciones indígenas*, 127.

106. *El Debate* (Oct. 9, 1896), quoted in del Pino, *Sublevaciones indígenas*, 126.

107. AHM, Leg. 1896, Caja 8 (letter from Ramón Guillén: Oct. 2, 1896).

108. *El Debate* (Dec. 24, 1896) quoted in del Pino, *Sublevaciones indígenas*, 133.

109. *El Comercio* (Oct. 6, 1896), quoted in del Pino, *Sublevaciones indígenas*, 131.

110. Cavero, *Monografía de la Provincia*, vol. 2, 51–52, 54–55, 58.

111. Cavero, *Monografía de la Provincia de Huanta*, vol. 2, 85–93.

112. Ibid.; *La República* (Feb. 20, 1897), quoted in del Pino, *Sublevaciones indígenas*, 136–137; AHM, Leg. 1897, Caja 3 (letter from D. J. Parra: Nov. 26, 1896); AHM, Leg. 1896, Caja 1 (letter from D. J. Parra: Dec. 17, 1896).

113. AHM, Leg. 1896, Caja 1 (letter from D. J. Parra: Dec. 17, 1896).

114. Cavero, *Monografía de la Provincia*, vol. 2, 107.

115. *La República* (Feb. 20, 1897), quoted in del Pino, *Sublevaciones indígenas*, 137.

116. ARA, Pref. Leg. 10 (OSH: Feb. 25, 1903).

117. ARA, Pref. Leg. 10 (OSH: Nov. 7, 1902); ARA, Pref. Leg. 11 (OSH: Mar. 10, 1907; May 13, 1907; Feb. 6, 1908).

118. *Registro Oficial* (Nov. 30, 1896), 1.
119. *Registro Oficial* (Aug. 27, 1897), 1. Descriptions of the ceremonies appear in Cavero, *Monografía de Huanta*, vol. 2, 111, 117.
120. González Prada, *Páginas Libres*, 107.
121. Nelson Manrique makes a similar argument in *Yawar Mayu: sociedades terratenientes serranas, 1879–1910* (Lima: DESCO Centro de Estudios y Promoción del Desarrollo, 1988).

CHAPTER TWO

1. A portion of this chapter appeared in Jaymie Patricia Heilman, "Por un imperio de ciudadanos: el movimiento del 'Tawantinsuyo' en el Ayacucho de los años 20," translated by María Gabriela Castro-Barrientos, in *Nuevas perspectivas sobre el 'oncenio' de Leguía*, edited by Paulo Drinot. (Lima: Instituto de Estudios Peruanos, forthcoming).
2. ARA, CSJ Leg. 409, Cuad. 5 (letter from Mariano Berrocal: Aug. 17, 1923).
3. See Jorge Basadre, *Historia de la República del Perú, 1822–1933* (Lima: Editorial Universitaria, 1983), vol. 13, 308; Dan C. Hazen, "The Awakening of Puno: Government Policy and the Indian Problem in Southern Peru" (Ph.D. Dissertation, Yale University, 1974), 153; Flores, *Buscando un Inca*, 254.
4. Discussions of the Tawantinsuyo Committee appear in de la Cadena, *Indigenous Mestizos*, 86–130; Carlos Arroyo, "La experiencia del Comité Central Pro-Derecho Indígena Tahuantinsuyo," *Estudios interdisciplinarios de America Latina y el Caribe* 15:1 (Jan.–June 2004): 1–24; Gerardo Leibner, "Radicalism and Integration: The Tahuantinsuyo Committee Experience and the 'Indigenismo' of Leguía Reconsidered, 1919–1924," *Journal of Iberian and Latin American Studies* 9:2 (Dec. 2003): 1–23; Steven Pent, "Bridging the Rural–Urban Divide: Mobilization and Citizenship of a Peruvian Peasant Organization" (M.A. thesis, University of California–Santa Barbara, 2007); Wilfredo Kapsoli, *Ayllus del sol: anarquismo y utopía andina* (Lima: TAREA Asociación de Publicaciones Educativas, 1984); Wilfredo Kapsoli, *Los movimientos campesinos en el Perú, 1879–1965*, 2nd ed. (Lima: Atusparia Ediciones, 1982).
5. Important works on Mariátegui include, but are hardly limited to, Alberto Flores Galindo, *La agonía de Mariátegui: la polémica con la Komintern* (Lima: DESCO, 1980); Aníbal Quijano, *Reencuentro y debate: Una introducción a Mariátegui* (Lima: Mosca Azul, 1981); Marc Becker, *Mariátegui and Latin American Marxist Theory* (Athens: Ohio University Center for International Studies, 1993); Jesús Chavarría, *José Carlos Mariátegui and the Rise of Modern Peru, 1890–1930* (Albuquerque: University of New Mexico Press, 1979).
6. De la Cadena, *Indigenous Mestizos*, 118–125.
7. Archivo General de la Nación (AGN), Ministerio de Trabajo y Asuntos Indígenas, Leg. 3.13.2.9 (Document titled "Declaración de Principios").
8. Kapsoli, *Ayllus del Sol*, 197–244.
9. José Luis Rénique, *La batalla por Puno: conflicto agrario y nación en los Andes Peruanos, 1866–1995* (Lima: IEP, 2003), 47–49, 75; Annalyda Álvarez-

Calderón, "'Es justicia lo que esperamos de Su Excelencia': política indígena en Puno (1901–1927)," in *Más allá de la dominación y la resistencia: Estudios de historia peruana, siglos xvi–xx*, edited by Paulo Drinot and Leo Garofalo (Lima: IEP, 2005), 312–341.

10. Kapsoli, *Ayllus del sol*; Rénique, *Batalla por Puno*, 60; Davies, *Indian Integration*, 54–55.

11. De la Cadena, *Indigenous Mestizos*.

12. Rénique, *Batalla por Puno*, 53.

13. Wilfredo Kapsoli, *El Pensamiento de la Asociación Pro-Indígena* (Cuzco, Peru: Centro Las Casas, 1980). On the Rumi Maki rebellion, see Nils Jacobsen, *Mirages of Transition: The Peruvian Altiplano, 1780–1930* (Berkeley: University of California Press, 1993), 339–343; Davies, *Indian Integration*, 54–55; Hazen, "Awakening of Puno," 141–146; Rénique, *Batalla por Puno*, 51–53.

14. Peter Blanchard, *The Origins of the Peruvian Labor Movement, 1883–1919* (Pittsburgh, PA: University of Pittsburgh Press, 1982).

15. AGN, Ministerio de Trabajo y Asuntos Indígenas, Leg. 3.13.2.9 (letter to Sr. Secretario General del Comité Central 'Pro-Derecho Indígena': June 21, 1920).

16. See Manuel Burga, "Las profetas de la rebelión, 1920–1923" in *Estados y naciones en los Andes: hacia una historia comparativa*, edited by Jean Paul Deler and Y. Saint-Geours (Lima: IEP, 1986), 480, 496; Kapsoli, *Movimientos campesinos*, 64; Basadre, *Historia*, 308; Hazen, "Awakening of Puno," 153; Flores, *Buscando un Inca*, 254.

17. AHM, Box 1923 (letter from Prefecto Accidental Boggio: Sept. 12, 1923; letter to Sr. Ministro del Estado: Aug. 31, 1923). For further discussion of the La Mar uprising, see Eric Mayer, "State Policy and Community Conflict in Bolivia and Peru, 1900–1980" (Ph.D. Dissertation, University of California–Santa Barbara, 1995), 277–315; Flavio Vila Galindo, *Los montoneros: Movimiento campesino de La Mar—Ayacucho, Peru* (Lima: n.p., 2000).

18. ARA, CSJ Leg. 409, Cuad. 5 (July 30, 1923).

19. ARA, CSJ Leg. 409, Cuad. 5 (Aug. 7, 1923); interview with Isidro Durán* (Mar. 14, 2003).

20. ARA, CSJ Leg. 409, Cuad. 5 (Aug. 17, 1923).

21. Ibid.

22. Photocopied document from Jorge Cárdenas's private collection in Carhuanca. This document is clearly from a court trial, but I have been unable to locate the original trial record.

23. AHM, Box 1923 (letter to Coronel Jefe del Gabinete Militar: Sept. 12, 1923).

24. ARA, Pref. Leg. 18 (Oficios de la Subprefectura de Cangallo [OSC]: Of. 180, June 10, 1924).

25. AHM, Box 1923 (letter to Coronel Jefe del Gabinete Militar: Sept. 12, 1923).

26. ARA, CSJ Leg. 409, Cuad. 5 (letters from Gerónimo Lara: July 30, 1923, August 7, 1923).

27. Interview with Isidro Durán* (Mar. 14, 2003); AHM, Box 1923 (letter from Prefecto Accidental Boggio: Sept. 12, 1923).

28. Interviews with Isidro Durán* (Mar. 14, 2003) and Modesto Ramos* (Oct. 4, 2003).

29. ARA, CSJ Leg 409, Cuad. 5 (Aug. 23, 1923). The edict appears in its entirety in ARA, CSJ Leg. 409, Cuad. 5 (undated document entitled "Declaración de Principios del Comité Central Pro-Derecho Indígena Tahuantinsuyo").

30. ARA, CSJ Leg. 409, Cuad. 5 (undated document entitled "Declaración de Principios del Comité Central Pro-Derecho Indígena Tahuantinsuyo").

31. Discussion of abusive authorities appears in Diez Hurtado, *Comunes y haciendas*, 197; Davies, *Indian Integration*, 81; Burga, "Profetas de la rebelión," 508.

32. ARA, SC Caja 16 (OCar 1923: Feb. 19, 1923).

33. ARA, SC Caja 16 (OCar 1923: Feb. 26, 1923).

34. ARA, Pref. Leg. 18 (OSC: Apr. 28, 1923).

35. ARA, SC Caja 16 (OCar: May 7, 1923).

36. Interview with Hernán Carrillo* (Mar. 14, 2003).

37. Augusto Cárdenas Zárate, "Sucesos Notables del Siglo" in *El Retorno: Boletin de la Comisión Pro Retorno al Distrito de Carhuanca*. No. 1 19-XII-1999, 4.

38. ARA, SC Caja 35 (OCar 1922: Dec. 12, 1922).

39. ARA, SC Caja 7 (OCar 1920: Jan. 30, 1920).

40. ARA, SC Caja 19 (Varios oficios: Sept. 13, 1920).

41. Quoted in Kapsoli, *Ayllus del Sol*, 29.

42. Quoted in de la Cadena, *Indigenous Mestizos*, 90.

43. ARA, Pref. Leg. 18 (OSC: Sept. 13, 1921).

44. ARA, SC Caja 19 (OCar 1920: May 11, 1920); ARA, SC Caja 46 (OCar 1921: Aug. 22, 1921).

45. ARA, CSJ Leg. 409, Cuad. 5 (letter from Fidel Gómez: Aug. 7, 1923).

46. ARA, CSJ Leg. 409, Cuad. 5 (letter from Severino Lara: Aug. 8, 1923).

47. ARA, CSJ Leg. 409, Cuad. 5 (letter from Rosa Meneses: Aug. 23, 1923).

48. Thurner, *From Two Republics*, 81–82.

49. ARA, CSJ Leg. 409, Cuad. 5 (letter from Severino Lara: Aug. 8, 1923).

50. Kapsoli, *Movimientos campesinos*, 74; Rénique, *Batalla por Puno*, 83–85; José Luis Rénique, "State and Regional Movements in the Peruvian Highlands: The Case of Cusco, 1895–1985" (Ph.D. Dissertation, Columbia University, 1988), 58; Flores Galindo, *Buscando un Inca*, 254.

51. Kapsoli, *Ayllus del sol*, 207.

52. ARA, Not. (Notary Ángel Arones) Leg. 364, Libro 2, Fol. 88 (Oct. 13, 1923).

53. ARA, Not. (Notary Francisco Mavila) Leg. 451, Libro 2, Fol. 218 (July 9, 1928); Not. (Notary Francisco Mavila) Leg. 452, Libro 1, Fol. 228 (Sept. 28, 1929); Not. (Notary Ángel Arones) Leg. 364, Libro 2, Fol. 158 (Aug. 11, 1924); Not. (Notary Ismael Berrocal) Leg. 277, Libro 3, Fol. 81 (June 7, 1929).

54. ARA, SC Caja 16 (OCar 1923: Apr. 23, 1923).

55. Interview with Ignacio Figueroa* (Oct. 2, 2003).

56. Interview with Gregorio Escalante* (Oct. 3, 2003).

57. ARA, SC Caja 16 (OCar 1923: Apr. 23, 1923).

58. ARA, SC Caja 46 (OCar 1926: May 5, 1926).

59. Alessandro Portelli, *The Death of Luigi Trastulli and Other Stories: Form and Meaning in Oral History* (Albany: State University of New York Press, 1991); Joanne Rappaport, *Cumbe Reborn: An Andean Ethnography of History* (Chicago: University of Chicago Press, 1994); Thomas Abercrombie, *Pathways of Memory and Power: Ethnography and History among an Andean People* (Madison: University of Wisconsin Press, 1998); Burga, "Las profetas de la rebelión," 512.

60. Thoughtful reflections on memory appear in Steve J. Stern, *Remembering Pinochet's Chile: On the Eve of London, 1998* (Durham, NC: Duke University Press, 2004).

61. On the relationship between political trauma and silence, see Jeffrey L. Gould and Aldo A. Lauria-Santiago, *To Rise in Darkness: Revolution, Repression, and Memory in El Salvador, 1920–1932* (Durham, NC: Duke University Press, 2008), 245–246.

62. ARA, CSJ Leg. 426, Cuad. 1 (passim: case initiated May 10, 1924).

63. Interview with Mercedes Cisneros* (Oct. 22, 2003).

64. Interview with Adolfo Urbana* (Feb. 17, 2003).

65. ARA, CSJ Leg. 426, Cuad. 1 (Testimony of Dominga Cordero: June 12, 1924).

66. Ibid.

67. Proyecto Especial de Titulación de Tierras (PETT) Luricocha (letter from Doroteo Silvera, Anacleto Carrasco, Nicanor Guerrero and Salome Pariona: Jan. 14, 1925).

68. Ibid.

69. Ibid. Description of the vial appears in Kapsoli, *Movimientos campesinos*, 52–53, 56.

70. Gow, "Yawar Mayu," 39–40.

71. See, for example, ARA, Pref. Leg. 13 (OSH: Jan. 16, 1926).

72. ARA, Pref. Leg. 13 (OSH: Jan. 30, 1926).

73. ARA, Pref. Leg. 13 (OSH: Jan. 24, 1924).

74. ARA, Pref. Leg. 13 (OSH: July 17, 1924).

75. ARA, Pref. Leg. 13 (OSH: Of. 160, Oct. 29, 1924).

76. ARA, Pref. Leg. 13 (OSH: Jan. 30, 1926).

77. ARA, Pref. Leg. 13 (OSH: Feb. 2, 1924).

78. ARA, Pref. Leg. 13 (OSH: Of. 24, Jan. 29, 1924; July 17, 1924).

79. ARA, Pref. Leg. 13 (OSH: Oct. 29, 1924).

80. ARA, Pref. Leg. 13 (OSH: Jan. 30, 1926).

81. For a different perspective, see Nelson Pereyra Chávez, "Los campesinos y la Conscripción Vial: Aproximaciones al estudio de las relaciones estado-indígenas y las relaciones de mercado en Ayacucho (1919–1930)," in *Estado y mercado en la historia del Perú*, edited by Carlos Contreras and Manuel Glave (Lima: Pontificia Universidad Católica del Perú), 334–350.

82. ARA, Pref. Leg. 12 (OSH: Oct. 16, 1923).

83. Ibid.
84. ARA, Pref. Leg. 12 (OSH: Jan. 21, 1923; Jan. 22, 1923).
85. ARA, Pref. Leg. 13 (OSH: Of. 20, Jan. 24, 1924).
86. ARA, Pref. Leg. 13 (OSH: Of. 26, Feb. 27, 1925).
87. Graham H. Stuart, "The Administration of President Leguía of Peru," *The American Political Science Review* 22:2 (May 1928), 416–420.
88. ARA, Pref. Leg. 13 (OSH: Jan. 21, 1924).
89. ARA, Pref. Leg. 13 (OSH: Of. 20, Jan. 24, 1924).
90. ARA, Pref. Leg. 13 (OSH: Of. 16, Jan. 21, 1924).
91. ARA, Pref. Leg. 102 (OGNGC: Aug. 31, 1927).
92. ARA, Pref. Leg. 13 (OSH: Feb. 4, 1926).
93. ARA, Pref. Leg. 13 (OSH: May 11, 1927).
94. See, for example, Xavier Albó, "El retorno del Indio," *Revista Andina* 9:2 (1991): 299–345.
95. García, *Making Indigenous Citizens,* 4–9; Shane Greene, "Getting over the Andes: The Geo-Eco-Politics of Indigenous Movements in Peru's 21st Century Inca Empire," *Journal of Latin American Studies* 38:2 (2006): 327–354.
96. Interview with Modesto Ramos* (Oct. 4, 2003).

CHAPTER THREE

1. Interview with Marcelino Lizarbe* (Sept. 24, 2003). A portion of this chapter appeared in Jaymie Patricia Heilman, "We Will No Longer Be Servile: 'Aprismo' in 1930s Ayacucho," *Journal of Latin American Studies* 38:3 (August 2006): 491–518.
2. The suggestion that APRA held little appeal in the south and to indigenous populations appears in Geoffrey Bertram, "Peru: 1930–1960" in *Cambridge History of Latin America,* vol. 8, edited by Leslie Bethell (Cambridge, UK: Cambridge University Press, 1991), 396.
3. Excellent regional analyses include Steve Stein, *Populism in Peru: The Emergence of the Masses and the Politics of Social Control* (Madison: University of Wisconsin Press, 1980); Peter F. Klarén, *Modernization, Dislocation, and Aprismo: Origins of the Peruvian Aprista Party, 1870–1932* (Austin: University of Texas Press, 1973); David S. Parker, *The Idea of the Middle Class: White-Collar Workers and Peruvian Society, 1900–1950* (University Park: Penn State University Press, 1998); David Nugent, *Modernity at the Edge of Empire: State, Individual, and Nation in the Northern Peruvian Andes, 1885– 1935* (Stanford, CA: Stanford University Press, 1997); Lewis Taylor, "The Origins of APRA in Cajamarca, 1928–1935," *Bulletin of Latin American Research* 19 (Oct. 2000), 437–459.
4. Stein, *Populism in Peru,* 102.
5. Ibid., 83–128.
6. Jeffrey L. Klaiber, "The Popular Universities and the Origins of Aprismo, 1921–1924," *Hispanic American Historical Review* 55 (Nov. 1975), 693–715.
7. Klarén, *Modernization, Dislocation, and Aprismo,* 129.
8. ARA, Pref. Leg. 19 (OSH: Mar. 10, 1932).

9. Jorge Basadre, *Perú, problema y posibilidad*, 4th ed. (Lima: M. J. Bustamente, 1994), 207–208.

10. Rénique, "State and Regional Movements," 107; Hazen, "Awakening of Puno," 291.

11. Hazen, "Awakening of Puno," 154; Kapsoli, *Ayllus del sol*, 161.

12. Davies, *Indian Integration*, 112–113.

13. *El Pueblo* (Nov. 28, 1934), 1. The first academic work to consider APRA in Ayacucho's countryside is Luis Miguel Glave and Jaime Urrutia, "Radicalismo político en élites regionales: Ayacucho 1930–1956," *Debate Agrario* 31 (Aug. 2000), 1–37. See also Jefrey Gamarra, "Estado, modernidad, y sociedad regional: Ayacucho 1920–1940," *Apuntes* 31 (July–Dec. 1992): 103–113.

14. *El Pueblo* (Dec. 4, 1934), 1; *El Pueblo* (Dec. 11, 1934); M. Gaspar Rojas, "La insurrección del Partido Aprista Peruano en Huamanga, 1934" (Bachelor's thesis, Universidad Nacional San Cristóbal de Huamanga, 1982); *El Pueblo* (Nov. 28, 1934; Dec. 4, 1934; Dec. 11, 1934). On the other coincident rebellions, see Frederick Pike, *The Politics of the Miraculous in Peru: Haya de la Torre and the Spiritualist Tradition* (Lincoln: University of Nebraska Press, 1986), 176.

15. ARA, SC Caja 23 (OCar 1932: Mar. 16, 1932).

16. ARA, SC Caja 23 (OCar Mar. 28, 1932; Mar. 16, 1932).

17. Carlos Contreras, *El Aprendizaje del capitalismo: estudios de historia económica y social del Perú republicano* (Lima: IEP, 1996), 229.

18. Interview with Emiliano Muñoz* (Oct. 13, 2003).

19. Migration figures are from Stein, *Populism in Peru*, 65, 70. For more on migration, see Sarah Lund Skar, *Lives Together—Worlds Apart: Quechua Colonization in Jungle and City* (Oslo: Scandinavian University Press, 1994); Florencia Mallon, *The Defense of Community in Peru's Central Highlands: Peasant Struggle and Capitalist Transition, 1860–1940* (Princeton, NJ: Princeton University Press, 1983), 247–267.

20. AGN, Ministerio de Trabajo y Asuntos Indígenas Leg. 3.13.2.2 (letter from Ramiro Prialé, Sept. 15, 1945). See also Adrian Alfredo Carbajal Quijano, *La población migrante carhuanquina en Lima en el proceso festivo patronal de la Virgen de Asunción* (Ayacucho, Peru: Informe de Investigación para el taller de UNSCH Seminario Anthropología-501, 1982).

21. ARA, CSJ Leg. 577, Cuad. 9 ("Cartilla Aprista": Dec. 23, 1933).

22. ARA, Pref. Leg. 19 (OSC: Mar. 10, 1932); ARA, SC Caja 44 (OCar: Sept. 3, 1934).

23. ARA, SC Caja 23 (OCar 1932: Mar. 26, 1932).

24. ARA, SC Caja 23 (OCar 1932: Aug. 18, 1932).

25. ARA, SC Caja 23 (OCar 1932: Aug. 20, 1932).

26. ARA, SC Caja 23 (OCar 1932: Apr. 17, 1932).

27. ARA, SC Caja 23 (OCar 1932: June 20, 1932).

28. ARA, CSJ Leg. 520, Cuad. 14 (letters from Francisco Chávez: Nov. 11, 1931; Nov. 14, 1931).

29. ARA, SC Caja 23 (OCar 1932: June 23, 1932). Romaní's other complaints appear in ARA, SC Caja 23 (OCar: Aug. 9, 1932); ARA, CSJ Cangallo, Leg. 1061 (passim: case initiated Oct. 13, 1932).

30. Quoted in Jeffrey Klaiber, *Religion and Revolution in Peru, 1824–1976* (Notre Dame, IN: University of Notre Dame Press, 1977), 162.

31. ARA, SC Caja 23 (OCar 1932: Aug. 5, 1932).

32. ARA, SC Caja 23 (OCar 1932: Oct. 17, 1932).

33. ARA, SC Caja 29 (Oficios Despachados 1937: Jan. 13, 1937).

34. ARA, SC Caja 29 (Oficios Despachados 1937: Apr. 10, 1937).

35. Mallon, *Defense of Community*, 279.

36. Klaiber, *Religion and Revolution in Peru*, 142; Vincent C. Peloso, *Peasants on Plantations: Subaltern Strategies of Labor and Resistance in the Pisco Valley, Peru* (Durham, NC: Duke University Press, 1999), 137; Diez Hurtado, *Comunes y haciendas*, 200.

37. On Champacancha, see ARA, SC Caja 28 (Mar. 30, 1933; Jan. 25, 1933; Feb. 23, 1933). For Champacancha's secret sale, see ARA, SC Caja 54 (Apr. 26, 1935). The notarial record of the initial sale appears in ARA, Notary Celso Bustios, Leg. 238 Fol. 1144 (Dec. 1, 1934); interview with Hernán Carrillo* (Feb. 17, 2003). On nationwide fights between communities and churches, see Mallon, *Defense of Community*, 277.

38. ARA, SC Caja 54 (OCar 1935: Apr. 26, 1935).

39. ARA, SC Caja 54 (OCar 1935: June 7, 1935); interview with Marcelino Lizarbe* (Sept. 24, 2003).

40. ARA, Pref. Leg. 20 (OSC: Sept. 24, 1937; June 2, 1938).

41. Interview with Marcelino Lizarbe* (Sept. 24, 2003).

42. ARA, SC Caja 51 (OCar 1938: Aug. 3, 1938).

43. Interview with Mercedes Cisneros* (Oct. 22, 2003).

44. ARA, CSJ Leg. 585 Cuad. 1 (testimony of Teófila Vega: Dec. 5, 1935).

45. ARA, SC Caja 29 (Oficios Despachados: May 3, 1937).

46. For sale details, see ARA, SC Caja 13 (OCar 1939: Mar. 20, 1939).

47. Interview with Emiliano Muñoz* (Oct. 13, 2003).

48. ARA, Notary Francisco Mavila, Leg. 455 Libro 2, Folio 328 (June 1, 1940).

49. ARA, SC Caja 54 (OCar 1935: May 27, 1935).

50. ARA, SC Caja 31 (OCar 1942: May 22, 1942).

51. ARA, CSJ Leg. 594 Cuad. 11 (testimony of Davíd Hiyo: Aug. 25, 1936).

52. ARA, Pref. Leg. 20 (OSC: Sept. 24, 1935).

53. ARA, Notary Manuel Ochoa, Leg. 383 Fol. 9 (Jan. 19, 1941).

54. Interview with Gregorio Escalante* (Oct. 3, 2003); ARA, Pref. Leg. 20 (OSC: Dec. 23, 1938; Aug. 2, 1938; Aug. 8, 1938).

55. ARA, Pref. Leg. 20 (OSC: Aug. 2, 1938).

56. ARA, Pref. Leg. 20 (OSC: Dec. 23, 1938).

57. Interview with Gregorio Escalante* (Oct. 3, 2003); ARA, SC Caja 5 (OCar 1940: Sept. 7, 1940); ARA, SC Caja 44 (OCar 1945: Nov. 17, 1945).

58. ARA, SC Caja 29 (Oficios Despachados 1937: Jan. 13, 1937).

59. ARA, Pref. Leg. 20 (OSC: Sept. 27, 1935).

60. ARA, SC Caja 29 (Oficios Despachados: Aug. 29, 1937).

61. ARA, SC Caja 13 (OCar 1939: Feb. 7, 1939).

62. ARA, Notary Ismael Berrocal, Leg. 279 Libro 2, Fol. 324 (Oct. 4, 1938).

63. Ibid.; ARA, Notary Franciso Mavila, Leg. 452 Libro 1, Fol. 178 (Apr. 13, 1929).

64. ARA, Pref. Leg. 20 (OSC: Mar. 16, 1936).

65. ARA, Pref. Leg. 20 (OSC: Dec. 23, 1938).

66. Interview with Emiliano Muñoz* (Oct. 21, 2003).

67. ARA, SC Caja 29 (Oficios Despachados 1937: Jan. 13, 1937).

68. ARA, SC Caja 6 (OCar 1936: Oct. 22, 1936).

69. ARA, Pref. Leg. 20 (OSC: Oct. 11, 1938).

70. ARA, SC Caja 8 (OCar 1944: Apr. 29, 1944).

71. ARA, SC Caja 44 (OCar 1945: Dec. 7, 1945).

72. See Chapter Six.

73. *Sierra* (PQ Apr. 1947), 2.

74. ARA, Pref. Leg. 14 (OSH: Dec. 9, 1934).

75. Earlier charges against Espino appear in ARA, CSJ Leg. 478 Cuad. 20 (passim: case initiated Sept. 10, 1928); CSJ Leg. 405, cuad. 4 (passim: case initiated July 1, 1923); CSJ Leg. 490, cuad. 14 (passim: case initiated March 26, 1929); CSJ Leg. 490, cuad. 9 (passim: case initiated Jan. 23, 1929); CSJ Leg. 428, cuad. 11 (passim: case initiated Oct. 6, 1925).

76. ARA, Pref. Leg. 14 (OSH: Dec. 18, 1934).

77. Ibid.

78. *Ayacucho* (Apr. 25, 1940), 1.

79. Glave and Urrutia, "Radicalismo político."

80. ARA, Pref. Leg. 14 (OSH: Dec. 9, 1934).

81. ARA, Pref. Leg. 104 (OGNGC: Dec. 11, 1935; Dec. 12, 1935).

82. ARA, Pref. Leg. 14 (OSH: Of. 702, Nov. 1936).

83. ARA, CSJ Leg. 562, cuad. 9 (passim: case initiated Dec. 1, 1934). For the impact of the Great Depression, see Klarén, *Modernization, Dislocation, and Aprismo*, 145–146; Mallon, *Defense of Community*, 268–307.

84. ARA, Pref. Leg. 14 (OSH: Oct. 8, 1936; Sept. 25, 1941).

85. ARA, Pref. Leg. 14 (OSH: Dec. 6, 1934; Nov. 25, 1936; July 6, 1937; Nov. 16, 1938; Jan. 30, 1939; June 28, 1940); ARA, Pref. Leg. 13 (OSH: Oct. 7, 1929).

86. ARA, Pref. Leg. 13 (OSH: July 15, 1929).

87. ARA, Pref. Leg. 13 (OSH: Feb. 22, 1929).

88. ARA, Pref. Leg. 14 (OSH: Dec. 6, 1934; Nov. 25, 1936; July 6, 1937; Nov. 16, 1938; Jan. 30, 1939; June 28, 1940); ARA, Pref. Leg. 13 (OSH: Oct. 7, 1929).

89. Taylor, *Shining Path*, 65.

90. See Chapter Seven.

91. For deeper reflections on the issue of family, see Jaymie Patricia Heilman, "Family Ties: The Political Genealogy of Shining Path's Comrade Norah," *Bulletin of Latin American Research* 29:2 (2010): 155–169.

CHAPTER FOUR

1. Interview with Luciana Arauja* (Sept. 12, 2003).

2. See Contreras, *Aprendizaje del capitalismo*, 214–272; Gonzalo Portocarrero and Patricia Oliart, *El Perú desde la escuela* (Lima: Instituto de Apoyo Agrario, 1989).

3. De la Cadena, *Indigenous Mestizos*; García, *Making Indigenous Citizens*.

4. Peter F. Klarén, *Peru: Society and Nationhood in the Andes* (New York: Oxford University Press, 2000), 298.

5. Ibid., 288–299. See also Nigel Haworth, "Peru," in *Latin America between the Second World War and the Cold War, 1944–1948*, edited by Leslie Bethell and Ian Roxborough (Cambridge, U.K.: Cambridge University Press, 1997), 170–189.

6. ARA, Pref. Leg. 15 (OSH: Apr. 16, 1946); Pref. Leg. 21 (OSC: Of. 928, Oct. 28, 1948).

7. ARA, SC Caja 5 (OCar 1940: Sept. 7, 1940).

8. ARA, Pref. Leg. 21 (OSC: Of. 173, Oct. 26, 1949).

9. ARA, Pref. Leg. 21 (OSC: Of. 181, Oct. 28, 1949).

10. ARA, SC Caja 47 (OCar 1949: June 17, 1949).

11. Interview with Ricardo Alvarado* (Oct. 6, 2003).

12. ARA, Pref. Leg. 20 (OSC: Jan. 24, 1938).

13. ARA, SC Caja 11 (OCar 1946: Mar. 26, 1946).

14. ARA, SC Caja 15 (OCar 1951: Aug. 28, 1951).

15. ARA, SC Caja 8 (OCar 1944: Oct. 1, 1944).

16. ARA, SC Caja 26 (OCar 1957: Oct. 11, 1957).

17. ARA, SC Caja 5 (OCar 1940: Nov. 29, 1940).

18. Interview with Enrique Canales* (Oct. 22, 2003).

19. Ibid.

20. Interview with Ricardo Alvarado* (Oct. 6, 2003).

21. Ibid.

22. Ibid.

23. Interview with Juana Romero* (Nov. 12, 2003).

24. Interview with Eugenia Alarcón* (Oct. 12, 2003).

25. Interview with Juana Romero* (Nov. 12, 2003).

26. ARA, CSJ Cangallo, Leg. 61, Exped. 87 (passim: case initiated Jan. 24, 1959).

27. Interviews with Augusta López* (Oct. 24, 2003) and Eugenia Alarcón* (Oct. 12, 2003).

28. ARA, SC Caja 31 (OCar 1947: Nov. 21, 1947).

29. ARA, SC Caja 11 (OCar 1946: Mar. 26, 1946).

30. ARA, SC Caja 31 (OCar 1947: Nov. 21, 1947); ARA, SC Caja 15 (OCar 1951: Nov. 23, 1951).

31. ARA, SC Caja 16 (OCar 1951: Oct. 13, 1951).

32. Interviews with Emiliano Muñoz* (Oct. 21, 2003) and Enrique Canales* (Oct. 22, 2003).

33. Roger Rasnake, *Domination and Cultural Resistance: Authority and Power among an Andean People* (Durham, NC: Duke University Press, 1988); Billie Jean Isbell, *To Defend Ourselves: Ecology and Ritual in an Andean Village*, 2nd ed. (Prospect Heights, IL: Waveland Press, 1985), 84–97; González-Castañeda, "Unveiling the Secrets of War," 189–193; La Serna, "Corner of the Living," 75–79, 92–95, 336–337; José Coronel, "Violencia política y respuestas campesinas en Huanta," in *Las rondas campesinas y la derrota de Sendero Luminoso*, edited by Carlos Iván Degregori (Lima: Instituto de Estudios Peruanos, 1996), 69.

34. Interview with Juana Romero* (Nov. 12, 2003).

35. Interview with Enrique Canales* (Oct. 22, 2003).

36. ARA, SC Caja 44 (OCar 1945: Apr. 14, 1945).

37. ARA, SC Caja 41 (OCar 1953: Mar. 6, 1953).

38. Interview with Juana Romero* (Nov. 12, 2003).

39. Interview with Ricardo Alvarado* (Oct. 6, 2003).

40. Interview with Emiliano Muñoz* (Nov. 12, 2003).

41. Interview with Ricardo Alvarado* (Oct. 6, 2003).

42. ARA, SC Caja 53 (Oficios de los Institutos Armados 1944: Dec. 7, 1944).

43. ARA, SC Caja 44 (OCar 1945: Apr. 17, 1945).

44. ARA, SC Caja 11 (OCar 1946: May 29, 1946).

45. ARA, SC Caja 44 (OCar 1945: Mar. 17, 1945).

46. ARA, SC Caja 43 (OCar 1950: Dec. 2, 1950).

47. ARA, Pref. Leg. 21 (OSC: Mar. 12, 1949).

48. William Roseberry, "Hegemony and the Language of Contention," in *Everyday Forms of State Formation: Revolution and the Negotiation of Rule in Modern Mexico*, edited by Gil Joseph and Daniel Nugent (Durham, NC: Duke University Press, 1994), 355–366.

49. ARA, CSJ Cangallo, Leg. 2, Exped. 56 (testimony of Epifanio Vásques: Jan. 19, 1943).

50. ARA, SC Caja 5 (OCar 1940: Dec. 23, 1940).

51. ARA, SC Caja 3 (OCar 1955: Nov. 23, 1955).

52. ARA, Pref. Leg. 104 (OGNGC: Nov. 18, 1946).

53. ARA, SC Caja 10 (OCar 1946: June 27, 1946).

54. ARA, CSJ Leg. 667, Cuad. 3 (letter from residents of Tiquihua: Aug. 3, 1940).

55. ARA, Pref. Leg. 104 (OGNGC: Dec. 17, 1946).

56. ARA, CSJ Cangallo, Leg. 40, Exped. 374 (testimony of Mariano Huaraca: Jan. 16, 1956).

57. ARA, CSJ Cangallo, Leg. 53, Exped. 701 (testimony of Germán Navarrete: June 12, 1957).

58. Interview with Ricardo Alvarado* (Oct. 6, 2003).

59. ARA, Pref. Leg. 104 (OGNGC: Feb. 7, 1947).

60. ARA, Pref. Leg. 104 (OGNGC: Dec. 13, 1947).

61. ARA, CSJ Cangallo, Leg. 47, exped. 86 (passim: case initiated Sept. 27, 1956); CSJ Cangallo, Leg. 47, Exped. 96 (passim: case initiated Sept. 29, 1956); CSJ Cangallo, Leg. 34 Exped. 84 (passim: case initiated Oct. 1, 1954).

62. ARA, CSJ Cangallo, Leg. 16, Exped. 68 (testimony of Sabino Soto: Aug. 9, 1950); ARA, SC Caja 47 (OCar 1949: Sept. 28, 1949).

63. ARA, CSJ Leg. 53, Exped. 701 (letter from Junta Administradora del Distrito de Carhuanca: Jan. 15, 1951). For a discussion of magic in relation to political trauma in El Salvador, see Gould and Lauria-Santiago, *To Rise in Darkness*, 248–252.

64. Interview with Hernán Carrillo* (Feb. 17, 2003).

65. Interview with Ignacio Figueroa* (Sept. 23, 2003).

66. Interview with Emiliano Muñoz* (Oct. 13, 2003).

67. Interview with Gregorio Escalante* (Oct. 3, 2003).

68. Interview with Ignacio Figueroa* (Sept. 23, 2003).

69. ARA, SC Caja 8 (OCar 1949: Dec. 12, 1949).

70. ARA, CSJ Cangallo, Leg. 4, Exped. 199 (letter from Rosalino Vega: June 8, 1949); ARA, SC Caja 8 (OCar 1949: Dec. 12, 1949).

71. ARA, CSJ Cangallo, Leg. 40, Exped. 747 (letter from Modesto Castillo and Moises Aguilar: Mar. 15, 1955).

72. Interview with Hernán Carrillo* (Apr. 25, 2003).

73. ARA, CSJ Cangallo, Leg. 17, Exped. 2 (letter from Benito Gutiérrez: Jan. 13, 1951).

74. ARA, CSJ Cangallo, Leg. 40, Exped. 747 (passim: case initiated May 13, 1955).

75. ARA, CSJ Cangallo, Leg. 4, Exped. 199 (testimony of Rosalino Vega: June 8, 1949).

76. ARA, SC Caja 8 (OCar 1949: Dec. 12, 1949).

77. Interview with Ignacio Figueroa* (Sept. 23, 2003).

78. Interview with Isidro Durán* (Mar. 14, 2003).

79. ARA, SC Caja 8 (OCar 1949: Dec. 12, 1949); ARA, CSJ Cangallo, Leg. 4, Exped. 199 (testimony of Rosalino Vega: June 8, 1949).

80. PETT Carhuanca (letter from Mariano Taipe: May 3, 1957).

81. Interview with Isidro Durán* (Mar. 14, 2003).

82. ARA, SC Caja 8 (OCar 1944: Oct. 31, 1944).

83. ARA, SC Caja 1 (OCar 1956: June 26, 1956).

84. ARA, SC Caja 16 (OCar 1951: Jan. 8, 1951).

85. ARA, SC Caja 5 (Informes emitidos 1940: Apr. 23, 1940).

86. Interviews with Maribel Quispe* (Dec. 14, 2002) and Teodoro Huamán* (Dec. 14, 2002).

87. ARA, Pref. Leg. 15 (OSH: July 10, 1941; Nov 13, 1941).

88. *Sierra* (PQSQ Jan. 1944), 7.

89. Ibid; *Sierra* (PQ Mar. 1948), 1.

90. ARA, Pref. Leg. 15 (OSH: Dec. 17, 1951; Jan. 5, 1952).

91. ARA, Pref. Leg. 14 (OSH: Mar. 28, 1941; July 14, 1941; July 23, 1941).

92. *Sierra* (PQ July 1949), 3.

93. *Sierra* (SQ Jan. 1958), 4.

94. ARA, Pref. Leg. 104 (OGNGC: June 26, 1940).
95. *Sierra* (PQ Jan. 1949), 4.
96. AGN, MDI, Paq. 425 (Of. 221, Nov. 4, 1942).
97. ARA, Pref. Leg.15 (OSH: Feb. 1944).
98. *Sierra* (PQ Mar. 1945), 4.
99. ARA, Pref. Leg. 15 (OSH: Of. 293, June 19, 1946).
100. Interview with Edgar Romero* (May 21, 2005).
101. *Labor* (May 19, 1947), 4.
102. Ibid.
103. Ibid.
104. ARA, Pref. Leg. 15 (OSH: Of. 64, Feb. 2, 1949).
105. ARA, Pref. Leg. 15 (OSH: Of. 225, May 8, 1949).
106. ARA, Pref. Leg 105 (OGNGC: Sept. 10, 1958).
107. ARA, SC Caja 33 (Oficios de Instituciones Armadas 1959: July 6, 1959; Sept. 10, 1959).

CHAPTER FIVE

1. This propaganda appeared on the door of a Carhuanca-born school-teacher.
2. See Jaymie Patricia Heilman, "Leader and Led: Hugo Blanco, La Convención Peasants, and the Relationships of Revolution" (Master's Thesis, University of Wisconsin–Madison, 2000); Hugo Blanco, *Land or Death: The Peasant Struggle in Peru* (New York: Pathfinder Press, 1972); Eduardo Fioravanti, *Latifundio y sindicalismo agrario en el Perú: el caso de los valles de La Convención y Lares* (Lima: Instituto de Estudios Peruanos, 1974).
3. Daniel Masterson, *Militarism and Politics in Latin America: Peru from Sánchez Cerro to Sendero Luminoso* (New York: Greenwood Press, 1991), 149, 173.
4. François Bourricaud, *Power and Society in Contemporary Peru*, translated by Paul Stevenson (New York: Praeger Publishers, 1970), 235.
5. Ibid. See also Fernando Belaúnde Terry, *Pueblo por pueblo*, 2nd ed. (Lima: Ediciones Minerva, 1995).
6. Pedro-Pablo Kuczynski, *Peruvian Democracy under Economic Stress: An Account of the Belaúnde Administration, 1963–1968* (Princeton, NJ: Princeton University Press, 1977), 60–61; Stefano Varese, *Witness to Sovereignty: Essays on the Indian Movement in Latin America* (Copenhagen: IWGIA, 2006). Ponciano del Pino's recent work echoes my findings about Belaúnde. See del Pino, "En busca del gobierno," 163–164.
7. Howard Handelman, *Struggle in the Andes: Peasant Political Mobilization in Peru* (Austin: University of Texas Press, 1974), 62–121, 129–150; Julio Cotler and Felipe Portocarrero, "Peru: Peasant Organizations," in *Latin American Peasant Movements*, edited by Henry A. Landsberger (Ithaca, NY: Cornell University Press, 1969), 297–322.
8. Handelman, *Struggle in the Andes*, 117, 120.
9. Masterson, *Militarism and Politics*, 213.

10. Leon Campbell, "The Historiography of the Peruvian Guerrilla Movement," *Latin American Research Review* 8 (Spring 1973), 45–70; Héctor Béjar, *Perú 1965: Apuntes sobre una experiencia guerrillera* (Montevideo: Sandino, 1969); Richard Gott, *Rural Guerrillas in Latin America* (Harmondsworth, U.K.: Penguin Books, 1973); Michael F. Brown and Eduardo Fernández, *War of Shadows: The Struggle for Utopia in the Peruvian Andes* (Berkeley: University of California Press, 1991).

11. Masterson, *Militarism and Politics*, 214–216.

12. *Obrero y Campesino* (July 1963), 4.

13. Ibid.

14. Ibid.

15. Ibid.

16. *Obrero y Campesino* (Oct. 1963), 2.

17. Ibid.

18. *Obrero y Campesino* (Oct. 1963), 1.

19. Interview with Antonio Cartolín (June 1, 2005).

20. *Obrero y Campesino* (Dec. 1963), 1; *Obrero y Campesino* (Oct. 1963), 2; *Obrero y Campesino* (Nov. 1964), 4; *Obrero y Campesino* (May 1965), 1.

21. ARA, SC Caja 30 (Oficios de los Institutos Armados 1962: Feb. 1962).

22. ARA, SC Caja 8 (OCar 1962: Mar. 21, 1962).

23. ARA, SC Caja 30 (Oficios de los Institutos Armados 1962: Mar. 14, 1962). See also Dionisio Ortiz Tello, "Pomacocha: del Latifundio a la Comunidad" (Bachelor's Thesis, Universidad Nacional San Cristóbal de Huamanga, 1968).

24. ARA, SC Caja 30 (Oficios de los Institutos Armados 1962: Mar. 14, 1962).

25. ARA, SC Caja 32 (Oficios de la Prefectura: Aug. 20, 1965).

26. Ibid.

27. Interviews with Cipriano Meneses* (Oct. 30, 2003), Adolfo Urbana* (Oct. 21, 2003), Enrique Canales* (Oct. 22, 2003), and Antonio Cartolín (June 1, 2005).

28. ARA, SC Caja 31 (Telegramas 1961: Sept. 18, 1961).

29. ARA, SC Caja 31 (Telegramas 1961: Sept. 19, 1961).

30. ARA, SC Caja 31 (Telegramas 1961: Sept. 21, 1961).

31. ARA, SC Caja 31 (Telegramas 1961: Sept. 18, 1961).

32. ARA, CSJ Cangallo, Leg. 8, Exped. 1 (testimony of Venancio Chávez: Aug. 20, 1965).

33. ARA, CSJ Cangallo, Leg. 8, Exped. 1 (testimony of Alejandro Mancilla: Oct. 20, 1965).

34. ARA, SC Caja 32 (Oficios de la Prefectura 1965: Aug. 19, 1965).

35. Interview with Cipriano Meneses* (Oct. 30, 2003).

36. ARA, CSJ Cangallo, Leg. 8, Exped. 1 (testimony of Quintin Arrieta: Apr. 19, 1965). Father Arrieta outlined the contents of complaints he had received from Cocha parents.

37. ARA, CSJ Cangallo, Leg. 8, Exped. 1 (testimony of Quintin Arrieta: Oct. 16, 1965).

38. *Obrero y Campesino* (Oct. 1963), 1.

39. Interview with Antonio Cartolín (June 1, 2005).

40. Interview with Ignacio Figueroa* (Sept. 23, 2003).

41. Interview with Hilario Calderón* (Oct. 22, 2003).

42. Interview with Esteban Licapa* (Oct. 5, 2003).

43. ARA, CSJ Cangallo, Leg. 8, Exped. 1 (testimony of Quintin Arrieta: Oct. 16, 1965).

44. ARA, SC Caja 32 (Oficios de la Prefectura 1965: Aug. 19, 1965); ARA, CSJ Cangallo, Leg. 8, Exped. 1 (testimony of Quintin Arrieta: Oct. 16, 1965).

45. ARA, CSJ Cangallo, Leg. 8, Exped. 1 Leg. 8, Exped. 1 (testimony of Quintin Arrieta: Oct. 16, 1965).

46. Interview with Melchora Gómez* (Mar. 15, 2003).

47. ARA, SC Caja 32 (Oficios de la Prefectura 1965: Aug. 19, 1965); ARA, CSJ Cangallo, Leg. 8, exped. 1 (passim: case initiated Oct. 11, 1965).

48. ARA, CSJ Cangallo, Leg. 8, Exped. 1 (letter from Venancio Chávez, Pedro Gómez, Antonio Vega, et al.: Aug. 18, 1965).

49. ARA, CSJ Cangallo, Leg. 8, Exped. 1 (passim: case initiated Oct. 11, 1965).

50. ARA, SC Caja 31 (Telegramas 1961: Aug. 13, 1961); ARA, SC Caja 7 (OCar 1964: May 24, 1964); interview with Rufina Enciso* (Mar. 14, 2003).

51. Interviews with Hernán Carrillo* (Feb. 17, 2003) and Adolfo Urbana* (Feb. 17, 2003).

52. Interview with Ricardo Alvarado* (Sept. 24, 2003).

53. Luis Allende Ayala's land purchases and sales are documented in ARA, Notary Ángel Arones, Leg. 373 folio 395 (Dec. 21, 1950); Leg. 371 Fol. 86 (May 21, 1945); Leg. 369 Libro 2 Fol.1 (Jan. 27, 1941); Leg. 372 Fol. 49 (Apr. 28, 1947); Leg. 371 Fol.184 (Oct. 12, 1945); Leg. 387 Fol. 100 (Aug. 16, 1947); Notary Manuel Ochoa, Leg. 387 Fol.104 (Aug. 18, 1947); Leg. 384 Fol.326 (Mar. 15, 1944); Leg. 386 Libro 2 Fol. 315 (Mar. 24, 1952); Leg. 386 Libro 2 Fol. 294 (Mar. 12, 1952); Leg. 386 Libro 2 Fol. 318 (Mar. 25, 1952); Leg. 383 Fol. 258 (Jan. 2, 1942); Leg. 383 Fol. 88 (May 20, 1942); Notary Alipio Remón, Leg. 393 folio 537 (July 23, 1969); Leg. 393 Fol. 537 (July 23, 1969); Leg. 392 Fol. 489 (July 25, 1967); Leg. 392 Fol. 492 (July 25, 1967).

54. Interview with Rufina Enciso* (Oct. 21, 2003).

55. *Paladín* (Feb. 3, 1968), 2.

56. ARA, SC Caja 7 (Varios oficios 1964: Oct. 29, 1963).

57. ARA, SC Caja 46 (OCar 1966: Jan. 15, 1966).

58. ARA, SC Caja 7 (OCar 1968: Oct. 25, 1968).

59. ARA, SC Caja 7 (OCar 1968: Nov. 18, 1968).

60. Bourricaud, *Power and Society*, 238.

61. Interview with Adolfo Urbana* (Apr. 25, 2003); ARA, SC Caja 8 (Oficios de los Institutos Armados 1961: Dec. 13, 1961; Dec. 14, 1961).

62. *Paladin* (Feb. 3, 1968), 2.

63. Interviews with Isidro Durán* (Apr. 25, 2003) and Adolfo Urbana* (Apr. 25, 2003).

64. Interview with Rufina Enciso* (Oct. 21, 2003).
65. Interviews with Isidro Durán* (Apr. 25, 2003) and Adolfo Urbana* (Apr. 25, 2003).
66. Interview with Calixto López* (Nov. 24, 2003).
67. Interviews with Isidro Durán* (Apr. 25, 2003) and Eugenia Alarcón* (Sept. 24, 2003).
68. Interview with Rufina Enciso* (Oct. 21, 2003).
69. ARA, SC Caja 32 (Varios Oficios: June 9, 1964).
70. Interview with Calixto López* (Nov. 24, 2003).
71. Interview with Isidro Durán* (Mar. 14, 2003); PETT Carhuanca (letter from Moises Ochoa: Aug. 28, 1965).
72. ARA, SC Caja 19 (Varios oficios: Sept. 3, 1966).
73. Interview with Ramón Palomino* (Sept. 24, 2003).
74. Interview with Isidro Durán* (Mar. 14, 2003); PETT Carhuanca (levantamiento catastral: July 31, 1967).
75. Rénique, *Batalla por Puno*, 154–155.
76. José Tamayo, *Historia social del Cuzco republicano* (Lima: n.p., 1978), 244. For continuing complaints, see PETT Contay (letter from Nicanor Villegas and Francisco Najarro, Aug. 12, 1967); ARA, SC Caja 6 (Varios oficios: Mar. 16, 1964).
77. See La Serna, "Corner of the Living," 185, for other references to the verga.
78. Interview with Emiliano Muñoz* (Oct. 13, 2003).
79. Interview with Juana Romero* (Nov. 12, 2003).
80. Interview with Rufina Enciso* (Mar. 14, 2003).
81. Ibid.
82. For a lengthy discussion of the La Torre family and its politics, see Heilman, "Family Ties."
83. Interview with Franco Silva* (May 24, 2005).
84. Interview with Edgar Romero* (May 26, 2005); Defensoría del Pueblo Centro de Información para la Memoria Colectivo y Derechos Humanos (CIMCDH), interview with Elena Iparraguirre, Mar. 12, 2003, folio 8.
85. Simon Enrique Sánchez Torres, *Huanta: Pueblo heroico—testimonio de luchas sociales, 1814–1969* (Lima: Ediciones Warpa, 1975); Fermín Rivera, *El movimiento campesino en la provincia de Huanta* (Ayacucho: UNSCH, 1970), 119–131; *Obrero y Campesino* (Nov. 1964), 4.
86. Interview with Antonio Cartolín (June 1, 2005).
87. Interview with Valentín Quintero* (Sept. 15, 2002); interview conducted by Caroline Yezer. I thank Caroline for letting me sit in on this interview.
88. Interview with Cirilo Reyes* (Sept. 16, 2003).
89. SH 1963 (Oct. 11, 1963).
90. SH 1963 (Jan. 4, 1963).
91. ARA, CSJ Huanta, Leg. 4, Exped. 941 (passim: case initiated June 14, 1963); ARA, CSJ Huanta, Leg. 4, Exped. 1076 (passim: case initiated Feb. 23, 1964); ARA, CSJ Huanta, Leg. 5, Exped. 1149 (passim: case initiated: May 24, 1963).

92. Rivera, *Movimiento campesino*, 117; interview with Eleodosia Sánchez* (Apr. 18, 2003).

93. ARA, CSJ Huanta, Leg. 10, Exped. 530 (letter from Jorge Urbina: Nov. 18, 1963).

94. ARA, CSJ Huanta, Leg. 10, Exped. 530 (passim: case initiated Nov. 18, 1963); CSJ Huanta, Leg. 10, Exped. 164 (passim: case initiated July 25, 1963).

95. ARA, CSJ Huanta, Leg. 10, Exped. 530 (letter from Central Social Cultural Huayllay: August 31, 1963).

96. ARA, CSJ Huanta, Leg. 10, Exped. 530 (letter from Cabo Comandante: Nov. 19, 1963). This letter describes Huayllay campesinos' requests.

97. Rivera, *Movimiento campesino*, 181. I have not found the documents quoted in Rivera's study, but the content of these petitions is consistent with the counteraccusations the Mavila hacendados made.

98. Rivera, *Movimiento campesino*, 181–191; the Mavilas' complaint appears in SH, Leg. 1944 (Jan. 4, 1964).

99. Rivera, *Movimiento campesino*, 182.

100. Interview with Mario Cavalcanti (June 16, 2005).

101. SH 1964 (Mar. 3, 1964; Aug. 13, 1964); SH 1963 (Oct. 5, 1963).

102. One of the very few studies devoted exclusively to the Belaúnde presidency is Kuczynski, *Peruvian Democracy*.

103. Linda J. Seligmann, *Between Reform and Revolution: Political Struggles in the Peruvian Andes, 1969–1991* (Stanford, CA: Stanford University Press, 1995).

CHAPTER SIX

1. CIMCDH: Expediente SR01DC002; interview with Melchora Gómez* (Oct. 22, 2003).

2. David Scott Palmer, "Revolution from Above: Military Government and Popular Participation in Peru, 1968–1972" (Ph.D. Dissertation, Cornell University, 1973), 90–91.

3. ARA, SC Caja 10 (Varios oficios: May 24, 1970).

4. CVR, *Informe Final*, Tomo IV, Cap. 1.1, 42. Ronald Berg demonstrates similar findings for Apurímac. See Berg, "Peasant Responses to Shining Path in Andahuaylas," in *Shining Path of Peru*, 2nd ed., edited by David Scott Palmer (New York: St. Martin's Press, 1994), 101–122.

5. PETT Carhuanca (Informe: May 18, 1971).

6. See Chapter Three.

7. ARA, SC Caja 34 (Oficios Remitidos: July 13, 1973); PETT Carhuanca (letter from Guido Malpartida: June 8, 1972); ARA, SC Caja 20 (Prefectura: Mar. 31, 1972); *ComunRuna* 1 (Aug. 1971), 14; interview with Enrique Canales* (Oct. 22, 2003).

8. PETT Carhuanca (letter from Daniel Guillén, Alejandro Alfaro, and Pedro Vega: Oct. 24, 1972).

9. Interview with Adolfo Urbana* (Nov. 3, 2003).

10. Héctor Béjar took a job with the military government, as did Trotskyist leader Ismael Frías.

11. PETT Carhuanca (letter from Edilberto Hiyo: Aug. 30, 1971).

12. ARA, SC Caja 34 (OCar 1973: Sept. 18, 1973).

13. PETT Carhuanca (letters from Daniél Guillén and Alejandro Alfaro: Dec. 8, 1972 and Dec. 15, 1972.)

14. ARA, SC Caja 9 (Varios Oficios: Jan. 24, 1976); ARA, SC Caja 22 (Varios oficios: Nov. 25, 1975).

15. Interview with Enrique Canales* (Oct. 25, 2003).

16. PETT Carhuanca ("Elecciones Comunales": Mar. 5, 1977).

17. Ibid.

18. For examples of complaints against authorities, see ARA, SC Caja 34 (Varios oficios: Feb. 20, 1973); ARA, SC Caja 36 (Varios oficios: July 13, 1972); ARA, SC Caja 22 (Varios oficios: May 16, 1975).

19. ARA, SC Caja 10 (Varios oficios: May 24, 1970).

20. ARA, SC Caja 2 (Informes mensuales: May 31, 1974).

21. ARA, SC Caja 31 (Oficios remitidos 1974: May 2, 1974).

22. ARA, CSJ Leg. 136, Cuad. 486 (passim: initiated May 10, 1975).

23. PETT Carhuanca (letter from Edilberto Hiyo: Nov. 30, 1971; letter from Victoria Ochoa: July 2, 1971; letter from Augusto Zárate: July 8, 1971; declaration of Pedro Félix Guillén: July 16, 1971).

24. *ComunRuna* 3 (December 1971–Mar. 1972), 13.

25. Interview with Adolfo Urbana* (Nov. 3, 2003). On the educational reform, see Judithe Bizot, *Education Reform in Peru* (Paris: UNESCO Press, 1975); Norman Gall, "Peru's Education Reform," *Fieldstaff Reports: West Coast South America Series* 21: 3–6 (Hanover, NH: American Universities Field Staff, 1974).

26. The Velasco government officially reclassified all "indigenous communities" as "campesino communities."

27. ARA, Fuero Privativo Agrario (FP), Leg. 15, Cuad. 18 (passim: case initiated May 28, 1979); PETT Carhuanca (letter from Edilberto Hiyo: Nov. 30, 1971).

28. PETT Carhuanca (letter from Victoria Ochoa: June 21, 1971; letter from Edilberto Hiyo: June 24, 1971; letter from Victoria Ochoa: July 2, 1971; declaration from Pedro Félix Guillén: July 16, 1971).

29. PETT Carhuanca (letter from Guillermo Aparicio Vega: Nov. 18, 1971).

30. Interview with Enrique Canales* (Oct. 22, 2003).

31. Interview with Adolfo Urbana* (Mar. 14, 2003).

32. PETT Carhuanca (letter from Néstor Cárdenas and others: May 24, 1972. See also "Pedido de disolución": Aug. 8, 1972).

33. PETT Rayme Alto (letter from Davíd Castillo and María Luisa Bustamente: May 18, 1971); ARA, FC, Leg. 206, Cuad. 7 (passim: case initiated Feb. 4, 1969); ARA, SC Caja 16 (Varios: Nov. 8, 1976); ARA, SC Caja 25 (Oficios: Feb. 15, 1970, Mar. 11, 1970); ARA, SC Caja 20 (Varios: Mar. 26, 1971,

Apr. 24, 1971); PETT Carhuanca (letter from Máximo Pariona: Aug. 31, 1971); ARA, FP, Leg. 64, Cuad. 6 (passim: case initiated Mar. 20, 1978).

34. PETT Carhuanca (letter from Cecilio Rojas: Sept. 4, 1975).

35. ARA, SC Caja 16 (Varios: Nov. 17, 1976, Jan. 26, 1977); ARA, FC, Leg. 45, Cuad. 7 (passim: case initiated Nov. 16, 1978); PETT Contay (letter from Fortunato Rua: Sept. 29, 1972).

36. ARA, FC, Leg. 206, Cuad. 7 (passim: case initiated Feb. 4, 1969); ARA, SC Caja 16 (Varios oficios: Nov. 8, 1976); ARA, SC Caja 20 (Varios oficios: Apr. 24, 1971); ARA, FP, Leg. 64, Cuad. 6 (passim: case initiated March 20, 1978).

37. PETT Carhuanca (letter from Edilberto Hiyo: May 31, 1972).

38. PETT Carhuanca (letter from Daniel Guillén: May 5, 1971).

39. ARA, SC Caja 49 (Varios oficios: December 11, 1979).

40. Interview with Juana Romero* (Nov. 12, 2003).

41. Interview with Natividad Vergara* (Oct. 4, 2003).

42. Interview with Constantino Rivera* (Mar. 14, 2003).

43. Interview with Gregorio Escalante* (Oct. 3, 2003).

44. Interview with Natividad Vergara* (Oct. 4, 2003).

45. ARA, FC, leg. 86, exped. 17 (passim: case initiated Nov. 29, 1949).

46. ARA, Notarial Records. To protect confidentiality, I am withholding the specific notarial reference for this quote.

47. Interview with Mercedes Cisneros* (Oct. 22, 2003).

48. ARA, SC Caja 16 (Varios oficios: Oct. 15, 1979; December 4, 1979).

49. Interview with Augusta López* (Oct. 24, 2003).

50. Interview with Adolfo Urbana* (Mar. 14, 2003).

51. Interview with Lucio Arroyo* (Oct. 17, 2003).

52. Interview with Jacinto Taboada* (Feb. 27, 2003).

53. Interview with Simon Retamoso* (Mar. 1, 2003).

54. Interview with Silvio Medina* (Sept. 17, 2003).

55. My argument benefited from a reading of Florencia Mallon's *Courage Tastes of Blood: The Mapuche Community of Nicolás Ailío and the Chilean State, 1906–2001* (Durham, NC: Duke University Press, 2005).

56. *Paladín* (June 25, 1969), 1; SH 1969 (June 13, 1969); Gall, "Peru's Education Reform," 7, 15.

57. Interview with Lucio Arroyo* (Oct. 17, 2003).

58. Interview with Silvio Medina* (Sept. 17, 2003).

59. The Peruvian Truth and Reconciliation Commission has argued that the 1969 uprisings inspired those who would soon form the PCP-SL. See CVR, *Informe Final*, Tomo III, 576. Carlos Iván Degregori makes a similar assertion in his influential book about the uprising *El surgimiento de Sendero Luminoso: Ayacucho 1969–1979* (Lima: IEP, 1990).

60. Interview with Mario Cavalcanti (May 23, 2005).

61. Interview with Lucio Arroyo* (Oct. 17, 2003).

62. Interview with Silvio Medina* (Sept. 17, 2003).

63. Degregori, *El surgimiento de Sendero Luminoso*, 51, 56, 58, 109; *Paladín* (July 12, 1969), 1; SH 1969 (Apr. 11, 1969; Apr. 24, 1969).

64. Degregori, *El surgimiento de Sendero Luminoso*, 63–65, 70; Gall, "Peru's Education Reform," 6, 15.

65. Gall, "Peru's Education Reform," 6.

66. Interview with Lucio Arroyo* (Oct. 17, 2003).

67. Interview with Silvio Medina* (Sept. 17, 2003).

68. Interview with Lucio Arroyo* (Oct. 17, 2003).

69. Interview with Silvio Medina* (Sept. 17, 2003).

70. Cynthia McClintock, *Peasant Cooperatives and Political Change in Peru* (Princeton, NJ. Princeton University Press, 1981), 34; José Matos Mar and Jose Manuel Mejía, *La reforma agraria en el Perú* (Lima: IEP, 1980); Peter S. Cleaves and Martin J. Scurrah, *Agriculture, Bureaucracy, and Military Government in Peru* (Ithaca, NY: Cornell University Press, 1978).

71. PETT Gervasio Santillana (Informe: Aug. 11, 1978).

72. Interview with Cirilo Reyes* (Feb. 15, 2003).

73. SH 1975 (December 25, 1975). For similar conflicts elsewhere, see McClintock, *Peasant Cooperatives*, 293; Douglas Horton, "Haciendas and Cooperatives: A Study of Estate Organization, Land Reform, and New Reform Enterprises in Peru," (Ph.D. Dissertation, Cornell University, 1976), 342.

74. SH 1977 (Mar. 15, 1977).

75. Interview with Silvio Medina* (Sept. 17, 2003).

76. SH 1977 (Mar. 15, 1977).

77. SH 1975 (May 5, 1975).

78. SH 1975 (Jan. 15, 1975).

79. PETT Gervasio Santillana (letter from Feudatarios of Coraceros: December 6, 1977).

80. SH 1977 (Mar. 21, 1977).

81. SH 1977 (Mar. 15, 1977).

82. Interview with Silvio Medina* (Sept. 17, 2003); Alfonso Geldres Cuadros and Abraham Vergara Rivera, "Realidad socio-económico de la Cooperativa Agraria de Producción Gervasio Santillana Ltda 2-8-VI-Huanta" (Bachelor's Thesis, Universidad Nacional San Cristóbal de Huamanga, 1981), 75, 79.

83. PETT Gervasio Santillana (letter from Augusto Oré, Rosa Robles, et al.: December 4, 1980).

84. José Coronel, *Campesinado y nación: a propósito del poder local en Huanta, 1990–1993* (Ayacucho: UNSCH, 1994), 25; Coronel, "Violencia política," 45.

85. PETT Huayllay (Informe: June 14, 1972). The document states the planned delivery date.

86. PETT Huayllay (Acta de Asamblea: Aug. 24, 1975).

87. SH 1976 (Apr. 9, 1976).

88. SH 1976 (Jan. 21, 1976).

89. Interview with Simón Retamoso* (Mar. 1, 2003).

90. SH 1975 (Sept. 30, 1975).

91. Interview with Simón Retamoso* (Mar. 1, 2003).

92. SH 1975 (Sept. 18, 1975).

93. SH 1975 (Sept. 29, 1975).
94. SH 1975 (Sept. 30, 1975).
95. Ibid.
96. SH 1979 (Mar. 10, 1979).
97. Interview with Simón Retamoso* (Mar. 1, 2003). For other blacklists, see Kimberly Theidon, "Traumatic States: Violence and Reconciliation in Peru" (Ph.D. Dissertation, University of California–Berkeley, 2002), 144–150.
98. Abraham F. Lowenthal, ed. *The Peruvian Experiment: Continuity and Change under Military Rule* (Princeton, NJ: Princeton University Press, 1975).
99. Seligmann, *Between Reform and Revolution*; Florencia Mallon, "Chronicle of a Path Foretold? Velasco's Revolution, Vanguardia Revolucionaria, and 'Shining Omens' in the Indigenous Communities of Andahuaylas," in *Shining and Other Paths: War and Society in Peru, 1980–1995*, edited by Steve J. Stern (Durham, NC: Duke University Press, 1998), 84–120; del Pino, "En busca del gobierno."

CHAPTER SEVEN

1. Interview with Melchora Gómez* (Mar. 15, 2003).
2. Discussions of teachers and the Shining Path appear in Carlos Iván Degregori, *Sendero Luminoso: II Lucha armada y utopia autoritaria* (Lima: IEP Documento de Trabajo, 1986), 6; Degregori, "Harvesting Storms," 128–130; Taylor, *Shining Path*, 91–95; Michael Smith, "Taking the High Ground: Shining Path and the Andes," in *Shining Path of Peru*, 2nd ed., edited by David Scott Palmer (New York: St. Martin's Press, 1994), 45–46.
3. CVR, *Informe Final*, Tomo I, Cap. 1, 61.
4. CVR, *Informe Final*, Tomo III, Cap. 3.5, 603; Degregori, *Ayacucho 1969–1979*, 253; Degregori, "The Origins and Logic of Shining Path," 60.
5. CVR, *Informe Final*, Tomo V, Cap. 2.1, 18.
6. Alan Angell, "Classroom Maoists: The Politics of Peruvian Schoolteachers under Military Government," *Bulletin of Latin American Research* 1:2 (1982): 2.
7. ARA, SC Caja 34 (Varios oficios: Oct. 24, 1973); ARA, SC Caja 22 (June 18, 1975); CVR, *Informe Final*, Tomo III, Cap. 3.5, 558.
8. Angel, "Classroom Maoists," 10; CVR, *Informe Final*, Tomo III, Cap. 3.5, 557.
9. CVR, *Informe Final*, Tomo III, Cap. 3.5, 554–555. On SUTEP activities in Cuzco, see Rénique, "State and Regional Movements," 240–241.
10. ARA, SC Caja 24 (Varios oficios: Sept. 13, 1972); SC Caja 34 (Oficios de la Prefectura: Aug. 14, 1973; October 25, 1973, Nov. 20, 1973); SC Caja 3 (Varios oficios: Nov. 14, 1975); SC Caja 9 (Varios oficios: Nov. 20, 1975); SC Caja 45 (Varios oficios: May 27, 1976); SC Caja 20 (Informe Mensual: Nov. 1972); SC Caja 27 (Oficios de la Prefectura: Aug. 1971); SC Caja 49 (Varios oficios: Sept. 1, 1971).
11. ARA, SC Caja 53 (Varios oficios: June 30, 1978; July 31, 1978); SC Caja 19 (Telegramas 1979: Aug. 10, 1979).

12. ARA, SC Caja 35 (Informes mensuales: Mar. 1979, Apr. 1979, May 1979, June 1979, July 1979, Aug. 1979); SC Caja 1 (Varios oficios: July 23, 1979).

13. ARA, SC Caja 53 (Varios oficios: Nov. 16, 1978); ARA, CSJ Cangallo, Leg. 174, Cuad. 197 (passim: case initiated Nov. 9, 1978).

14. ARA, SC Caja 53 (Oficios recibidos: Nov. 22, 1978; Nov. 24, 1978).

15. ARA, SC Caja 35 (Informes mensuales: Nov. 1978; Dec. 1978; Jan. 1979; Feb. 1979; Mar. 1979). Quote from the Mar. 1979 informe.

16. ARA, SC Caja 35 (Informe mensual: Apr. 1979).

17. ARA, SC Caja 35 (Informe mensual: May 1979).

18. ARA, SC Caja 35 (Informe mensual: June 1979, July 1979).

19. ARA, SC Caja 1 (Oficios de la Prefectura: July 24, 1979).

20. ARA, SC Caja 1 (Oficios de la Prefectura: Oct. 19, 1979).

21. ARA, SC Caja 1 (Varios oficios: Feb. 19, 1979); SC Caja 35 (Informes mensuales: Mar. 1979).

22. ARA, SC Caja 35 (Informes mensuales: July 1979).

23. ARA, SC Caja 1 (Varios oficios: Aug. 21, 1979).

24. Ibid. See also ARA, SC Caja 35 (Informes mensuales: Aug. 1979).

25. Gustavo Gorritti, *The Shining Path: A History of the Millenarian War in Peru.* Translated by Robin Kirk (Chapel Hill: University of North Carolina Press, 1999), 47.

26. Ibid., 46–52.

27. Theidon, *Entre prójimos*, 35.

28. ARA, SC Caja 1 (Prefectura: Oct. 17, 1973).

29. ARA, CSJ Cangallo, Leg. 174, Cuad. 197 (letter from Melano Muñoz: Nov. 9, 1978).

30. Ibid.

31. Interview with Adolfo Urbana* (Nov. 3, 2003).

32. Interview with Adolfo Urbana* (Mar. 3, 2003).

33. Interview with Valentín Samanes* (Oct. 5, 2003).

34. Interview with Melchora Gómez (Sept. 23, 2003).

35. Interview with Tomás Nuñez* (Oct. 21, 2003).

36. Interview with Hilario Calderón* (Oct. 22, 2003).

37. Examples include ARA, SC Caja 47 (OCar 1949: October 11, 1949); ARA, Pref. Leg. 20 (OSC: February 12, 1945).

38. PETT Carhuanca (letter from Pedro Guillén, Reynaldo Barrientos, Jorge Cárdenas, and Cecilio Morales: Aug. 28, 1972).

39. Interview with Adolfo Urbana* (Oct. 21, 2003).

40. Interview with Ignacio Figueroa* (Sept. 23, 2003).

41. Interview with Hilario Calderón* (Oct. 22, 2003).

42. ARA, SC Caja and date of document withheld.

43. ARA, SC Caja and date of document withheld.

44. ARA, SC Caja and date of document withheld. Capitalization in the original.

45. ARA, SC Caja and date of document withheld.

46. Interview with Patricio Cornejo* (Sept. 24, 2003).

47. ARA, SC Cajas and dates of documents withheld.

48. Interview with Melchora Gómez* (Mar. 15, 2003).

49. Interview with Hilario Calderón* (Oct. 22, 2003).

50. Interview with Melchora Gómez* (Mar. 15, 2003).

51. Interview with Adolfo Urbana* (Apr. 25, 2003).

52. CVR, *Informe Final*, Tomo V, Cap. 2.1, 18.

53. Interview with Valentín Samanes* (Oct. 5, 2003).

54. Interview with Tomás Nuñez* (Oct. 21, 2003).

55. Interview with Patricia Quispe* and Celestino Maldonado* (Oct. 22, 2003).

56. Interview with Teodoro Velásquez* (Oct. 19, 2003).

57. ARA, SC Caja 1 (Varios Oficios: Aug. 21, 1979).

58. ARA, SC Caja 51 (Varios Oficios: Dec. 26, 1979). The original complaint was dated Aug. 23, 1979.

59. Interview with Adolfo Urbana* (Oct. 21, 2003).

60. ARA, SC Caja 1 (Varios oficios: Oct. 25, 1979).

61. ARA, SC Caja 51 (Varios oficios: Dec. 26, 1979).

62. Interview with Adolfo Urbana* (Oct. 21, 2003).

63. CIMCDH: Interview 200649 (Mar. 20, 2002); Interview 200575 (Mar. 5, 2002); Interview 200633 (Mar. 18, 2002); Interview 200615 (Mar. 14, 2002); Interview 200565 (Mar. 1, 2002).

64. Ibid.

65. For a discussion of community reconciliation issues, see Theidon, *Entre Prójimos*.

66. Interview with Franco Silva* (May 24, 2005).

67. Ibid.

68. Coronel, *Campesinado y nación*, 70; Coronel, "Violencia política," 43.

69. Scholarly Resources Inc., *Documenting the Peruvian Insurrection* (Woodbridge: Primary Source Microfilm, 2005), Reel 12, folder 2, document entitled "Abimael Guzmán."

70. *Caretas* (Dec. 6, 1982), 14.

71. Coronel, *Campesinado y nación*, 23, 24.

72. CIMCDH: Interview 200719 (May 6, 2002).

73. CIMCDH: Interview 200521 (May 21, 2002).

74. CIMCDH: Interview 200649 (March 20, 2002).

75. For a sensitive consideration of PCP-SL violence in other parts of Peru, see Ponciano del Pino, "Family, Culture, and 'Revolution': Everyday Life with Sendero Luminoso," in *Shining and Other Paths: War and Society in Peru, 1980–1995*, edited by Steve J. Stern (Durham, NC: Duke University Press, 1998), 158–192.

76. *Equis X* 327 (February 7, 1983), 20.

77. Interview with Luciana Arauja* (Sept. 12, 2003).

78. Interview with Ignacio Figueroa* (Sept. 23, 2003).

79. Interview with Modesto Ramos* (Oct. 4, 2003).

80. Interview with Pastora García* (Oct. 4, 2003).

81. Interview with Ignacio Figueroa* (Sept. 23, 2003).
82. Ibid.
83. Interview with Patricia Quispe* (Oct. 22, 2003).
84. Interview with Ignacio Figueroa* (Sept. 23, 2003).
85. Interview with Juana Romero* (Nov. 12, 2003).
86. Interview with Modesto Ramos* (Oct. 4, 2003).
87. *Equis X* 327 (February 7, 1983), 20.
88. Interview with Modesto Ramos* (Oct. 4, 2003).
89. Interview with Ignacio Figueroa* (Sept. 23, 2003).

CONCLUSION

1. Interview with Isaac Escobar* (May 21, 2001).
2. Billie Jean Isbell, "Shining Path and Peasant Responses in Rural Ayacucho," in *The Shining Path of Peru*, 2nd ed., edited by David Scott Palmer (New York: St. Martin's Press, 1994), 79; Berg, "Peasant Responses," 113–115.
3. Steve J. Stern, "Conclusion," in *Shining and Other Paths: War and Society in Peru, 1980–1995*, edited by Steve J. Stern (Durham, NC: Duke University Press, 1998), 470.
4. Carl von Clausewitz, *On War* (New York: Penguin, 1968 [1832]), 119.
5. Theidon, *Entre prójimos*, 233, 256.
6. Recent contributions to the study of Andean peasant politics appear in Nils Jacobsen and Cristóbal Aljovín de Losada, eds., *Political Cultures in the Andes, 1750–1950* (Durham, NC: Duke University Press, 2005).
7. See Stern, "New Approaches to the Study of Peasant Rebellion and Consciousness: Implications of the Andean Experience," in *Resistance, Rebellion and Consciousness in the Andean Peasant World*, edited by Steve J. Stern (Madison: University of Wisconsin Press, 1987), 3–25.
8. Julio Cotler, "Mécanica de la dominación interna y del cambio social en la sociedad rural," in *Perú problema: 5 ensayos*, edited by José Matos Mar (Lima: Moncloa Editores, 1968).
9. Nelson Manrique, "The War for the Central Sierra," in *Shining and Other Paths: War and Society in Peru, 1980–1995*, edited by Steve J. Stern (Durham, NC: Duke University Press, 1998), 193–223.
10. La Serna, "Corner of the Living."
11. Eric Wolf, *Peasant Wars of the Twentieth Century* (New York: Harper and Row, 1969), 301.
12. Degregori, "Harvesting Storms," 138.
13. Berg, "Peasant Responses," 118.
14. Degregori, *Sendero Luminoso I*, 6
15. Berg, "Peasant Responses to Shining Path in Andahuaylas," 118.
16. CVR, *Informe Final*, Tomo I, Cap. 3, 155–193.
17. Poole and Rénique, "New Chroniclers of Peru," 144.
18. de la Cadena, "From Race to Class."
19. Interview with Hernán Carrillo* (Feb. 17, 2003).

20. Interview with Porfirio Quispe* (Oct. 21, 2003).

21. Mariana Gálvez is a pseudonym.

22. A useful—if polemical—discussion about Andeanism appears in Orin Starn's "Missing the Revolution: Anthropologists and the War in Peru," *Cultural Anthropology* 6:1 (1991): 63–91.

Bibliography

ARCHIVES

AGN—Archivo General de la Nación
AHM—Archivo Histórico Militar
APBN—Archivo Público de la Biblioteca Nacional
ARA—Archivo Regional de Ayacucho
CIMCDH—Defensoría del Pueblo Centro de Información para la Memoria
Colectivo y Derechos Humanos
PETT—Proyecto Especial de Titulación de Tierras, Ministerio de Agricultura,
Ayacucho
SH—Subprefectura Huanta

SECONDARY SOURCES

Abercrombie, Thomas. *Pathways of Memory and Power: Ethnography and
History among an Andean People.* Madison: University of Wisconsin Press,
1998.
Aguirre, Carlos. *The Criminals of Lima and Their Worlds: The Prison Experience, 1850–1935.* Durham, NC: Duke University Press, 2005.
Albó, Xavier. "El retorno del Indio." *Revista Andina* 9:2 (1991): 299–345.
Álvarez-Calderón, Annalyda. "'Es justicia lo que esperamos de Su Excelencia':
política indígena en Puno (1901–1927)." In *Más allá de la dominación y la resistencia: estudios de historia peruana, siglos xvi–xx,* edited by Paulo Drinot
and Leo Garofalo, pp. 312–341. Lima: Instituto de Estudios Peruanos, 2005.
Anderle, Ádám. *Los movimientos políticos en el Perú entre las dos guerras
mundiales.* Havana: Casa de las Américas, 1985.
Angell, Alan. "Classroom Maoists: The Politics of Peruvian Schoolteachers under Military Government." *Bulletin of Latin American Research* 1:2 (May
1982): 1–20.

Arroyo, Carlos. "La experiencia del Comité Central Pro-Derecho Indígena Ta-huantinsuyo." *Estudios interdisciplinarios de America Latina y el Caribe* 15:1 (January–June 2004): 1–24.

Basadre, Jorge. *Historia de la República del Perú, 1822–1933.* Lima: Editorial Universitaria, 1983.

———. *Perú, Problema y Posibilidad,* 4th ed. Lima: Fundación M. J. Bustamante de la Fuente, 1994.

Becker, Marc. *Mariátegui and Latin American Marxist Theory.* Athens: Ohio University Center for International Studies, 1993.

———. *Indians and Leftists in the Making of Ecuador's Modern Indigenous Movements.* Durham, NC: Duke University Press, 2008.

Béjar, Héctor. *Perú 1965: Apuntes sobre una experiencia guerrillera.* Montevideo: Sandino, 1969.

Belaúnde Terry, Fernando. *Pueblo Por Pueblo,* 2nd ed. Lima: Editorial Minerva, 1995.

Berg, Ronald. "Peasant Responses to Shining Path in Andahuaylas." In *Shining Path of Peru,* 2nd ed., edited by David Scott Palmer, pp. 101–122. New York: St. Martin's Press, 1994.

Bertram, Geoffrey. "Peru: 1930–1960." In *Cambridge History of Latin America,* edited by Leslie Bethel, pp. 385–450. Cambridge, U.K.: Cambridge University Press, 1991.

Bizot, Judithe. *Educational Reform in Peru.* Paris: UNESCO Press, 1975.

Blanchard, Peter. *The Origins of the Peruvian Labor Movement, 1883–1919.* Pittsburgh, PA: University of Pittsburgh Press, 1982.

Blanco, Hugo. *Land or Death: The Peasant Struggle in Peru.* New York: Pathfinder Press, 1972.

Bobrow-Strain, Aaron. *Intimate Enemies: Landowners, Power, and Violence in Chiapas.* Durham, NC: Duke University Press, 2007.

Bourricaud, François. *Power and Society in Contemporary Peru.* Translated by Paul Stevenson. New York: Praeger Publishers, 1970.

Brown, Michael, and Eduardo Fernández. *War of Shadows: The Struggle for Utopia in the Peruvian Amazon.* Berkeley: University of California Press, 1991.

Burga, Manuel. "Las profetas de la rebelión, 1920–1923." In *Estados y naciones en los Andes: hacia una historia comparativa,* edited by Jean Paul Deler and Y. Saint-Geours, pp. 463–517. Lima: Instituto de Estudios Peruanos, 1986.

Burga, Manuel, and Alberto Flores Galindo. *Apogeo y crisis de la República Aristocrática: oligarquía, aprismo y comunismo en el Perú, 1895–1932.* Lima: Ediciones Rikchay Perú, 1980.

Campbell, Leon. "The Historiography of the Peruvian Guerrilla Movement." *Latin American Research Review* 8 (Spring 1973): 45–70.

Carbajal Quijano, Adrian Alfredo. *La población migrante carhuanquina en Lima en el proceso festivo patronal de la Virgen de Asunción.* Ayacucho, Peru: Informe de Investigación para el taller de UNSCH Seminario Anthropología-501, 1982.

Cavero, Luis E. *Monografía de la Provincia de Huanta.* Lima: n.p., 1953.

Chavarría, Jesús. *José Carlos Mariátegui and the Rise of Modern Peru, 1890–1930*. Albuquerque: University of New Mexico Press, 1979.

Clausewitz, Carl von. *On War*. Harmondsworth, UK: Penguin, 1968. (Originally published in 1832.)

Cleaves, Peter S., and Martin J. Scurrah. *Agriculture, Bureaucracy, and Military Government in Peru*. Ithaca, NY: Cornell University Press, 1980.

Comisión de la Verdad y Reconciliación. *Informe Final: (Perú, 1980–2000)*. Lima: Universidad Nacional Mayor de San Marcos, 2004. Available at: www.cverdad.org.pe

Contreras, Carlos. *El aprendizaje del capitalismo: estudios de historia económica y social del Perú republicano*. Lima: Instituto de Estudios Peruanos, 2004.

Coronel, José. *Campesinado y nación: a propósito del poder local en Huanta: 1990–1993*. Ayacucho: UNSCH, 1994.

———. "Violencia política y respuestas campesinas en Huanta." In *Las rondas campesinas y la derrota de Sendero Luminoso*, edited by Carlos Iván Degregori, pp. 29–116. Lima: Instituto de Estudios Peruanos, 1996.

Cotler, Julio. "Mécanica de la dominación interna y del cambio social en la sociedad rural." In *Perú problema: 5 ensayos*, edited by José Matos Mar, pp. 153–197. Lima: Moncloa Editores, 1968.

Cotler, Julio, and Felipe Portocarrero. "Peru: Peasant Organizations." In *Latin American Peasant Movements*, edited by Henry A. Landsberger, pp. 297–322. Ithaca, NY: Cornell University Press, 1969.

Coxshall, Wendy. "From the Peruvian Reconciliation Commission to Ethnography: Narrative, Relatedness, and Silence." *PoLar: Political and Legal Anthropology Review*, 28:2 (November 2005): 203–222.

Davies, Thomas. *Indian Integration in Peru: A Half-Century of Experience, 1900–1948*. Lincoln: University of Nebraska Press, 1974.

Degregori, Carlos Iván. *Sendero Luminoso: I. Los hondos y mortales desencuentros*. Lima: IEP Documento de Trabajo, 1985.

———. *Sendero Luminoso: II. Lucha armada y utopia autoritaria*. Lima: IEP Documento de Trabajo, 1986.

———. *El surgimiento de Sendero Luminoso: Ayacucho 1969–1979*. Lima: Instituto de Estudios Peruanos, 1990.

———. "The Origins and Logic of Shining Path: Two Views." In *The Shining Path of Peru*, 2nd ed., edited by David Scott Palmer, pp. 51–62. New York: St. Martin's Press, 1994.

———. "Harvesting Storms: Peasant Rondas and the Defeat of Sendero Luminoso in Ayacucho." In *Shining and Other Paths: War and Society in Peru, 1980–1995*, edited by Steve J. Stern, pp. 128–157. Durham, NC: Duke University Press, 1998.

de la Cadena, Marisol. "From Race to Class: Insurgent Intellectuals *de provincia* in Peru, 1910–1970." In *Shining and Other Paths: War and Society in Peru, 1980–1995*, edited by Steve J. Stern, pp. 22–59. Durham, NC: Duke University Press, 1998.

————. *Indigenous Mestizos: The Politics of Race and Culture in Cuzco, 1919–1991*. Durham, NC: Duke University Press, 2000.

del Pino, Juan José. *Las Sublevaciones indígenas de Huanta*. Ayacucho, Peru: n.p., 1955.

del Pino, Ponciano. "Family, Culture, and 'Revolution': Everyday Life with Sendero Luminoso." In *Shining and Other Paths: War and Society in Peru, 1980–1995*, edited by Steve J. Stern, pp. 158–192. Durham, NC: Duke University Press, 1998.

————. "'En busca del gobierno': Comunidad, política, y la producción de la memoria y los silencios en Ayacucho, Perú, siglo XX." Ph.D. Dissertation, University of Wisconsin–Madison, 2008.

Deustua, José, and José Luis Rénique C. *Intelectuales, indigenismo y descentralismo en el Perú, 1897–1931*. Cusco: Centro de Estudios Rurales Andinos "Bartolomé de las Casas", 1984.

Diez Hurtado, Alejandro. *Comunes y haciendas: procesos de comunalización en la sierra de Piura (siglos xviii al xx)*. Piura, Peru: CIPCA, 1998.

Díaz Martínez, Antonio. *Cangallo: latifundio y comunidad*. Ayacucho, Peru: UNSCH,1968.

————. *Ayacucho: hambre y esperanza*. Ayacucho, Peru: Ediciones Waman Puma, 1969.

Drinot, Paulo. "For Whom the Eye Cries: Memory, Monumentality, and the Ontologies of Violence in Peru." *Journal of Latin American Cultural Studies* 18:1 (March 2009): 15–32.

Fioravanti, Eduardo. *Latifundio y sindicalismo agrario en el Perú: el caso de los valles de la Convención y Lares (1958–1964)*. Lima: Instituto de Estudios Peruanos, 1974.

Flores Galindo, Alberto. *La agonía de Mariátegui: la polémica con la Komintern*. Lima: DESCO, 1980.

————. *Buscando un Inca: identidad y utopía en los Andes*, 4th ed. Lima: Editorial Horizonte, 1994.

Gall, Norman. "Peru's Education Reform." *Fieldstaff Reports: West Coast South America Series* 21:3–6. Hanover, NH: American Universities Field Staff, 1974.

Gamarra, Jefrey. "Estado, modernidad, y sociedad regional: Ayacucho 1920–1940." *Apuntes* 31 (July–Dec. 1992): 103–113.

García, María Elena. *Making Indigenous Citizens: Identities, Education and Multicultural Development in Peru*. Stanford, CA: Stanford University Press, 2005.

Gaspar Rojas, M. "La insurección del Partido Aprista Peruano en Huamanga, 1934." Bachelor's thesis, Universidad Nacional San Cristóbal de Huamanga, 1982.

Geldres Cuadros, Alfonso, and Abraham Vergara Rivera, "Realidad socioeconómico de la Cooperativa Agraria de Producción Gervasio Santillana Ltda 2-8-VI-Huanta." Bachelor's thesis, Universidad Nacional San Cristóbal de Huamanga, 1981.

Glave, Luis Miguel, and Jaime Urrutia. "Radicalismo político en élites regionales: Ayacucho, 1930–1956." *Debate Agrario* 31 (August 2000): 1–37.

González-Castañeda, Olga. "Unveiling the Secrets of War in the Peruvian Andes." Ph.D. Dissertation, Columbia University, 2006.

González Carré, Enrique, Jaime Urrutia, and Jorge Lévano P. *Ayacucho: San Juan de la Frontera de Huamanga.* Lima: Banco de Crédito del Perú, 1997.

González Prada, Manuel. *Páginas libres; Horas de lucha.* Caracas: Biblioteca Ayacucho, 1985.

Gorriti, Gustavo. *The Shining Path: A History of the Millenarian War in Peru.* Translated by Robin Kirk. Chapel Hill: University of North Carolina Press, 1999.

Gotkowitz, Laura. *A Revolution for Our Rights: Indigenous Struggles for Land and Justice in Bolivia, 1880–1952.* Durham, NC: Duke University Press, 2007.

Gott, Richard. *Rural Guerrillas in Latin America.* Harmondsworth, UK: Penguin Books, 1973.

Gould, Jeffrey L., and Aldo A. Lauria-Santiago. *To Rise in Darkness: Revolution, Repression, and Memory in El Salvador, 1920–1932.* Durham, NC: Duke University Press, 2008.

Gow, Rosalind. "Yawar Mayu: Revolution in the Southern Andes, 1860–1980." Ph.D. Dissertation, University of Wisconsin–Madison, 1981.

Greene, Shane. "Getting over the Andes: The Geo-Eco-Politics of Indigenous Movements in Peru's 21st Century Inca Empire." *Journal of Latin American Studies* 38:2 (2006): 327–354.

Handelman, Howard. *Struggle in the Andes: Peasant Political Mobilization in Peru.* Austin: University of Texas Press, 1974.

Haworth, Nigel. "Peru." In *Latin America between the Second World War and the Cold War, 1944–1948*, edited by Leslie Bethell and Ian Roxborough, pp. 170–189. Cambridge, UK: Cambridge University Press, 1997.

Hazen, Dan C. "The Awakening of Puno: Government Policy and the Indian Problem in Southern Peru, 1900–1955." Ph.D. Dissertation, Yale University, 1974.

Heilman, Jaymie Patricia. "Leader and Led: Hugo Blanco, la Convención Peasants, and the Relationships of Revolution." Master's Thesis, University of Wisconsin–Madison, 2000.

———. "We Will No Longer Be Servile: 'Aprismo' in 1930s Ayacucho." *Journal of Latin American Studies* 38:3 (August 2006): 491–518.

———. "Family Ties: The Political Genealogy of Shining Path's Comrade Norah." *Bulletin of Latin American Research* 29:2 (2010): 155–169.

———. "Por un imperio de ciudadanos: el movimiento del 'Tawantinsuyo' en el Ayacucho de los años 20," translated by María Gabriela Castro-Barrientos. In *Nuevas perspectivas sobre el 'oncenio' de Leguía*, edited by Paulo Drinot. Lima: Instituto de Estudios Peruanos, forthcoming.

Hinojosa, Iván. "On Poor Relations and the Nouveau Riche: Shining Path and the Radical Peruvian Left." In *Shining and Other Paths: War and Society in*

Peru, 1980–1995, edited by Steve J. Stern, pp. 60–83. Durham, NC: Duke University Press, 1998.

Horton, Douglas E. "Haciendas and Cooperatives: A Study of Estate Organization, Land Reform and New Reform Enterprises in Peru." Ph.D. Dissertation, Cornell University, 1976.

Husson, Patrick. *De la guerra a la rebelión: Huanta, siglo xix.* Cusco: Centro de Estudios Regionales Andinos "Bartolomé de Las Casas," 1992.

Isbell, Billie Jean. *To Defend Ourselves: Ecology and Ritual in an Andean Village*, 2nd ed. Prospect Heights, IL: Waveland Press, 1985.

———. "Shining Path and Peasant Responses in Rural Ayacucho." In *The Shining Path of Peru*, 2nd ed., edited by David Scott Palmer, pp. 77–100. New York: St. Martin's Press, 1994.

Jacobsen, Nils. *Mirages of Transition: The Peruvian Altiplano, 1780–1930.* Berkeley: University of California Press, 1993.

Jacobsen, Nils, and Cristóbal Aljovín de Losada, eds. *Political Cultures in the Andes, 1750–1950.* Durham, NC: Duke University Press, 2005.

Kapsoli, Wilfredo. *El pensamiento de la Asociación Pro Indígena.* Cusco, Peru: Centro de Estudios Rurales Andinos "Bartolomé de las Casas," 1980.

———. *Los movimientos campesinos en el Perú, 1879–1965*, 2nd ed. Lima: Atusparia Ediciones, 1982.

———. *Ayllus del sol: anarquismo y utopía andina.* Lima: TAREA Asociación de Publicaciones Educativas, 1984.

Kirk, Robin. *The Monkey's Paw: New Chronicles from Peru.* Amherst: University of Massachusetts Press, 1997.

Klaiber, Jeffrey L. "The Popular Universities and the Origins of Aprismo, 1921–1924." *Hispanic American Historical Review* 55:4 (November 1975): 693–715.

———. *Religion and Revolution in Peru, 1824–1976.* Notre Dame, IN: University of Notre Dame Press, 1977.

———. *The Catholic Church in Peru, 1821–1985: A Social History.* Washington, DC: Catholic University of America Press, 1992.

Klarén, Peter F. *Modernization, Dislocation, and Aprismo: Origins of the Peruvian Aprista Party, 1870–1932.* Austin: University of Texas Press, 1973.

———. *Peru: Society and Nationhood in the Andes.* New York: Oxford University Press, 2000.

Kuczynski, Pedro-Pablo. *Peruvian Democracy under Economic Stress: An Account of the Belaúnde Administration.* Princeton, NJ: Princeton University Press, 1977.

La Serna, Miguel. "The Corner of the Living: Local Power Relations and Indigenous Perceptions in Ayacucho, Peru, 1940–1983." Ph.D. Dissertation, University of California-San Diego, 2008.

Leibner, Gerardo. "Radicalism and Integration: The Tahuantinsuyo Committee Experience and the 'Indigenismo' of Leguía Reconsidered, 1919–1924." *Journal of Iberian and Latin American Studies* 9:2 (December 2003): 1–23.

Lowenthal, Abraham F., ed. *The Peruvian Experiment: Continuity and Change under Military Rule.* Princeton, NJ: Princeton University Press, 1975.

Mallon, Florencia E. *The Defense of Community in Peru's Central Highlands: Peasant Struggle and Capitalist Transition, 1860–1940.* Princeton, NJ: Princeton University Press, 1983.

———. *Peasant and Nation: The Making of Postcolonial Mexico and Peru.* Berkeley: University of California Press, 1995.

———. "Chronicle of a Path Foretold? Velasco's Revolution, Vanguardia Revolucionaria, and 'Shining Omens' in the Indigenous Communities of Andahuaylas." In *Shining and Other Paths: War and Society in Peru, 1980–1995,* edited by Steve J. Stern, pp. 84–120. Durham, NC: Duke University Press, 1998.

———. *Courage Tastes of Blood: The Mapuche Community of Nicolás Ailío and the Chilean State, 1906–2001.* Durham, NC: Duke University Press, 2005.

Manrique, Nelson. *Las guerrillas indígenas en la guerra con Chile: campesinado y nación.* Lima: Centro de Investigación y Capacitación, 1981.

———. *Yawar Mayu: sociedades terratenientes serranas, 1879–1910.* Lima: DESCO Centro de Estudios y Promoción del Desarrollo, 1988.

———. "The War for the Central Sierra." In *Shining and Other Paths: War and Society in Peru, 1980–1995,* edited by Steve J. Stern, pp. 193–223. Durham, NC: Duke University Press, 1998.

Masterson, Daniel M. *Militarism and Politics in Latin America: Peru from Sánchez Cerro to Sendero Luminoso.* New York: Greenwood Press, 1991.

Matos Mar, José, and José Manuel Mejía. *La reforma agraria en el Perú.* Lima: Instituto de Estudios Peruanos, 1980.

Matto de Turner, Clorinda. *Aves sin nido.* Caracas: Biblioteca Ayacucho, 1994. (Originally published in 1889)

Mayer, Eric. "State Policy and Community Conflict in Bolivia and Peru, 1900–1980." Ph.D. Dissertation, University of California–Santa Barbara, 1995.

McClintock, Cynthia. *Peasant Cooperatives and Political Change in Peru.* Princeton, NJ: Princeton University Press, 1981.

Méndez, Cecilia. "The Power of Naming, or the Construction of Ethnic and National Identities in Peru: Myth, History, and the Iquichanos." *Past and Present,* 171:1 (May 2001): 127–160.

———. *The Plebeian Republic: The Huanta Rebellion and the Making of the Peruvian State, 1820–1850.* Durham, NC: Duke University Press, 2005.

Milton, Cynthia. "At the Edge of the Peruvian Truth Commission: Alternative Paths to Recounting the Past." *Radical History Review* 98 (May 2007): 3–33.

Mitchell, William P. *Peasants on the Edge: Crop, Cult, and Crisis in the Andes.* Austin: University of Texas Press, 1991.

Nugent, David. *Modernity at the Edge of Empire: State, Individual, and Nation in the Northern Peruvian Andes, 1885–1935.* Stanford, CA: Stanford University Press, 1997.

Ortiz Tello, Dionisio. "Pomacocha: del Latifundio a la Comunidad." Bachelor's Thesis, Universidad Nacional San Cristóbal de Huamanga, 1968.

Palmer, David Scott. *"Revolution from Above": Military Government and Popular Participation in Peru, 1968–1972.* Dissertation Series, No. 47. Ithaca, NY: Cornell University Latin American Studies Program, 1973.

Pareja Pflucker, Piedad. *Terrorismo y sindicalismo en Ayacucho, 1980.* Lima: Empresa Editorial Ital Perú, 1981.

Parker, David S. *The Idea of the Middle Class: White-Collar Workers and Peruvian Society, 1900–1950.* University Park: Penn State University Press, 1998.

Peloso, Vincent C. *Peasants on Plantations: Subaltern Strategies of Labor and Resistance in the Pisco Valley, Peru.* Durham, NC: Duke University Press, 1999.

Pent, Steven. "Bridging the Rural–Urban Divide: Mobilization and Citizenship of a Peruvian Peasant Organization." M.A. thesis, University of California–Santa Barbara, 2007.

Pereyra Chávez, Nelson. "Los campesinos y la Conscripción Vial: Aproximaciones al estudio de las relaciones estado-indígenas y las relaciones de mercado en Ayacucho (1919–1930)," in *Estado y mercado en la historia del Perú*, edited by Carlos Contreras and Manuel Glave, pp. 334–350. Lima: Pontificia Universidad Católica del Perú.

Perú, *Censo nacional de población y ocupación, 1940, Vol. 6 Departamentos: Ica, Huancavelica, Ayacucho.* Lima: Dirección de Estadística, 1944.

Pike, Fredrick B. *The Politics of the Miraculous in Peru: Haya de la Torre and the Spiritualist Tradition.* Lincoln: University of Nebraska Press, 1986.

Poole, Deborah. "Performance, Domination and Identity in the *Tierras Bravas* of Chumbivilcas (Cusco)." In *Unruly Order: Violence, Power, and Cultural Identity in the High Provinces of Southern Peru*, edited by Deborah Poole, pp. 97–132. Boulder, CO: Westview Press, 1994.

Poole, Deborah, and Gerardo Rénique. "The New Chroniclers of Peru: U.S. Scholars and Their 'Shining Path' of Peasant Rebellion." *Bulletin of Latin American Research* 10: 2 (1991): 133–191.

Portelli, Alessandro. *The Death of Luigi Trastulli and Other Stories: Form and Meaning in Oral History.* Albany: State University of New York Press, 1991.

Portocarrero, Gonzalo, and Patricia Oliart. *El Perú desde la escuela.* Lima: Instituto de Apoyo Agrario, 1989.

Quijano, Aníbal. *Reencuentro y debate: Una introducción a Mariátegui.* Lima: Mosca Azul, 1981.

Rappaport, Joanne. *Cumbe Reborn: An Andean Ethnography of History.* Chicago: University of Chicago Press, 1994.

Rasnake, Roger Neil. *Domination and Cultural Resistance: Authority and Power among an Andean People.* Durham, NC: Duke University Press, 1988.

Rénique C., José Luis. "State and Regional Movements in the Peruvian Highlands: The Case of Cusco, 1895–1985." Ph.D. Dissertation, Columbia University, 1988.

———. *La batalla por Puno: conflicto agrario y nación en los Andes Peruanos, 1866–1995.* Lima: IEP Ediciones, 2004.

Ritter, Jonathan. "A River of Blood: Music, Memory and Violence in Ayacucho, Peru." Ph.D. Dissertation, University of California–Los Angeles, 2006.

Rivera, Fermín. *El movimiento campesino en la provincia de Huanta.* Ayacucho, Peru: UNSCH, 1970.

Roseberry, William. "Hegemony and the Language of Contention." In *Everyday Forms of State Formation: Revolution and the Negotiation of Rule in Modern Mexico*, edited by Gilbert M. Joseph and Daniel Nugent, pp. 355–366. Durham, NC: Duke University Press, 1994.

Ruiz Fowler, José R., *Monografía histórico-geográfica del Departamento de Ayacucho.* Lima: Imprenta Torres Aguirre, 1924.

Sala i Vila, Núria. *Selva y Andes: Ayacucho, 1780–1929, historia de una región en la encrucijada.* Madrid: Consejo Superior de Investigaciones Científicas Instituto de Historia, 2001.

Sánchez Torres, Simon Enrique. *Huanta: Pueblo heroico—testimonio de luchas sociales, 1814–1969.* Lima: Ediciones Warpa, 1975.

Scarritt, Arthur. "The Rattle of Burnt Bread: Indigenous Immobilization and Land Loss in the Peruvian Highlands, 1982–2003." Ph.D. Dissertation, University of Wisconsin–Madison, 2006.

Scholarly Resources Inc., *Documenting the Peruvian Insurrection.* Woodbridge, CT: Primary Source Microfilm, 2005.

Seligmann, Linda J. *Between Reform and Revolution: Political Struggles in the Peruvian Andes, 1969–1991.* Stanford, CA: Stanford University Press, 1995.

Skar, Sarah Lund. *Lives Together—Worlds Apart: Quechua Colonization in Jungle and City.* Oslo: Scandinavian University Press, 1994.

Smith, Michael L. "Taking the High Ground: Shining Path and the Andes." In *The Shining Path of Peru*, 2nd ed., edited by David Scott Palmer, pp. 33–50. New York: St. Martin's Press, 1994.

Starn, Orin. "Missing the Revolution: Anthropologists and the War in Peru." *Cultural Anthropology* 6:1 (February 1991): 63–91.

———. "Villagers at Arms: War and Counterrevolution in the Central-South Andes." In *Shining and Other Paths: War and Society in Peru, 1980–1995*, edited by Steve J. Stern, pp. 224–260. Durham, NC: Duke University Press, 1998.

Stein, Steve. *Populism in Peru: The Emergence of the Masses and the Politics of Social Control.* Madison: University of Wisconsin Press, 1980.

Stern, Steve J. *Peru's Indian Peoples and the Challenge of Spanish Conquest : Huamanga to 1640.* Madison: University of Wisconsin Press, 1982.

———. "Beyond Enigma: An Agenda for Interpreting Shining Path and Peru, 1980–1995." In *Shining and Other Paths: War and Society in Peru, 1980–1995*, edited by Steve J. Stern, pp. 1–12. Durham, NC: Duke University Press, 1998.

———. "Conclusion." In *Shining and Other Paths: War and Society in Peru, 1980–1995*, edited by Steve J. Stern, pp. 470–476. Durham, NC: Duke University Press, 1998.

———. "New Approaches to the Study of Peasant Rebellion and Consciousness: Implications of the Andean Experience." In *Resistance, Rebellion and*

Consciousness in the Andean Peasant World, edited by Steve J. Stern, pp. 3–25. Madison: University of Wisconsin Press, 1987.

———. *Remembering Pinochet's Chile: On the Eve of London, 1998.* Durham, NC: Duke University Press, 2004.

Stuart, Graham H. "The Administration of President Leguía of Peru." *The American Political Science Review* 22:2 (May 1928), 416–420.

Tamayo Herrera, José. *Historia Social Del Cuzco Republicano.* Lima: n.p., 1978.

Taylor, Lewis. *Bandits and Politics in Peru: Landlord and Peasant Violence in Hualgayoc, 1900–30.* Cambridge, UK: Centre of Latin American Studies University of Cambridge, 1987.

———. "The Origins of APRA in Cajamarca, 1928–1935." *Bulletin of Latin American Research* 19:4 (October 2000): 437–459.

———. *Shining Path: Guerrilla War in Peru's Northern Highlands, 1980–1997.* Liverpool, UK: Liverpool University Press, 2006.

Theidon, Kimberly. "Traumatic States: Violence and Reconciliation in Peru." Ph.D. Dissertation, University of California–Berkeley, 2002.

———. *Entre prójimos: el conflicto armado interno y la política de la reconciliación en el Perú.* Lima: Instituto de Estudios Peruanos, 2004.

Thurner, Mark. *From Two Republics to One Divided: Contradictions of Postcolonial Nationmaking in Andean Peru.* Durham, NC: Duke University Press, 1997.

Varese, Stefano. *Witness to Sovereignty: Essays on the Indian Movement in Latin America.* Copenhagen: IWGIA, 2006.

Vila Galindo, Flavio. *Los montoneros: movimiento campesino de La Mar, Ayacucho, Peru.* Lima: n.p. 2000.

Walker, Charles. *Smoldering Ashes: Cuzco and the Creation of Republican Peru, 1780–1840.* Durham, NC: Duke University Press, 1999.

Wolf, Eric. *Peasant Wars of the Twentieth Century.* New York: Harper and Row, 1969.

Yezer, Caroline. "Anxious Citizenship: Insecurity, Apocalypse and War Memories in Peru's Andes." Ph.D. Dissertation, Duke University, 2007.

Index

Abad, Julian (subprefect), 36
Abandon: Aristocratic Republic and, 16, 22–23, 40–41; Ayacucho department and, 6, 89, 203n28; Belaúnde and, 123, 137; Champacancha and, 89; civil guard withdrawal and, 173–74, 176; education and, 100; impunity and, 24, 26, 33, 192, 196; Luricocha and, 10, 63, 91; Revolutionary Government of the Armed Forces and, 148, 151; rule by, 9, 10, 34; Shining Path and, 178, 185, 188; and tinterillos, 113; and varayocs, 106
Abercrombie, Thomas, 57
Acción Popular: anti-Indianism and, 199; compared to other political parties, 3, 9, 193; and Cooperación Popular, 134, 146; dominance in Carhuanca, 133; highway construction and 123, 134–39, 145–46; local notables in, 121, 133–134, 137–140, 147, 152; Luricochano support for, 143; progress and, 134; Shining Path and, 147; Trotskyists and, 125, 128, 140
Administration and Vigilance Councils, 150, 152–153, 156–157, 166
Agrarian production cooperatives, 165–167, 171, 182, 186
Agrarian reform: Belaúnde and 122, 124, 142–146; and Cangallo Peasant Federation, 126; and Federation of Huanta Peasants, 142; by 1962 military government, 122; by Revolutionary Government of the Armed Forces, 144, 149, 157–158,

161, 164–168, 170–171; Trotskyists and 125, 130, 142
Aibar, César, 116–118, 142–143
Aibar, Santiago, 116–118
Alcohol, 32, 48, 66–67. *See also* Chicha
Alfaro, Dionisio, 75, 81, 99, 107
Allende, Francisco, 19, 27, 31, 61
Allende, Luis (priest), 29–34, 55, 131
Allende Ayala, Luis: abuses of, 134–135, 153–154, 160; Acción Popular and, 133–135, 137; anti-Indianism and, 199; and APRA, 98; land acquisitions by, 31, 55, 222n53; land conflicts and, 130–132, 160; murder of, 148, 159–160, 183, 192; and teachers, 99; as a tinterillo, 107
Alliances, between local and national elites, 16, 40
Alvarado, Ricardo (pseudonym), 99–101, 104–105, 133
Añaños, Albino, 47
Andahuaylas, 18, 29, 31, 86, 171
Animals. *See* livestock
Anti-Indianism, 12, 198–200
Appointments, of authorities: in Aristocratic Republic, 10, 22, 29–30, 32; in 1920s, 53, 61; in 1930s, 85–86, 89–90; in 1960s, 139–140; and Revolutionary Government of the Armed Forces, 152, 154, 168–170
APRA (Alianza Popular Revolucionaria Americana): and antifascism, 116; and anti-Indianism, 199; and authorities, 75, 78–80; and Bustamante y Rivero, 97–98; in Cangallo, 98; in Carhuanca, 71–72, 74–89 passim; Catholic Church and, 80;

Ocopa, 23, 103, 106
Odría, Manuel, 98, 118
Ongoy, 125
Oral history, 2, 14, 17, 44, 57, 133, 161–162, 186. *See also* Memory

Paladín, 134, 136
Palomino, Benigno, 60–61
Pampa Cangallo, 49
Pampamarca, 49, 56–57, 59
Pampay I (hacienda), 6; agrarian reform in, 161–162, 165; Belaúnde and, 146; hacendados and, 142; Shining Path and, 185–186
Pampay II (hacienda), 145–146
Pantani, Ezequiel, 165–167
Parra, Domingo J., 38–40
Partido Comunista del Perú, 72–73, 97, 117–118, 141
Partido Comunista del Perú-Bandera Roja, 141
Partido Comunista del Perú-Sendero Luminoso (PCP-SL). *See* Shining Path
Partido Comunista del Perú-Unidad, 128, 141, 191. *See also* Stalinists
Partido Obrero Revolucionario-Trotskista (POR-T), 124, 128, 142, 192
Pasture rights, 160, 166–167. *See also* livestock
Patiño, Cirilo, 49, 52–54, 56–57, 154
Patria Nueva, 46
Patronato de la Raza Indígena, 46, 55
PCP-SL. *See* Shining Path
Peasants: identity of, 10–12; labor of, 5–7, 11, 66, 144, 153, 159; politics of, 7–10; unions of, 121–123, 125–126, 141
People's War, 1, 4, 160, 191; abusive notables and, 41; anti-Indianism and, 3, 198; civil guard withdrawal and, 178, 183; flight to Lima and, 161; history and, 8, 193–194
Pereyra Chávez, Nelson, 212n81
Peru: Aristocratic Republic and, 16, 19–20, 40; Ayacucho in, 4; nation-state formation of, 8; political efforts to transform, 8, 42–43, 50, 77, 92, 123–124, 147, 170–171, 193, 196–197; politics in, 2–3, 8; rule in, 9–10, 34, 195; Shining Path and, 1
Peruvian Communist Party. *See* Partido Comunista del Perú

Peruvian Restoration Party, 98
Pévez, Juan Hipólito, 55
Piérola, Nicolás, 17, 36–39
Piura, 20, 42, 73
Police. *See* Civil guard
Politics, 7–9, 192–194, 196–198, 203n20; during Aristocratic Republic, 15–22, 30, 33, 39–41. *See also names of specific parties and movements*
Pomacocha, 126–127, 178
Poole, Deborah, 33, 198, 204n6
Popular Cooperation. *See* Cooperación Popular
Popular Schools, 184
Popular Universities, 72
Populism, 71–72, 123
POR-T. *See* Partido Obrero Revolucionario-Trotskista
Portelli, Alessandro, 57
Poverty: Carhuanca and, 11; education and, 101; imprisonment and, 25; land conflicts and, 160; migration and, 76; military conscription and, 21; Peru and, 120, 194; Tawantinsuyo movement and, 42; taxation and, 54–55, 63
Prado, Manuel, 97
Prado, Pedro, 128, 130, 179–183
Priests: abuses by, 15, 30, 32, 45, 86, 89, 115–116, 181; appointments of, 30; Champacancha and, 80-84; children of, 31, 107; Luricochanos' struggle for better, 93–94, 116, 192; migration of, 11, 86; political involvement of, 30–31; prestige of, 31–32; tinterillos and, 111; Trotskyists and, 129, 131–132; wealth of, 31–32
Progressive Mutualist Society of Carhuanca Towns and Annexes, 87–88
Propaganda: Acción Popular, 120, 220n1; APRA, 73–74, 76–77, 91–92; Shining Path, 175–76, 182; Trotskyist, 129
Provincial Democratic Anti-Fascist Committee, 116
Pseudonyms, 14, 201n1
Puno, 21, 42, 45–46, 55, 58, 63, 139
Puquio, 22–23

Qachir, 142
Quechua language, 12, 42, 49, 53, 82, 87, 100, 133, 144, 153, 170, 199
Quijana, Alejandro, 159, 183, 200

Urbana, Adolfo (pseudonym), 60, 156, 161, 185
Urbanization, 71, 134
Urbina, Feliciano, 35
Urrutia, Jaime, 91

Vanguardia Revolucionaria, 171
Varayocs: abuse of, 19, 27–28, 51–52, 103–106, 134; APRA and, 75, 78, 80; in Aristocratic Republic, 19–20, 24; defined, 19; disappearance of, 103, 106; duties of, 20, 104; illiteracy and, 52, 103, 119; prestige of, 27, 103–105, 115; protests by, 19, 27, 51–52, 105–106, 114
Varese, Stefano, 123
Velasco Alvarado, Juan: agrarian reform and, 144, 149, 157, 161–162, 170; coup of 1968 and, 146, 148, 170; memories of, 149, 161–162, 192; ouster of, 149, 173; SUTEP and, 174. *See also* Revolutionary Government of the Armed Forces
Verga. *See* Whips
Víctor Fajardo, 107, 150, 179, 203n20
Vilcashuamán (district), 21, 48–49, 180, 184; civil guard withdrawal from, 177–178; highway to Carhuanca, 136, 138; student strike in, 176
Vilcashuamán (province), 6, 202n15, 203n17
Violence: against authorities, 9; against gamonales, 9, 27; against hacendados, 144–145; by Apristas, 79, 117; by authorities, 27, 93; by gamonales,

16–17, 23, 26–27; by Shining Path, 2–3, 41, 149, 162, 172, 184, 188, 190–194, 198, 200; by students, 175–177; by teachers, 100; by tinterillos, 109, 112; by Trotskyists, 131–132. *See also* Military Repression, Murder
Virán (hacienda), 5, 18, 27, 29, 75, 132
Virgin de Asunción, 30, 87, 190, 200
Vischongo, 176–178, 203n17
Von Clausewitz, Carl, 193

Walker, Charles, 8
War of the Pacific, 4, 15–17, 34–36, 38, 40
Water, 11, 104, 134–135, 152, 164, 166
Whips, 139–140
Witchcraft, 109, 113, 132, 219n63
Wolf, Eric, 196
Women: abusive authorities and, 28, 60, 111; in APRA, 91–92; as authorities, 139–140; education and, 101–102; gamonales and, 18, 111–112; hacendados and, 18, 28, 144; in land struggles, 82; rape, 32, 38, 101–102, 182; Tawantinsuyo movement and, 44, 50, 70. *See also* Mothers
World War II, 97

Yezer, Caroline, 3, 223n87

Zárate, Alejandro, 60
Zárate, Salomón, 78–80, 82, 89
Zárate, Teófila, 60, 82
Zulén, Pedro, 45